People of Sunlight
People of Starlight

Barrenland Archaeology
in the Northwest Territories of Canada

Bryan C. Gordon

Mercury Series
Archaeological Survey of Canada
Paper 154

Canadian Museum of Civilization

© Canadian Museum of Civilization 1996

CANADIAN CATALOGUING IN PUBLICATION DATA

Gordon, Bryan H. C.

People of sunlight: people of starlight:
Barrenland archaeology in the
Northwest Territories of Canada

(Mercury series, ISSN 0316-1854)
(Paper/Archaeological Survey of Canada,
ISSN 0317-1854; no. 154)
Includes an abstract in French.
Includes bibliographical references.
ISBN 0-660-15963-5

1. Northwest Territories — Antiquities.
2. Indians of North America —
Northwest Territories — Antiquities.
3. Inuit — Northwest Territories — Antiquities.
4. Barren ground caribou — Northwest Territories.
5. Hunting and gathering societies —
Northwest Territories.
6. Excavations (Archaeology) — Northwest Territories.
I. Canadian Museum of Civilization.
II. Title. III. Title: Barrenland archaeology in the
Northwest Territories of Canada.
IV. Series. V. Series: Paper (Archaeological Survey of
Canada); no. 154.

E99.S65G67 1996   971.'9'401   C96-980191-2

 PRINTED IN CANADA

Published by
Canadian Museum of Civilization
100 Laurier Street
P.O. Box 3100, Station B
Hull, Quebec
J8X 4H2

Senior production officer: Deborah Brownrigg
Cover design: Expression Communications Inc.

Front cover:
According to one Dene legend, caribou arose from
the Milky Way, which is composed of individual stars
interpreted as a herd of caribou. In this drawing by
Mearle Gordon Roy, the herd is descending from the
Milky Way in late autumn before spending the winter
with the people of sunlight and starlight in the forest.

OBJECT OF THE MERCURY SERIES

The Mercury Series is designed to permit the rapid
dissemination of information pertaining to the
disciplines in which the Canada Museum of
Civilization is active. Considered an important
reference by the scientific community, the Mercury
Series comprises over three hundred specialized
publications on Canada's history and prehistory.

Because of its specialized audience, the series
consists largely of monographs published in the
language of the author.

In the interest of making information available
quickly, normal production procedures have been
abbreviated. As a result, grammatical and
typographical errors may occur. Your indulgence is
requested.

Titles in the Mercury Series can be obtained by
writing to:
Mail Order Services
Canadian Museum of Civilization
100 Laurier Street
P.O. Box 3100, Station B
Hull, Quebec
J8X 4H2

BUT DE LA COLLECTION

La collection Mercure vise à diffuser rapidement le
résultat de travaux dans les disciplines qui relèvent
des sphères d'activités du Musée canadien des
civilisations. Considérée comme un apport important
dans la communauté scientifique, la collection
Mercure présente plus de trois cents publications
spécialisées portant sur l'héritage canadien
préhistorique et historique.

Comme la collection s'adresse à un public spécialisé,
celle-ci est constituée essentiellement de
monographies publiées dans la langue des auteurs.

Pour assurer la prompte distribution des exemplaires
imprimés, les étapes de l'édition ont été abrégées.
En conséquence, certaines coquilles ou fautes de
grammaire peuvent subsister: c'est pourquoi nous
réclamons votre indulgence.

Vous pouvez vous procurer la liste des titres parus
dans la collection Mercure en écrivant au :

Service des commandes postales
Musée canadien des civilisations
100, rue Laurier
C.P. 3100, succursale B
Hull (Québec)
J8X 4H2

Canadä

Abstract

Hunters of the Beverly caribou range of Canada's Northwest Territories have been dependent on and influenced by seasonal migrations for 8,000 years. Historical records document that the Dene conformed to a seasonal cycle in response to caribou movements: four out of five nineteenth-century baptismal certificates show Dene births in February, March and April in the winter-range forest – nine months after massed herds were intercepted at tundra water crossings, nine months after nutritionally fit caribou provided adequate fat to allow Dene women to conceive. Prehistoric evidence agrees with historic observations. The herd influenced people, and the people adapted to the herd. Rangewide archaeological sites extend from the northern calving ground, south along the migration border to the boreal forest. Sizes of ancient camps mimic density of caribou at any given point in the range. Sites are small near the calving ground, large and stratified at major water crossings near the treeline where the herd massed, and small again in the forest where the herd dispersed over the winter range.

This study analyzes and compares over 13,000 artifacts representing 1,002 hunting camps of four major archaeological traditions. Although there are characteristic tool traits in each tradition, similar types of tools reflect a common seasonal lifestyle. Men's and women's tools co-occur throughout range and cultural sequence, evidence of the interactive nature of caribou hunting and processing. Cross-culturally, tool size, shape, breakage, hafting and chipping pattern are specific to summer-occupied tundra or winter-occupied forest. In winter, for example, people conserved their tools while modifying them for use with mittened hands. In summer, they took advantage of plentiful raw materials, altering tools to fit antler and bone hafts. A total of 131 radiocarbon estimates dates the cultural sequence. Northern Plano (8,000 to 7,000 years ago) arrived soon after deglaciation and evolved into Shield Archaic (6,500 to 3,500 years ago), which represents forest dwellers during a continuing warm period. Pre-Dorset (3,450 to 2,650 years ago), the only non-Indian culture, came from the north in response to a worldwide climatic deterioration. Taltheilei (2,600 years ago to the present) appeared when climate warmed; it expanded during its Middle Phase when its people took maximum advantage of tundra water crossings. Late Taltheilei persisted, to develop into the modern Dene.

Résumé

Les chasseurs de la chaîne Caribou, dans les Territoires du Nord-Ouest, au Canada, se sont adaptés aux migrations saisonnières de la harde de caribous de Beverly et ils en ont vécu pendant 8000 ans. D'après les documents historiques, le activités annuelles des Dénés suivaient un cycle saisonnier conforme aux déplacements des caribous. Quatre certificats de baptême sur cinq du XIXe siècle témoignent de naissances chez les Dénés en février, mars et avril, dans la forêt de leur territoire d'hivernage, neuf mois après l'interception des grandes hardes aux traverses de rivières de la toundra, neuf mois après que les femmes dénées eurent mangé le gras de caribou qui leur était nécessaire pour concevoir. Les évidences préhistoriques concordent avec les observations historiques. Les gens se sont adaptés à la harde. Les sites archéologiques parsèment la chaîne de montagnes, depuis la région de mise bas des caribous au nord, le long du corridor de migration au sud jusqu'à la forêt boréale. La taille des anciens campements correspond à la densité des caribous n'importe où sur le territoire. Les sites sont petits près des lieux de mise bas, grands et stratifiés aux principales traverses de rivières près de la limite des arbres où la harde se rassemblait et, de nouveau, petits dans la forêt où la harde se dispersait pour l'hiver.

Cette étude analyse et compare plus de 13 000 objets provenant de 1002 campements de chasse qui relèvent de quatre principales traditions culturelles. Bien que chaque tradition comporte des caractéristiques propres pour ses outils, des outils similaires témoignent d'un mode de vie saisonnier commun. Les outils qui servaient aux activités des hommes et à celles des femmes se retrouvent également sur tout le territoire et dans toute la série culturelle, ce qui met en évidence l'interaction entre la chasse et l'apprêt du caribou. Indépendamment des cultures, la taille, la forme, les cassures, l'emmanchement et les modèles de taille des outils sont spécifiques à l'occupation estivale de la toundra ou à l'occupation hivernale de la forêt. En hiver, par exemple, on modifiait les outils pour les prendre avec des mitaines. En été, dans la toundra, on profitait de l'abondance des matières premières et on faisait des manches d'outils en andouiller ou en os. Des datations au carbone 14 (131) permettent de dater la série culturelle. La culture Plano (il y a 7000 à 8000 ans) est apparue dans le Nord après la déglaciation. Elle est devenue la culture Archaïque du Bouclier (il y a 3500 à 6500 ans), advenue pendant une période ininterrompue de chaleur. La culture prédorsétienne (il y a 2650 à 3450 ans), la seule culture non indienne, vint du Nord à la suite d'une détérioration climatique d'envergure universelle. La culture Talthéiléi (il y a 2600 ans) fit son apparition lorsque le climat se réchauffa de nouveau; elle s'étendit durant sa Phase moyenne, quand les gens tirèrent avantage des traverses de rivières dans la toundra. Les Talthéiléiens récents sont devenus les Dénés d'aujourd'hui.

This book is dedicated to the memories of my daughter,
Charlotte Amy, and her fiancé, John Stack. Charlotte
loved the Barrenlands and wanted to return.

Thelon River

by Peter S. Jull

Van Gogh's orchard river
In the heart of light,
Light-scaled waters,
And the endless land
Rolling
To some consummation
With the sky,
Is medium for newer signals
Than among the Congo's leaves
Black figurings
Or horrid groans.

Here we have nothing
But the cropless land
Bleak-hilled,
And the distance
Of the sun's
Blind radiation,
Far and wide.

Here we are nothing
But the herds
In graceful
Listlessness,
Moving finger
Dallying across
The land.
The voice upon the waters,
More direct,
Spoke in thunder,
Gestured in fire,
But in the everlasting
Weakness
Of our wider world,
Desultory predation,
Cleaning a telescope
Or mending a tent,

It's satisfying to wait
And maybe let
Our culture's flow
Bring meat to the crossing
And blood to the bow.
Or maybe, half-asleep,
It will pass by.

Watching
On the hill
I see the tent-ring
Below
From former days
When the herds moved
Numberless
And the camps were full;
I also see
The haze line
On horizons
And the river's glare
Like ice
Light-sheeted in the spring-
My eyes
Drop away
From visions of
So much gold.

We were the people,
And we are, still,
And if we wait,
Doubtful,
The tides of imagination
Striking from the land,
A single heat-clap
To transfigure all,
Once again we'll be
The first survivors
In a newer world.

(Reprinted with permission of Robert F.J. Shannon, editor, *North-Nord Magazine*
(1967 Spec. Ed.), Indian and Northern Affairs).

Chapter 4 - The Late Phase of the Taltheilei Tradition

Chapter 5 - The Middle Phase of the Taltheilei Tradition

Chapter 6 - Early and Earliest Phases of the Taltheilei Tradition

Chapter 7 - General Taltheilei and Middle Plains Indian Phases

Chapter 8 - The Pre-Dorset Tradition

Chapter 9 - The Shield Archaic Tradition

Chapter 10 - The Northern Plano Tradition

Chapter 11 - Conclusions and Related Research

For initiating the project, I thank Ben Strickland, an amateur archaeologist from Livingstone, Montana, who retrieved artifacts from the Thelon Game Sanctuary in 1969 while with a Calgary Zoo muskox program. He brought them to the attention of Eric Harvey, Harry Chritchley and Hod Meech of the Riveredge Foundation of Calgary. Mr. Chritchley informed Profs. Jane and David Kelley of the Dept. of Archaeology, U. of Calgary. The Kelleys recommended me to Riveredge and suggested the Thelon Game Sanctuary study as a topic for my doctoral thesis.

Riveredge Foundation funded the first two years in 1970 and 1971. The Canadian Museum of Civilization provided the bulk of funding from 1973 through 1983. Additional financial assistance was provided by Opportunities for Youth and COSEP.

A 17-year project requires more assistance than can adequately be remembered. I regret if I omit any in this list of those who made our work possible and more pleasant:

- Harry Critchley of the Riveredge Foundation provided lab space after the first field seasons and encouraged me.
- Dept. of National Defense officers and technicians in Ottawa, Namao and Yellowknife (especially 435 Squadron) air-dropped three years of equipment, food and fuel.
- University of Calgary, Dept. of Archaeology provided camping and excavation equipment in the first two years.
- Prince of Wales Northern Heritage Center in Yellowknife provided canoe storage and logistic suppport.
- Don and Ann Gordon of Edmonton fed and housed crew members enroute to field.
- Julie and Bob Woodland of Yellowknife housed crews in 1970-1.
- Adelaide Chaffee and Fred Riddle provided hospitality on Damant Lake.
- Hank and Tom Foess assisted the Howard Lake survey (Whitefish Lake - 1976).
- Assistants and students at the former Museum of Man, now the Canadian Museum of Civilization (CMC) washed, labelled and catalogued artifacts.
- David Laverie of CMC drafted maps, charts and illustrations.
- Luke McCarthy of CMC made artifact casts from Thelon materials which were used in displays.
- Rachel Perkins of CMC constructed a database to correlate site material with artifact storage cabinets.
- Dan Murphy and Jim Griffin of the Information Services Division advised on tool databases and computer induced graphs.
- Mark Allston, Mark Blok, Cindy Brouse and Melanie Zahab, volunteers at CMC, assisted in completing the data base.
- Harry Foster of Photographic Services, CMC, photographed artifacts (see photo credits).
- Dr. James Wright, CMC, provided background on the Grant Lake area and many hours of discussion about the movements of prehistoric peoples in the Barrens.
- Dr. George McDonald, Executive Director, CMC, encouraged me throughout this work.

Most of all I would like to thank the crews who endured long days of survey and digging at the height of black-fly and mosquito seasons. They are:

- 1970 Warden's Grove crew: James Firth, Marjory Gordon, Michael Groarke, Luther Meyer and Brian Yorga surveyed and tested 51 sites, some as far as Hoare Lake. Dr. John Dennis made a botanical survey from the Hanbury River down the Thelon as far as Hornby's cabin.
- 1971 Warden's Grove crew: Priscilla Bickel, Steven and Virginia Burger, James Firth, Marjory Gordon, Jeffrey Hunston, Robert Janes, Philip Kettles, Luther Meyer and Brian Yorga excavated two major sites, KjNb-6 and 7, and found and tested 18 new sites.
- 1973: Morgan Jones assisted me in the Back River Survey.
- 1973-74: Frank Metcalf, canoist, surveyed Thelon River from Hornby Point to Beverly Lake.
- 1974 Migod Site crew at Grant Lake (Dubawnt River): Charles Arnold, Marjory Gordon, Jean and Paul Kay (geographers), David Morrison and Jane Sproull excavated Migod Site.
- 1975: Milton Wright and I surveyed the forested Taltson River from Noman Lake south to Nonacho Lake and east to Gray Lake while Frank Metcalf and Henning von Krogh surveyed Firedrake Lake on the upper Dubawnt,
- 1976 Warden's Grove crew: Margaret Barlow, Rick Blacklaws, Marjory Gordon, Caroline Kobelka, Frank Metcalf, and David Morrison excavated KjNb-7. Rick surveyed Whitefish Lake with me while David Morrison and Frank Metcalf surveyed the Elk River branch of the Thelon headwaters from Damant Lake to Warden's Grove.
- 1977 Whitefish Lake crew: Margaret Barlow, Marjory Gordon, Debbie and Laurie Jackson, and Jane and Callum Thomson dug KeNi-2, 4 and 5. Laurie and I also surveyed Cree Lake and River in northern Saskatechewan.
- 1978 Lake Athabasca crew: Marjory Gordon, Yvonne Marshall and Andrew Stewart surveyed the south shore of Lake Athabasca from William River east to Fond-du-lac village.
- 1982: Marjory, Bruce and Charlotte Gordon assisted in surveying Mary, Mosquito and Sid lakes.
- 1983 Mosquito Lake crew: Irma Eckert, Marjory, Bruce and Charlotte Gordon, and Andrew Stewart excavated KdLw-l.

I am endebted to Elizabeth Charron, Andrew Stewart and David Morrison for editorial comments, and Ryan Dyck and Patrick Zakher for appendicizing and shrinking the many tables, customizing older PCX maps using CorelDraw 4 and assisting with layout. Sterling Presley made the photomicrographs. Richard Morlan initiated the formatting of the manuscript in MS-Word for publication. Patrick Zakher customized the formatting of all chapters and used the software to generate the tables of contents and appendix, and caption and cite the figures. Henning von Krogh took some of the photographs in the text as a member of my 1975 crew. The Canadian Armed Forces took the airphoto of site KeNi-4 at Whitefish Lake (Plate i.1). I thank Father Mousseau of the Oblates of Mary Immaculate Archives in Yellowknife for kind permission to reprint those photographs cited with Oblate permission. Other photographs are cited on their right margins, except those taken by archaeological crew members. A quarter century of field work involves many people outside my summer crews and winter museum assistance. If I have missed someone, I apologize.

According to Hearne (1958 Glover ed., pp. 221-2, the Dene origin of the caribou is the *Aurora Borealis*, which they call *etthen* or caribou. I once heard of a similar legend that they arose from the

Milky Way, which, unlike the Aurora, is composed of individual stars which may be interpreted as a herd of caribou, but I have not found the source. Mearle Gordon Roy drew the cover of the herd descending from the Milky Way in late autumn at treeline, before spending the winter with the Dene in the forest. When the stars are very bright, caribou are plentiful in that part of the Beverly range, but the Dene never entertained the idea of sampling this celestial food. Rather, the Milky Way guided them to their more worldly staff-of-life as it roamed the winter forest. A book title and special colouring effects to the cover were later added to Mearle's drawing.

My wife Marjory, helpmate, critic and confidante, was with me from initial planning to completion of this work.

Introduction

'The narrows, known as Taltheilei, at the eastern end of (Great Slave) lake, are the point at which contact with the ordinary life of the North ceases. From this point on the traveller strikes dim trails that lead off into the Unknown - hunting trails for the Dogrib, Yellowknife, and Slave Indians, in the days before the trading post and the fur catch changed them from nomads, wandering clear across the Barren Lands to the Arctic itself...' London *Times*, Dec. 13, 1924 (anon.)

This is a study of peoples for whom those "dim trails" gave access to a land well-known to them, a land which served to provide all of their needs by way of the migrating Beverly caribou population. Following and intercepting migrating caribou was not a departure from, but an intimate part of, their "ordinary life". Field research and historic accounts corroborate the fact that human behavior was so dependent upon herd movement on the Barrenlands of Canada, that, had caribou vanished, people would have perished.

Ethnographic observation of the Dene (J.G.E. Smith:1975) elaborated upon the direct link between "Caribou-Eater" Dene (or Northern Indians) and caribou of the Beverly and Kaminuriak populations. Parker (1972b:10), through observing tagged animals, found these two caribou populations each maintained a 94 per cent homogeneity even though their winter range overlapped. As alternate sources of fish and game were absent or insufficient to provide necessities provided by caribou (hide for tents, clothing and nets; antler for tools and sufficient meat for nutritional needs), the Dene were not arbitrary in their summer/winter nomadic cycle. These people of sunlight, people of starlight, were in tune with the Beverly and Kaminuriak herds (J.G.E. Smith: 1975: 392, 405, 417, 421), following them across the Barrens in the long warm days of summer and into the forest during the short, cold days of winter. Dene hunters alternated, according to season, from as much as twenty-four hours of sunlight, hampered by little but subdued twilight, to as much as eighteen hours of moonlight and subdued twilight, enhanced by the reflection from the whiteness of snow. In the brightness and plenty of the summer, when the caribou herds massed, food supply was adequate. The people gathered together for mass hunts at river crossings (Fig. ii), dressing in leather costume with porcupine quillwork and bright embroidery. In the dimness and hardship of winter when herds dispersed, meat was scarce and people broke up into smaller family groups to make utilitarian undecorated clothing. Nutrition suffered and starvation was not unknown.

This same cycle and discrete band/discrete herd association (Gordon, 1975: 75-90) has been seen ethnographically, as well as archaeologically since deglaciation 8,000 years ago. The observations of Smith were echoed in the results of my studies of Pre-Dorset toolkits. Sites were distributed within each of the four major Barrenland caribou ranges and not between them. Pre-Dorset tools and toolkits showed greatest similarity within each of the ranges and greatest differences between different ranges. A similar discrete band/discrete herd association occurs in the Beverly range for all the remaining cultures.

Smith (1975) noted that when caribou herds disperse in the winter forests, Dene bands dispersed as well, in attempts to maximize food resources. Without a doubt, nutritional fitness of the animals and availablity at various parts of their migration route influenced nutrition of the Dene and their predecessors. Human nutrition, as derived from a single primary food resouce (caribou) in turn influenced the yearly cycle, including childbearing. This is another aspect of the dependence of discrete bands upon discrete herds which undoubtedly extended into prehistoric times and adds to an understanding of prehistoric population dynamics.

The direct historic approach seemed the most efficient way to integrate the massive amounts of Beverly range archaeological material open to interpretation. I tried to approach my work without preconceptions, and more in the nature of pure research, and alert to ethnographic correlates. I tried to observe as broadly as possible and let available material lead the way.

My study of the prehistory of the Beverly range, extending back thirty years, expanded with progress in other disciplines, such as J.G.E. Smith's work with the Dene and Parker's (1972) and Miller's (1974, 1976) work with the caribou. Samuel Hearne's (1958) description of his 1769, 1770, 1771 and 1772 journey across the Barrenlands provided invaluable confirmation of caribou and Dene movements before life was disrupted by the fur trade. Studies of the work of earlier archaeologists and of Beverly range artifacts allowed defination of tradition and phase-specific toolkits. The recognition of seasonal differences between forest and tundra toolkits of each phase or tradition came only recently, after examining extensive artifact databases. Studies on human birth cycles also stress a correlation between human and caribou migratory patterns. While floor plans of artifacts and features may increase our understanding of settlement patterns and placement of work stations in sites, they will be covered in a future volume. Gender-related tool distributions in these floor plans will also be compared.

I follow a specific analytic approach in my study of the various peoples, ranging from the Taltheilei (historic through 2600 B.P.) through the Pre-Dorset, the single Inuit-type tradition. The same approach is traceable through Shield Archaic (3500 to 6500 B.P.) and Northern Plano (7000 to 8000 B.P). Each phase and tradition is dated by radiocarbon and lies within the Beverly range. Each artifact is analyzed by type: point, scraper, knife, chitho or hide abrader, wedge, ground tools (adze, axe, chisel, gouge, pick), core, hammerstone, whetstone, edge grinder, spokeshave, shaft polisher, pushplane, saw, pointed tools (awl, drill, graver), ochre, firecracked rock, bone, wood and metal. Each chapter includes a short description of general tool trends, noting seasonal difference. I compare all tools in the final chapter, summarizing cross-cultural seasonal trends.

Separating mixed surface collections into phases, traditions and culture is effected with little difficulty in the case of culturally distinct artifacts such as projectile points. But what about unassigned tools in many mixed collections? Fifty thousand Barrenland surface artifacts appeared undiagnostic, but knives and scrapers superficially unspecific to phase or tradition were too numerous to ignore without detailed examination. I attempted to assign general surface artifacts by examining scrapers and knives from known cultural contexts, i.e., stratified levels. Using multiple metric (length, width, thickness, weight) and descriptive attributes (plan, section, base, tip, midsection, primary and secondary retouch, basal alteration, notches, stems or shoulders, thinning, edge-wear, thinning, grinding, fluting, tapering, etc.), I was able to assign 6,715 artifacts in terms of attribute combinations, using 6,385 stratified artifacts in large tool-specific databases on a best-match basis (Table i). Descriptive attributes within each category were held constant while I gradually opened a window of metric measurements. Parameters were tight (within mm) as I slowly diverged from the mean until surface artifacts closely correlated with those defined in cultural context. While comparisons were empirical rather than statistical, most phase assignments were clear. Assigning artifacts to multiple phases was rare because their differences are distinct, even in common artifacts like Middle Phase knives and big triangular Early Phase scrapers.

Artifact description	Excavated	Surface
points	380	1221
scrapers	847	1405
knives	1297	1867
chithos	168	185
hammerstones	38	36
pushplanes	34	111
wedges	78	147
whetstones	20	20
planes	28	75
burin planes	26	83
burin slotters	28	86
burin spalls	18	10
plane spalls	117	66
slotter spalls	28	31
miscellaneous	60	151
adzes and fragments	125	117
cores and fragments	185	92
flakes	2402	716
bone fragments	420	123
wood fragments	44	120
metal fragments	42	53
Total	6385	6715

Table i. Excavated and surface artifacts in 1002 sites in the Beverly caribou range.

In this book of over 300 pages, there are 101 maps, 57 black and white photographs and 5 line drawings and an index. *Note that artifacts in all photographs are reduced to three-fourths of natural size.*

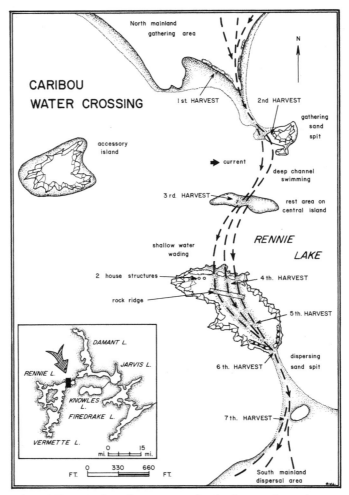

Figure i. Example of a caribou water crossing showing seven harvesting axes from north to south.

Chapter 1

The Beverly Caribou Range - Natural Environment

The Barrenlands

The term "barren grounds", first noted by Hearne on March 21, 1770 and Hudson Bay Company factors at Fort Prince of Wales (Hearne 1958:12), and perpetuated by Tyrrell (1898) and Hanbury (1904:36), denote that area of Canada bordered by the Mackenzie Valley, Arctic Ocean and Hudson Bay of the Northwest Territories and the provinces of Saskatchewan and Manitoba. It has also been called the Barrens, Barrenlands, Arctic Prairies and *dechinule* or "land of little sticks" by the Dene, with modern usage favoring the Barrenlands.

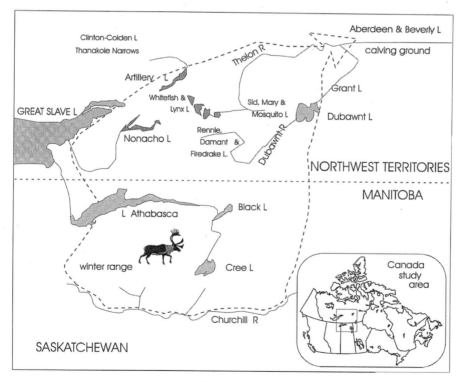

Figure 1.1. The Beverly caribou range.

The Barrenlands enclose the Bluenose, Bathurst, Beverly and Kaminuriak caribou ranges, which extend from deep within the forests of the Mackenzie Valley and Prairie provinces north onto the tundra. The two eastern ranges of Beverly and Kaminuriak are south of the Arctic Circle on a 300-700 m (960-2,250 ft.) high plateau cut by fast rivers flowing to the Mackenzie River, the Arctic Ocean and Hudson Bay. These eastern ranges are in the eastern Mackenzie and Keewatin Districts and the north halves of Saskatchewan and Manitoba (Fig. 1.1).

Figure 1.2. An esker used as a caribou migration path.

Beverly Geography, Geology, Climate, Fauna and Flora

The Beverly range has flat 150 m high north, central and south drainages separated by low hills. The north tundra drainage flows via the Back River to Chantry Inlet on the Arctic Ocean. The forested central drainage flows via the Thelon to Baker Lake, Chesterfield Inlet and Hudson Bay. The south drainage flows via Artillery and Athabasca Lakes to Great Slave Lake and the Mackenzie. The central and south drainages are separated by a 450 m divide north of Lake Athabasca.

A mantle of boulders or glacial erratics, cobbles, sand and thin acid soil cover the surface of the range. Eskers, remnants of rivers which ran under glaciers, snake their way across forest and tundra (Fig. 1.2). Barchan dunes mark the northern desert on the south shore of Lake Athabasca. Beach ridges showing the 8,500 year-old shores of Glacial Lakes Thelon, Dubawnt and McConnell (East Arm of Great Slave Lake) bear no human sign (Fig. 1.3). Beneath glacial deposits is unfossiliferous flat sandstone bedrock over Pre-Cambrian granite, undulating acidic diorite and granodiorite (Wright 1967:47). The Pre-Cambrian granite is some of the oldest rock in the world.

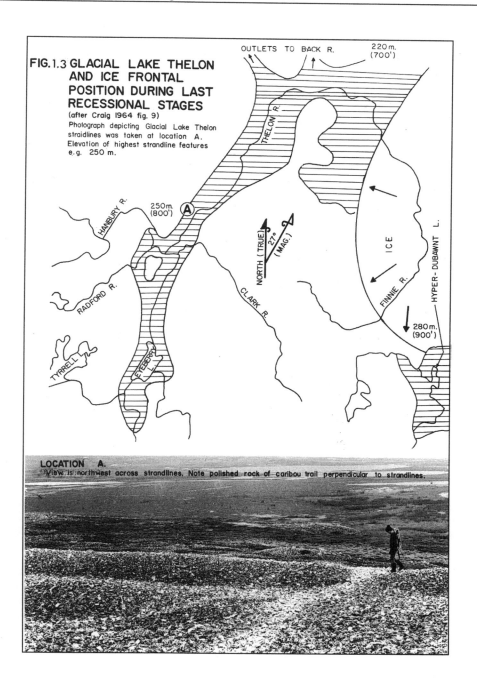

FIG. 1.3 GLACIAL LAKE THELON AND ICE FRONTAL POSITION DURING LAST RECESSIONAL STAGES
(after Craig 1964 fig. 9)
Photograph depicting Glacial Lake Thelon straidlines was taken at location A. Elevation of highest strandline features e.g. 250 m.

LOCATION A.
View is northwest across strandlines. Note polished rock of caribou trail perpendicular to strandlines.

Deglacial warming 5,000-7,000 years ago saw soil development and a 200 km treeline advance during Northern Plano and Shield Archaic human occupation. Tundra soils with buried spruce cones, bark and wood overlain by pollen and *Sphagnum* spores mark the advance. Tree lichens and fast growing shrubs and grasses provided food for the first caribou. An upper zone devoid of tree pollen signals a very cold 3,500-2,200 year-old Pre-Dorset occupation. Above are signs of tree advance marking the warm 750 year-old Taltheilei occupation, while a stable cool period extending to the present denotes ancestral Dene (Gordon 1975:51).

In each range, the treeline separating northern tundra and southern spruce forest is more transition than boundary because the forest has clearings, while the tundra has outlying tree stands in protected river valleys like the Thelon. Forest and tundra separation results from change in soil development and plant growth traceable to the division between arctic and continental air masses. Today's prevailing cold dry northwest winds force the continental air mass south in winter, only to return with short temperate summers. Mean monthly tundra temperature does not exceed 4°C (Terasmae 1961:669) except for July-August, when ambient temperatures range 15-27° max. and 5-18° min., and soil temperatures range 10-21, 3-12 and 0-9°C at depths of 1, 10 and 20 cm (Dennis 1970). Soil thawing of only 12 cm under *Sphagnum* and 1 m under spruce, and a low annual precipitation (25 cm; half as snow) retard plant growth. Ridges have shrubs on undeveloped brunisols and regosols. Bogs have cottongrass on gleyed brunisols and peaty gleysols, and flood plain has willow. Long hours of summer sunlight result in undulating grassy tussocks competing for light. Photoperiodism or seasonal differences in sunlight also affects birth spacing in caribou, with notable effects also in humans in conjunction with nutrition.

Compared to tundra, the forest has more frost-free days (≤80), precipitation (32-40 cm; 60% in May-Sept. Showers peak in July) and snowfall (125-150 cm), but less severe blizzards. Black Lake in the forest has mean January and July temperatures of -29 and 15°C (Minni 1976). Unlike the tundra, trees reduce wind speeds to 8-16 km per hour, making life more bearable. Snow and forest-cover insulation are important for caribou winter shelter.

Spring ice breakup occurs first on small streams and lakes, followed by Thelon, Dubawnt and Back River breakup from early to late June, when runoff remains high for 1-2 weeks. Spring is earlier in the southwest, and Beverly, Aberdeen and Schultz Lakes in the northeast may be frozen until July, but navigable shorelines may open by early July. Wind-driven floes then rapidly shatter on shore. Freezup reverses the process, with small lakes freezing about the end of September, followed by big lakes and rivers. Lake ice may be 50 cm thick by November 10 and 2 m thick by December 1. Ice remains later on tundra lakes and freezeup is earlier, a warning to travellers arriving too early from the forest or departing too late from the tundra. The Meadowbank area of Back River and the Schultz rapids above Baker Lake never freeze completely.

Climate, exposure, soil and permafrost affect floral range. A warmer climate and thicker soil results in more plant species in the forest than tundra. *Sphagnum* moss is common to both, but *Cladonia*, *Cetraria* and *Stereocaulon* lichen grow on spruce and jackpine (*Pinus banksiana*), while tundra crustose lichen is limited to excrescences on dry sandstone ridges. Black and white spruce (*Picea mariana* and *P. glauca*) and aspen (*Populus tremuloides*) are common in the forest but confined to protected tundra valleys, with dwarf and paper birch (*Betula glandulosa* and *B. papyrifera*) in isolated patches. Other forest trees are balsam poplar (*Populus balsamifera*), Alaska and water birch (*Betula neoalaskana* and *B. occidentalis*), alder (*Alnus rugosa*) and tamarack (*Larix laricina*). It is hard for trees to grow on tundra due to dryness as well as cold. Signs of winter dessication are reddish mountain cranberry (*Vaccinium vitis-ideae*) and crowberry (*Empetrum nigrum*) on hillsides and mixed red and green needles under spruce.

Caribou (*Rangifer tarandus groenlandicus)* was the main game, but tundra muskox (*Ovibos moschatus*) and hare (*Lepus arcticus*), and forest moose (*Alces alces*), black bear (*Ursus americanus*), snowshoe hare (*Lepus americanus*), beaver (*Castor canadensis*), muskrat (*Ondatra zibethicus*), woodchuck (*Marmota monax*) and porcupine (*Erethizon dorsatum*) were sometimes hunted. Rangewide game birds were permanently-residing willow and rock ptarmigan (*Lagopus lagopus* and *L. mutus*), migratory Canada, white-fronted and snow geese (*Branta canadensis, Anser albifrons and Chen caerulescens*), whistling swan (*Olor columbianus*), oldsquaw, mallard, pintail and other ducks (*Clangula hyemalis, Anas platyrhynchos, A. acuta,* etc.), herring gull (*Larus argentatus*) and various loons (Gavia spp.). Rangewide game fish are round and lake whitefish (*Prosopium cylindraceum* and *Coregonus clupeaformis*), lake trout (*Salvelinus namaycush*), pike (*Esox lucius*) and grayling (*Thymallus arcticus*). Char (*Salvelinus alpinus*) is in arctic drainage lakes, while walleye (*Stizostedion vitreum*) and several suckers (*Catostomus* spp.) are in forest lakes.

Tundra predators are wolverine (*Gulo luscus*), grizzly bear (*Ursus horribilis*), red and Arctic fox (*Vulpes fulva* and *Alopex lagopus*) and wolf (*Canis lupus*). Forest predators are wolf, wolverine (*Gulo gulo*), otter (*Lutra candensis*), fisher and marten (*Martes pennanti* and *M. americana*), and mink, weasel and ermine (*Mustela vison, M. rixosa* and *M. erminea*). Rangewide raptors are peregrine and gyrfalcon (*Falco peregrinus* and *F. rusticolus*), bald and golden eagle (*Haliaetus leucocephalus* and *Aquila crysaëtos*), rough-legged hawk (*Buteo lagopus*), jaeger (Stercocarius spp.), and many owls and hawks. Other birds include gulls, Arctic and common tern (*Sterna paradiseae* and *S. hirundo*), bittern (*Botaurus lentiginosus*), common crow and raven (*Corvus brachyrhynchos* and *C. corax*). But for wood frogs and Canadian toads (*Rana sylvatica* and *Bufo americanus hemiophrys*), amphibians and reptiles are absent in the Beverly range.

Caribou Adaptation

Human existence as embodied in Beverly archaeology is based on tundra caribou or *Rangifer tarandus groenlandicus*. Compared to woodland caribou or *Rangifer tarandus tarandus,* it is smaller with larger, rounder and more bent, but less palmated antlers. After the mid-Pleistocene and appearing contemporaneously, *Rangifer* (caribou and reindeer) became the most important game for northern people. It tolerates temperature ranges of 83°C (150°F), and is well-adapted to short warm summers and long cold winters. Its best adaptation is adaptability itself (Bergerud 1974:582), thriving on sparse forest and tundra plant species on frozen soils.

Hormonal change caused by pregnancy and photoperiodism arouses the migration impulse in caribou cows. Habitual return to a specific calving ground in May may relate to a learned homing capacity for direction and a phylogenetic imprinting which directs the herd past landmarks (Fig. 1.4; Banfield 1961; Bergerud 1974:575). On its route the herd forms subherds which seasonally vary by age and gender. After calving, spring cow subherds form midsummer cow-calf subherds. In early May, bull subherds stop short of the calving ground, joining cow-calf subherds in late June. Together, they move to treeline as one vast herd which fissions into small subherds in August. After entering the forest, rutting subherds reappear in September and October at treeline before returning to the forest as tiny winter subherds.

Figure 1.4. Caribou migration trails on the tundra, Thelon River.

Wolf predation regulates herd size by calf deaths (often indiscriminately). Although wolves pup south of the herd calving ground, wolf kills rise as cows and calves group against mosquitoes and wolves as they move south (Parker 1972a:81). Grouping reunites previous winter subherds and enhances herd stability (Bergerud 1974; Miller 1974:62), but wolves isolate the weak, slow and sick (Parker 1972a:33; Calef and Heard 1980:593). After wolves, calf deaths are due to abandonment, stillbirth, pathologies, pneumonia, malnutrition and injuries (Miller and Broughton 1974:4). Humans, the second major predator, kill fewer calves than wolves because they cannot accompany spring migration over snowy terrain. Unfortunately, as counts show in buried levels, not enough bone and teeth (esp. calf) are preserved in the acid soil to estimate herd recruitment or reduction. Insects, the third predator, weaken rather than kill, but do not hatch until summer. Animal loss by predation is offset somewhat by the caribou's ability to adapt to several habitats (Murdoch and Oaten 1975).

In June, grassy plants form half of the diet; in July, twigs and leaves; in September, mushrooms, and in winter, tree lichens. Ice-covered, deep, late winter snow covering lichens and plants make caribou move to bare southwest slopes (Miller 1976:6,24). Fewer available calories cause weight loss (McEwan and Whitehead 1970:905). With spring thaw, caribou again eat twigs and leaves; later sedge and cottongrass. The minimal carrying capacity of winter forest controls herd size, not the 35-45% richer summer diet.

Figure 1.5. The KeNi-4 crossing at Whitefish Lake.
In July, caribou from the calving ground 300 km east, crossed the dunefield, trying to bypass the manmade brush fences on the hill before reaching the sandspit on the far left. The hill has five archaeological levels while the dunefield had thousands of surface artifacts.

Band-herd Affiliation and Herd Following

Signs of human band and caribou herd affiliation have been accumulating since humans and caribou first entered the Barrenlands. Piled slab *inukshuit* made by Thelon and Dubawnt River hunters mark the route of the herd returning to the forest (Morrison 1981). That hunters followed it, is seen in distinctive Eyeberry Lake quartzite from the heart of the range being carried several hundred km south to Lake Athabasca (Wright 1975). Archaeological levels separated by wind-blown sand contain caribou hunting and processing tools that became instrumental in testing the idea of herd following. Archeological sites were preserved because sand from glacial lakes blown in from adjacent dunefields covered the tools of each culture (Fig. 1.5). This separation between levels permitted the defining and radiocarbon dating of tools used by subsequent hunting bands, with those at the bottom or 2 m level being 8,000 years old.

The affiliation of human bands with specific herds means a separation from other bands and herds, a segregation reflected in different but contemporaneous tool styles in the four herd ranges (Gordon 1975). This herd separation even exists in the rutting area used by both Beverly and Kaminuriak caribou, where 94% of all ear-tagged caribou return to their herd after mingling (Parker 1972b). It follows, therefore, that as hunting camps of past bands are confined to the modern caribou range, band-herd affiliation would consequently have existed throughout prehistory, resulting in herd following (Gordon 1975).

The concept of herd following has been argued for many years. Nineteenth century diffusionists and 20th century environmentalists used it to explain supposed artifact similarity over wide areas of Ice-Age Europe. It is seldom referred to in archaeological contexts, as alternate game was usually available. When used, it is confounded. Burch's (1972) Caribou Inuit study misconstrued herd following as herd accompaniment, which is clearly absurd given the sustained pace of migration. His evidence in that study was obscured by effects from past tribal animosity. Historic Caribou Inuit were prevented from herd following by their traditional Dene enemies who were confined to the winter range by the fur trade (Gordon 1990:399-400). When they eventually starved on the tundra, the Inuit were relocated to coastal villages. Ironically, Burch (1976, quoted in Smith 1978) mentions Dene hunters following the herd onto the tundra to the calving ground, which suggests they used the whole range. Had Burch known at that time that the Dene were free to follow the herd for two thousand years without impediment from Inuit, he would have found herd following realistic. Unfortunately, he did not know of the many Dene and earlier tundra camps that demonstrate the full seasonal cycle.

Given the time depth represented in this study, did herds always migrate along the same corridors? Several biological papers suggest variability in herd movement from year to year (Heard and Calef 1986). I have little doubt that modern seasonal movements vary due to overhunting, forest fires and human impingement on caribou range, but calving ground locations have remained stable for centuries, based on aerial survey and the archaeological record. Surface and stratified sites on the modern corridor contain tools and bone from all phases which prove long term use.

Herd following is rejected by some historians embellishing a feast and famine concept by focussing their research on rare fur trade accounts of chaotic winter subherd movement near forts. By exterminating local subherds to provide meat to traders, Indians destroyed local migration, leading to the assumption that the main migration vanished and that herds are unpredictable. Away from forts, the major migration continued, with meat-sharing between bands established in central crossing camps surrounded by small camps. Ironically, predictability is even rebuffed by some Dene villagers who avoid these crossings because they require boats, spears and long waits. Instead, they fly to open areas peripheral to the treeline and rely on distant shooting.

That cached meat could permit sedentary bands is unlikely because rock caches are absent on the tundra, and tree caches are rare in the forest. I believe old or sick people incapable of the long treks summered in the forest, subsisting on berries, fish and forest game, but their number and energy needs are tiny compared to those of herd followers. In late spring, the Dene followed the herd to the calving ground but did not accompany it; in autumn, both returned to the forest. Herd following was aided by hoof marks in mud and polished bedrock and verbal accounts of past movement. Strangest of all, the earliest most-cited Dene observer, Samuel Hearne, documented herd following two centuries ago: "As their whole aim is to procure a comfortable subsistence, they take the most prudent means to accomplish it; and by *always following the lead of the deer,* are seldom exposed to the griping hand of famine" (Hearne 1958:83; emphasis mine).

Since 1970, my crews and I have recorded 1002 sites with 13,100 culturally assigned artifacts, most of which are on the tundra. The largest sites are just north of treeline and well beyond the winter range. They are also the most transiently occupied because the herd crosses them over 2-3 days. Their size is due to the intense activity occurring during their short occupation. If the band did not follow the herd, how do we explain these tundra sites? That these transient camps were used over the centuries is apparent in stratified bone and tool levels to depths exceeding 2 m and ages to 8,000 years (Fig. 1.6). Along the 600 km migration route, hundreds of ancient camps from all time periods where other game or caching were absent, prompted Burch (1991:439-444) to retract his denunciation of herd following.

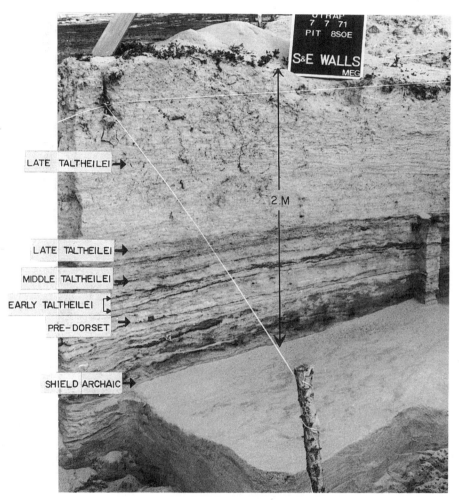

Figure 1.6. Major cultural levels in the Junction site.
KjNb-6 was the first major site to be excavated, providing dated artifacts for culturally assigning surface
artifacts

Rather than canoe the rivers, the Dene and their predecessors followed the herd overland through the north and central drainages in the summer and over frozen rivers and lakes of the south drainage in winter and spring. On May 20th, 1771, Hearne noted that the Dene carried one-man canoes hundreds of km in order to intercept the herd at a crossing (Hearne 1958:62). Mobility had its costs, however, and invalids and the aged paid the dearest cost under severe conditions. The Dene were also forced to contend with seasonal inconsistencies of abundant meat and fat in summer, and almost none in spring. To endure the trials of life on the move, possessions had to be light, as tents and poles, bedding, vessels, dried meat and babies were carried by hand or sled. But herd following had its rewards: semi-permanent access to a travelling and seemingly endless meat supply, more access to seasonal and geographical resources such as berries, migratory birds and fish; soapstone, chert and quartzite for tool-making; birchbark for baskets, and spruce root for nets and line.

The affiliation of a band with a specific herd was also responsible for the development of distinctive local dialects and a kinship that was unique to the range (Gordon 1975). An example of these distinctions is evidenced by the Kaminuriak band comprising the Hatchet and Duck Lake and Barren Lands local bands. Each band is sororal, where a woman may marry her sister's widower, leviradical, where a man may marry his brother's widow, and patrilateral, where women are exchanged through cross-cousin marriage. But the Caribou-Eater in the adjacent Beverly range are neither sororal nor leviradical, with rare patrilocality. Rather, they are bilaterally-related, with bride going to the groom's band (Smith 1978). Such distinctions support the concept of restricted past contact, a constraint also appearing in tool styles and trade goods which are suitable for testing past herd following.

Caribou	Spring	Summer	Autumn	Winter
♂ meat	low	high	rut tainted	dropping
♀ meat	low	low	high	dropping
♂/♀ meat	moderate	rising	high for size	high for size
♂ fat	very low	rising	very heavy	none
♀ fat	dropping	none	rising	high
♂/♀ fat	moderate	rising	high for size	high for size
fish	low	high	dropping	low
birds	rising	low	none	none
berries	none	low	none	none
muskox	none	low	none	none
beaver	low	none	none	low
bear	low	none	none	low

Table 1.1. Value/access/choice of pre-contact Dene food.
♂ & ♀ = bulls & pregnant cows. ♂/♀ = few non-pregnant cows and yearlings. Beaver and bear were hunted in winter forest.

It appears that human mobility is highest in summer, lowest in winter and sporadic at treeline as caribou enter the forest in August and return to tundra for October rut. Bands did not remain at treeline to conduct both tundra and forest forays because there is no evidence of long occupation. Instead, camps at small stream crossings were used sporadically to hunt subherds dispersed widely east and west. Spring forays north onto tundra had to align with the main migration path, while fall forays deep in the forest involved meandering animals. It was far better to hunt at the large productive camps north of treeline at north-south water-crossings where the Thelon River bends east towards the calving ground at Beverly Lake.

Human Seasonal Nutrition and Birth Spacing

Ethnographic accounts of Dene dependence on caribou suggest potential seasonal change in the nutrition of caribou and hunter. As human seasonal nutrition depends on herd seasonal nutrition to maximize weight and the ratio of fat to meat, cows and bulls were preferred in different seasons (Table 1.1). Bulls were best in summer and early fall, but the efforts of November rutting resulted in the consumption of back fat reserves and also tainted the meat. Cows were better in late fall and mid-winter, while smaller, non-pregnant cows and yearlings had fat that lasted until spring. Fat is crucial to diet and especially for human conception, but was available mainly in summer and autumn. Seasonally, the Dene diet was balanced by eating everything edible. In summer, fall and winter, meat provided protein, fat, iron, vitamin A, riboflavin and niacin. The heart, liver and kidneys gave vitamin C and thiamine. Blood was rich in protein and iron; intestine and stomach contents added calcium, carbohydrates and fiber. Back fat provided vitamins A, E and K, while soft bone ends gave calcium and phosphorous, and the eyes gave vitamin A. Seasonally-available fish, birds, berries, muskox, beaver and bear supplemented diet, but had limited effect on annual nutrition.

Nutrition peaked in July-August when caribou were killed by the hundreds. Meat was eaten raw, dried in strips, or powdered with fat and berries to make pemmican, a convenient, light, nutritious trail food that gave energy for herd-following. When the herd scattered in the winter forest, pemmican became depleted and malnutrition increased. By early spring, people were starving because fish, bear, beaver and birds were few, thin or unavailable. At this time, weight loss caused mainly by fat absence would stress lactating mothers, as seen in other studies by Frisch (1988), and this absence of dietery fat lowered fertility among the Dene.

Birth spacing in most hunting, fishing, gathering and pastoral peoples relate more to female nutrition than cultural factors like birth control, spousal separation and frequency of intercourse (Rosetta 1992:83). Fertility decreases under chronic malnutrition in proportion to food deprivation. Even short term malnutrition impairs ovarian function, disrupts menstruation and lowers the fertile lifespan. A turn-of-century north Greenland study showed Polar Inuit women did not menstruate over a 4-month winter period (Cook 1894a, 1894b, 1897). In addition, very few cyclic menses occurred among 1950-60's breast-feeding Inuit (Otto Schaefer, pers. comm. to Condon 1991:292). The link between nutrition and fertility results in later Dene puberty, earlier menopause and fewer children. Women lactated for 3-4 years, rarely having more than five children in 20 reproductive years (Mason, in Jenness 1955; Hearne 1958:201). Dene seasonal nutrition determined both health and fertility.

To test fertility and birth spacing among herd followers, hundreds of 19th and early 20th century Roman Catholic baptisms showing Dene birth dates in the Beverly and Kaminuriak winter ranges were scanned by computer. They indicate 4 of 5 babies were born in February, March and April, with an April peak (Sister Rose Arsenault, pers. comm.; see also Fig. 1.7). A very steep conception peak occurred in July-August on the tundra, when fat from hundreds of caribou was plentiful, with births in the northern forest nine months later. By late summer, mothers moved north again, carrying their infants in their parkas. Although herd-following by these Dene never attained the magnitude taken by their ancestors, most hunted close to the big mid-route sites where past harvesting intensified. Their mothers and ·

grandmothers obviously had also been subject to summer food peaks and spring deficits causing birth spacing. Their cycle of July-August conception and March-April birthing meshes well with the caribou cycle, just as it undoubtedly did for earlier peoples. As meat and fat are critical to human reproduction, seasonal camp locations offer clues to the reproductive state of Dene women. We shall return to this in the last chapter after site locations of all phases are discussed.

Fr. P. Duchaussois.
Reprinted with permission of Oblate Archives, Yellowknife.

Figure 1.7. Dene babies born about February to April. Baby in foreground is in a moss bag.

Chapter 2

Exploration within the Beverly Caribou Range

Early European Exploration

Henry Hudson, believing that his 1609 voyage to the New World was a failure, undertook a second voyage to find a passage to China. He sailed through Hudson Strait with hope, only to find a large inland sea and a western land beyond. Hudson, his seven-year-old son, and some sick sailors were set adrift in a small open boat by a mutinous crew, but despite this, his discovery became known. Years later, Groseilliers and Radisson brought a load of furs to London from Hudson Bay and convinced a group of London merchants of the potential for profit. With the incorporation of the Hudson's Bay Company in 1670, the stage was set for the exploration of the land west of the Bay. A fort was erected at York Factory near the Nelson River. From this fort, company personnel travelled north to Baker Lake and south into what is now Manitoba. In 1689, although he tried, Henry Kelsey (1929:25) failed to meet any Dene with which to trade. By 1694, English influence was interrupted when York Factory was taken and held by the French for some twenty years.

After James Knight reclaimed York Factory in 1714, he wanted to rebuild and extend the English trade network. To that end he assigned William Stuart and a band of Crees to accompany Thanadelthur, a Dene "Slave Woman" who had escaped from the Cree (van Kirk 1974). She was to act as interpreter and liaison with her people. Efforts were jeopardized by distance, sickness, anger, fear and hunger. When the bodies of nine Dene slaughtered by the Crees were found, Thanadelthur alone followed the large band of retreating Dene and convinced them to return. Ten days later, she negotiated a peace with the Cree and brought her people into the fur trade.

The quest of the Hudson Bay Company for fur, copper, and a Northwest Passage was the stimulus for Hearne being sent out from Fort Prince of Wales (on Churchill River) from 1769-1772. Native copper was already known and unprofitably obtained (Glover in Hearne 1958: xii). Increased trade resulting from the journeys was negligible. The Passage was undescribed and unperceived. But Hearne's journals of his travels across the Barrenlands provide our only descriptions of Dene life before it was irrevocably changed by the fur trade. Amidst Hearne's records of his travels are insights into the dependence of Dene upon caribou, observations of items of material culture, attitudes, shamanism, etc.

My own exploration of Hearne's work led me to explore herd following and to indirectly find a title for this book. In 1771 and 1772, Hearne and a Dene party lead by Matonabbee, hiked from Fort Prince of Wales to the Coppermine and back. While unsuccessful in finding a copper mine, an entry in Hearne's diary mentions an encounter with Caribou-Eater Dene who had followed the Beverly herd south from the Thelon River. This is the first documented evidence of herd following in the Beverly range (Hearne 1958:175-177; entry for Feb.15-24, 1772) . It is also the last because the historic Caribou Inuit ascended this previously held Dene Thelon River territory from the Beverly Lake calving ground past Thelon Bluffs and Crossing-Place-of-Deer to Lookout Point (Tyrrell 1902; map). Dene contact was absent because they had deserted the area at Hornby Point and Warden's Grove around 1800 A.D. for the southern fur trade.

In 1796, David Thompson entered the south winter range of the Beverly caribou by descending the turbulent Fond-du-Lac River from Reindeer and Wollaston Lakes to Black and Athabasca Lakes (Thompson 1916). By 1804, the Northwest Company's Fort Fond-du-Lac, built in 1800, folded in competition with Hudson's Bay Fort Chipewyan. Fort Chipewyan at the west end of Lake Athabasca had better access south of the range via the Churchill River and La Loche and Peter Pond portages.

Western trade routes from the Athabasca, Clearwater, Slave and Peace Rivers to the fur-rich Mackenzie drainage bypassed most Dene (Fig. 2.1). Furthermore, trade items were little needed by the Caribou Eater Dene. Instead, they depended directly upon the caribou and needed little more than a metal hatchet, ice-chisel, file and knife to replace their less efficient stone counterparts (Hearne 1958:51). These simple trade items could be traded over large distances, keeping the Caribou Eater as isolated herd followers until the late 19th century.

In 1832, George Back descended the Slave River to Great Slave Lake and sailed through to the East Arm where he built Fort Reliance. From there, he pulled his boats up Lockhart River waterfalls to Artillery Lake, portaged the height-of-land and descended the Great Fish or Back River to Chantry Inlet on the Arctic Coast. The location of his encounters first with the Dene and then with the Inuit mark the west and north borders of the Beverly range. He was followed by adventurers and trophy muskox hunters who sought an easier route to Artillery Lake and the Barrenlands. They eventually followed an old Indian portage route that Back had missed, naming it after the adventurer, Warburton Pike.

The east border and interior were visited by Father Alphonse Gasté, O.M.I., in 1868. Unlike Hearne, who encountered the Dene at Dubawnt Lake, Gasté saw the Caribou Inuit (Mary-Rousselière 1970:3-17). In 1894, J. B. Tyrrell (1898) of the Geological Survey of Canada descended the Dubawnt River after crossing the height-of-land from Black Lake. He too found Inuit at Dubawnt Lake, and recognizing the change from Hearne's day, suggested that they had occupied the area shortly after the Dene left.

David Hanbury and J.W. Tyrrell in 1901 and 1903 crossed Pike's Portage and mapped the Hanbury and Thelon Rivers to Baker Lake. Adventurers Radford and Street crossed the Hanbury to Bathurst Inlet in the early 20th century.

Charles Camsell of the Geological Survey struck north from Lake Athabasca in the far southwest of the Beverly winter range, crossing a portage that now bears his name. John Hornby and two youths, Harold Adlard and Edgar Christian, arrived at Hornby Point via the Hanbury and Thelon Rivers, but arrived too late to intercept the migrating caribou. In the winter of 1927, they starved to death just weeks before the caribou returned in spring (Whalley 1962).

The Beverly range is a mosaic of Cree, Dene, Inuit, English and French names that reflect original peoples, as well as exploration and history. Dene names such as Thelon (whitefish) River and Dubawnt (ice-shore) Lake (Avaaliq'uuq or far off lake in Inuktitut), and Inuktitut lakes like Kamilukuak (broad river) are on the same maps as British names like Clinton-Colden and Baker Lakes and the Back River. Most recently, the Thelon headwater lakes of Rennie, Jarvis and Knowles were named to honour downed World War II aviators, but native people retain their descriptive names of places that were renamed by the Canada Permanent Committee on Geographical Names in Ottawa. The Dene and Inuit call the Back 'Thlewey-cho-dezeth' (Great Fish) or 'Kuu' (the river). The Dene occupied both forest and tundra, but now use only southern Keewatin in fall hunts. This area is now claimed by Inuit who occupied it historically but were relocated to Hudson Bay villages in the 1950's due to starvation. The Churchill River separates the Dene and the forest Cree and demarcates the southern limit of caribou migration. The central Barrenlands were mapped before World War II by Guy Blanchard of the Topographic Survey. The RCAF photographed the entire Beverly range in the 1950's.

Figure 2.1. Two dog teams on the Mackenzie River.

Fr. P. Duchaussois.
Reprinted with permission of Oblate Archives, Yellowknife.

Previous Archaeological Research

Initial archaeological research did not penetrate the Beverly range due to sheer distance and transport cost. A lack of comparative peripheral artifacts made cultural identification tenuous, resulting in dubious long distance comparison of projectile points to those named Alberta, Scottsbluff, Agate Basin and Yuma in the North American Plains. Later, artifacts collected through geological exploration were compared with controlled stratigraphic material excavated in the 1970's.

R.S. MacNeish (1951:31) was the first to record sites in the range at IgNj-1 at Black Lake and IhNk-1 at Stony Rapids near Lake Athabasca. At its Artillery Lake and Lockhart River west border, he defined the Artillery, Lockhart and Taltheilei complexes, now part of the Taltheilei tradition. His Whitefish complex, said to be from the Whitefish Lake esker, is intrusive because its Plains arrowheads were brought north by a Yellowknifer, and none like them appear at Whitefish Lake (Fig. 2.2).

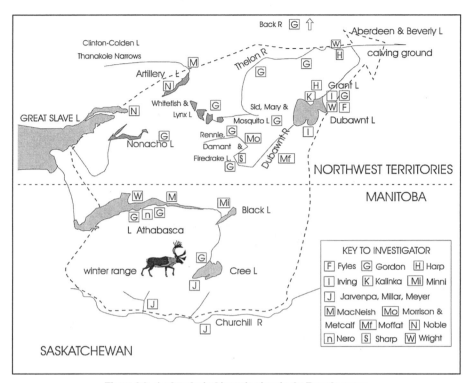

Figure 2.2. Archaeological investigations in the Beverly range.

John Fyles (pers.comm., 1988) of the Geological Survey noted Dubawnt and Thelon River sites in 1954 as part of Operation Baker. He not only found sites near the remote Beverly Lake calving ground, but paved the way for investigations by Moffatt and Harp (1959), Irving (1968) and Wright (1976) by finding the important Grant Lake KkLn-1 site. In 1955, while portaging from the Chipman River and canoeing down the Dubawnt, Moffatt found 9 sites at Chipman (IhNg-1) and Dubawnt Rivers (KeLt-2, KjLn-1), and Selwyn (JbNc-1), Boyd (JjMu-1), Barlow (JlMs-1 & 2), Carey (KaLu-1) and Grant Lakes (KkLn-2). Moffatt and Fyle's Agate Basin points inspired Elmer Harp (1959, 1961) to visit Grant Lake. Using its points and tools from 13 Beverly and 9 Aberdeen Lake sites, Harp defined five cultural phases: Archaic and Late Archaic Indian separated by Pre-Dorset, and Thule leading to historic Caribou Inuit. Later field work identified his Archaic phases as Northern Plano and Shield Archaic, and his Late Archaic as Taltheilei, named earlier by MacNeish (Wright 1972a; Gordon 1976).

In 1960-1963, Robert Nero of the Saskatchewan Provincial Museum found sites on the Crackingstone Peninsula and Cantara Bay on the north and south shores of Lake Athabasca. His points are described in Wright's synthesis of Lake Athabasca prehistory (1975:105-128), and are Plains Besant, Pelican Lake and Taltheilei. In 1963, Irving (1968) revisited Grant Lake and examined KeLq-1 and KgLo-1 on the Slow River south of Dubawnt Lake. His work resulted in a tentative synthesis of eastern Barrenland prehistory. To the west, MacNeish's Artillery Lake study was continued by William Noble, who in 1966-1969 surveyed its western shore south to Pike's Portage (Noble 1971). In the absence of datable buried levels, he organized his complexes according to the beach ridges of Pike's Portage, which mark glacial rebound after the draining of Glacial Lake McConnell.

LdLl-2, the northernmost site with all four Beverly traditions, was found by Harp on Aberdeen Lake in 1958 (Wright 1972a). Here, Wright identified Northern Plano, late Shield Archaic, Pre-Dorset and Taltheilei, plus historic Caribou Inuit. His Plano material was surface, while his Shield Archaic gave an aberrent date of only 1000 B.C.

Access to the center of the Beverly range came following a 1969 Calgary Zoo program to collect muskox calves in the Sanctuary. An amateur archaeologist accompanying the biologists, Ben Strickland, forwarded tools he found to the Riveredge Foundation. It alerted University of Calgary archaeologists, and a year later a Canadian Forces 435 Squadron Hercules at Edmonton parachuted supplies for three seasons into Warden's Grove. The Thelon River project ended in 1976, finding four large stratified sites with Taltheilei, Pre-Dorset and Shield Archaic levels, and providing a dated tool base for assigning surface tools from the remaining 64 sites.

Surveys from Warden's Grove basecamp took us downriver to Hornby Point, upriver to the Dickson Canyon of the Hanbury River, overland south to the Clarke River, and north to Steele Lake. In 1973-1974, the lower Thelon River was surveyed downstream from Hornby Point, past Thelon Bluffs and Ursus Island to Beverly Lake, where all traditions are represented. In 1973, the Back River or north border of the range was surveyed from McKinley River to Garry Lake. Several sites there may be Dene, but most were historic Uvaliarlit, a sub-group of the Netsilik Inuit.

Meanwhile, surveys continued in more accessible points of the south range. Wright (1975) surveyed Lake Athabasca, finding Pre-Dorset, Early, Middle and Late Taltheilei, and possibly, Shield Archaic, the latter a first in the Mackenzie drainage. In 1972-1974, Minni (1976) found Taltheilei, Pre-Dorset and Northern Plano at nearby Black Lake, her Agate Basin point marking a change in game from prairie bison to caribou about 8,000 years ago.

In 1974, radiocarbon dates at the Grant Lake Migod site showed a 6,500-3,500 B.P. Shield Archaic occupation, and added an important Plano date (Gordon 1975:93). They suggest the Dubawnt valley was the main early caribou migration route before the Thelon valley was adopted in Pre-Dorset and Taltheilei times. The 18th-19th century changes from Taltheilei Dene to Caribou Inuit noted by Hearne on July 30, 1770, and Tyrrell on August 18, 1893 near Grant Lake (Tyrrell 1911:96) support an 1800 A.D. Migod Late Taltheilei radiocarbon date (S-1158b/NMC-831). This marks decimation of the Dene on the tundra by disease, as well as their exodus for the fur trade in the northern forest.

In 1975, we surveyed little-known Caribou-Eater territory at the Dubawnt, Thelon and Taltson headwaters (Fig. 2.3). Gordon and Wright followed the forested Taltson from Noman Lake south to Nonacho Lake and east to Gray Lake. Metcalf and von Krogh portaged between Firedrake Lake on the Dubawnt headwaters to Jarvis Lake on the Thelon. Both recorded sites at Damant, Rennie and Knowles Lakes on the upper Thelon. Significant finds were Plains and Late Taltheilei notched points, a few Pre-Dorset tools, and Dene standing tepee poles, historic graves and a 1930's family supply box with embroidery, sewing and shotgun reloading equipment. The very rich sites at Firedrake Lake suggest it was not only a Dene center, but was used by hunters of all four prehistoric traditions. That it remains Dene is seen anecdotally. The footprints, test pitting and singing across the lake by two huge crew members of my second team badly scared local hunters. From their antics, the hunters thought they were bushmen or *bekaycho* and would have shot them on sight (Sharp 1988). Fortunately, my crew members continued their survey north to our camp at Rennie Lake.

Figure 2.3. Archaeological site at a minor caribou water-crossing in the forest, upper Thelon River.

In 1976, excavations were resumed in KjNb-7 at Warden's Grove. More Shield Archaic, striated Pre-Dorset and Taltheilei tools were dated. A bottom Shield Archaic level dated 4,050 B.C. In August, KeNi-4 was found and tested at Whitefish Lake, 100 km southwest, followed by a survey of Lynx and Howard Lakes, where we found tools of all traditions. The Elk branch of the upper Thelon was canoed from Damant Lake to Warden's Grove by Frank Metcalf and David Morrison, with side trips to Jim, Mantic and Sid Lakes. Finds include sites of all traditions, and several historic Dene camps.

In 1977, Late Taltheilei sites HjNo-1 and HkNh-5 were found at Cree Lake in northern Saskatchewan. This was followed by Late, Middle and Early Taltheilei sites IdNl-1 and IdNl-2 on the Pipestone branch of Cree River. Later in the summer, we returned to Whitefish Lake to dig KeNi-2, 4 and 5. Noteworthy finds were Plano points, a Plains Middle period Duncan point dating 2200 B.C., and more Middle and Early Taltheilei tools and dates.

In 1977, Hans Kalinka recorded historic Caribou Inuit sites at Aberdeen Lake where the Thelon and Dubawnt merge, while Tom Foess found a long Dene metal lancehead at KcNe-1 below Whitefish Lake (ASC Archives). Henry Sharp added early and late historic Dene sites at Firedrake Lake. According to 1978 ASC archival data, Kalinka found a Caribou Inuit whalebone sled runner at the Grant Lake inflow, and KkLn-18 at the Chamberlin River. Rob Common, overwintering at Warden's Grove, found a Middle Taltheilei point at KkNb-23 (ASC Archives), near the remains of an incinerated Soviet nuclear-powered satellite.

In 1978, we surveyed the sand dunes along the south shore of Lake Athabasca from William River east to Fond-du-Lac village, adding more Northern Plano, Shield Archaic, Pre-Dorset and Early, Middle and Late Taltheilei sites to the south range database. Athabasca and Black Lake Northern Plano also helped trace early hunter movement from the Plains through the boreal forest to the tundra.

In 1982, we surveyed Mary, Mosquito and Sid Lakes on an unnamed Dubawnt headwater river; our goal to trace Northern Plano north to Grant Lake. The earliest tools were, however, Shield Archaic. Perhaps Northern Plano hunters continued directly north from Black Lake via the Dubawnt proper, a poorly surveyed area. Pre-Dorset and Taltheilei tools were numerous in 56 sites. Another Dene camp was found, while Pre-Dorset at KcLw-2 at the Mary Lake outflow dated 2,745±250 B.P. (S-2224). KdLw-1, dug in 1983 at a north Mosquito Lake caribou crossing, had a bottom level with likely Shield Archaic quartzite flakes dating 6,710±140 B.P. (S-2191). This underlay a Pre-Dorset level dating 3,550±125 B.P. (S-2193), while above were Early and Earliest Taltheilei levels dating 2,485±85 and 2,800±110 B.P. (S-2493 and S-2192). Near the surface were Middle, Late and historic Taltheilei levels.

In the mid-1970's, David Meyer (1979, 1983) surveyed part of the Churchill River valley in northwest Saskatchewan, later adding the Haultain River south of Cree Lake, and finding several Taltheilei points. In 1979-80, James Wilson (1981) discovered a few more sites at Little Gull and Archibald Lakes and on the west bank of the MacFarlane River on Lake Athabasca.

In 1982, David Morrison and Frank Metcalf surveyed part of the Lockhart river, finding the first Shield Archaic point on the Mackenzie drainage.

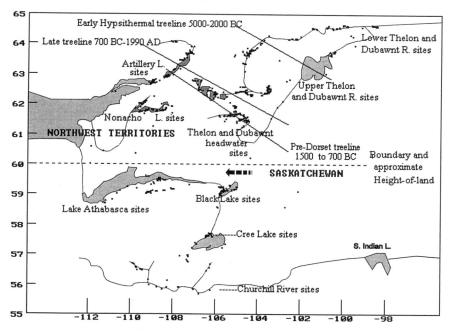

Figure 2.4. Distribution of 1002 Beverly sites.

James Millar (1983) excavated two Late Taltheilei campsites on the Kisis Channel of the Churchill River near Buffalo Narrows, northern Saskatchewan. His stratified sites are important because they set one culture relative to another in time, while marking the southern limit of the Beverly range. His materials add significant new data to my forest database, lending credence to comparative studies for the entire range. The Late Taltheilei people who lived at his sites, and later Dene people in the same locale, mainly fished and hunted boreal fauna such as moose, but they also hunted caribou. The sites give time depth to the southern extreme of Dene occupation. As in Hearne's time, the Churchill River separated the ancestors of both the Dene and Cree.

With broadened surveys of the range, dated materials from buried components provided a means for reinterpreting some incipient work. I interpreted MacNeish's strange Artillery Lake stemmed points as Middle Taltheilei, shouldered points as Early Taltheilei, and big crude side-notched Lockhart points as Late Taltheilei. All represent the material culture of ancient Dene Indians. Noble's Canadian Tundra tradition was separated into its Taltheilei Indian and Pre-Dorset components. David Morrison and Frank Metcalf's find of a side-notched point on the Mackenzie drainage extended the range of Shield Archaic peoples.

Mapping Caribou Hunting Camps in Forest and Tundra

At first glance, it is easy to assume that the 1,002 archaeological sites in Fig. 2.4 represent sites selected because they were accessible along rivers or beside lakes; i.e., the archaeologist could get to them easily. Such is not the case, as our surveys were unconfined to lake and river banks, and many were done overland on foot (Fig. 2.5). Even during "time off" from major excavations, twenty km hikes to inland areas were common, and resulted in sparse and small sites. Site distribution from these many years of survey and excavation probably are an accurate representation of reality.

Unsurveyed areas include the height-of-land north of Lake Athabasca and most of the Dubawnt River. The height-of-land is a mosaic of tiny lakes, glacial-debris strewn waterways and rocky hills. A few tiny camps exist on its edges, but surveying here may not be worth the expense of helicopters, the only aircraft capable of landing there. The Dubawnt demands the combined canoeing skills for large lakes and whitewater, and would require air-lifting boats capable of handling both types of water.

If any comparison were to be made between tundra sites, treeline sites and forest sites, I needed a geographic indicator that would be consistent through time. The treeline itself can be plotted deep into the past using radiocarbon-dated buried stumps, cones, bark and needles. It's advance in extended warm periods and recession during prolonged cold affected site location.

The post-glacial treeline retreated 200 km about 3,500-3,000 years ago to Kasba Lake, Manitoba (Sorenson et al. 1971) during the Pre-Dorset period. It advanced to Ennadai Lake about 2,700 years ago during a warm period when the Earliest Taltheilei phase replaced Pre-Dorset. Conditions stabilized 2,200-1,800 years ago during Middle Taltheilei, but 1,100 years ago the forest re-advanced 100 km. It returned 50 km to Kasba Lake 800 years ago, then readvanced to Ennadai Lake where it remains. Major shifts of 200 km occurred before and after Pre-Dorset, with much smaller shifts across the present treeline in Taltheilei. Treelines were parallel throughout prehistory because the range is quite flat and mean temperature isotherms are parallel.

Figure 2.5. A caribou drivelane on the upper Thelon River.

Southern sites were always forested, northern sites were always on tundra, but intermediate sites were forested from 6,000-3,000 B.C., tundra covered at 1,500-700 B.C., reforested at 700 B.C.-1,200 A.D. and at treeline from 1,200 A.D. to the present. Some spruce between Warden's Grove and Hornby Point are 400 years old, 60 cm wide at breast height and 20 m tall, while other trees are 150-200 years old and smaller (Dennis 1970). Warden's Grove probably began in the warm post-glacial and was widely used by all peoples, as seen in its big stratified sites with rich charcoal layers. Named after Warden Knox who monitored muskox in the newly-created Thelon Game Sanctuary in the 1930's, it separated from continuous forest during the cold Pre-Dorset period. From the Grove, driftwood floats downriver to the Beverly/Aberdeen Lake calving ground, where it was collected at *Akilineq* by Inuit from Bathurst Inlet and Coronation Gulf (Stefansson 1919). Except along the treeless Back River, both Inuit and Indians had access to wood for making tent poles, sled runners and tools. Both built campfires near treeline, but where firewood was scarce, hearths are tiny or absent.

The presence of wood made forest conditions for hunters markedly different from that of the tundra. Its importance is easily taken for granted until hunters need wood on the tundra for warmth and cooking. While tiny willow and heather cooking fires were used, no longer are there poles to support a tent, runners for sledges, shafts for spears and arrows, and most importantly of all, a hearth for warmth, cooking and fellowship. So important was the treeline that the largest hunting camps were near it, and are easily found in the open ground cover.

In all periods, herd and hunter lived the cold half-year (November-April) in the sheltered forest and the warm half-year (May-October) on the tundra. As wood access changed with the treeline, its effects on material culture and camp location were crucial. To show this, I divided forest and tundra using three past treelines (Fig. 2.4).

Chapter 3

Historic Dene and Caribou Inuit

European trade goods mark Dene emergence from the prehistoric Late phase (1300-200 years ago) of the Taltheilei tradition. Contemporary with the Dene are the Caribou Inuit descendents of a coastal Thule tradition that entered the north Beverly range. Their tools are not prehistoric, but are included here because they ended the long tradition of herd following by preventing the Dene from pursuing the caribou north in summer.

Historic Dene

European goods were carried inland by the Cree and Dene well in advance of Hudson Bay Company personnel. Traded for fur and meat, these iron, steel, brass, copper, cloth, pottery and glass items are found among the collapsed poles of tent rings and mixed with quartzite tools in top archaeological levels (Fig. 3.1). Too recent for radiocarbon-dating, they and their users are described by Hearne (1958) who visited forest and tundra, and Mackenzie (1801) who crossed the forest (Table 3.1). Absent stratigraphically, but recorded historically, are perishable crude wood paintings, quillwork, moosehair embroidery, double paddles borrowed from the Caribou Inuit and birchbark boiling baskets from the Cree (Gordon 1977:73).

Bathurst range	Beverly tundra	Beverly forest	Kaminuriak range
Hearne (1958) Mackenzie (1801)	(S-1007 & S-1160) at the Migod site KkLn-4 at Grant Lake on the Dubawnt River. (S-712) at KjNb-7 at Warden's Grove on the Thelon River.	(Gak-3797) at IgOc-1 on Lake Athabasca	Hearne (1958)

Table 3.1. **Dene historic references and radiocarbon estimates too recent for dating.** All are "modern" dates.

Figure 3.1. Copper and steel pots and kettles traded from the Hudson's Bay Company simplified cooking for the Dene.

Dene on the Tundra

On February 24, 1772, Hearne (1958:176) encountered a Caribou-Eater family that had followed the caribou south from their Warden's Grove tundra camp on the Thelon River. He also found the Dene at Lake Dubawnt on his first Coppermine attempt in 1769 A.D., just as we found their tundra tools there and at Sid, Mary and Mosquito Lakes in the 1970's. Two years later, he and those Dene familar with the tundra passed the Artillery Lake sites (Fig. 3.3) on their way to Bloody Falls on the Coppermine River. When ethnologist Ernest Burch (1972:340) studied the Caribou Inuit, the Dene had not inhabited the tundra for almost two centuries, but historic accounts (Smith 1970:315) and archaeological data provide evidence of their earlier presence. Tundra artifacts are listed in Table 3.2.

Dene Tools and the Treeline

Tundra sites are larger but fewer than forest sites, confirming Hearne's observations that large groups assembled to hunt caribou at tundra water-crossings. The smaller number of tundra sites suggest lessened emphasis as the fur trade drew the Dene south. In fact, most tundra sites are near treeline in the Sid-Mary-Mosquito Lakes cluster, with other tundra sites north or west at Artillery and Clinton-Colden Lakes, the Thelon River from Warden's Grove to Beverly Lake, and Grant Lake. One large forest cluster is at Damant, Rennie, Knowles and Firedrake Lakes, an area still used sporadically by Dene who fly in from Black Lake and Stoney Rapids in northern Saskatchewan. Others are at Whitefish and Lynx Lakes, Noman-Nonacho and Gray Lakes, Athabasca, Cree and Black Lakes, with scattered sites at south Artillery Lake and along the upper Churchill River. The straight line on my maps from mid-Artillery Lake, past Sid, Mary and Mosquito Lakes, approximates the treeline.

Until the discovery of the tundra camps, it was assumed that Dene forest hunters gathered at treeline to intercept the southward-bound caribou (Smith 1978:84). The large number of treeline sites reveal hunter movement south from summer tundra to winter forest (Fig. 3.2). Few represent late winter camps because hunters cannot sustain the pace of pregnant cows moving north through deep snow nor accept the risk of crossing rivers covered with dangerous candle ice. My data suggest hunting families began to follow the herd in late May and June after lakes were clear of ice. Of 203 sites, 156 are in forest and 47 are on tundra (Fig. 3.3).

Mixed with bone and wood in some tundra and many treeline and forest sites, are metal and plastic trade goods. Forest trade items of brass, copper, steel and glass predominate because they are closer to fur trade routes (Table 3.2; Fig. 3.4. KjNb artifacts are from Warden's grove tundra; KeNi and KcNg artifacts are from forest camps at Whitefish and Lynx Lakes).

Tundra artifacts	Forest artifacts
brass and bone arrowheads KjNb-7:17-1 and KjNb-7:31-7 at Warden's Grove, upper Thelon River	brass buttons and cartridges in JkOg-1:2, JjNh-5:48 and JkNg-5:12 at Rennie, Nonacho and Damant Lakes ♠
tubular beads KjNb-7:31-9b, 31-8 and 31-10 from brass kettles at Warden's Grove, upper Thelon River	copper lanceheads and thick fragments KcNg-3:37, KeNi-4C:1-31 and KeNi-4C:1-32 at Lynx and Whitefish Lakes ♠
kettle fragments at KkLn-4 and KcLw-1 at Grant and Mosquito Lakes	kettle fragments in the top level of KeNi-4 at Whitefish Lake ♠
iron band KiNb-1:2 at Eyeberry Lake, Thelon River	steel trap JlNg-10:10 at Damant Lake, upper Thelon River ♠
steel axe cut peg KjNb-7:31-8	steel knife JdOx-1 on the Taltson River below Nonacho Lake ♠
recent U-shaped 3-rock hearth, level -1 of KkLn-4 at Grant Lake	steel gas drum cap JlNg-4:3 at Damant Lake ♠
bone and wood in LaLg-2 at Mary Lake	steel strike-a-light at Mantic Lake, upper Thelon River
bone and wood at LbLw-1 above the junction of the Thelon and Tammarvi Rivers (Tyrrell 1902)	plastic transmitter part JlNg-5:17 at Damant Lake ♠
Caribou Narrows historic camps KkNj-7 and KlNj-4 on Clinton-Colden Lake (ASC Archives).	glass beads from a family chest left at Sparrow Bay at Nonacho Lake ♠

Table 3.2. Dene artifacts (see Figs. 3.4 & 3.10). ♠=treeline site

Reprinted with permission of the Hudsons Bay Company Archives, Provincial Archives of Manitoba N5832

Figure 3.2. Dene camps at treeline.

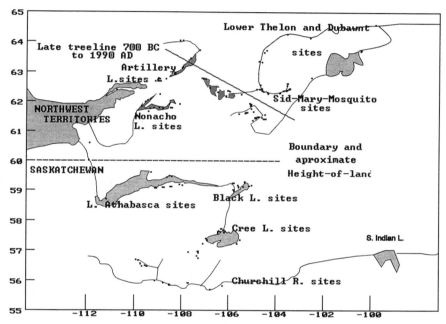

Figure 3.3. Distribution of 203 Dene camps and the Late treeline.

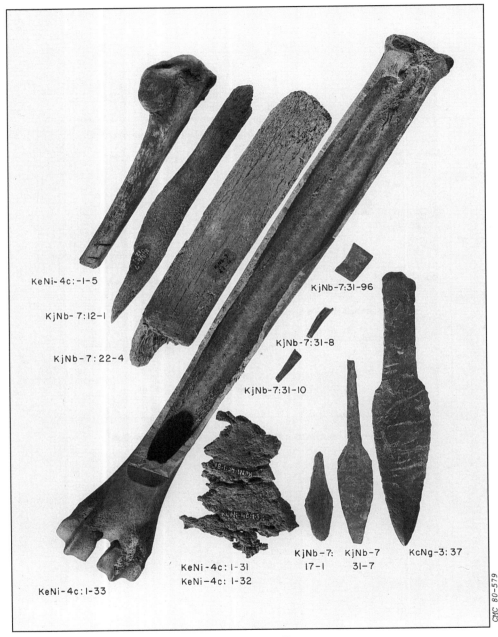

Figure 3.4. Dene artifacts.

Analysis of projectile points

The tool most distinctive and easily identified to a hunting culture is the projectile point. Metal and bone points are depicted but not compared in the tables because they are few and vary from short arrowheads to long lanceheads (Fig. 3.4 bottom). Though historic, sheet brass arrowhead KjNb-7:31-7 (84.5x15.9x1.5 mm & 6 g) was in a Late Taltheilei level, suggesting very early tundra trade with the Hudson Bay Company before Hearne. Native copper surface point KcNg-3:37 (126x26x4.5mm & 51.9 g) is alternately ground and was used on a short forest lance. KjNb-7:17-1 (41x12x3 mm & 0.66 g) is a short bone arrowhead. Five points are from four scattered tundra sites at KiNk-10 on Lockhart River, KjNb-6 & 7 at Warden's Grove (3), and KkLn-17 at Grant Lake. Lance and arrowheads at the large KjNb-7 river-crossing suggest caribou were taken while crossing the Thelon to the south bank, before they dispersed. Eight points are in forest sites at KeNo-32 on the East Arm of Great Slave Lake, KeNi-4 (2) and KcNg-3 at Lynx-Whitefish Lakes on the upper Thelon, JjNh-14 and JiNd-1 at Damant-Firedrake Lakes on the upper Dubawnt, and HcOi-2 at Saleski Lake on the Churchill River (Fig. 3.5)

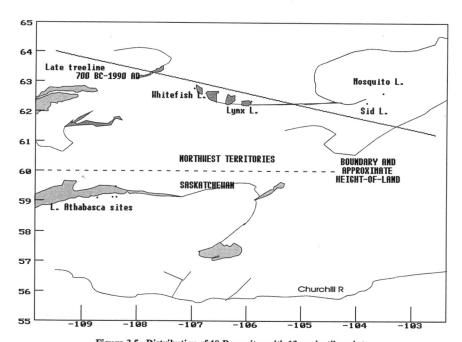

Figure 3.5. Distribution of 10 Dene sites with 13 projectile points.

Untanged corner or side-notched quartzite or metal spadelike points superficially resemble those of Woodland Cree and Plains Indians living near the Churchill River (Table 3.3). Most are biconvex with unground flat bases, a few of which taper. Three are shouldered, two each are eared or broken, four are tanged, one is fully ground, and one at Lockhart River is also a knife. Their mean, maximum and minimum measurements and standard deviations are in Table 3.4.

Traits	Forest total (8)	Tundra total (5)
Material	2 copper; 2 quartzite;1 each of quartz, shale, basalt, chert	2 quartzite and 1 each of chert, brass and bone
Plan	6 spadelike and 2 lanceolate	3 spadelike and 2 lanceolate
Section	6 biconvex and 2 biplanar	3 biconvex and 2 biplanar
Taper	6 tapered to tip and 2 parallel-sided	2 tapered to tip; 1 to haft and 1 is parallel-sided
Basal edge	4 unground , 1 ground flat and 3 unground round	1 unground and 2 ground flat; 1 unground and 1 ground tang
Base plan	5 unground side-notched, 2 parallel tang; 1 unground square	2 ground side-notch; 2 tapered tang,1 unground corner-notch
Base traits	2 eared and 1 fully ground	1 hafted knife made from a side-notched point
Shouldered	2	1

Table 3.3. Comparing Dene forest and tundra points.

Est	No.	Min.	Max.	Mean	S.D.	Exclude	No	Min.	Max.	Mean	S.D.	Exclude
L	4	40.6	110.0	59.25	33.87	none	6	19.4	49.29	39.00	10.75	none
W	4	12.1	59.99	30.12	20.72	none	6	14.4	30.00	24.18	5.73	none
T	4	2.90	10.93	7.08	3.33	none	6	2.70	8.07	6.00	1.86	none
Wt	3	0.66	7.28	4.91	3.69	1	5	2.30	10.01	6.61	2.86	1

Table 3.4. Dene tundra (left) and forest (right) stone point measurements (mm & g).
Exclusions are due to incompleteness from breakage

Analysis of scrapers

Scrapers are used to remove fat and membrane from hides and to soften garments, moccasins, tents and bags by flexing. Striae are on some of their abruptly retouched bits, their orientation, depth and width showing scraper direction and pressure. Endscrapers heavily and obliquely applied to grit-covered skin have deep oblique striae, while wider sidescrapers exert less pressure and are less worn and rarely striated.

Two smaller stratified scrapers were used to assign eight surface ones (Table 3.5 top). KeNi-4C:-1-12 at Whitefish Lake is square, tortoise-backed, ground based, unserrated and striated. KdLw-1:358 at Mosquito Lake is rhomboid, tortoise-back, crude and unserrated.

STRATIFIED (2)	Min.	Max.	Mean	SURFACE (8)	Min.	Max.	Mean
Length	21.42	31.37	26.40	Length	27.37	60.93	47.44
Width	27.90	33.15	30.53	Width	18.29	49.80	36.62
Thickness	5.97	10.17	8.07	Thickness	6.00	17.68	10.57
FOREST (8)	Min.	Max.	Mean	TUNDRA (2)	Min.	Max.	Mean
Length	27.37	60.93	44.77	Length	21.42	52.77	37.10
Width	18.29	49.80	36.04	Width	27.10	40.99	34.45
Thickness	6.00	17.68	10.49	Thickness	5.97	10.83	8.40

Table 3.5. Dene scraper measurements (mm & g) by provenience and range.

Two scrapers are from two tundra sites at Mosquito and Sid Lakes; eight from forest sites at Whitefish, Lynx and Athabasca Lakes (Fig. 3.6). All are unspurred. Forest scrapers are larger (Table 3.5 bottom), half of their bases are dorsally retouched, while tundra bases are unretouched. Plans are rhomboid or unknown due to fragmentation (1 each), ovoid or tearshaped (3 each) and rectangular (2). Sections are planoconvex (6), tortoise-backed (2) and tabular or keeled (1 each). One scraper is serrated, four are on naturally tapered flakes (2 ground, 2 unground) and five have dorsally retouched bases. Half have cortex, none are striated, and bits are very worn (3), worn (6) or unworn (1).

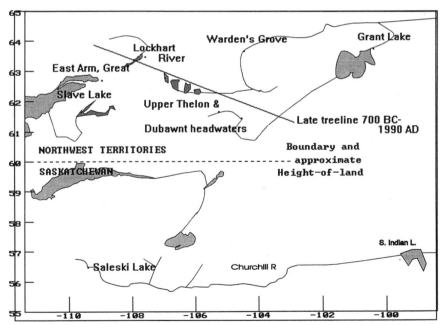

Figure 3.6. Distribution of eight Dene sites with 10 scrapers.

One combination, five end and two side scrapers were found, all surface except those from forest sites KcNf-4 and KeNi-4 (2 each) at Lynx-Whitefish Lakes, with one each in IgOe-1 & 2, IgOe-6 and IiOc-4 on Lake Athabasca. KcNf-4:23, from an historic tent ring, is on a beige cortex tearshaped planoconvex serrated unworn spall. KeNi-4:275 is on a black and red iron axe fragment. KeNi-4B:3 is of pink and gray mottled chert and IgOe-6:2 is a crude black chert pebble.

Analysis of knives

Four stratified knives are used to classify six surface ones (Table 3.6 top). Four tundra ones are from KiNk-1 and KdLw-1 at Lockhart River and Mosquito Lake. Six scrapers are from forest sites KeNi-4 and JlNg-10 at Whitefish and Damant Lakes (Table 3.6 bottom and Fig. 3.7). Eight are quartzite; two are metal: JlNg-10:10, a perforated steel trap fragment; and KeNi-4:1311, a bifacially ground copper blade with a 4 mm drillhole and blunt square ends. There are too few stone forest and tundra knives to compare.

STRATIFIED (4)	Minimum	Maximum	Mean	SURFACE (6)	Minimum	Maximum	Mean
Length	one estimate of 50mm			Length	one estimate of 119.63mm		
Width	20	45	32.50	Width	25.28	59.99	36.86
Thickness	4.22	11.78	8.20	Thickness	1.41	10.93	6.98
FOREST (6)	Minimum	Maximum	Mean	TUNDRA (4)	Minimum	Maximum	Mean
Length	no estimate possible			Length	no estimate possible		
Width	no estimate possible			Width	19.59	59.99	39.79
Thickness	7.94	11.78	9.69	Thickness	4.22	10.93	7.92

Table 3.6. Dene stone knives (mm & g) by provenience and range.

All four excavated knives are transversely or obliquely broken. All are beige quartzite bifaces - three at tundra site KdLw-1 and one at forest site KeNi-4 (Fig. 3.7). They include a base, two tips and a flat tapered unground base-midsection. Two are lanceolate, one is ovoid and one is fragmented. KdLw-1:1095 is serrated and KdLw-1:343 is worn but unstriated. Except for KiNk-10:38, the six surface knives are from forest sites. All are bifacial with unground base, except unifacial KeNi-4B:5. KiNk-10:38 was an alternately retouched side-notched point. Three knives are lanceolate; one is rectangular. The fully ground copper and side-notched knives are complete, except for two midsections and a tip; all are worn. The four knives with tips are one notched, pointed and sharp; two pointed and worn, and one of square dull copper. All four are without striae. KeNi-4B:22 of white quartzite is very thick (10.41 mm) for its length. The large range of knife plans and usage is due to diverse application, the transition from stone to metal, and conversion from side-notched projectile points.

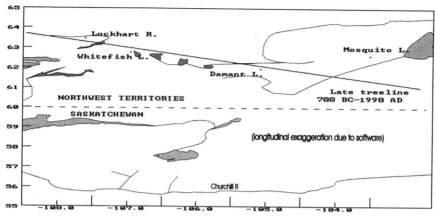

Figure 3.7. Distribution of four Dene sites with 10 knives.

Analysis of chithos

Chithos are usually flat sandstone discs used after scrapers to soften hides. As only one fragment of 10 is from a tundra site (KdLw-1:1106; Mosquito Lake), range comparison is meaningless. All forest chithos are from sites at the following lakes: Cree (HiNi-1 & HjNo-2); Athabasca (IgOg-16), southeast Lynx (KcNf-3 & 4 - 5 chithos) and Whitefish (KeNi-4). All are worn, ovoid, flat, beige sandstone, except HjNo-2:49, a green-black basalt tear-shaped cortex spall by Cree Lake Lodge, and one of pink quartzite on southwest Lake Athabasca. KcNf chithos have blunt backs for handling. Chithos in KcNf-4:24 tent ring 3 were used to classify four surface ones. The mean size of forest chithos is 116.2 x 81.3 x 10.9 mm & 153.6 g.

Analysis of detritus

Flake detritus results from tool-making, its size and quantity showing degree of reduction and availability of stone. Of 82 tundra flakes and 31 forest flakes, 16 are surface and 97 are buried (Fig. 3.8). From bags of uncounted flakes, 62 representative tundra flakes include one of basalt, six of chert (mostly gray), one of white quartz and 54 of quartzite (mostly beige, but also gray & pink). Four flakes are cobble cortex spalls. Twenty-four forest flakes include eight of basalt (mostly gray), five of chert (black or gray), one of white quartz, eight of quartzite (mixed colours) and two of black or gray shale. Four flakes are worked; three are cobble spalls. Tundra flakes are smaller (Table 3.7), with most at KdLw-1 on Mosquito Lake. Larger forest flakes are mainly at Whitefish Lake site KeNi-4. Cobbles for knapping were abundant at both sites, with knappers sharpening and conserving tools more at Mosquito Lake, as seen in smaller flakes. But size may also relate to knapping preference, as the more plentiful Whitefish basalt was harder to reduce.

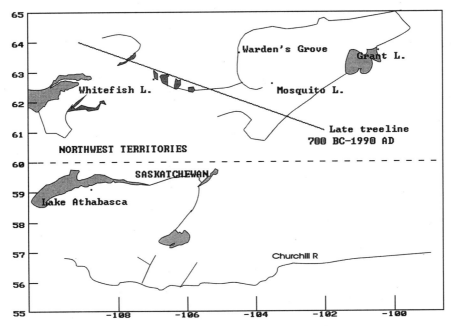

Figure 3.8. Distribution of 5 Dene sites with 113 flakes.

TUNDRA (62)	Minimum	Maximum	Mean	FOREST (24)	Minimum	Maximum	Mean
Length	7.85	59.65	25.90	Length	20.43	55.50	33.20
Width	3.95	47.79	21.07	Width	14.23	34.20	22.94
Thickness	0.97	19.19	5.63	Thickness	2.10	17.80	6.77

Table 3.7. Comparing Dene tundra and forest flakes (mm & g) (their numbers are bracketted).

Analysis of miscellaneous stone artifacts

Mosquito Lake tundra site KdLw-1 has a quartzite core and fragment; Whitefish Lake forest site KeNi-4 has three basalt and quartzite fragments. Bar whetstone KeNi-4B:36, with wide striated groove, is of worn ochre-stained pink sandstone measuring 78x51x11 mm. Dene fire-cracked rock was identified only at KdLw-1.

Analysis of metal artifacts

The Dene used steel, iron, brass and copper trade items (Figs. 3.9-3.10). Many steel and iron ones have rusted away, but their use as knives, hatchets and axes are implied in cutmarks on sticks, logs and stumps. Of the 77 metal items in 30 sites, 53 were surface and 24 were buried; all mainly from forest sites. Tundra finds are at Thanakoie Narrows near Clinton-Colden Lake, Eyeberry and Mantic Lakes on the upper Thelon River and Mosquito Lake on the upper Dubawnt. Forest sites extend from

Pike's Portage to Lynx-Whitefish and Rennie-Damant Lakes on the upper Thelon, to Firedrake Lake on the upper Dubawnt. Southerly sites are at Tsu and Gray Lakes on the Taltson, to Athabasca, Stony, Black and Cree Lakes, Buffalo Narrows and Fort Chipewyan.

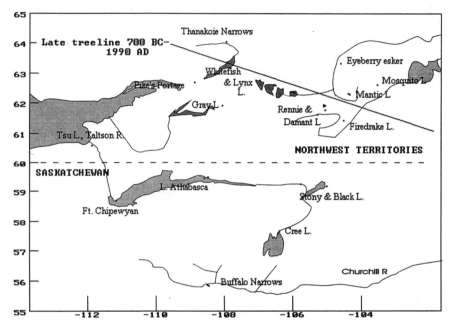

Figure 3.9. Distribution of 30 Dene sites with 77 metal objects.

Tables 3.8a-b show trade metal dispersion, half of tundra metal being native copper and a fourth is iron. The rest are brass and steel fragments. Two-thirds of forest metal is brass and steel, then lead, iron and copper. The absence of tundra lead sinkers relates to the inconvenience of transporting this heavy metal, plus a lack of interest in fishing by the Dene. Copper is more plentiful on the tundra due to nearby placer sources at Bathurst Inlet and Coppermine River.

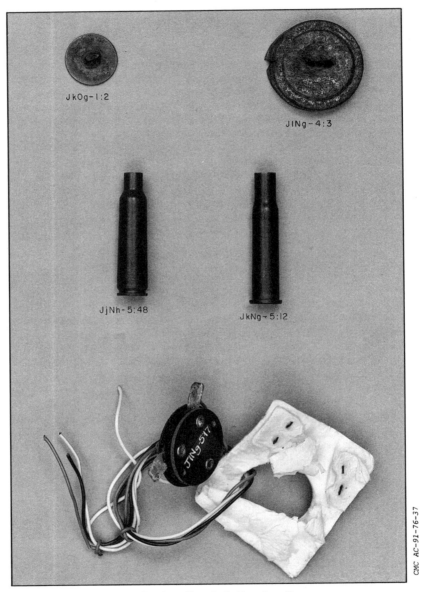

Figure 3.10. Historic artifacts in the Beverly caribou range.

METAL OBJECT	LOCATION	MEASUREMENTS (mm/g/calibres) and REMARKS
copper arrowhead	JiNd-1:12 at Firedrake Lake	39x13x2/3. Tanged and ground
1944 copper cent	IiOc-1 at Lake Athabasca	(Wright 1975). Associated with bead
10 copper fragments at Whitefish and Mantic Lakes	KeNi-4C:1-31/32; KbNa-16:2 and 3a-g; and KbNb-4:4	Fig.3.4 (bottom) measures 39x19x3/7
copper lancehead	KcNg-3:37 at Lynx Lake	126x26x5/52 (Fig.3.4 bottom)
brass art piece	IeOs-1:4 at Fort Chipewyan on Lake Athabasca	16x15x2/4 (resembles a gunflint)
arrowhead of rolled brass	KjNb-7:31-7 at Warden's Grove, Thelon River	85x16x2/6 (Fig.3.4 bottom)
brass buttons	GlOc-2:1 and JkOg-1:2 (Fig. 3.10)	22mm diameter (Millar 1983)
brass sheet and hook	KdLw-1:1094 on Mosquito Lake	39x25x1/3 and 27x19x2/?
20 cartridge cases; various calibers. Also JkOi-2 and Whitefish Lake	JkNg-5, JjNh-5, IhNk-2, KcNf-5 and KeNj-1 at Lynx, Damant, Rennie and Stony Lakes (Fig.3.9)	.22 (6), 30-30 (5), 250-3000 (2; Fig.3.10), .44 (2), 45-90 (1), 30'06 (2) and .270 (1?)
steel knife	JdOx-1:2 at Tsu Lake cabin, Taltson River	see Bielowski 1984
steel drum seal	JlNg-4:3 at Damant Lake (Fig. 3.10 top)	37mm diameter x 4mm
strike-a-light and prong	KbNb-4:1 & 16 at Mantic Lake	86x44x5/45 and 70x7x3/5
.44 calibre bullet mold	JlOa-2:1 at Gray Lake	like pair of pliers
knife from trap	JlNg-10:10 at Damant Lake	63x25x3/12 (from spring portion)
iron scraper	KeNi-4:275 at Whitefish Lake	34x50x6/41 (resembles axe bit)
9 steel fragments (see locations) and rivet KeNi-4B:27 from Whitefish Lake	LaNl-2 at Thanakoie Narrows; KcNi-3:49 at Lynx Lake; KdLw-1:1094 at Mosquito Lake	57x13x3/8 and 60x17x3/15, etc. Made from traps, except rivet.
2 steel washers	IiOd-2 at Lake Athabasca	52x52x4/48 (Wright 1975)
steel screw	KcNf-4:45 at Lynx Lake	109x15x7/11. Bird bunt
7 steel/iron nails; HjNo-2 and KcNb-28	Gloc-1 at Buffalo Narrows and Cree & Jim Lakes	shingle, common, forged square-section and unknown
steel spoon	IiOd-2 at Lake Athabasca	from can (Wright 1975)
2 lead sinkers	HjNo-2 at Cree Lake (plus lead foil)	90x17x15/138 and 49x9x9/16
.22 calibre lead slug	KcNf-4:43 at Lynx Lake	13x10x5/3 (in tent ring)
lead musketballs at IhNg-2 at Black Lake	and GlOc-2 at Buffalo Narrows	14x13x3/5:12x12x6/4 (Minni 1976 & Millar 1983)
plastic and steel	JlNg-5:17 at Damant Lake (Fig.3.10 radio part)	12x39mm diameter/14 g tube socket and battery

Table 3.8a. Dene metal objects.
length/width/thickness/weight in mm & g

Material	Range total	Forest total	Tundra total
brass	24(31)	22(38)	2(11)
copper	14(18)	4(07)	10(53)
iron	12(16)	7(12)	5(26)
lead	9(12)	9(16)	
steel	18(23)	16(28)	2(11)
Total	77(100)	58(101)	19(101)

Table 3.8b. Types of metals in Dene forest and tundra sites (no. and frequency).

Analysis of bone and antler artifacts

Archaeological bone is mostly Dene because podzol soil acids dissolve older bone unless it is frozen. Bone is in tundra sites at Thanakoie Narrows, KjNb-6 & 7 and Elk River on the upper Thelon, and Grant and Mantic-Sid-Mosquito-Mary Lakes on the Dubawnt (Fig. 3.11). Forest bone is from Nonacho-Noman Lakes on the Taltson, Whitefish-Lynx Lakes on the Thelon, Rennie-Damant Lakes on the Elk and Firedrake Lake on the Dubawnt. Southern forest sites with bone are at Athabasca, Black, Key and Cree Lakes on the Mackenzie system, and Buffalo Narrows on the upper Churchill.

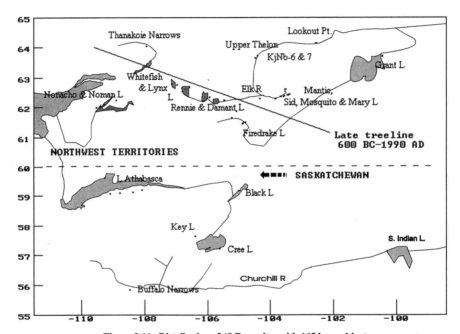

Figure 3.11. Distribution of 48 Dene sites with 165 bone objects.

In 48 sites were 165 bone objects (103 surface; 62 buried). They include 132 bone fragments, 22 teeth, four jaws, a moose tibia, a caribou astragalus and sesamoid, and a dozen tools. Tools are five awls (Fig. 3.4, KjNb-7:12-1), three hide beamers (Fig. 3.4, KeNi-4C:1-33), a gouge, two handles (Fig. 3.4, KjNb-7:22-4) and a caribou antler spatula at KdNi-3. Two awls have round triangular sections and round and pointed ends (Fig. 3.12). KeNi-4:1-5 is a steel cut-marked left humerus of a common or yellow-billed loon (Fig. 3.4 top). Most beamers on split caribou metapodials are used for removing hair from wet hides (e.g., KeNi-4:1-33). A split moose metatarsal beamer, and grooved, pointed and spatulate tools of unknown use, are from GlOc-21 at Buffalo Narrows (Millar 1983:199). JjNh-3:50 is a gouge on a hack-marked lanceolate concavoconvex antler.

Reprinted with permission of Oblate Archives, Yellowknife. Henry Jones, photographer.

Figure 3.12. Using an awl to fasten the ends of a birch bark basket.

Cutmarks are on a caribou metacarpal, a large mammal rib, a snowshoe hare or loon longbone, and a burnt fragment from JlNg-8 on north Damant Lake. All were mixed with knives and preforms, cores and used flakes. KcNf-4 tent ring 2 has 16 bone segments and two caribou ribs, while ring 3 has a bone and wood fragment. On the northwest arm of Firedrake Lake, JiNe-4 has many caribou jaws, skulls and wood chips in a 13 by 30 m area of old campfires dating prior to 1935.

Analysis of wood artifacts

Most wooden objects in campsites are recent Dene, older wooden items having decomposed in the acid soils (Fig. 3.13). Wood distribution resembles that of bone, with tundra sites at Thanakoie Narrows, KjNb-7, and Grant and Jim-Mantic-Mary-Mosquito Lakes. Forest sites are at Pike's Portage and Artillery, Whitefish-Lynx-Howard, Rennie, Firedrake, Athabasca, Middle-Black and Cree Lakes, and Elk and Cree Rivers. Of 50 surface and 18 buried objects from 40 sites, 57 include four arrows and five bows, two birchbark canoes and many rolls, a canoe mold, a charcoal sample, a club, a piece of coal, 17+ grave fences and crosses, several hearths, one lobstick marker tree trimmed of its upper branches, a fork for holding pots or retrieving boiling rocks (pot boilers) to place them in baskets, 11 skin stretchers, two meat racks, several poles, a post, a shaft and eight tent stakes. Tundra and forest items are in Table 3.9 top and bottom, respectively.

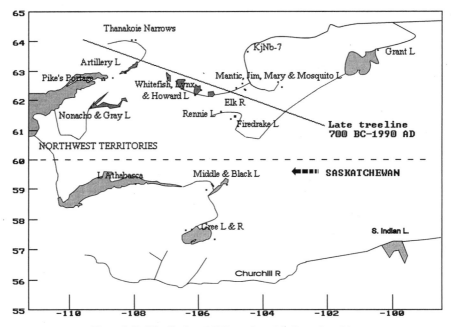

Figure 3.13. Distribution of 40 Dene sites with 68 wooden objects.

WOOD ARTIFACT	LOCATION	ASSOCIATION/REFERENCE
bent pot holder	KkLn-5 on Grant Lake	tent poles and frames and cabins
long bent shaft	KcNb-13 at Mantic-Jim Lakes	unknown use
tanged, flattened skin stretcher	in KcNb-18 tent ring on Mantic-Jim Lakes	tent peg
2.5 cm squared shaft	KcNc-9, junction of Elk and Thelon Rivers	2 cut fragments
cut birchbark	JkOc-9 on southeast Gray Lake, Taltson River	near standing tepee without cover
7 arrow fragments (one 32 cm long)	KcNf-4 tent ring on Lynx Lake. 8 mink? skin stretchers	screw bunt (Table 3.8a), two clubs, a stake and two bows
1.5m post. Side 1 reads "UV Oct.16,1942" ; Side 2 reads "N. A. L. LaFleur"	KbNg-1 on southwest Howard Lake	Dartmouth canoists during World War 2
fallen poles over 2 tent rings	KbNg-2 on southwest Howard Lake	much flaking detritus
3 bark canoes (1 ribless), creche and tent rings with poles	JiNf-13, on northwest arm of Firedrake Lake. Wood cut with beaver-tooth adze	fired stones, 'shaking tent' rings, cut stumps, and stone and bone fragments
meat-drying racks	Nonacho and Athabasca Lakes	recent Dene camps

Table 3.9. Dene wood in tundra (top) and forest (bottom).

Analysis of miscellaneous artifacts

Other miscellaneous artifacts only at forest sites are two white clay smoking pipes with late corner-notched points from GlOc-1 and 3 at Buffalo Narrows, Churchill River (Millar 1983:207), plus another pipe from GlOc-21. Glass shards were at Black and Athabasca Lakes in IhNh-10 and IiOd-2. Chinaware was reported from KeNo-15 near Fort Reliance (Noble 1971:102-135). A radio battery came from a cabin at JiNc-1 on Firedrake Lake. Snowshoes were used, but not preserved (Fig. 3.14).

Fr. P. Duchaussois. Reprinted with permission of Oblate Archives, Yellowknife.

Figure 3.14. Two hunters with snowshoes for powder snow.

Analysis of domiciles and graves

Cabins and transient camps belong to semi-sedentery forest fur trappers, while older tundra tent rings prevail at Thelon and Dubawnt water-crossings (Fig. 3.16; Tables 3.10a-b). Historic accounts show skin tents evolved to canvas tents and cabins. From treeline, cabins extend south from Fort Reliance, Snowdrift, Lynx-Rennie-Firedrake and Nonacho-Gray Lakes, to Tsu Lake and Fort Smith on the Taltson and Slave Rivers. They extend further to the Black, Cree, LaLoche and Peter Pond Lakes, and the Cree, Haultain and Churchill Rivers. Non-Christian graves are simple mounds or log outlines on the ground. Christian graves are coffin burials with cross and picket fence. In Table 3.10c, both are arranged mapwise from northwest to southeast. At Nonacho, Noman, Black, Firedrake and many unnamed other forest lakes, there are both Christian and non-Christian burials; the latter are undated. Christian graves date after 1800 A.D., when the Hudson Bay Company reached Lake Athabasca, with missionaries, fifty years later. Roman Catholic priests canoed the Churchill River and Lake Athabasca, some preaching deep in the forest. For example, in the late 1890's, a large group of Dene were met by a priest at Solitude Lake at the height-of-land between Cree Lake and the Churchill drainage.

TUNDRA TENT RINGS	LOCATION	ASSOCIATION/REFERENCE
2 at KdNb-1	junction of Elk and Thelon Rivers	Tyrrell 1902
several at LbLw-1	junction of Thelon and Tammarvi Rivers	Tyrrell 1902
several at LaLt-5	Lookout Point, Thelon River	drift fence for channelling caribou (Tyrrell 1902)
fallen tent poles	Markham Lake on Dubawnt River	Harp 1959
FOREST TENT RINGS	**LOCATION**	**ASSOCIATION/REFERENCE**
10 at KeNp-2	southwest Artillery Lake	cache pits and hearths (Fig. 3.15 right)
few at KgNl-3	Twin Butte on Artillery Lake	recent age (Noble 1971)
few tent frames	Firedrake Lake on Dubawnt River	
1 at JkOc-8	standing tepee poles on Gray Lake	60-90 year-old square cans
frame at JjNj-1	esker in north Rennie Lake	
implied at JjNh-10	Rennie Lake outlet	notched sharpened tent stakes
many at JiNf-1 and 12	campfires; northeast arm of Firedrake Lake	hunting blind. Trees>100 years (Sharp1988b)
"magic shaking tent" at JiNf-10	northeast arm, Firedrake Lake. Site 3	nearby "Inuit grave" (Sharp 1988b)
JiNf-13,16,18 &19; also meat drying racks	13 tent rings on northwest arm of Firedrake Lake (Sharp 1988)	2 bark canoes, beaver tooth adze, poles, cache and 13 bull antlers with skulls
many at JjNe-7	north shore of Firedrake Lake. Site T19S.	(Sharp 1988b)
? at HiNi-3	Wheeler Esker on Cree Lake	cut wood artifacts (J & B)
1 at HkNn-4	Cree Lake, northern Saskatchewan	muskrat bone (J & B)

Table 3.10a. Dene tundra and forest tent rings.
Unreferences items are the author's; J & B=Jarvenpa and Blumbach 1988.

Cabins (number)	Location	Type of Association and Reference
many at KeNo-1 and 19	also Old Ft Reliance, East Arm,Great Slave L.	Noble (1971:102-135)
1 at KcNu-1	near Snowdrift on Great Slave Lake	
1 at JaOx-1	Slave River near Fort Smith on Slave River	Heitzman 1980
1 at JdOx-1 and JkOf-1	Tsu Lake on Taltson River	HBC metal knife (see Heitzman above)
1 at JkOi-2	isthmus between Hjalmar and Nonacho Lakes	
2 at KbNh-1	southwest Lynx Lake	
1 at JjNc-4	northeast arm of Firedrake Lake	
many at JiNe-3	northeast arm of Firedrake Lake	also fences (Sharp 1988b)
many at JiNf-9 and 15	northwest arm sites #2 & T15, Firedrake Lake	also bark canoe. Sharp (1988b)
1 each at JiNf-19 and JkNf-7	Firedrake and Jarvis Lakes. Sites #'s 22 & 23	also canoe and beaver tooth adze (Sharp 1988b)
1 each at HhNs-1 and 2	Stony Narrows on Cree Lake	13 *features* and 14 *structures* (J & B)
1 at HiNr-1 and 2	Hudson Bay Island on Cree Lake. Site #21	13 *features* and 9 *structures* (J & B)
many at HjNm-1 and 2	Barkwell Bay on Cree Lake	also 1 at HjNn-4 (J & B)
? at HjNo-2, 3 and 6	Cree Lake sites #17 and 18	35 *features* and 33 *structures* (J & B)
1 at HkNn-1, 2 and 9	Widdess Bay, Cree Lake sites #19 & 20)	16 *features* and 13 *structures* (J & B)
1 at IgNi-6	Black Lake	(Minni 1976:34-37)
many at IgNk-2, 3 and 6	Black Lake	copper pot fragments and lead musketballs (Minni 1976)
IhNg-1 and IhNh-1 and 2	IhNk-8 to 11 at Black Lake	many cabins (Minni 1976)
? at HfNt-1, 2 and 4	Haultain River	also 27 *features* and 25 *structures* (J & B)
? at HeNt-1	Haultain River	also 3 *features* and 2 *structures* (J & B)
Bell camps 1 and 2	Haultain River (site #7)	also 1 *feature* and 1 *structure* (J & B)
HcOj-1 and HcOi-1	Laloche Lake, Churchill River (1 each)	see also HdOj-1 and HdOk-1 to 4 (J & B)
1 each at HeOk-1 and 2	Rendezvous Lake, Churchill River	(J & B)
GlOe-1 and GlOg-1	Peter Pond Lake, Churchill River	1 cabin each (J & B)
? at GlNv-1	Alexander Point, Churchill River site #32	3 *features* and 3 *structures* (J & B)
? at GlNw-1	Little Cow Island, Churchill River site #31	1 *feature* and 1 *structure* (J & B)
? at GkNm-3	union of Souris and Churchill Rivers site #36	9 *features* and 8 *structures* (J & B)

Table 3.10b. Dene forest cabins.
Like artifact scatters, dog shelters and hitching posts (Fig. 3.17) and drying racks, *Features* and *Structures* are 2 or 3-dimensional, respectively. J & B=Jarvenpa & Blumbach 1988; unref. items are the author's. HBC= Hudson's Bay Company

Figure 3.15. Dene tents on Great Slave Lake

Burial type	Location	Type of Association and Reference
cemetery at KfNm-15	Timber Bay, Artillery Lake	Christian (Noble 1971:102-135)
grave at KfNm-16	Timber Bay, Artillery Lake	Christian (Noble 1971:102-135)
grave at KgNl-6	west-central Artillery Lake	Christian (Noble 1971:102-135)
cemetery at KeNo-21	Pike's Portage, East Arm, Great Slave Lake	Christian (Noble 1971:102-135)
grave at KeNn-1	Pike's Portage, East Arm, Great Slave Lake	Christian (Noble 1971:102-135)
grave at KaNp-3	east side, north Nonacho Lake	quartzite flakes and scraper
child's grave at KbNo-1	Noman Lake spit	Christian. In 1940's camp
cemetery at JkOh-15	east Nonacho Lake	Christian. South of tourist fish camp
grave or shaking tent at JiNf-10	northeast arm of Firedrake Lake	regarded magical. Low stone wall on hill (Sharp 1988
grave at IgNg-1	Black Lake, northern Saskatchewan	Christian rosary and line of stones
grave at IfNk-2	Black Lake, northern Saskatchewan	Christian picket-fence periphery
grave at IgNj-6	Black Lake, northern Saskatchewan	Christian picket-fence periphery
child's grave at IhNj-5	Black Lake, northern Saskatchewan	in tree (Minni 1976:34-40)
grave at IgNj-12	Black Lake, northern Saskatchewan	(Minni 1976:34-40)
grave at IhNh-2	Black Lake, northern Saskatchewan	(Minni 1976:34-40)

Table 3.10c. Dene graves. Unreferenced items are author's.

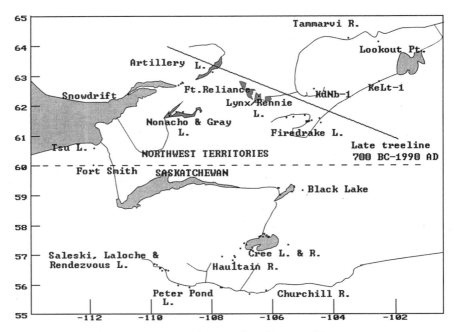

Figure 3.16. Distribution of 77 Dene sites with tents, cabins or graves.

Figure 3.17. "Hitching posts" for sled dogs at Firedrake Lake.
Dene still use the area for autumn caribou hunting

Conclusions Regarding Site Distribution and Artifacts

Table 3.11 summarizes differences in Dene settlement patterns in the forest and tundra. As the forest was affected earliest and heaviest by fur trade and church influences, it had a higher population with a more visible legacy in the form of widely scattered trade copper and iron items, cabins and graves. But of the remaining stone tools, it can be seen that forest points, scrapers and flakes have greater retouch, possibly in keeping with difficulties in procuring new replacement stone because it was snow-covered or faraway in tundra quarries.

Trait	Forest range	Tundra range	Remarks
dating	post-1750 A.D.	post-1800 A.D.	more forest occupation
distributio	very widespread	less widespread	retraction to forest
points	smaller	larger	more forest retouch
scrapers	larger. More dorsally retouched bases	smaller. More unretouched bases	too few to compare. More forest retouch
knives			too few to compare
chithos	only one	eight	too few to compare
flakes	smaller	larger	more forest conservation
bone	caribou	caribou and other	used in many tools
wood	distributed like bone	distributed like bone	used in many tools
metal	brass and steel	copper and iron	separate trading influences
domicile	mostly cabins	mostly tents	mobility and wood
graves	interment	open-air	Christian church influence in forest

Table 3.11. Dene forest and tundra tool and trait comparison.
Unlisted data alike in both ranges. No wedges found

Historic Caribou Inuit

Lured by the fur trade, the Dene took up year-round residence in the forest. Their abandonment of the tundra left an enormous area uninhabited the whole year, a gap soon filled by Caribou Inuit. The Caribou Inuit had traded their traditional maritime lifestyle to subsist on caribou which, due to its migration, enticed the Inuit farther and farther southwest towards the forest where the Dene dwelled. The Inuit spread from the Beverly Lake calving ground 100 km upriver to the Crossing-Place-of-Deer (Tyrrell 1902, map; Fig. 3.18), but were stopped by those Caribou-Eater not drawn to the fur trade. Accounts exist of mutual Dene and Inuit avoidance after spotting the others' campfire smoke (Blanchet 1928:8; Smith & Burch 1979:76-101), but other accounts, some fanciful, state both claimed the land and died in the resulting skirmish (Mallet 1930:31-41).

Until their relocation to coastal villages in the 1950's, the Caribou Inuit were regarded as successful inland hunters. But this was not so, because the Dene prevented them from following the caribou to their winter range, ultimately starving them. Herd followers without suitable alternate game cannot adapt if they are not free to roam the whole range.

Several theories have been proposed to explain Caribou Inuit origins. The primitiveness of their tools suggested to Birket-Smith (1929) that they had occupied the Barrenlands for centuries. Taylor (1968) and Burch (1978) opt for a northern link with Netsilik Inuit occupying Boothia Peninsula and King William Island. The Netsilik are nomadic seal hunters who use sea ice igloos extensively, but their dialect resembles that of the Caribou Inuit. Linnamae and Clark (1976) favour a connection with Hudson Bay coastal Inuit, based upon contemporaneous surface dwellings of both groups and their eastern proximity.

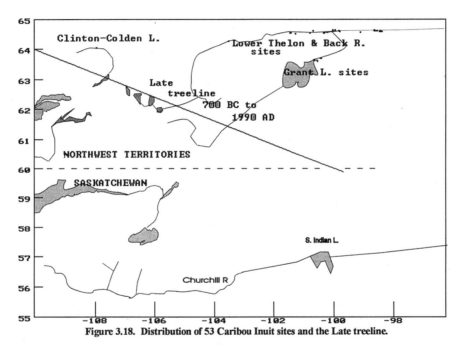

Figure 3.18. Distribution of 53 Caribou Inuit sites and the Late treeline.

I favour Taylor and Burch's proposal of a northern link using archaeological evidence and historic accounts of Inuit camps. The river-crossing of Nadlok on the Burnside just south of the Arctic Circle has Copper Inuit artifacts with coastal affinities (Gordon 1988), but is also on a southeast trade route between the Coppermine River placer deposits and Beverly Lake (Stefannson 1919). Nadlok's abandonment just before the Caribou Inuit occupied Beverly tundra about 1825 A.D., is contemporary with copper in a Caribou Inuit tool at Grant Lake. As other deposits are rare or absent, copper was likely carried past Nadlok by the Copper Inuit in the process of becoming the Caribou Inuit, a process hastened by annual travel to the copper source.

Although rare with a southern and eastern spread, Caribou Inuit copper is thinly distributed north of the treeline. When Grant Lake was surveyed by the Tyrrells in 1896, they found Hearne's Dene had been replaced by Caribou Inuit (Tyrrell 1898, 1902). Several decades after Hearne, Inuit camps were found on the Back River (Back 1836). Except for two tent rings at Thanakoie Narrows near

Clinton-Colden Lake (Morrison 1982), sites cluster on the lower Back, Thelon and Dubawnt Rivers (Fig. 3.19). These sites are near Stefannson's (1919) *Akilinik* (*Akilineq*) camp at Beverly Lake which traded copper for driftwood for making tent poles, sledges and spears. Site contents from northwest (top) to southeast are in Table 3.12.

SITE	LOCATION and ASSOCIATED SITES	CONTENTS, REFERENCE and ASSOCIATED MATERIAL
LaNl-2	Clinton-Colden Lake	tent rings. Also LaNl-3
LgLr-1	east bank of the Consul River at the Back River	Utkuhikhalingmiut Iniut tent camp (Fig. 3.19)
LiLl-1	northwest of Sand Lake. Also LiLm-1	Back River Caribou Inuit
LjLm-1	32 km south of Garry Lake	rings, hunting blinds and *inukshuit*
LjLs-1	McKinley and Back Rivers. Also LjLt-1 to 7	rings, blinds, snow goggles and *inukshuit*
LkLs-1	5 km above confluence of Back and Bullen Rivers	tent rings
LlLo-2	Pelly-Garry Lakes. Also LlLr-1	tent rings. Also LlLq-1 & 2
LcLa-1	10 km above Aberdeen Lake.	tent rings (Harp 1961)
LdLh-2	Aberdeen Lake. Also LdLh-3 and 5	6 rings and 6 cairns (Harp 1961)
LdLj-1	south Aberdeen Lake at the Narrows	tent rings (Harp 1961:21)
LdLl-1	southwest Aberdeen Lake	notched spadelike point (Wright 1972a)
LdLl-2	west Aberdeen Lake	rings, wood fragment, cloth and point (Wright 1972a)
LdLl-4	south Beverly Lake at the Narrows. 75m row of hopping stones with cairn	5 knives, 3 scrapers,core, 4 choppers, ground slate rubbing stone, rings (ASC artifact accession 1400; Harp 1961)
LdLo-2	0.5km to Beverly Lake; 5-6 km to *Akilineq*	caches, rings; drilled, zigzag & dowelled wood kayak rest (Harp 196
LdLo-3	0.5km to LdLo-2	rings. Also LdLo-4 point (Harp 1961)
LdLo-5	northwest bank of Beverly Lake	rectangular sod hut (Harp 1961)
LdLp-1	1.6km above Thelon Bluffs with caribou drive lan	slate knife, cutting block with bored holes and steel cutmarks
LaLt-5	by Lookout Point on theThelon River	tent rings and drift fence
LdLq-3	Ursus Island on the Thelon River	40cm long side-notched and rivetted steel lancehead (trade item)
LdLq-2	Ursus Island on the Thelon River	tent rings. Also LdLq-4
LdLp-1	Pingawalook site at Thelon Bluffs (Tyrrell 1902)	drift fence, meat caches and stone slab igloo.
KkLn-1	Grant Lake. Also KkLn-5 and14 wooden toggle	meat caches, rings, hunting blinds, copper riveted knife (Wright 1975

Table 3.12. Caribou Inuit tundra sites separated into Back, Thelon and Dubawnt drainages.
All references are the author's unless noted.

AC–3–K75–4

Figure 3.19. Caribou Inuit tent ring on the middle Back River.

Chapter 4

The Late Phase of the Taltheilei Tradition

Dating and Distribution

In the Little Ice Age of 300-700 years ago, the Greenlandic Norse disappeared and the Canadian coastal Thule retreated inland to become Copper and Caribou Inuit. Late Taltheilei bands adapted the bow and notched arrows from Prairie Indians in the forest to hunt caribou, using the bow horizontally like their Dene descendents and Inuit (Thompson 1916:166). On the tundra the bow, as discussed under points, improved hunting away from traditional water-crossings where lances were still used. Surface arrow and lance heads were identified using stratified specimens (Fig. 4.1).

Late Taltheilei is 200-1,300 years old, based on 38 radiocarbon dates. Beverly dates agree with 185-1,230 and 220-1,290 year-old Bathurst and Kaminuriak dates.[1] Beverly forest sites date generally later, around 390-1,275 years old, with fewer 220-1,150 year old tundra dates (Table 4.2). Unlike those of the Dene, Late phase site locations overlay those of earlier cultures on the herd migration route, being more numerous at the centre of the range (Fig. 4.2). Sites are at Rennie-Lynx-Firedrake, Mantic-Sid-Mary, Black and Cree Lakes, then divide according to the Haultain and Mudjatik River valleys before ending at Saleski Lake, Buffalo Narrows and Churchill River. Of 93 tundra and 154 forest sites, camps outside this route at Artillery, Clinton-Colden, Grant, Barlow, Boyd, Nonacho and Athabasca Lakes represent hunters of smaller subherds. Late phase hunters are the last bands of herd followers before the fur trade and White-introduced diseases ended most aspects of traditional life.

Figure 4.1. Surface artifacts, including those of Late Taltheilei, were assigned to phase and tradition using similarities to stratified dated material.

---

[1] Blakeslee (1994:205) cautions against the use of Gakushuin dates for constructing archaeological chronologies. The four dates for the Bathurst and Kaminuriak caribou ranges fit the regional chronology and have acceptable standard deviations.

BATHURST RANGE	BEVERLY TUNDRA	BEVERLY FOREST	KAMINURIAK RANGE
185 B.P. no sigma. (I-4375). KeNw-3, north arm, Great Slave Lake 190±100 B.P. (S-476) in LbPf-5 at Snare Lake 210±80 B.P. (S-474) in LbPf-2 at Snare Lake 670±70 B.P. (Gak-1865) at KePl-1, north arm, Great Slave Lake (Frank Channel complex 1230±180 B.P. (Gak-1866) in LcPc-7 at Winter Lake, Mackenzie District, NWT. Windy Point component (all above are Noble 1971 and pers. comm.)	220±105 B.P. (S-1158b) at KkLn-4 at Grant Lake 265±85 B.P. (S-1159) at KkLn-4 500±95 B.P. (I-5335) in KjNb-7 at Warden's Grove, Thelon R. 590±60 B.P. (S-649) in KjNb-6 at Warden's Grove, Thelon R. 845±115 B.P. (S-717) at KjNb-7 1010±70 B.P. (S-1021) at KkLn-4 at Grant Lake, Dubawnt Lake 1020±230 B.P. (S-1156a) in KkLn-4 at Grant Lake 1045±95 B.P. (S-1009) at KkLn-4 at Grant Lake, Dubawnt R. 1150±85 B.P. (S-716) at KjNb-7 at Warden's Grove, Thelon R.	390±65 B.P. (S-1155) at JjNk-2 at Rennie Lake, Elk River 405±40 B.P. (S-1259) at KeNi-4 at Whitefish Lake, Thelon R. 535±60 B.P. (S-1139) at JkNf-1, Jarvis Lake, Elk River 540±95 B.P. (I-4550) in KfNm-3 on Artillery Lake (Noble 1971) 610±110B.P. (Gak-3799) at IjOg-2 on Lake Athabasca (Wright 1975) 630±90 B.P. (S-1156) at JjNk-2, Rennie Lake, upper Thelon R. 715±60 B.P (S-1136) in JjNd-1, Firedrake Lake, Dubawnt R. 875±95 B.P. (S-587) in KfNm-3 at Artillery Lake (Noble 1971) 880±130 B.P.& 1010±160 (I-4973) in KeNo-2 at Fort Reliance on East Arm of Great Slave Lake (Noble 1971) 940±50 B.P. (S-1142) & 1030±65 B.P. (S-1141) in JiNc-3 and JiNf-7, upper Thelon R. 1035±70 B.P. (S-1441) & 1040±80 B.P. (S-1530) & 1055±60 B.P. (S-1529) in KeNi-4 at Whitefish Lake, Thelon R. 1260±170 B.P. (Gak-3798) in IgOo-1 at Lake Athabasca (Wright 1975) 1275±75 B.P. (S-2240), Buffalo Narrows, Saskatchewan (Millar 1983)	220±95 B.P. (I-4149) in Shethanei Narrows site, Manitoba (Nash 1975) 460±80 B.P. (Gak-2342) at Egenolf Lake site, Manitoba (Nash 1975:31) 625±90 B.P.(I-5239) in JqLp-1 at Mountain Lake, Keewatin District (Nash 1975:152) 770±80 B.P. (Gak-2341) at Shethanei Lake, Manitoba 775±90 B.P. (I-630) in Caribou Hill site, Keewatin District 990±110 B.P. (I-3032) and 1290±110 B.P. (I-3033) at Duck Lake Narrows, Manitoba (Nash 1975:85)

Table 4.1. Late phase radiocarbon dates
(unreferenced dates are the author's)

Late Phase Material Culture

The most important difference between Late Taltheilei and earlier phases, and in fact with all earlier traditions, is tool quality and symmetry, especially points and knives, but also many scrapers and chithos. Most Late phase stone, bone and wood tools are poorly made and asymmetric. They differ from Dènè tools primarily in the absence of European metal (Fig. 4.3). I analyze them using common attributes like plan, section, colour, material, length, width and thickness, as well as specific attributes such as traits for tip, midsection and base in points; retouch and wear in knives and scrapers, etc. As attribute tables are repeated for all tool types and cultures, they are in the Appendix. Since tables in the text and the Appendix complement one another, *table numbering in the text is not sequential*.

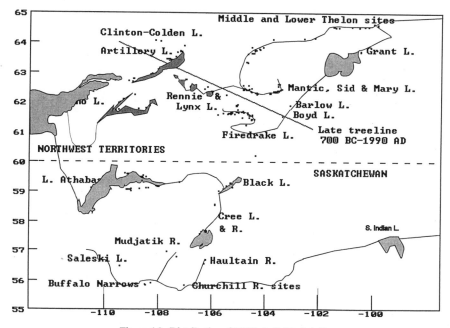

Figure 4.2. Distribution of 247 Late Taltheilei sites.

Analysis of Projectile points

The plans of Late phase stone points vary more than earlier phases due to the adoption of the bow and various arrowhead notching techniques from the south. Unless broken or retouched all have sharp tips, basal striking platforms and vary in size from lanceheads to tiny arrowheads. Fig. 4.4 shows 14 points with corner and side-notched, tanged, stemmed and fishtailed bases from forest sites KeNi-4, JkNf-1 & 2, JjNk-2, JjNe-1 and KcNc-9, and tundra sites KjNb-6 & 7 and KkLn-4. Most points are short, crudely retouched and asymmetrically variable in plan. Of 1061 Beverly range points, 359 are Late phase, their distribution seen in Fig. 4.5, and of these, 226 are side or corner-notched and 127 are unnotched.

Notched points are more plentiful and dispersed than unnotched ones (Tables 4.2a-b). Location and radiocarbon dates suggest notched points spread consistently and quickly over the range, from Buffalo Narrows on the Churchill River as far as Clinton-Colden Lake in the extreme northwest, with heavy numbers along the whole Thelon River. They are plentiful at Jarvis Lake on the migration path, with scattered concentrations at Athabasca and Artillery Lakes representing the hunting of subherds. Unnotched points did not reach Artillery and Clinton-Colden Lakes or Black Lake-Chipman River, but were found at Aberdeen Lake on the lower Thelon. Unnotched points at Buffalo Narrows, where notching was introduced, may appear contradictory, but these points dating from the oldest Late phase sites of 1275 years ago, represent the earlier change from lance to arrowhead (Fig. 4.6). Except for points on the shores of large lakes, most were found at water-crossings. A comparison of the number of notched and unnotched points suggests that archery and lancing were both used at water-crossings. Arrows were used for longer range shooting as caribou leave the water, but they were also used on corralled animals in pounds (Hearne 1958:50).

Figure 4.3. While the Dene had many metal artifacts, their Late Taltheilei ancestors used stone tools, some of which are emanating from the side wall of a sand blowout.

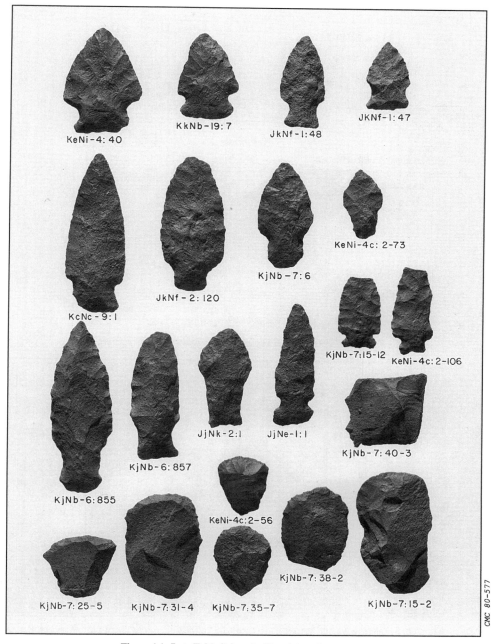

KeNi-4: 40

KkNb-19: 7

JkNf-1: 48

JKNf-1: 47

KcNc - 9: 1

JkNf - 2: 120

KjNb - 7: 6

KeNi-4c: 2-73

KjNb-7:15-12

KeNi-4c: 2-106

KjNb-6: 855

KjNb- 6: 857

JjNk-2:1

JjNe-1: 1

KjNb- 7: 40-3

KeNi-4c: 2-56

KjNb-7: 25-5

KjNb-7: 31-4

KjNb-7:35-7

KjNb-7: 38-2

KjNb-7: 15-2

CMC 80-577

Figure 4.4. Late Taltheilei projectile points and scrapers.

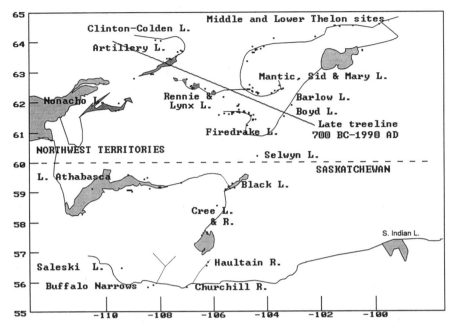

Figure 4.5. Distribution of 149 Late Taltheilei sites with 359 points.

Figure 4.6. The change from Middle Taltheilei lances to Late Taltheilei arrows allowed Late phase bowmen to hide behind piled boulder hunting blinds to shoot caribou at longer range.

No.	northwest tundra (37)	No.	northeast tundra (36)	No.	south-central tundra (18)
5	Clinton-Colden Lake, Lockhart R.	9	Aberdeen Lake, Thelon River	3	Eyeberry Lake, Thelon River
4	Thanakoie Narrows, Lockhart R.	1	Ursus Island, Thelon River	1	Mosquito Lake, Dubawnt River
14	north Artillery Lake, Lockhart R.	4	Thelon Bluffs, Thelon River	1	Barlow Lake, Dubawnt River
9	Warden's Grove, Thelon River	11	Grant Lake, Dubawnt River	6	Mantic & Jim Lakes, Thelon River
4	Grassy Island, Thelon River	1	Lookout Point, Thelon River	4	Mary Lake, Dubawnt River
1	Hornby Point, Thelon River	10	upper Thelon and Elk Rivers	3	Sid Lake, Dubawnt River
No.	northwest forest (56)	No.	middle forest (68)	No.	southeast forest (16)
4	south Artillery Lake, Lockhart R.	17	Damant Lake, Thelon River	1	Pipestone River on Cree River
3	Nonacho Lake, Taltson River	28	Jarvis Lake, Thelon River	2	Cree Lake and Cree River
27	Lake Athabasca	10	Firedrake Lake, Dubawnt River	2	Haultain River, Churchill River
1	Rennie Lake, Thelon River	4	Boyd and Selwyn Lakes, Dubawnt	3	Saleski Lake, Churchill River
21	Whitefish & Lynx Lakes, Thelon	10	Black Lake and Chipman River	8	Buffalo Narrows, Churchill River

Table 4.2a. Late Taltheilei tundra (91) and forest (141) notched points.

No.	northwest tundra (16)	No.	northeast tundra (15)	No.	south-central tundra (10)
15	Warden's Grove, Thelon River	4	Aberdeen Lake, Thelon River	3	Eyeberry Lake, Thelon River
1	Grassy Island, Thelon River	1	Ursus Island, Thelon River	2	Barlow Lake, Dubawnt River
		4	Grant Lake, Dubawnt River	3	Mantic & Jim Lakes, Dubawnt R.
		6	upper Thelon and Elk Rivers	2	Sid and Mary Lakes, Dubawnt R.
No.	northwest forest (22)	No.	middle forest (39)	No.	southeast forest (25)
3	Nonacho Lake, Taltson River	11	Damant Lake, Thelon River	1	Pipestone River on Cree River
4	Lake Athabasca	18	Jarvis Lake, Thelon River	1	Cree Lake and River
5	Rennie Lake, Thelon River	6	Firedrake Lake, Dubawnt River	1	Saleski Lake, Churchill River
10	Whitefish & Lynx Lakes, Thelon	4	Black Lake and Chipman River	22	Buffalo Narrows, Churchill River

Table 4.2b. Late Taltheilei tundra (41) and forest (86) unnotched points.

In attempting to visualize the change from lance to arrowhead, I separated the larger unnotched from smaller notched points, as the former are likely derived from Middle phase lanceheads (Tables 4.2c-d).

Estimated	Number	Min.	Max.	Mean	S.D.	Excluding
Length	215	19.48	89.94	44.07	11.98	11 fragments
Width	222	12.48	36.93	20.93	4.07	4 fragments
Thickness	220	3.53	11.18	6.85	1.49	6 fragments
Weight	97	1.00	23.00	5.91	3.59	129 fragments

Table 4.2c. Late phase notched arrowhead data (mm & g).

Estimated	Number	Min.	Max.	Mean	S.D.	Excluding
Length	109	18.00	90.00	48.82	14.12	24 fragments
Width	121	14.00	38.91	21.50	4.53	12 fragments
Thickness	127	0.60	11.00	7.09	1.64	6 fragments
Weight	53	2.00	60.00	8.60	8.54	80 fragments

Table 4.2d. Late phase unnotched lancehead data (mm & g).

In keeping with local sources, quartzite was used in most tundra points, but one tenth of forest points are chert or sandstone, with some shale. Tundra points are white, then beige and gray; forest points are gray, then white and beige. Just as the type of stone varies more in forest points, so also does texture. Of the 41 found, 15 from forest sites are banded, 10 are mottled and three are veined, while 10 tundra points are banded, two are mottled and one is speckled (Tables 4.3a-b, Appendix[2]). Spadelike or notched plans outnumber lanceolate ones. Other plans are triangular JiNc-1:12 & pentagonal IgOh-1:2 at Firedrake and Athabasca Lakes, plus two indeterminate fragments. Most sections are biconvex, but some forest planoconvexity is due to flat-cleaving schist, sandstone and siltstone (Tables 4.4 & 4.5).

Half of forest tips and one third of tundra tips are pointed. The rest are retouched or broken, like half of tundra tips. Numerous round, serrated and square point tips in the forest have special uses. Serrated KcNi-4:5 has deep narrow side-notches for hafting as a knife, while square tipped JkNf-5:2 and JkNg-3:1 from Damant Lake are bashed, like tundra point KkNj-1:1 from Clinton-Colden Lake. Of seven points accidentally burinated at the tip by striking rock, five are from tundra sites. More forest than tundra points taper to tip, while basally tapered and parallel sided points are evenly divided (Tables 4.6 and 4.7).

The basal plan of points coincides with size and haft, varying more in forest than tundra due to diverse raw material, especially on newly introduced arrowheads. Lanceheads are wider, with square, stemmed, flared or wide expanding bases. Arrowhead bases are side or corner-notched or fish-tailed, while parallel or tapered tanged bases may be either, depending on their length. Tanging and stemming may be holdovers from Middle phase. Unground and ground notches are popular in forest and tundra, respectively. Unground stems also increase in forest points, but some of the six from GlOc-20 & 21 at Buffalo Narrows may be knives (e.g., #10-24; Millar 1983). Unground flared point GlOb-1:1 was found nearby at Churchill Lake, while ground corner-notched KfNm-20:3 is from southwest Artillery Lake.

---

[2] Common tables are appendicized; summary tables are not.

There are equal ratios of forest and tundra ground basal edges, but there are twice as many tundra unground round bases. A fourth of forest points are shouldered compared to a tenth of tundra ones. Rare single shoulders, as on points at JlNg-6 & 8 on Damant Lake (Tables 4.8-10), may indicate a shift to double shoulders, as in the Early to Middle Taltheilei transition.

The usual breakage in Late phase points is transverse, then diagonal and semi-diagonal, with longitudinal breaks common in tundra points. Longitudinal breakage includes burination or elongate spalling from an edge or face by accident or intention. When hinge fractures occur, double burination seems intentional but rare. The ratio of point notches, ears, tangs, thinning, burning, patination, weathering and end-thinning in both forest and tundra sites is similar. Most points used as other tools ("as is" or retouched) are knives with striated or worn edges or side-notches. Only one occurs per site: Grant Lake bipolar wedge KkLn-4:965-1 (Gordon 1976:158), Mary Lake bifacial scraper KcLx-2:84 and Selwyn Lake notched point-endscraper JbNc-1:2. All are from the Dubawnt valley, while the Damant Lake gravers are from the Thelon valley (Tables 4.11-14).

Lanceheads are longer, barely wider and thicker, and much heavier than arrowheads. Tundra points are slightly longer, wider, thicker and heavier than forest points (Tables 4.15a-b).

Analysis of scrapers

Scrapers are mainly on flat, rhomboid, unretouched, beige quartzite flakes (Fig. 4.2 bottom; six from tundra site KjNb-7 and one from forest site KeNi-4). Their common plan and basal width suggest hafting in a caribou rib marrow cavity, while wear and striae infer an acute angle of application above the hide. Some are also spurred awls or gravers (e.g., KjNb-7:25-5); others are discoidal or square (e.g.s, KjNb-7:38-2 and 31-4). Many scrapers have unifacial bases like KeNi-4C:2-56, while several bases are bifacial.

Phase-specific traits on 68 stratified scrapers (36 tundra; 32 forest[3]) at KeNi-4, KdLw-1, KjNb-6 and 7, KkLn-4 and Buffalo Narrows were used to classify 85 surface ones (13 T; 72 F[4]), resulting in sparse dispersion on the upper Thelon River and Artillery and Cree Lakes, but with clusters along the treeline and at Lake Athabasca (Fig. 4.7).

Half of forest scrapers are quartzite compared to 86% of tundra scrapers. One fifth each of forest scrapers are chert, quartz and other stone, suggesting a wide range of source material compared to scrapers made from quartzite cobbles at tundra river sources. Scrapers are arranged by main colour[5], with white popular, then gray and beige. A fifth of tundra scrapers are orange from quartzite. Forest ones are of diverse stone: 14 banded, 5 mottled, 7 speckled and 4 veined. Diverse forest scraper shapes include rhomboids, rectangles and squares[6] found mainly at Buffalo Narrows and Whitefish and Athabasca Lakes and ulu-like GlOc-20:3-5 at Buffalo Narrows (Tables 4.16a-4.17a). As tundra scrapers

---

[3] hereafter abbreviated as T (tundra) or F (forest).

[4] Assuming artifacts indistinguishable from one another are of the same culture, databases of stratified dated artifacts with metric and 10-20 descriptive fields were used to classify 6,715 of 50,000 surface artifacts on a best-match basis. Seriously divided searches were rare because culturally-specific traits exist even in common artifacts such as Middle Taltheilei knives that are stemmed and Early phase scrapers that are large and triangular). See Introduction.

[5] e.g.s, beige, beige-orange or beige and orange are classed under the main colour name of beige.

[6] these are classed as 4-sided in the tables. Triangles and tearshapes are 3-sided.

include tearshapes and triangles found mainly at KjNb-7 and KkLn-4, their difference may be seasonal, as easier to haft 4-sided scrapers are prominent in the winter forest where mittens were worn. Basally worn and retouched 3-sided socketted scrapers are on the summer tundra. Winter 4-sided and summer 3-sided scraper and knife handle distributions will be compared in later chapters.

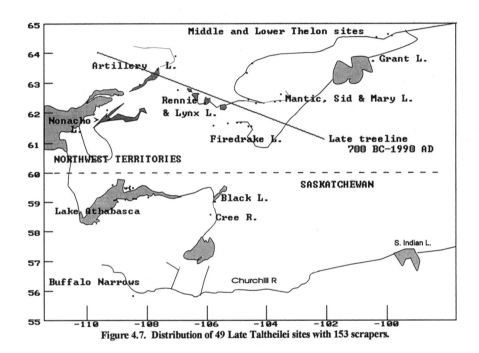

Figure 4.7. Distribution of 49 Late Taltheilei sites with 153 scrapers.

The length of 4-sided scrapers is alike in both ranges, but 3-sided scrapers are markedly shorter in tundra sites, perhaps from both bit wear and basal retouch to fit bone and antler sockets. In fact, deeply striated bits occur only in tundra sites KjN-6 and 7, and infer heavy oblique scraper application over hides (Gordon 1975:220). Half of all scrapers are flat, but forest ones are more keeled, mainly at Lake Athabasca, while planoconvexity is high at Buffalo Narrows. Tundra scrapers are more tortoise-shaped, mainly at KjNb-7. Forest scrapers are twice as serrated, especially at Lake Athabasca. Most unretouched forest bases are unground, while over one-third of tundra bases are worn. Over one-third of all bases have dorsal retouch, but very few have bifacial retouch or double bits. Dorsal and bifacial retouch is similar in tundra sites KjNb-6 & 7 and forest sites at Buffalo Narrows and Lake Athabasca, with cortex prominent in forest scrapers. Half of forest bits and two-thirds of tundra bits are worn, with some at KjNb-6 & 7 and Grant Lake, very worn. Big striking platforms suggest a fifth of all scrapers were made from thinning flakes struck from bifacial cores or knives, a method evident at Buffalo Narrows and Lake Athabasca forest sites and Grant Lake tundra sites. Single spurs are uncommon but are on 14% of the tundra scrapers, mainly at KjNb-6 & 7, and 9% of forest scrapers. Double spurs are rare but prevail at KjNb-7. Compared to tundra scrapers, forest ones are larger, unspurred, striated, worn or retouched, but more serrated, 4-sided, cortexed, keeled and planoconvex. Tundra ones are more 3-sided, tortoise-backed and basally ground (Tables 4.17b-4.26b).

Analysis of knives

Late Taltheilei knives are cruder with less retouch than those of earlier phases. Many broken ones littering the ground imply easy manufacture and discard. Mainly used as butchering tools for caribou, knives were also used on other game, fish, birds and sundry tasks. Most are ovoid, except some like semilunar KjNb-7:33-35 (Fig. 4.8 left), square-based lanceolate KjNb-7:17-33 (center) and round tipped KeNi-4C:2-105 (top). Some bases were ground to protect their hafting sinew from wear. In knives retouched from tip-midsection to break, missing bases are assumed to be retouched, but if retouch ended before the break, bases are assumed to be unretouched. Blunted hafts and backs are tabled as ground, and round ends may not be bases, as sharp round tips occur. Some tanged and stemmed bases have pointed tips, while others may be round but sharp.

Two hundred and eight stratified knives were used to assign 92 surface ones in 57 sites (Fig. 4.9). As Beverly knives have fewer phase-specific traits than scrapers, their identification as Late phase makes them appear sparse. However, enough exist to form a tundra cluster of butchering sites at Mantic-Sid-Mary Lake on the tundra, with scattered sites on the Thelon River and Artillery and Grant Lakes. Forest clusters are at Athabasca and Firedrake Lakes; single sites are at Whitefish, Nonacho-Gray and Cree Lakes and Buffalo Narrows.

Tundra knives are almost entirely quartzite (mostly beige), but forest ones are gray, white and beige quartzite, quartz and chert. Two distinctive red quartzite knives at LdLl-2 at Aberdeen Lake imply re-use of an earlier Shield Archaic cobble source found by Wright (pers. comm. 1996). Forest knives are mainly unifacial unworked fragments. Three-fourths of tundra knives are transversely or diagonally broken with edge fragments, bases and base-midsections exceeding tip-midsections and tips. A third of knives are ovoid or 4-sided in forest or 3-sided in tundra sites, like scrapers. Like points and scrapers, forest knife plans greatly vary, with a fifth discoid with planoconvex section. About one-third have bifacial retouch. Like scrapers, uniface forest knives are serrated; tundra knives are worn or wind-abraded. Half of forest bases are unground and bifacially retouched, versus a third of tundra ones, and more forest bases are both unground and unifacial. Round tips are twice as common in forest sites and may relate to planing wood, while square tips conform with the pattern of 4-sided forest tools. A tenth of tundra tips are unworn and pointed, a sign of early breakage and discard (Tables 4.27a-4.36).

Cortex on the dorsal face, basal edge and platform of forest knives support a unifacial trend, while twice as many tapered, round, square or tanged bases are unground like scrapers. Forest knives are smaller and have more raised lateral (rather than basal) platforms than knives of all phases (Tables 4.37-4.42b). Several Buffalo Narrows forest knives may be hand-hafted as they have blunt backs and unground bases. Jarvis Lake point JkNf-5:7 has striae parallel to its edge like a knife. Forest knives are more diverse, unifacial, 4-sided, planoconvex, serrated, worn, cortexed and backed, with more tips. Tundra knives are more bifacial, ovoid, ground, broken and larger, with more bases and rounder tips (Table 4.43)

Figure 4.8. Late Taltheilei knives and chithos.

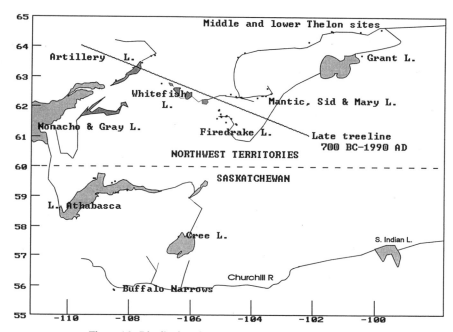

Figure 4.9. Distribution of 57 Late Taltheilei sites with 300 knives.

Analysis of chithos

Twenty-two chithos are dispersed on upper Thelon River tundra, including Mosquito and Grant Lakes, while 85 forest ones are at Whitefish-Lynx, Cree, Firedrake and Athabasca Lakes and Buffalo Narrows. Three-fourths are sandstone (e.g., thin flat worn bifacially retouched tundra KjNb-7:31-20; Figs. 4.8 and 4.10). Some tundra chithos are quartzite. Forest ones at Buffalo Narrows are diverse stone and one at Whitefish Lake is of gneiss. Like points, scrapers and knives, chitho material and type vary more in forest sites. More than half of forest and a third of tundra chithos are beige; a fourth of tundra ones are gray. Twenty of unknown colour are from a Buffalo Narrows collection that was unavailable for study. Three-quarters of forest chithos and two-thirds of tundra ones have bifacially worked and worn edges. Unifacial tundra chithos are common, reflecting quartzite, which unlike sandstone, has no parallel cleavage (Tables 4.44a-45). Almost all forest chithos are complete with breakage high in tundra. More tundra chithos are 4-sided. Forest ones are rounder, the opposite of other tools (Fig. 4.11). Winter chithos at Buffalo Narrows are D-shaped, perhaps for gripping with mitted hands in winter. Three-fourths of forest chithos and two-thirds of tundra ones are flat due to linearly cleaved schist and gneiss. Chithos of undulating section in sites KjNb-6 & 7 may be due to Warden's Grove tundra source material. Half of chithos have cortex. Like points, scrapers and knives, forest chithos are smaller. More forest chithos are bifacial, diverse, flat and worn; more tundra chithos are unifacial, broken and larger (Tables 4.46-4.52).

Difference	Forest knives	Tundra knives	Remarks
stone and colour	diverse stone; gray	beige quartzite	locally available material
faciality	more unifacial	less unifacial	less forest preparation and breakage risk (conservati
fragmented	less	more	more available tundra stone due to no snowcover
plan	more 4-sided. More tips	more ovoid. More bases	good winter hand grip. Tundra bases returned to cam
section	more planoconvex	less planoconvex	planoconvex tools are often only unifacially prepared
wear	more	few are sand-blasted?	more forest use on hard frozen carcasses?
bifacially retouched bas	more unground	more ground	more tundra socket preparation and wear
edge	more serrated	less serrated	serrated for cutting frozen meat in winter forest?
tip	many are rounded	a few are round	rounded for multiple task of wood planing?
longitudinal breaks	less	more	breakage by hitting surface rock at tundra crossings
cortex	more	less	less forest breakage risk and more unifaciality
back	some are backed	none are backed	protected hand or mit for winter cutting?
size	smaller	larger	more forest use, sharpening and stone conservation

Table 4.43. Comparing Late Taltheilei forest and tundra knives.

Difference	Forest chithos	Tundra chithos	Remarks
stone and colour	gray schist and gneiss	beige sandstone	locally available material
bifaciality	twice that of tundra	half that of forest	good schist or gneiss cleavage, versus poor sandstone cleavage
fragmented	almost all are complete	3/4 are complete	break-resistant forest schist and gneiss, versus tundra sandstone
plan	rounder	more 4-sided	faster wear and rounding on gneiss and friable schist
section	more tabular	less tabular	typical forest schist and gneiss cleavage
wear	greater	less	more use or greater visibility of dark forest schist and gneiss
size	smaller	larger	more forest use, retouch and wear on friable schist and gneiss

Table 4.52. Comparing Late Taltheilei forest and tundra chithos.

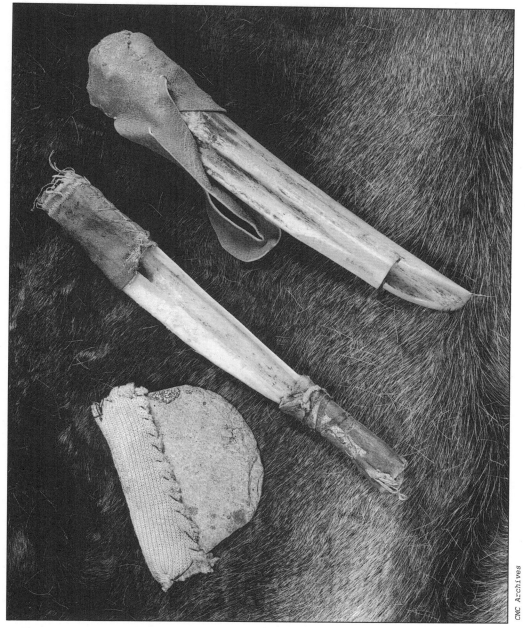

CMC Archives

Figure 4.11. Rounded Late Taltheilei chithos changed to Dene chithos with a cloth back to protect the user. Beamer and flesher to the right.

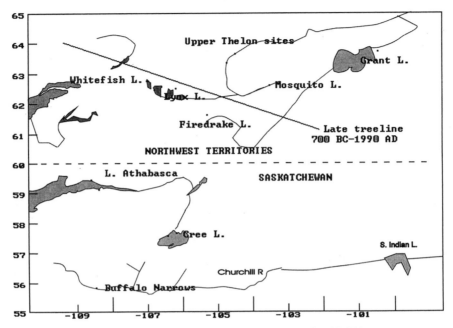

Figure 4.10. Distribution of 17 Late Taltheilei sites with 107 chithos.

Analysis of wedges

Wedges are long, bipolarly-struck, shock-resistant quartz or quartzite rectangles. Used for splitting wood, bone and antler, wedges resemble bipolarly-struck flakes, but with smashed edges; some even laterally. Their resemblance to flakes likely resulted in sparse recognition in the large upper Thelon and Mosquito and Grant Lakes surface collections and at Lake Athabasca, Cree River and Buffalo Narrows forest sites (Fig. 4.12). As a tool of convenience, they are local stone. Tundra wedges are mainly beige quartzite; forest ones are quartz and chert of varying colour. Forest wedges are one-fifth 3-sided and one-fourth parallelogram. Tundra ones are one-fourth square and one-fifth each of rhomboid or ovoid-biconvex. Forest sections are more rhomboid; tundra ones are one-third each of biconvex, planoconvex and triangular. Forest scarring is channelled concave or flat columnar; tundra scarring is mixed. Both are bipolarly percussed, some on all edges (double bipolar), while a tenth have unipolar percussion. Forest wedges are larger; tundra ones, more 4-sided or round (Tables 4.53a- 4.59).

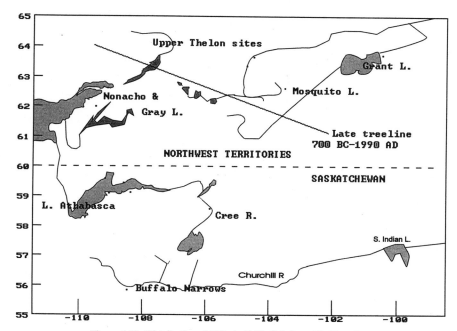

Figure 4.12. Distribution of 13 Late Taltheilei sites with 31 wedges.

Difference	Forest wedges	Tundra wedges	Remarks
stone and colour	white and clear quartz	gray quartzite	locally available material
flake scars	more channelled and columnar	less channelled and columnar	due to locally available material. Like Early phase ,but unlike Middle phase and Shield Archaic
percussion	bipolar and unipolar	bipolar and discoidal	wood versus tundra antler use? Like other phases
plan	more parallelogram, 3-sided and asymmetric	more square or round and symmetric	more resistant compact plan for hard tundra antler splitting?
section	1/3 are rhomboidal	planoconvex or triangular	more resistant compact section for hard tundra antler splitting?
size	larger	smaller	like other phases. Less forest wear on soft wood?

Table 4.59. Comparing Late Taltheilei forest and tundra wedges.

Analysis of adzelike tools

Nine sites have 21 adze flakes, chisels and gouges (14 F,7 T; 10 buried, 11 surface; Table 4.60; Fig. 4.13). Dispersed shock-resistant basalt was favoured, each artifact thin section showing a separate source. Half of forest items are brittle lamellar gray or black shale, while quartzite ratios are alike. Due to windblown sand abrasion, only one tundra adze flake has striae, while 14% each of forest adzelike tools have longitudinal or diagonal striae from manufacturing and use. Forest tools are also widely ground and polished; 14% with specifically ground areas. Hinge fracturing from adze sharpening is only on three forest flakes. Forest adze flakes are larger, perhaps due to work on softer wood (and less sharpening, versus hard tundra bone or antler) or their unworkable shale. Tundra flakes are small due to their more workable basalt. Forest adzes are 3-4 sided. The tundra adze is lanceolate with perpendicular sides. The Lake Athabasca chisel has a sharp 30 degree bit and steep sides. Tundra gouge KjNb-7:41 has no handle but its width, thickness and bit angle resemble forest gouge KdNi-3:16 (Table 4.61-69d).

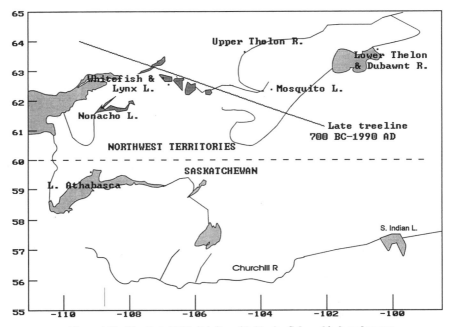

Figure 4.13. Nine Late Taltheilei sites with 21 adze flakes, chisels and gouges.

Adzelike artifact	R	Length	Width	Thickness	Weight/g	Plan	Section	Bit angle	Platform
IjOg-2:9 adze	F	142.8	73.1	28.4	362	rectangle	round back	45	45
JkOe-4:1 adze	F	111.9	55.0	18.8	146	tearshape	biconvex	60	
KeNi-4A: 2-26 adze	F	-79.7 frag.	-69. frag.	-34 frag.	-165 frag.	ovoid	round back	50	65
KcLw-24:44 adze	T	134.1	64.0	42.7	454	lancelike	round back	50	75
IjOg-2:1 chisel	F	103.6	40.3	11.1	64.6	rectangle	rectangle	30	80
KdNi-3: 16 gouge	F	50.6	28.6	10.6	16.2	rectangle	concavoconvex	30	
KjNb-7:41 gouge	T	-42.2 frag	36.0	12.5	-18. frag	lancelike	biconvex	30	

Table 4.69c. Forest and tundra adzelike tools by range, shape, bit angle and platform (see Glossary for terms).

Difference	Forest	Tundra	Remarks
stone and colour	half are gray shale	black basalt	locally available stone
plan	lanceolate	rectangular	may be insignificant due to small sample
striae	more variable	less variable	special forest uses on wood. Like Early Taltheilei
sharpening flakes	larger and fewer	smaller and more	available stone for tools? Soft forest wood. vs. hard tundra antler
grinding & polishing	heavy & widespread	rare and restricted	soft forest wood versus hard tundra antler. Like Middle Taltheilei
hinging	forest only	absent	small sample?
size	larger	smaller	less adze sharpening for soft forest wood. Like other phases

Table 4.69d. Comparing Late Taltheilei forest and tundra adzelike tools.

Analysis of cores

Cores were prepared by Taltheilei people until metal replaced stone tools in the 18th to 19th centuries. Except bladecores, they are quite simple (e.g., KjNb-6:48-1; Fig. 4.14 bottom left). Tundra cores (21 F; 36 T) are at Sid Lake and KjNb-6 & 7 on the upper Thelon and Grant and Mosquito Lakes on the Dubawnt. Forest cores (21) are at Whitefish Lake, Lynx Lake KbNf-1 & KcNf-5 and GlOc-20 & 21 at Buffalo Narrows (Fig. 4.15). Almost all tundra and over half of forest cores are quartzite (mainly beige), then white veined quartz in forest and banded chert on tundra (Tables 4.70a-c).

In this and later chapters, core plan and section are what I perceive as the core before flake or blade removal, based on scar orientation and remaining cortex. Half of tundra cores are lightly flaked and retain the roundness, curved striking platforms and cortex of abundant river cobbles. Half of forest cores were 3-4 sided, but two-thirds retain a round face. Half of cores are blocky; the remaining forest and tundra cores are conical or lenticular. Bladelike scars in a fifth of forest cores are due to quartz cleavage. Forest cores are smaller due to heavier flaking (resulting in serration), and cortex trimming done perhaps on the tundra before transport. Two edgeworn forest cores may have been choppers for breaking frozen caribou joints. Plan and wear suggest a tenth of tundra cores are also pushplanes or knives. Another is a unipolarly pocked hammerstone. One small bashed forest core has the bipolar columnar flaking of a wedge (Tables 4.71-4.83d).

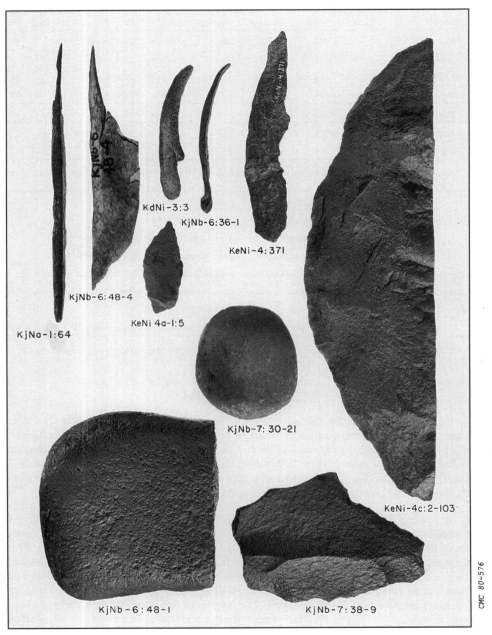

KdNi-3:3

KjNb-6:36-I

KjNb-6:48-4

KeNi-4:371

KeNi 4a-I:5

KjNa-I:64

KjNb-7: 30-21

KeNi-4c:2-103

KjNb-6:48-I

KjNb-7:38-9

CMC 80-576

Figure 4.14. Late Taltheilei needle, awls, copper fragment, adze flake, hammerstone, worked flake and core fragment (clockwise). Adze at right was in disturbed part of Late phase level and is Pre-Dorset.

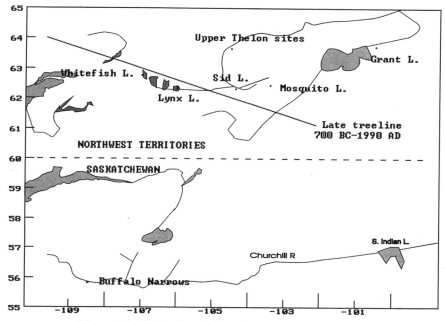

Figure 4.15. Distribution of 11 Late Taltheilei sites with 78 cores.

Difference	Forest cores	Tundra cores	Remarks
stone/colour	1/2 are white quartz	beige quartzite	locally available material
texture	banding present	veining present	locally available material
plan	3-4 sided	half are round cobbles	different cleavage. Unlike cores of other phases
section	biconvex and planoconvex	half are round	different cleavage. Unlike cores of other phases
profile	lenticular/conical/boatshape	some conical	different cleavage. Unlike cores of other phases
flake scars	some are bladelike	almost all are flakelike	different cleavage. Like Early; unlike Middle phase
platform	1/3 are single	3/4 are along a curve	different cleavage. Like other phases & Shield Archaic
depleted	almost all	one-fourth	more forest reduction like all phases and traditions
multi-use	one wedge	diverse tools	more tundra uses like all phases except Shield Archaic
serration	common	uncommon	more forest reduction like all phases and traditions
hinging	half	one-tenth	different cleavage and more forest reduction
battering & polarity	less than 2/3 are unipolar; more bipolar flaking	4/5 are worn & unipolar; less bipolar flaking	different cleavage and more forest reduction
edge wear	10% are worn	almost all are worn	more tundra cores are used as tools
cortex	half	one-fifth	less forest breakage risk, but more conservation
size	smaller	larger	more forest reduction like Early, but not Middle phase

Table 4.83d. Comparing Late Taltheilei forest and tundra cores.

Analysis of detritus

Of several tons of surface and stratified flakes at Whitefish, Athabasca, Grant and Mosquito Lakes, Buffalo Narrows and Warden's Grove (Fig. 4.16), 134 each were randomly collected from forest and tundra sites, catalogued separately from flake bags and compared. They include 139 regular, 126 worked and 3 sharpening flakes. Of the 507 detrital entries, the remaining 239 entries include flake bags and smaller flake batches (site location and weight only). More forest flakes are white; more tundra flakes are beige. Of 18 forest flakes, four are banded, one each are mottled-speckled and two are veined, while ten tundra ones are only banded. Tundra flakes are larger (Tables 4.84a-4.85b). Of the 126 worked flakes, two were snapped, leaving 124 for measuring. Forest worked flakes are also smaller (Tables 4.86a-b). As all flake bags are from tundra sites, range comparison is impossible, but their minimum, maximum and mean weights and standard deviation (abbrev. as min., max., mean and S.D. in later chapters) are 1.5, 9591, 765 and 1604. Their large standard deviation emphasizes the great variation in Late phase flaking stations.

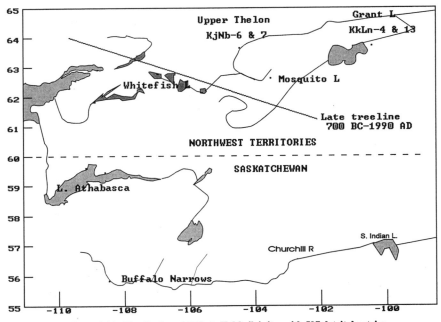

Figure 4.16. Distribution of 11 Late Taltheilei sites with 507 detrital entries.

Analysis of hammerstones

Of five surface and 17 buried hammerstones in four forest and two tundra sites (Fig. 4.17), most tundra and two-thirds of forest hammerstones are quartzite, with one of granite in both ranges, and one of sandstone in the forest. Half of forest ones are beige, versus two-thirds of tundra ones, with other colours alike. Tundra ones are smaller and 3-4-sided or round. Forest ones are larger, ovoid or 3-sided; opposite to cores and suggesting non-interchangability. They are also easily discarded, while cores are reduced. That more tundra hammerstones are bipolarly pocked; forest ones more equatorial, could be construed that forest ones are also net weights, but their pocking at one spot suggests they were really anvils for carefully reducing tools or cores (Tables 4.87a-4.91c).

Difference	Forest	Tundra	Remarks
stone/colour	mixed; half are beige	beige quartzite	locally available material. More forest selection
plan/section	mixed; many are ovoid	half are 4-sided	more forest selection. Like Pre-Dorset and Shield Archaic
pocking	2/3 are unipolar or equatorial	unipolar or bipolar	forest anvil use like other Taltheilei phases and Shield Archaic
size	larger	smaller	anvil use like other phases; unlike Pre-Dorset and Shield Archaic

Table 4.91c. Comparison of Late Taltheilei forest and tundra hammerstones.

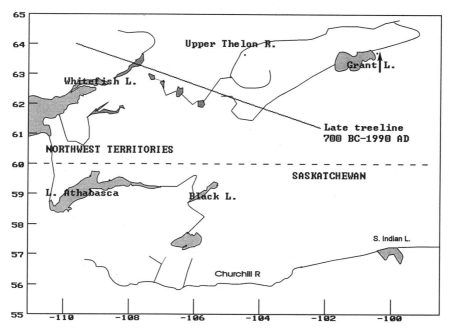

Figure 4.17. Distribution of 6 Late Taltheilei sites with 22 hammerstones.

Analysis of whetstones

Except for Lake Athabasca, whetstones (9 buried; 8 surface) are dispersed in 12 sites near treeline from Noman, Nonacho, Whitefish and Lynx Lakes to the Elk River (Fig. 4.18). Only four tundra whetstones may relate to plentiful but unidentified fine-grained sandstone fragments as sharpening alternatives. Most are multi-coloured sandstone and schist. More forest whetstones are obliquely worn bars; more tundra ones are longitudinally worn. Some double as chithos. A forest one has a wide, striated, shaft-smoothing groove. A rangewide lack of notches in whetstones suggests their carriage in pouches (Fig. 6.14; KbNo-1:1 right). Forest ones are larger, perhaps because they are barlike and longer (Tables 4.92a-4.101c).

Difference	Forest whetstone	Tundra whetstone	Remarks
stone/colour	multi-coloured sandstone and schist	multi-coloured sandstone and schist	locally available material
plan/section	bar type and biplanar	variable	seasonally different tasks
multi-use	also as chitho	also chitho, but tools more variable	seasonally different tasks like Middle phase
wear	heavy edge and face wear	longitudinal edge striae and wear	seasonally different tasks
size	larger	small	seasonally different tasks

Table 4.101c. Comparing Late Taltheilei forest and tundra whetstones.

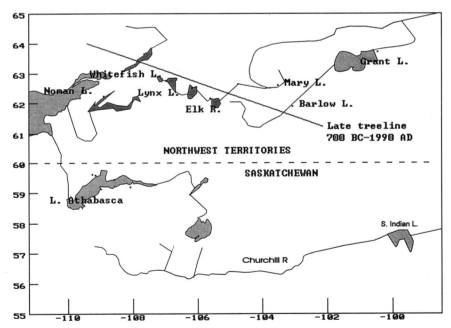

Figure 4.18. Distribution of 12 Late Taltheilei sites with 17 whetstones.

Analysis of skin flexers

The proximity to treeline of flexers in Mantic and Mary Lake tundra sites, and Whitefish (3), Jarvis (6) and Rennie (3) Lake forest sites, is compatible with late summer and early fall hide-working (Fig. 4.19). As tundra flexers are slightly longer and thinner, but much narrower and lighter, they may have been applied to thin summer skins for some reason unknown to me. However, as only three occur, some heavily polished scrapers may also have been used as skin flexers (Tables 4.102a-b).

Analysis of miscellaneous artifacts

Miscellaneous artifacts are separated by double lines in Table 4.102c. Both tundra quartzite spokeshaves, KkLn-4:889 at Grant Lake is half the size of KbNa-21:37 at Mantic Lake. Mosquito Lake shaft polishers are alike in size, colour and material, but KdLw-1:373 has a wide groove for spearshafts and KdLw-1:374, a narrow groove for arrowshafts. The other tundra and forest pushplanes, awls and gravers are too few and diverse to compare, but awls are rangewide, while shaft polishers occur only at KdLw-1 and pushplanes mostly in KjNb-6 & 7. The Hudson Bay Company copper kettle fragment indicates trade in advance of traders, but copper was also brought from Coppermine placer deposits, and pounded and rolled into various handles. Two tundra and forest gravers are on points. Three pieces of fire-cracked rock are from a KeNi-4 level. Forest antler spatula KdNi-3:3 is seen in Fig. 4.10 top.

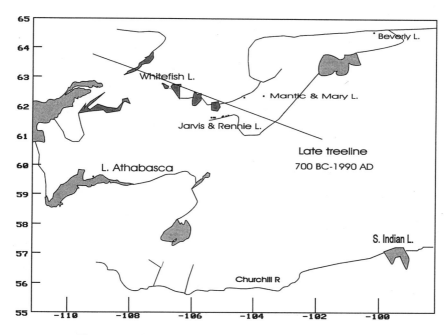

Figure 4.19. Distribution of 12 Late Taltheilei sites with 16 skin flexers.

Analysis of bone debris

About 3 kg of bone (caribou where identifiable) are from forest site KeNi-4 and tundra sites KjNb-7 and KkLn-4. KeNi-4 has 136 entries (1,959 g), including unknown tool KeNi-4:2-18 (Table 4.102), 25 bones (752 g), 87 bags with 679 unmeasured fragments (993 g) and 24 teeth and jaws (209 g). The 36 KjNb-7 entries (1,468 g) contain an intrusive Dene bone point, a cut-marked rib (12 g), 11 bags with 19 bones (527 g), 22 bone bags of 236 unmeasured fragments (926 g) and several teeth (3 g). KkLn-4 entries (79 g) are 6 bones (34 g), 5 bone bags with 155 fragments (43 g), and four tooth fragments (2 g).

I wanted to explore seasonally diverse human nutrition, but small unequal bone samples from game prevent range comparison. Tiny bone fragments and bone meal suggest human tundra fat deficits at KkLn-4 and KjNb-7, but their locations at major water-crossings nullify this suggestion. A fat deficit is more apt to occur in late winter or early spring in the northern forest, but acidic soils there would have dissolved residual bone in all sites except those with deep strata that are frozen for most of the year. Such a situation exists in the KeNi-4 forest site at a main crossing. But, it has big fragments (mean=62x21x6.5 mm & 6.5 g, while tundra sizes vary (KjNb-7 & KkLn-4 means are 48x15x5.2mm & 4.6 g & 24x12x4.7mm & 1.6 g), making rangewide comparison impossible (Tables 4.103a-c).

As all parts of the caribou skeleton are at major water-crossings, carcasses were not carried far. KeNi-4 had a broken left scapula, scapular fragments, left distal and proximal right humeri, proximal left humeral head, left humerus with impact scar on its post-medial corner, two left and a right radio-ulni, right metacarpal, distal metacarpal, calcined vertebra, rib, pelvis, left pelvic acetabular socket, left fibula, distal and metapodial fragments, left metatarsal with distal impact scar, nine metatarsal fragments, three right metatarsi, a left distal ulna, five phalanges, right astragalus and cut-marked astragalus, naviculo-cuboid and left cuboid. Jaws and teeth include three mandibles with PM-2, 3 & 4 and M1 & 2, a mandible with PM-2, 3 & 4 and M1, a maxilla with PM-2, 3 & 4 and M1 & 2, and a partial maxilla with PM's. They also include two calf mandibles with either PM-3 & 4 or M2 & 3, a mandible with M1, 2 & 3, a mandible with M2 & 3, 2 mandibles with lower PM2-3 fragments, four lower PM's, a calf lower M3, and teeth sectioned for determining season of caribou death (i.e., season of hunter kill or site occupation) - two isolated ones and several, including an M3, from two mandibles.

Caribou bones at the KjNb-7 crossing include four right proximal ulnar fragments, distal humerus, right distal tibia, two vertebral fragments, three rib fragments, metatarsus, distal metatarsus, three left metatarsi, metatarsal fragment, metapodial fragment, two left distal metapodials, two right calcani, right cubo-navicular, two left and a right astragali, phalange and proximal first phalange. Teeth and jaws include two left mandibular fragments, a right mandible, and four teeth.

Late phase caribou bones at the smaller KkLn-4 crossing are appendicular, suggesting another stage of carcass processing. They include a right distal radius, a left tibia, a burnt left astragalus, a left calcaneous, a left talus, medial phalange and a phalange. KkLn-4 is hard against a hillside, with a camp space about a km away. Perhaps the meat-rich appendages were stripped right at the crossings, with the axial skeleton returned to camp or thrown into the river. Teeth and jaws include two partial mandibles with PM-3 & 4 and M1 & 2, and PM-3 & 4.

Artifact	Size (mm/g)	Description
KkLn-4:889 T	19.4x19.2x9.38/3.5	spokeshave; also endscraper
KbNa-21:37 T	38.7x31.2x7.2/7.7	spokeshave/endscraper; rectangular quartzite. Big spur and lateral concavity
KdLw-1:373 T	55.4x34.7x15.3/45	shaft polisher; wide groove for spearshaft. Sandstone.
KdLw-1:374 T	54.2x37.6x12.7/40	shaft polisher; narrow groove for arrowshaft. Sandstone.
KjNb-6:40-27 T	fragment 19.3mm thick	pushplane; tearshaped, tortoise-backed, abruptly retouched quartzite
KjNb-7:4-1 T	59.79x32.69x13/21	pushplane; lanceolate, tortoise-backed, hafted, lightly retouched quartzite
KjNb-7:30-14 T	35x22 wide, thick fragment	pushplane; keeled rectangular, abruptly retouched quartzite
KbNe-4:2 T	62.9x29.5x13.7/28	pushplane; assigned to phase using stratified pushplane KjNb-7:4-1
KlNa-1:69 T	113x6x2/14. Square section	awl; rolled placer copper. Also under placer copper.
KjNb-6:48-4 T	99x19x5.6/4.2	awl; polished caribou bone fragment
KjNb-6:36-1 T	60x7.5x3.6/6.6	awl; on fragment of Hudson's Bay Company copper trade kettle
IdNl-1:10 F	50x15x9.5/8.6	awl; quartzite and planoconvex
KeNi-4:358 F	48x8x3/2	awl; typical rotational striae, but also transverse striae. Basalt
KlNa-1:69 T	113x6x2/14	placer copper; rolled, with square handle. Also under awl.
KdNi-3:3 T	54x12x82.9	spatula, marrow type of antler (Fig. 4.14 top)
KjNb-7:11-15 T	53x 25.3x11.8/14.1	graver; worn with unground base. Pre-Dorset type chert
JkNg-3:15 F	22x16x7/3	graver on wide, ground and asymmetric, side-notched, quartzite point
JlNg-8:15 F	40x24x8/9	graver on unground, tanged, quartzite point base
KeNi-4:2-18 F	92.4x12.7x2.8/4.4	bone tool; unidentified caribou bone
KeNi-4:C1-18 F	104x57x19/105	fire-cracked rock of quartzite is rangewide but stratified at Whitefish Lake
KeNi-4:C1-19 F	99x52x28/161	fire-cracked rock of quartzite is rangewide but stratified at Whitefish Lake
KeNi-4:C-1-5 F	67x48x29/107	fire-cracked rock of sandstone is rangewide but stratified at Whitefish Lake

Table 4.102c. Late Taltheilei miscellaneous artifacts. T=tundra; F=forest

Analysis of metal

Copper objects are two awls (one placer and undepicted, the other a Hudson's Bay Company kettle fragment; Table 4.102c). Also included are a placer copper tool handle; a semilunar piece of unknown use (KeNi-4:371 is 84.8x14.9x1.6mm/70g; Fig. 4.14 top); and four KeNi-4C fragments. Fragment #1-7 weighs 50 mg, #1-8 consists of three tiny fragments weighing 2.5 g, #1-31 is 39.4x19.2x2.8mm/7g; and #1-51 is 10.1x9.8x1.6mm/0.7g.

Conclusions on Late Phase Artifacts

Points, knives, chithos, adze flakes, cores, flakes, hammerstones and whetstones are smaller in the forest because they were sharpened and used repeatedly from autumn to spring as new stone became inaccessible under snow or was hundreds of km away in tundra quarries (Table 4.103d). Forest scrapers are serrated with a narrow grip for removing frozen or dried membrane while wearing mittens. Tundra knife bases and base-midsections exceed tip-midsections and tips, a sign of tip breakage at rock-strewn water-crossings and the return of hafted bases to camp for remounting. Forest chithos are smaller due to more intensive winter hide-working. Forest wedges may have been larger due to milder use on wood, with less extensive sharpening, rather than hard tundra antler. Their many types of sections may relate to various wooden hafts and applications, as do their higher ratios of channel (concave) and columnar (flat) flake scars. Amorphous tundra scars may result from splitting antler and bone. A tenth of wedges have unipolar percussion for soft wood splitting, while discoidal percussion allows tundra antler or bone to be split by dispersing the striking points over the periphery of the wedge and extending its life. Forest flexers had longer tangs for softening frozen winter clothing prior to use. More forest adzelike artifacts are thinned by grinding and use. Tundra adzes are thinned by flaking. A profusion of round cores, half of them in tundra sites, concurs with plentiful round quartzite cobbles suitable for tool-making at tundra river-crossings. Battered depleted forest cores imply stone conservation due to distant sources or snowcover, or cobble cortex trimming before their transport south in autumn. Tundra regular and retouched flakes are correspondingly larger due to quarry access. Based on pocking, forest and tundra hammerstones seem to have different uses, with an emphasis on their use as anvils in the forest. Finally, all parts of the caribou skeleton occur at major forest and tundra water-crossings.

Trait	Forest range	Tundra range	Remarks
C14 dates	390 to 1275 years BP	220 to 1150 years BP	continuous herd following from Middle Taltheilei phase
cortex	more	less	less forest breakage risk
points	smaller arrowheads. More unifacial types	larger lanceheads. Few unifacial types	forest influence of more retouch and Plains notching and flatness
scrapers	4-sided. Larger. More serration, spurring, wear, cortex and ground bases. Planoconvex and keeled	3-sided. Smaller. Less serration, wear, spurring, ground bases and striae. Smaller and tortoise-backed	more tundra use. Less forest retouch. Seasonally different use, haft and size
knives	more unifacial, serration, wear, 4-sided, cortex, tips and backing. Fewer breaks. Smaller	less unifacial, serration, wear, 4-sided, cortex, tips and backing. More breaks. Larger	less forest preparation and use, but on frozen meat. More tundra rock breakage
chithos	some schist. More bifaciality, wear and plans, but less breakage. 4-sided. 1/4 have undulating section. Smaller	some quartzite. Less unifaciality, wear and plans, but more breakage. Rounded 1/3 have undulating section. Larger	forest schist but most sandstone. More tundra breaks and forest use. Seasonally different hafting
wedges	quartz. Channel/columnar scars. Unipolar percussion. Asymmetric. Flatter. Larger	quartzite. Amorphous scars. Discoidally struck. Symmetric. Not flatter. Smaller	local stone and use on forest wood versus tundra antler
sharpening adze flakes	silicious shale. More regular striae than wear. Smaller	basalt. More cross-striae than wear. Larger	soft wood versus hard antler or bone reduction. More forest use
cores	quartz. 3-4 sided. Some bladelike. Cortex. Smaller and depleted	quartzite. Rounded. More flakelike. Diverse use. Larger	more forest quartz bladelike cleavage
flakes	smaller	larger	more forest tool and core reduction
hammer-stones	1/2 are ovoid. Equatorially-pocked. Smaller	1/2 are 4-sided. End-pocked. Larger	more forest use as anvils for tool reduction
whetstone	less wear. Smaller	more wear. Larger	tundra tools need keener edge or are of harder stone
flexers	larger	smaller	seasonally different lengths
bone	less broken	more broken	sample too small for speculation

Table 4.103d. Comparing Late Taltheilei forest and tundra tools.
Unlisted data can be assumed to be similar.

Chapter 5

The Middle Phase of the Taltheilei Tradition

Dating and Distribution

Beneath Late phase levels in stratified sites KjNb-5 to 7 and KkLn-4 are thick Middle phase beds dating 1,300 to 1,800 years ago. The other radiocarbon dates are on single buried levels at Rennie, Jarvis and Firedrake forest sites (Table 5.1). Most tundra dates in stratified levels dated not only a ton or so of quartzite debris from tool-making, but many symmetrical ground stemmed lanceheads, knives and triangular scrapers - artifacts with culturally-specific traits for assigning thousands of surface tools in hundreds of sites. That this phase saw the greatest range exploitation of all Beverly people under a warm stable climate is seen in the largest number, variation and distribution of bifacial butchering knives. Most big tundra water-crossings are at Warden's Grove, Hornby and Lookout Points, Ursus Island and Beverly Lake, while small site clusters are at north Artillery and Mantic-Mary-Sid-Mosquito Lakes (Fig. 5.1). Big forest water-crossings are at Whitefish-Lynx and Damant-Rennie-Firedrake Lakes; small site clusters are at south Artillery and Noman-Nonacho-Gray Lakes. Sites are absent on the Churchill, but some are at Athabasca, Black and Cree Lakes, and Cree River. Three sites in the Bluenose and Kaminuriak ranges are dated, but dates are absent in Saskatchewan.

Middle Phase Material Culture

Analysis of projectile points

Except for two notched types, points (113 F; 315 T) in a third of Middle phase sites have the size and ground stem of lanceheads rather than large arrowheads. Phase assignment of spadelike KbNf-1:13 at Lynx Lake and notched chisel-like KdNc-3:1 is based on their similarity, and an associated Middle phase stemmed pentagonal point. KdNc-3 is above Eyeberry Lake and below Jim Lakes. Both are upriver from Warden's Grove (Fig. 5.5). Most points are lanceolate (Figs. 5.2 & 5.3 top), then ovoid (Fig. 5.2 left middle), pentagonal (Figs. 5.2 & 5.4 bottom), stemmed (Figs. 5.2 right middle and 5.4 top half), tanged (Fig. 5.4 third row) and uni-shouldered (Fig. 5.4 top).

BLUENOSE HERD	BEVERLY TUNDRA	BEVERLY FOREST	KAMINURIAK
1380±105 B.P. (S-466) in MkPk-7 on the Coppermine River (McGhee 1970)	1085±80 B.P. (S-720) in KjNb-6 at Warden's Grove, Thelon River	1320±90 B.P. (S-1156) in JjNk-2 at Rennie Lake, Elk River	1630±135 B.P. (I-2086) in JjLk-4 at Henik Lake, Keewatin District (Irving 1968:45)
	1175±105 B.P. (S-630) in KjNb-5 at Warden's Grove	1340±50 B.P. (S-1140) in JkNf-1 on Jarvis Lake, Elk River	1800±95 B.P. (I-5240) in JqLp-1 in Keewatin District (Nash 1975:152)
	1450±95 B.P. (I-5334) in KjNb-6	1350±80 B.P.(S-1528) in KeNi-5 at Whitefish Lake, Thelon River	
	1465±95B.P. (S-736) in KjNb-7 at Warden's Grove, Thelon River	1390±50 B.P. (S-1143) in JjNe-6 at Jarvis Lake, Elk River	
	1480±95 B.P. (I-5333) in KjNb-6	1740±110B.P.(S-1137) in JjNd-1 at Firedrake Lake, Dubawnt River	
	1515±110 B.P.(S-733) in KjNb-6		
	1555±90 B.P. (I-5977) in KjNb-6		
	1555±75B.P. (S-1008) in KkLn-4 at Grant Lake, Dubawnt River		
	1600±65 B.P. (S-718) in KjNb-6		
	1625±130 B.P.(S-977) at KkLn-4 at Grant Lake, Dubawnt River		
	1695±110B.P. (S-629) in KjNb-6		
	1775±100B.P. (S-732) in KjNb-6		
	1780±215 B.P.(S-734) in KjNb-6		
	1790±45 B.P. (S-650) in KjNb-6		
	1915±140 B.P.(S-663) in KjNb-6		

Table 5.1. Middle phase radiocarbon dates.

Tundra points are scattered at many large and small water-crossings. Forest points cluster near treeline, perhaps because lances were useless farther south at frozen crossings and were replaced by snares. Points are mainly quartzite, but forest points are more gray chert and shale like Late phase. A fourth of tundra points are beige or white (Tables 5.2a & b), while most rangewide points are biconvex and lanceolate (Tables 5.3 & 5.4; top of Figs. 5.2 & 5.3). Forest plan variation resulted from repeated sharpening of lanceolates, forming a pentagonal shape (bottom of Figs. 5.2 & 5.4). More forest tips are tapered or pointed compared to tundra ones, which are broken from striking surface rock at crossings. Forest and tundra ratios of points with parallel sides and round, serrated and flat tips are alike, but fewer forest bases are ground, and a fourth are square. Several forest bases are linked to Late Taltheilei with notches and tangs (Fig. 5.4 third row), but their basal edges are ground flat, unlike the Late phase. Conversely, a few single and double shoulders mark continuity from Early phase (Fig. 5.4 top). Compared to forest points, tundra points are more transversely and semi-diagonally broken, with burination appearing to be accidental, as seen in long tip scars from hitting surface rock. Forest and tundra points differ in earing (6 & 2%) and end-thinning (4 & 3%), which may relate to seasonally different hafts, and in patination (4 & 2%). Burning, heat treating and tanging are mainly at Granite Falls and nearby Mantic Lake. Except for a forest scraper, chisel and tundra gouge, altered points are mainly wedges, knives, burins or gravers, as seen in their striae or retouch, and occur equally in both forest and tundra. Forest points are shorter, probably the result of resharpening when raw material was inaccessible (Tables 5.3-5.14c).

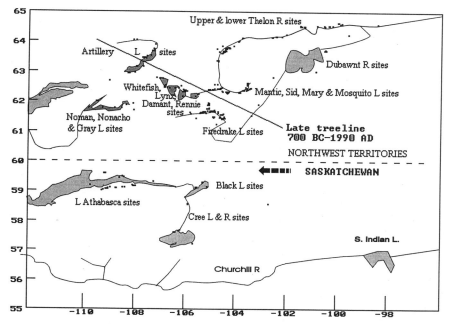

Figure 5.1. Distribution of 355 Middle Taltheilei sites.

Forest points, mainly near treeline, are pentagonal, rarely heat treated, planar, and taper towards the tip from square midsections and bases. Larger scattered tundra points are beige quartzite, biconvex lanceolates that taper from midsections and round bases (Table 5.14c).

Difference	Forest points	Tundra points	Remarks
distribution	near treeline	widespread	treeline focus in autumn; dispersed tundra water-crossings in summer
stone/colour	more variety. Gray	less variety. Beige	locally available material
plan	some pentagonal	some heavy & lanceolate	more forest tip sharpening creates pentagonal plan
section	some are planar	biconvex	influenced by flat side-notched points of overwintering Plains Indians?
taper	more towards tip	more to base	more forest tip sharpening consistent with pentagonal shaping
basal grinding	more square	more round	seasonally differing hafts. More forest basal spurring and thinning
breakage	more transverse	less transverse	hitting exposed rock at tundra water crossings
patination	less rare	more rare	consistent with heat treating Granite Falls & Mantic Lake forest tools?
size	smaller	larger	more forest retouch due to limited stone access under snowcover

Table 5.14c. Comparing Middle Taltheilei forest and tundra points.

Figure 5.2. Middle Taltheilei projectile points.

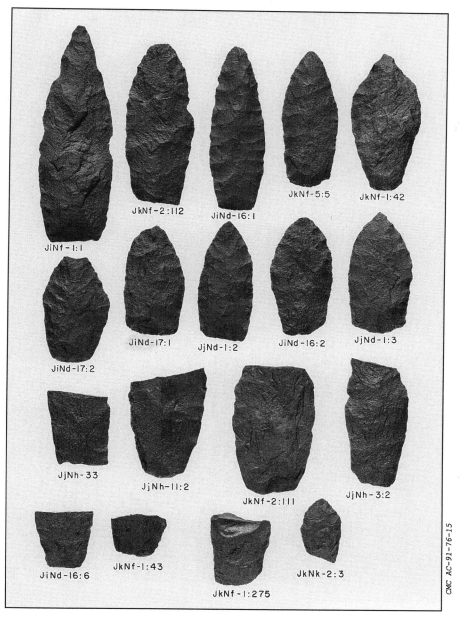

JkNf-2:112

JiNd-16:1

JkNf-5:5

JkNf-l:42

JiNf-l:l

JiNd-17:2

JiNd-17:1

JjNd-l:2

JiNd-16:2

JjNd-l:3

JjNh-33

JjNh-ll:2

JkNf-2:lll

JjNh-3:2

JiNd-16:6

JkNf-l:43

JkNf-l:275

JkNk-2:3

CMC AC-91-76-15

Figure 5.3. Middle Taltheilei projectile points (cont'd).

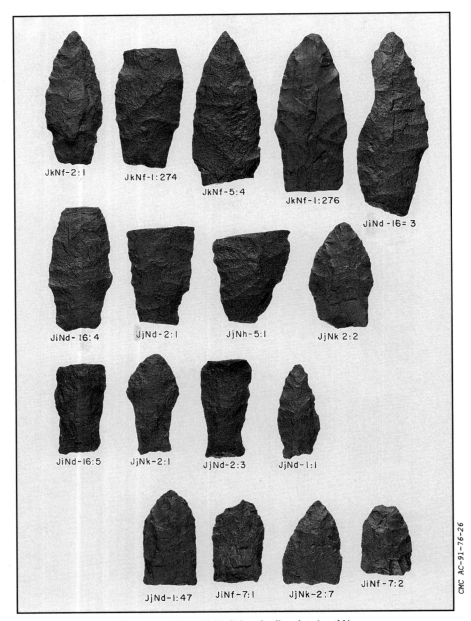

JkNf-2:1   JkNf-1:274   JkNf-5:4   JkNf-1:276   JiNd-16= 3

JiNd-16:4   JjNd-2:1   JjNh-5:1   JjNk 2:2

JiNd-16:5   JjNk-2:1   JjNd-2:3   JjNd-1:1

JjNd-1:47   JiNf-7:1   JjNk-2:7   JiNf-7:2

CMC AC-91-76-26

Figure 5.4. Middle Taltheilei projectile points (cont'd.).

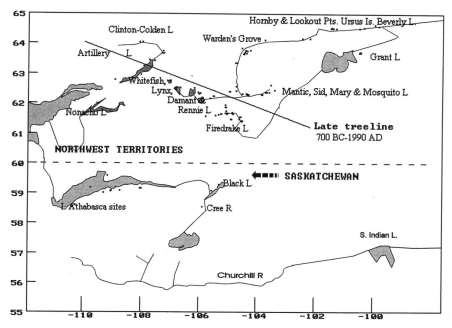

Figure 5.5. Distribution of 122 Middle Taltheilei sites with 428 points.

Analysis of scrapers

Middle phase scrapers appear more dispersed than Late ones because their distinctive large size and triangular shape permitted a greater phase assignment of surface finds. Like points, they are in 40% of Middle phase sites (441 F; 540 T; Fig. 5.6). Mainly quartzite, more tundra scrapers are beige than forest ones, which are more mottled or banded, reflecting available rock. Four-sided forest scrapers and 3-sided tundra ones may relate to hand or wood hafting in the forest, and antler or bone socketting on the tundra (Fig. 5.7 top center). Rangewide sections (mostly tabular) and serration are too alike to compare, but dual-bitted and discoid scrapers are only in the forest. Bases, most dorsally retouched, are more ground or worn on the tundra from socket mounting. Rangewide cortex, wear and striae are alike, but more forest scrapers made from knife sharpening flakes retain their original biface platforms. They also have more single or dual engraving spurs like those in Dene forest sites in Alaska, the Yukon and Fisherman Lake, N.W.T. (Fig. 5.7 top, Tables 5.15 to 5.26d; Millar 1968:Figs. 40 to 42). Forest scrapers are shorter.

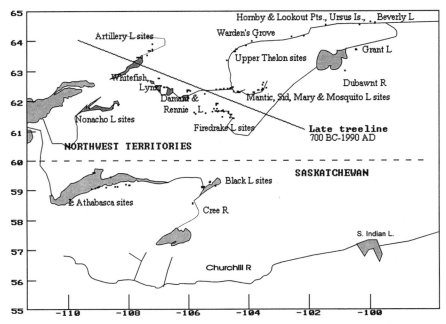

Figure 5.6. Distribution of 143 Middle Taltheilei sites with 981 scrapers.

Difference	Forest scrapers	Tundra scrapers	Remarks
distribution	near treeline*	widespread*	hide preparation heavy at treeline and light at tundra water-crossings
stone & colour	some are gray quartz*	beige quartzite*	locally available material
texture	banded and mottled*	speckled*	locally available material
plan	more 4-sided*	more 3-sided*	hand or wood forest hafting, versus tundra bone/antler socketting
section	more keeled/planoconvex	more tortoise-backed	hand or wood forest hafting, versus tundra bone/antler socketting
cortex	more*	less*	forest breakage risk from thinning is reduced by leaving more cortex
basal wear	less due to wood haft?*	more due to bone haft?*	hand or wood forest hafting, versus tundra bone/antler socketting
biface platform	more knife thinning*	less knife thinning*	more forest retouch needed from heavier tool use and sharpening
spurring	more, unlike Late phase	less, unlike Late phase	more forest graver use
size	shorter*	longer*	more forest sharpening due to limited stone access

Table 5.26d. Comparing Middle Taltheilei forest and tundra scrapers (* like Late and Early Taltheilei).

KkLn-4:816a

KjNb-7:33-79a

KjNb-7:33-49

KjNb-7:25-4

KjNb-7:38-24

KjNb-7:19-136

KjNb-7:16-16

KjNb-6:49-19

KjNb-7:33-17

KkLn-4:730

KjNb-6:40-4

KkLn-4:777

KbNb-8:19
KbNb-8:20

KbNa-19:5

KcNf-3:8

CMC 80-575

Figure 5.7. Middle Taltheilei scrapers and knives.

KjNb-6:679

KjNb-7:41-53

KjNb-7:33-12

KcNf-3:7

KeNi-4:1349
KeNi-4:1350

CMC 80-590

Figure 5.8. Middle Taltheilei symmetrical knives.

KjNb-7: 34-15

KjNb-7; 7-40

KdNc-2: 3

KjNb-7: 35-9

KjNb-6: 17-4

KjNb-7: 23-31

KjNb-7: 10-13

KeNi-4c: 3-56

CMC 80-588

Figure 5.9. Middle Taltheilei knives and gravers.

KeNi-4c: 3-54

KkLn-4: 675-2a

KkLn-4: 699a

KjNb-7: 38-32a

KjNb-6: 20-40

KjNb-6: 23-9a

CMC 80-591

Figure 5.10. Middle Taltheilei needle, awls, chitho, hammerstone and edge abrader.

Analysis of knives

Phase-specific ground stem knives (411 F; 954 T) are dispersed at most sites like points and scrapers, with the addition of Grant, Markham and Barlow Lakes (Fig. 5.11). Plans are mainly ovoid and lanceolate (Figs. 5.8-9), and even notched (KjNb-7:23-31) or tanged (tiny copper KeNi-4C:3-56). Eighty-eight percent of all burnt and shattered knives are in a few square meters in Warden's Grove sites KjNb-5 (16 knives) and KjNb-7 (8 knives), and suggest some form of ritual. Three burnt scrapers and two burnt points surround the KjNb-7 knives, while KjNb-5 knives are confined to a hearth. It might appear they were heated to improve their retouching quality through vitrification, but they were already finely retouched and likely broken through firing, as seen in the close proximity of their multi-coloured components. Both Back (1836:447) and Jenness (1956:28) comment on destroying a person's property at death. If such a custom existed prehistorically, what easier way to destroy tools than by breaking them by burning.

More tundra knives are broken; some are split. Rangewide sections have similar ratios of wear and retouch. More unworn unifaces with ground bases are in tundra sites. More serrated preforms are in forest sites. Perpendicular scraper-type striae are confined to forest knives JkNf-5:29, JjNe-6:7 and JiNe-1:27 at Jarvis Lake. Square, flat and round edges are more common in forest knives. Two-thirds of forest and half of tundra platforms are removed, suggesting a rangewide manufacturing technique. Forest knives are smaller but appear heavier due to three choppers from Lake Athabasca and Thelon River (weight more than 400 g; Tables 5.27a-5.42c).

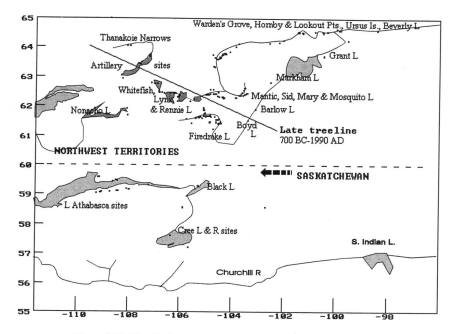

Figure 5.11. Distribution of 241 Middle Taltheilei sites with 1365 knives.

Difference	Forest knives	Tundra knives	Remarks
stone and colour	gray quartzite*	beige quartzite*	locally available material
face and cortex	like tundra (unlike Late phase)	like forest (unlike Late phase)	similar seasonal knife reduction
complete	half are complete	1/4 are broken lengthwise*	from hitting exposed tundra rock
plan/section	more semilunar or planoconvex	less semilunar/planoconvex@	forest flatness like Plains points?
serration	common. On preforms^	scarce. On platforms^	cutting frozen forest meat?
ground base	uncommon@	common@	from tundra bone/antler sockets
square, flat & round base & tip	common^	uncommon^	forest hand or wood hafting
midsection and tip	more serration*	less serration*	cutting frozen forest meat?
striae	one Jarvis Lake knife-scraper	none	some heavy use in forest
blunt backs	present@	rare@	for forest hand-hafting?
platform	only 1/3 have platforms	1/2 have platforms	more forest basal retouch
size	smaller*	larger*	more forest sharpening & use

Table 5.42c. Comparing Middle Taltheilei forest and tundra knives (@like Late,^Early or *Late & Early phases).

Analysis of chithos

Sandstone chithos occur throughout the Taltheilei tradition, but surface ones have few distinguishing traits for phase assignment (Fig. 5.10; KjNb-7:38-32a). Nonetheless, by combining all traits in Figs. 5.43b-5.50c, I assigned chithos (88 F; 27 T) in 11 sites in the forest at Black, Whitefish and Athabasca Lakes and on tundra at KjNb-6 & 7, and Grant and Mantic-Mary-Mosquito Lakes. Most forest sandstone chithos at Whitefish Lake are either surface and sand-abraded, or worn by gritty prime fall hides at treeline, but nine of 18 KjNb-6 & 7 chithos are quartzite with possible special tundra use (Fig. 5.12). More forest chithos are spalled; more tundra chithos are halved from striking surface rock. Rangewide chithos are usually round or ovoid, but 3-sided and bell-shaped ones occur in tundra sites. Forest chithos are smaller, flat and worn, with more cortex. Tundra chithos are wavy and unworn.

Difference	Forest chithos	Tundra chithos	Remarks
stone and colour	beige sandstone^	beige with some quartzite^	locally available material
faciality	bifacial*	1/4 are unifacial*	forest bifaciality from laminar sandstone
fragmented	1/2 are complete@	1/3 are complete@	more tundra breakage from exposed rock
plan and section	round and tabular@	ovoid and tabular@	
cortex	more	less	more forest conservation and less breakage risk
wear	almost all are worn@	2/3 are worn@	more forest use and retouch
size	smaller*	larger*	more forest wear and sharpening

Table 5.50c. Comparing Middle Taltheilei forest and tundra chithos (@like Late,^Early or *Late & Early phases).

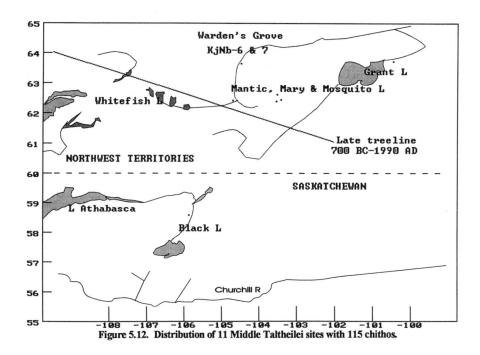

Figure 5.12. Distribution of 11 Middle Taltheilei sites with 115 chithos.

Analysis of wedges

Wedges (22 F; 28 T in 23 sites) cluster near treeline, KjNb-6 & 7 at the Warden's spruce grove, and at Thelon Bluffs and Aberdeen Lake near the Inuit trading site of *Akilineq* mentioned in Chapter 1. Oddly, none were found in Saskatchewan despite extensive field survey (Fig. 5.13). Wedge concentration at wood sources suggests shaft, board and handle production, while much smaller Grant Lake and Back River wedges suggest the making of harder tundra antler and bone needles, awls and other tools. Tundra wedges are also bipolarly percussed with columnar flake scars, while forest percussion is unipolar with rhomboid flake scars from splitting wood. Most wedges are quartzite of square plan and biconvex section (Tables 5.51a-5.56c).

Difference	Forest wedges	Tundra wedges	Remarks
stone	quartz; some chert@	almost all quartzite@	locally available material
colour	more orange^	more white^	locally available material
plan, size, flakescar	more rhomboid and bigger with less columnar & channelled flakescars*	more shapes and smaller with more columnar & channelled flakescars*	forest hand or wood hafting, versus tundra bone or antler socketting
percussion, section	uni- & bipolar@. More convex	discoidal@. Less convex	forest wood use, vs. tundra antler

Table 5.56c. Comparing Middle Taltheilei forest and tundra wedges
(@like Late,^Early or *Late & Early phases, except for range reversal of wedge size & flake scars).

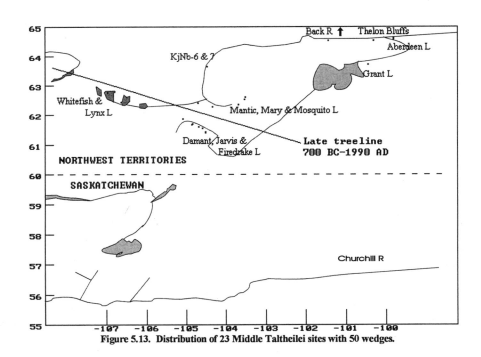

Figure 5.13. Distribution of 23 Middle Taltheilei sites with 50 wedges.

Analysis of adzelike artifacts

Adzelike artifacts include rangewide adze flakes, three tundra chisels and a gouge (Table 5.57). Like wedges, adze sharpening flakes occur near wood sources and are half the size of tundra ones at Grant Lake. The faces of those at wood sources are obliterated by grinding striae used to shape the adze bit. Unground lightly worn tundra flakes suggest adze shaping by chipping rather than grinding, with adzes directly applied to hard bone or antler. The more precise shaping of adzes used on wood may be for special applications, although a platform groove on a tundra flake suggests careful limiting of the bit size. All flakes are basalt except two silicious shale tundra flakes. Striae suggest one chisel was transversely sharpened; the other longitudinally (Tables 5.57-5.66b).

Type of tool	Range total	Forest total	Tundra total
adze flakes	47(92)	4(100)	43(91)
chisel	3(06)		3(06)
gouge	1(02)		1(02)
Total	51(100)	4(100)	47(99)

Table 5.57. Comparing the number of Middle Taltheilei adzelike tools.

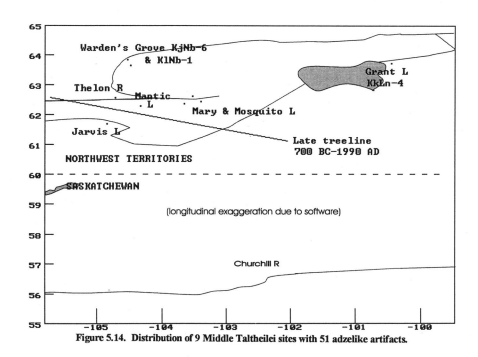

Figure 5.14. Distribution of 9 Middle Taltheilei sites with 51 adzelike artifacts.

Split chisel KcLw-1:128 (estimated width & length) with no basal edge, was near KcLw-24:4 at Mary Lake and of similar thickness and width (Table 5.66c). KcLw-24:4 has longitudinal use striae, and KcLw-1:128 has transverse grinding striae. KdNc-3:1 on the upper Thelon River is smaller and unstriated like a Shield Archaic point midsection. Warden's Grove gouge KlNb-1:2 on a unifacial unstriated point base resembles KdNc-3:1 in size but not in shape.

Artifact	Range	Length (mm)	Width (mm)	Thickness (mm)	Weight (g)	Plan	Section	Bit	SPA
KcLw-1:128	T	65.59 broken	46.07 broken	13.33	41.6 fragment	ovoid	biconvex	20	
KcLw-24:4	T	88.54	52.06	13.85	70.3	lanceolate	keeled	50	30
KdNc-3:1	T	56.95	27.02	7.81	14.2	triangular	biplanar	40	
KlNb-1:2	T	53.11	24.40	7.30	11.1	lanceolate	biconvex	60	

Table 5.66c. Middle phase chisels (top) and gouge. Bit=bit angle & SPA=platform angle.

Difference	Forest adzes	Tundra adzes	Remarks
stone and colour	1/2 are of gray silicious shale	black basalt	locally available material
striae	more variable	less variable	special forest applications?^
grinding	widespread	restricted	wood versus bone or antler usage^
polishing	heavy and widespread	facial ridges	wood versus bone or antler usage^
size	larger	smaller	less adze sharpening for soft forest wood versus hard tundra antler
grooved platform	none	only one	greater tundra adze sharpening for antler^

Table 5.66d. Comparing Middle Taltheilei forest and tundra adze flakes (^like Early phase).

Analysis of cores

All cores are from buried levels, with most at Warden's Grove, and isolated finds at Grant and Whitefish Lakes (4 F; 58 T; Fig. 5.15). Like flakes and other tools, most are quartzite. Half of forest cores are white, half of tundra ones are beige. Most cores have flake scars, but a tenth of tundra ones have blade scars. Bipolar cores are confined to tundra, with more curved platforms indicating their cobble origin. Tundra cores are also more battered at one end. A tenth of tundra edges are sand abraded. Most forest cores, but only one-fifth of tundra cores, are depleted. Several tundra cores are also pushplanes, knives or cleavers. A forest core is also a hammerstone. More forest cores are serrated and may have been used for scraping frozen hide. Hinging is only on one tundra core (Tables 5.67a-5.81b).

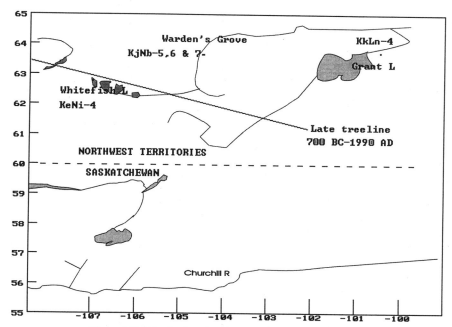

Figure 5.15. Distribution of 5 Middle Taltheilei sites with 62 cores.

Difference	Forest cores	Tundra cores	Remarks
quartzite	white*	beige; 1/5 are banded*	locally available material. More forest selection
plan/section	once were varied cobbles^	remained 4-sided after reduction^	locally available material. More forest selection
flake scars	all are flakelike#	a tenth are bladelike#	more frequent blade scars on tundra
platform	fewer are along a curve*	more are along a curve*	more tundra blade scars on curved platforms
depleted	most*	only 1/5 are depleted*	more forest reduction for making tools from flakes
multi-use	one hammerstone@	10% are pushplanes, knives or cleavers	more tundra multiple use tools
serration	more*	less*	forest use on frozen hide as scrapers?
edge wear	unworn@	a tenth are worn@	more tundra sand abrasion rather than wear?
size	larger#	smaller#	forest cores larger due to harder cobble reduction

Table 5.81c. Comparing Middle Taltheilei forest and tundra cores
(@like Late,^Early or *Late & Early phases; # unlike either).

Analysis of detritus

Detritus includes stratified flakes, flake bags, worked flakes and sharpening flakes from one forest and seven tundra sites (Fig. 5.16). Their material and site distribution resemble that of cores. Most are beige quartzite from KjNb-5 to 7, KkLn-4 & 13, KeNi-4, KdLw-1 and KbNb-17. Some flake bags contain tundra chert and forest quartz and sandstone. Of 598 representative flake entries, 47 forest flake bags weigh 2079 g, with min., max. and mean measurements (mm) and S.D. of 0.75, 472.4, 44.2 and 74.1; 174 tundra bags weigh 336,280 g, with analogous values of 0.13, 21,773, 1932.6 and 3801.2. One hundred and sixty-seven whole regular and sharpening flakes and 39 retouched flakes indicate forest flakes are smaller. All 19 complex flake tools are from tundra sites KjNb-6 & 7, and include a chopper, chisel, two chithos, eight knives and seven scrapers. As these sites overlook a major water-crossing, I suggest flakes were retouched for prompt use and discarded before hunters followed the caribou south. Compared to regular or worked flakes, the smallness of tundra bifacial sharpening flakes suggests an origin in the thinning or sharpening of medium to big knives (Table 5.82a-5.84c).

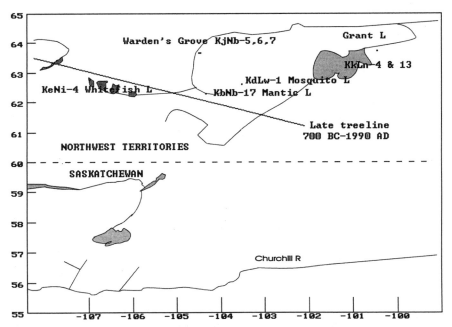

Figure 5.16. Distribution of 8 Middle Taltheilei sites with 598 detrital entries (flakes/flakebags).

Analysis of hammerstones

Six surface and 7 buried hammerstones (5 F & 8 T) are from Athabasca (4) and Artillery Lakes (1), KjNb-7 (5), KdLw-1 (2) and KjNb-6 (Fig. 5.17). All are quartzite except one of sandstone at Lake Athabasca. Most forest ones are pink; tundra ones are beige or gray. Forest hammerstones retain the roundness of their river cobble origin and have the equatorial pocking and larger size representative of their use as anvils (Tables 5.85a-5.89b).

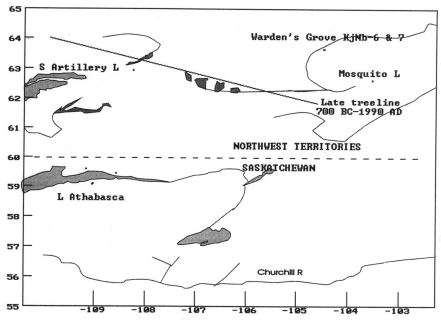

Figure 5.17. Distribution of 8 Middle Taltheilei sites with 13 hammerstones.

Difference	Forest hammerstones	Tundra hammerstones	Remarks
stone	some sandstone	all quartzite	locally available material. More forest selection
colour	pink (1 banded)	beige or gray	locally available material
plan and section	4-sided in both	rounded in both	locally available material. Like other traditions
pocking	2/3 unipolar or equatorial	2/3 are unipolar	more forest tasks, including use as anvils, like other phases
size	larger	smaller	like cores, and opposite Middle phase tools generally

Table 5.89c. Comparing Middle Taltheilei forest and tundra hammerstones.

Analysis of whetstones

KkLn-4:666-2a, an un-notched 5.76 mm thick pink sandstone bar fragment, is from Grant Lake. Its thick polished flat face and chitho edge is depicted in Gordon (1976:141).

Analysis of pushplanes

Dispersed pushplanes (30 F; 89 T; their numbers are bracketted) are at forest sites at Firedrake-Jarvis-Rennie-Damant (18), Whitefish-Lynx-Howard (6), Athabasca (4) and Nonacho (1) Lakes, and Pipestone River (1). Tundra sites are at Warden's Grove KjNb-4 to 7 (57), KkNb-3 & 10 (7), KlNa-1 (1), Sid (1), Mosquito (2) and Grant Lakes (1), and the lower Thelon (20) (Fig. 5.18). Most are biege or orange quartzite, except six tundra chert planes and one of gray shale. Most are rectangular or ovoid. Triangular ones are confined to tundra sites. Half of these are tortoise-backed, but keeled ones are common in forest. All planes have equal end and side retouch, but forest ones are smaller with more bit retouch and cortex. Forest planes are shaped via big, thin and bashed platforms opposite their keels. Tundra platforms are normal with less overall retouch (Tables 5.90a-5.101c).

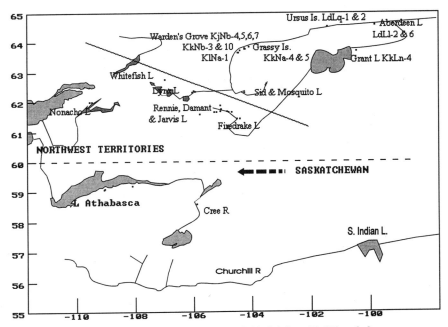

Figure 5.18. Distribution of 40 Middle Taltheilei sites with 119 pushplanes.

Difference	Forest pushplane	Tundra pushplane	Remarks
stone and colour	gray quartzite	some coloured chert	locally available material
plan	ovoid and 4-sided	some 3-sided	winter wood or hand hafting, versus summer bone or antler socketting
section	mostly keeled	mostly tortoise	winter wood or hand hafting, versus summer bone or antler socketting#
thin haft	very high	moderate	winter wood or hand hafting, versus summer bone or antler socketting#
serration	very high	moderate	serrated for planing soft forest wood
ventral retouch	mainly on the bit	more unretouched	for use on soft forest wood
cortex	more	less	less forest breakage risk. Less available raw material due to snowcover
platform	big, thin & bashed	normal	poor forest quartzite cleavage
thinning	dorsal haft	mostly unthinned	winter wood/hand hafting vs. summer bone/antler socket. Like Early phase
size	smaller	larger	more forest conservation and less wear from wood #

Table 5.101c. Comparing Middle Taltheilei forest and tundra pushplanes (# unlike Early phase).

Analysis of gravers

Unlike rotationally-striated, long round awls and drills, gravers are simple flake spurs that wear linearly through dragging along a bone or antler surface to cut shallow grooves. Six tundra gravers are dispersed at Warden's Grove (3) and Mantic (1), Mary (1) and Grant (1) Lakes, while four forest gravers are at Whitefish (2), Damant (1) and Jarvis (1) Lakes (Fig. 5.19). A graver is seen in Fig. 5.9 bottom right. Seven surface points and a sidescraper also are gravers, three from KjNb-6 & 7 levels. KjNb-6:20-10 has a spokeshave concavity between its spurs, with both sides retouched and planelike wear on a side. KjNb-7:10-13 is ovoid with a long spur and curved platform (Fig. 5.9 bottom). KjNb-7:22-12 is tearshaped and biconvex. Forest gravers are smaller (Tables 5.102a-b).

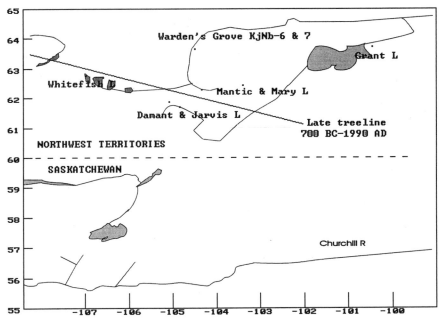

Figure 5.19. Distribution of 8 Middle Taltheilei sites with 10 gravers.

Analysis of skin flexers

Flexers are in all Beverly traditions and phases. They are long tools with rounded striated ends from flexing or softening skins (like the edges of chithos). They are also on long points, knives, spokeshaves and the ends of bar whetstones. Thirteen flexers (8 F & 5 T) are from Firedrake (1), Jarvis (4), Damant (3), Mantic (1) and Mosquito (4) Lakes. Their treeline focus suggests special late summer and early fall hide-working (Fig. 5.20). Like gravers, forest flexers are smaller than tundra flexers (Tables 5.103a-b).

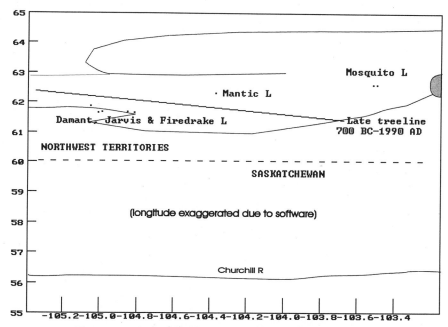

Figure 5.20. Distribution of 8 Middle Taltheilei sites with 13 skin flexers.

Analysis of bone and teeth

Bones, fragments and bags of counted bones include 76 entries from four stratified sites. Forest site KeNi-4 at Whitefish Lake has 43 entries and tundra sites KjNb-6 & 7 at Warden's Grove and KdLw-1 at Mosquito Lake have 26, 5 and 2 entries (Fig. 5.21). KeNi-4 has 26 caribou jaws and 153 molars and premolars (199 g) and 601 bones (791 g). The latter include 64 long bone fragments, right distal ulna, two distal metapodials, five distal metacarpals or metatarsals, distal tibia, astragalus, right calcaneus and left navicular - all caribou. KjNb-7 has no jaws or teeth, but 823 bones (1536 g) include a left unciform, magnum, cuneiform, scaphoid, right radius and many long bone fragments - primarily caribou. KdLw-1 has two tiny bone fragments weighing 0.1 g, plus 7.3 g of bone powder, suggesting bone crushing for fat extraction. KkLn-4 has 186 long bone fragments (122 g).

Unless frozen , acid soil quickly dissolves bone, but even then, thawed bone from permafrost levels is an irretrievable paste. Consequently, low bone yields do not correspond with actual caribou harvesting. Such is the case for the Middle phase which has the thickest levels and most sites of all phases and traditions, suggesting the heaviest caribou harvesting.

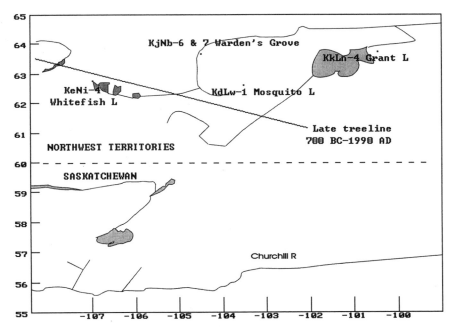

Figure 5.21. Distribution of 4 Middle Taltheilei sites with 76 bone/tooth entries.

Analysis of wood and metal

Spruce includes a 7.4 g charcoal sample and five wood fragments (0.3 g) in KeNi-4 level 3 at Whitefish Lake, 18 fragments (666.7 g) in level 2a of KjNb-7 at Warden's Grove and a 20 mg fragment in level 4 of KkLn-4 at Grant Lake. Copper entries in level 3 of KeNi-4 are an eyeless needle (44.3x6.2x2.2mm/1.6g; Fig. 5.10 top; Gordon 1976:Plate 28 bottom), a cold-hammered sheet awl (35.4x8.6x2.6mm/2.6g), a snapped point (33.6x11.4x1.4mm/1.6g), a piece of sheet (33.2x20x1mm/22 g) and 31 fragments (40.5 g).

Awls and needles are vital women's tools in a society where tailored clothing was needed in a harsh environment, but few occur in Taltheilei due to their type of material (Fig. 5.22). Hudson Bay Company steel needles rusted quickly, and bone needles and awls dissolved in the acid soil (a bone awl is in Late Taltheilei). Basalt and quartzite awls are in Early Taltheilei levels, but the Middle Taltheilei copper needle and awl are the earliest surviving Barrenland examples due to their resistant material.

Analysis of miscellaneous artifacts and art

Miscellaneous items are edge grinders (Fig. 5.10; KjNb-6:23-9a), spokeshaves, a denticulate, saws, objects interpreted as art on form and retouch, red sand and unidentified fur (Table 5.104).

Artifact	Size (mm/g)	Description
JlNg-8:43 F	67.2x36.5x6.2/17.7.Green-beige mudstone	edge grinder. Fine horizontal and vertical grinding grooves
KeNi-4:1563 F	91x-79.8x14.2/>121. Beige sandstone	edge grinder. Main and few minor grooves on broken chitho
KdLw-1:1149 T	20.1x16.5x6.4/2.2. Beige sandstone	edge grinder. V-shaped groove
KjNb-6:23-9a T	162x108.2x39.1/889. Gray sandstone	edge grinder. Wide central groove. Stratified level 3
KeNi-4:851 F	87.8x38.5x15.7/54. Beige quartzite	spokeshave on surface point
KjNb-6:40-36 F	62.7x37.9x11.3/25. Gray-green quartzite	spokeshave notched at end. Stratified level 3
KjNb-7:23-13 T	24x16x4.5/>1.7. Beige quartzite	denticulate fragment. Shallow unifacial notches rule out saw usage
KcNf-17:2 F	52.3x34.7x6.7/12. White chert	saw. Shallow bifacially chipped sawing notches
IhOa-2:129 F	65.3x43.5x9.3/25.3. Gray banded chert	saw. Shallow bifacially chipped sawing notches
LdLp-1:89 T	75.3x30.4x11.8/9.6. Gray quartzite	awl. Spur opposite cortex platform. Cult. affil. using knife KjNb-6:44-7
KkLn-4:675-2a T	63x12.4x4.8x>5.4. Black slate	awl. Joins awl fragment 679-2a? (Fig. 10, top)
KeNi-4C:3-54 F	44x6.2x2.2 /?	broken eyeless copper needle
KkLn-4:780 T	45x28.8x10.18/13. White/purple quartzite	art object on parallelogram knife
KdLw-1:1155 T	25.23x24.7x5.9/5.3. Beige quartzite	art object on wedge
KkNj-10:1 T	49.7x44.6x13.4/37. White quartzite	art object on parallelogram knife
KdLw-1 T	52.6 g of red sand and 1.4 g of fur	from ochre? From garment?

Table 5.104. Comparing Middle Taltheilei miscellaneous artifacts.

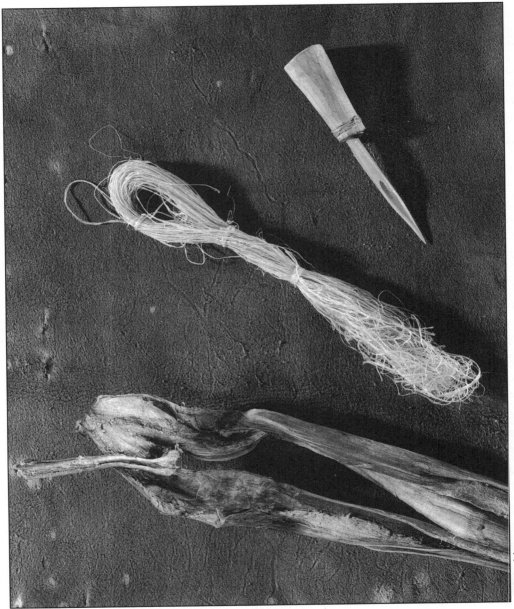

CMC Archives

Figure 5.22. Although bone needles and awls are unpreserved in Middle Taltheilei, a bone awl similar to the one at right may have been used. Back sinew at left was defibrillated into sinew strands (center) for sewing.

Conclusions On Middle Taltheilei Artifact Comparisons

Forest points, scrapers, knives, chithos, flakes, pushplanes, gravers and flexers are smaller, perhaps because they were sharpened more and retained longer due to inaccessible raw material under snowcover or hundreds of km away in tundra quarries. Scrapers and knives are serrated and 4-sided for easier winter hand gripping and use on frozen hides and meat. More tundra knives are broken, with split tips resulting from hitting surface rock. More forest chithos are flat and worn. Tundra chithos are wavy and unworn due to ample sandstone and less use. More widespread cortex in forest chithos is a sign of lower breakage risk because it confined sharpening to the edge. Forest wedges and adzes may be larger, as they wear less on soft wood than tundra antler. Depletion and smaller size of forest cores agree with their suggested maximum usage due to difficulties in stone replenishment from snow-covered or distant tundra quarries. Forest hammerstones are larger, due perhaps to their use as anvils in conjunction with a billet. Socketted triangular tortoise-backed pushplanes in tundra sites may be better suited to shaping antler, while keeled serrated ones may have been hafted in a split branch for shaping wood. Heavy wear on tundra bits suggests harder antler (Table 5.105).

Trait	Forest range	Tundra range	Remarks
C14 dates	1320-1740 years ago	1085-1915 years ago	herd following continuous from Early phase
cortex	more	less	more forest uniface tools
points	more types. Some pentagonal and flat. Tapered tip. More square based. Some are arrowheads	larger but fewer types. Lanceolate and biconvex. Tapered to rounded basal edge. Most are lanceheads	more forest retouch and the introduction of the bow and arrow from wintering Plains Indians
scrapers	shorter. 4-sided. More ground and spurred. Keeled and planoconvex	longer. 3-sided. Fewer ground spurs Tortoise shaped	more forest retouch and seasonal hafting differences
knives	smaller. More serrated. Less ground More square based and backed	larger. Less serrated. More ground Fewer square based. More platforms	more forest retouch and seasonal differences in base, serration, etc.
chithos	smaller. More sandstone. Rounder. More bifacial retouch and wear	larger. More quartzite. Less bifacial and ovoid. More breaks	more forest retouch and more tundra breaks
wedges	more chert and quartz. More convex Unipolar/bipolar percussion. Larger	quartzite. More channel and columnar scarring. More types. Discoidal plan	differences in hardness of forest wood, versus tundra bone & antler
adze flake sharpening	larger. Shale. More ground and polished	smaller. Basalt. Less ground and polished	differences in hardness of forest wood, versus tundra antler
cores	big cobbles. Flakelike. Used & serrated	4-sided worn quartzite. Some bladelike	different stone sources
flakes	smaller	larger	more forest reduction
hammerstones	larger. More sandstone. 4-sided-pocked	smaller. Quartzite. Round. End-pocked	different rock source & forest anvils
pushplanes	ovoid or 4-sided. Keeled. More cortex and bashed platforms	bigger. 3-sided. Tortoise plan. Less thinning, serration and retouch	more forest retouch and seasonally different use
gravers/flexers	smaller	larger	more forest retouch

Table 5.105. Comparing Middle Taltheilei forest and tundra tools. Unlisted data is similar in forest and tundra tools.

Chapter 6

Early and Earliest Phases of the Taltheilei Tradition

Dating and Distribution

The nature of Earliest phase tool styles and radiocarbon dates stimulated speculation on Dene origin. Radiocarbon dates of 2,575 and 2,570 years ago in forest sites KeNi-4 and JjNi-2, and 2,485 and 2,605 years ago in tundra sites KdLw-1 and KkLn-4 suggest rapid inroads of the Beverly range by a small band of hunters quickly adapting to herd following (Fig. 6.1). After the end of the cold Pre-Dorset period, these first Taltheilei people likely entered the range via the east-flowing Peace River, which pierces the Rockies and flows past Lake Athabasca. The Early phase people are included here because they descend from the Earliest phase pioneers.

The Early phase lasted 1,800-2,450 years ago, based on four radiocarbon dates west of the range, eight tundra dates at Grant Lake and Warden's Grove, nine forest dates at Whitefish, Nonacho, Lynx and Rennie Lakes, but none to the east (Table 6.1). Western dates are from sites with shouldered Early phase points at Bloody Falls near the Coppermine delta (McGhee 1970), Fisherman Lake in the southwest District of Mackenzie (Millar 1968) and Artillery Lake, which had a contaminated sample in a subsurface hearth (Noble 1971). Early phase points occur east in the Kaminuriak range but their sites are not radiocarbon dated.

Early-Earliest sites occupy the complete range, with a Churchill River occupation on its Haultain tributary. Tundra sites cluster at north Artillery Lake, Warden's Grove, Ursus Island-Thelon Bluffs, and Jim-Sid-Mantic-Mary-Mosquito, Grant and Beverly-Aberdeen Lakes, with a few sites at Caribou Narrows-Lockhart River, and Eyeberry and Barlow Lakes and Slow River. Forest sites focus at south Artillery, Lynx-Whitefish-Howard, Nonacho, Damant-Jarvis-Rennie-Knowles-Firedrake, Black and Athabasca Lakes, with some sites at Cree Lake and Cree River. Stratified sites with Earliest Taltheilei levels are at Rennie and Whitefish Lakes in the forest, and Grant and Mosquito Lakes on the tundra (Fig. 6.2).

Figure 6.1. Earliest Taltheilei pioneers and their caribou herd used this esker in the southern range as a migration route.

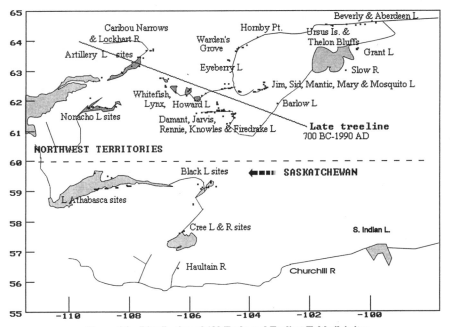

Figure 6.2. Distribution of 189 Early and Earliest Taltheilei sites.

Analysis of Early and Earliest Phase Material Culture

The transition from Earliest to Early phases involves an increase in lance diameter. Narrow thick tangs and incipient notching (Fig. 6.7 top) widen into thin shoulders (Figs. 6.3 & 6.4 top). The transition from Early to Middle phases occurs in several dozen uni-shouldered or stemmed points, sharing both levels (e.g.s, JkNg-3:14, KjNb-6:428, KeNi-4:300 & 872; Fig. 6.2 middle). Full transition is exemplified in Figs. 6.3 top & bottom and Fig. 6.4 top. Early points seem more dispersed (167 F & 63 T; Fig. 6.5) than the general site distribution (Fig. 6.2), because some sites without points had many phase-specific knives (Fig. 6.5).

Analysis of Early phase points

Like tools of other phases, points are beige quartzite with a few of white chert and gray shale. Points are biconvex shouldered lanceolates, except for a few pentagonal, rectangular, notched and incipient tanged varieties (Fig. 6.4 top). Tundra points are longer where tips are intact. They have more parallel sides with less evidence of sharpening. Two-thirds of forest and half of tundra bases are ground square, with reverse ratios for ground stems. Basal edges are mainly ground flat, with more variety in tundra bases. Like other phases, tundra points have more transverse breaks, less earing, multiple use, and rare burination (Tables 6.2a-6.14c).

N.W.T. (WEST)	BEVERLY NORTH	BEVERLY SOUTH	N.W.T. (EAST)
875±95 B.P. (S-587) 400 B.C. to 0 A.D. estimate from surface contaminated hearth in KfNm-3 on Artillery Lake (Noble 1971) 1790±70 B.P. (S-465) in MkPk-6 on the north Coppermine River (McGhee 1970) 1930±160 B.P. (I-319) and 2265±385 B.P. (S-703) on the Mackenzie complex, Fisherman Lake, N.W.T. (Millar 1968 and Wilmeth 1976, pers. comm.)	1915±80 B.P. (S-1020) in KkLn-4 at Grant Lake on the Dubawnt River 1970±120 B.P. (S-631) in KjNb-3 at Warden's Grove, Thelon River 1985±80 B.P. (S-1019) in KkLn-13 at Grant Lake, Dubawnt River 2075±115 B.P. (S-1024) in KkLn-4 at Grant Lake 2240±75 B.P. (S-1022) in KkLn-4 at Grant Lake 2345±170 B.P. (S-737) in KjNb-7 at Warden's Grove, Thelon River 2355±80 B.P. (S-715) in KjNb-7 2440±120 B.P. (S-711) in KjNb-7	1545±55 B.P. (S-1438) in KeNi-4 at Whitefish Lake, upper Thelon River 1775±60 B.P. (S-1138) in KaNp-1 at Nonacho Lake, Taltson River 1855±130 B.P. (S-1439) in KeNi-5 at Whitefish Lake 2020±110 B.P. (S-1257) in KbNg-6 at Lynx Lake, upper Thelon River 2145±125 B.P. (S-1157) in JjNi-2 at Rennie Lake, Elk River 2385±170 B.P. (S-1437) at KeNi-4 at Whitefish Lake 2390±105 B.P. (S-1436) in KeNi-4 at Whitefish Lake 2475±60 B.P. (S-1440) at KeNi-4 at Whitefish Lake 2545±160 B.P. (S-1260) at KeNi-4 at Whitefish Lake	undated
	Early phase - 1800 to 2450 years ago.		
	2485±85 B.P. (S-2493) in KdLw-1 at Mosquito Lake, upper Dubawnt R. 2605±205 B.P. (S-1025) in KkLn-4 at Grant Lake, Dubawnt River	2575±80 B.P. (S-1531) in KeNi-4 at Whitefish Lake 2570±120 B.P. (S-135) in JjNi-2 at Rennie Lake, Elk River	
	Earliest phase - 2450 to 2600 years ago.		

Table 6.1. Early and Earliest Taltheilei radiocarbon dates.
(Unreferenced dates are the author's)

Figure 6.3. Early Taltheilei projectile points.

eNi-4c:4-153

KbNb-8:44

KeNi-4:1403

KeNi-4c:4-l50

JjNi-2:4

KeNi-4c:4-5

KkLn-4:5ll

KkLn-4:532

KeNi-4c:4a-l2

KeNi-4c:4-l58

KjNb-7:30-l25

KeNi-4c:4-l09

KjNb-7:5-l9

KeNi-4c:4-l40

KjNb-7:30-l07

KeNi-4c:453

KeNi-4c:4-l22

KjNb-7:3-20

KeNi-4c:4-l2l

KjNb-7:30-l08

KjNb-7:5-20

CMC 80-586

Figure 6.4. Early Taltheilei points, wedges and scrapers.

Difference	Forest points	Tundra points	Remarks
quartzite	beige and gray *	beige and white	locally available material
plan and section	less lancelike*. More notching	more lancelike*. Less notching	influence from Earliest Taltheilei
breakage	less	more	seasonally different stone access
taper	more towards tip*	more towards base *	more forest use and sharpening
square based and eared	more*	less*	seasonally different hafts
multiple use	more	less	restricted forest material under snow
size	smaller*	larger*	more forest use and sharpening

Table 6.14c.   Comparing Early Taltheilei forest and tundra points (*like Middle phase).

Analysis of Earliest phase points

Earliest phase points are thicker, narrower and less shouldered than Early phase points (Fig. 6.7 upper, to Fig. 6.3). Few occur (3 F; 20 T), befitting their introduction, but Earliest and Early site distribution overlaps. Isolated forest finds at Rennie-Jarvis-Firedrake Lakes, and tundra finds at Warden's Grove and Grant and Aberdeen-Beverly Lakes, suggest continuous herd following to the Early phase (Fig. 6.6 to Fig. 6.5). Traits are mostly untabled due to the small number of points, but most are biconvex, quartzite and beige. Most forest tips are pointed; tundra tips, crushed or burinated. Most sides are parallel, but a third of tundra ones retain their taper. Most tangs are parallel, with one third of tundra bases square. Tundra points are smaller, and more broken, burinated and altered to other tools (Table 6.15-6.25c).

Difference	Forest points	Tundra points	Remarks
colour, plan and section	same	same	standardized production and use
intentional burination	absent	present	tundra burins used on bone or antler?
tang	parallel	1/3 are square based	attachment to shaft directly in forest and via bone socket in tundra
ground based and eared	more^	less^	forest grinding and earing to retain and protect sinew binding shaft
shouldered	all double	some single	shoulders to retain forest sinew and adjust tundra socket
broken or burinated	less	more	impact on more plentiful tundra surface rock?
multiple use	none@	wedge and burin@	tool conversion from broken tundra points?
size	smaller^	larger^	more forest use and sharpening

Table 6.25c.   Comparing Earliest Taltheilei forest and tundra points (^ like Middle and Early phases; @ unlike either).

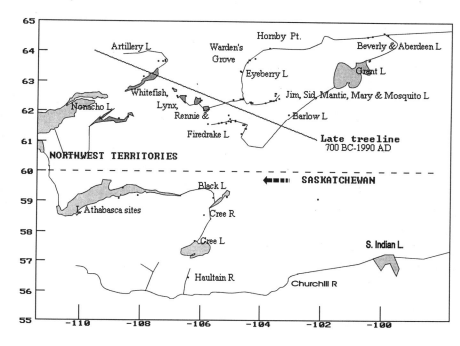

Figure 6.5.
Distribution of 82
Early Taltheilei
sites with 330
points.

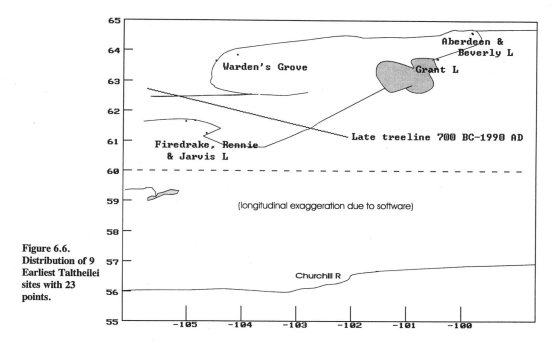

Figure 6.6.
Distribution of 9
Earliest Taltheilei
sites with 23
points.

KkLn-4:381

KkLn-4:368
KkLn-4:680

KkLn-4:378

KkLn-4:374

KkLn-4:369

KkLn-4:397

KkLn-4:380

CMC 80-578

Figure 6.7. Earliest Taltheilei points, wedges, scraper and knives.

Analysis of Early phase scrapers

Scraper examples are in Fig. 6.4 bottom half, and Fig. 6.9 (KkLn-4:364d top left). Tundra clusters are at Warden's Grove and Sid-Mantic-Jim-Mary-Mosquito and Aberdeen-Beverly Lakes, with small sites at north Artillery and Grant Lakes and Slow River. Big forest clusters are at Damant-Jarvis-Firedrake, Athabasca and Black Lakes. Isolated finds are at Whitefish-Lynx, Nonacho and Cree Lakes and Pipestone River (Fig. 6.8). Plan, size and spurs vary (e.g., KeNi-4C:4-158, Fig. 6.4 left center).

Most Early phase scrapers are quartzite, but a third of forest ones are chert. Most forest scrapers are beige or gray; tundra ones are beige or white. Half of forest and a third of tundra scrapers are rhomboid, while some tundra scrapers are triangular and flat. Like other tools, forest sections vary more. Most scrapers are flat, but forest backs are rounder or keeled. More forest scrapers are serrated. About half of all bases are dorsally retouched, but unground in forest and ground in tundra scrapers. Three-fourths of all bits are worn, with a few very worn. Like knives and points, most hafts are ground, but unground hafts are more common in forest scrapers, as are biface thinning platforms. Single spurs are five times more common than double spurs in both forest and tundra sites. Forest scrapers are shorter, with greater width and thickness due to rhomboid plans and keeled or tortoise sections (Tables 6.26a-6.37c).

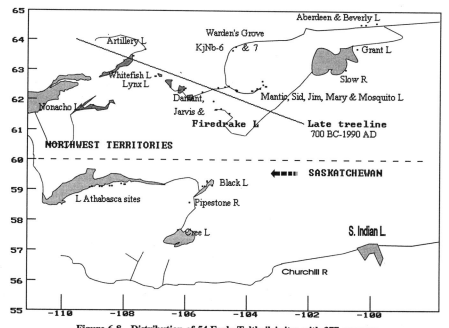

Figure 6.8. Distribution of 54 Early Taltheilei sites with 377 scrapers.

Difference	Forest scrapers	Tundra scrapers	Remarks
stone and colour	more gray quartzite*	more beige quartzite*	locally available material
texture	1/3 are mottled*	1/5 are speckled*	locally available material
plan and section	more rhomboid and keeled#	more triangular and flat#	seasonally different hafting
serration	more	less	use on frozen hide?
haft	less grinding and wear*	more grinding and wear*	heavy tundra socket wear
biface platform	more knife reduction*	less knife reduction*	more forest sharpening
spurring	like tundra (other phases differ)	like forest (other phases differ)	rangewide engraving
size	shorter*	longer*	more forest sharpening

Table 6.37c. Comparing Early Taltheilei forest and tundra scrapers (*like Middle phase; #like Middle and Earliest).

Analysis of Earliest phase scrapers

Of three surface and five buried quartzite scrapers (2 F & 6 T) from KeNi-4, KjNb-6 and KkLn-4, forest ones are rhomboid; tundra ones are mainly triangular. Tundra sections vary; two-thirds are flat and a sixth each, round or biconvex. Forest scrapers are flat. Scrapers have no cortex or striae, but most have dorsal retouch and a forest one has bifacial retouch. Forest scrapers are smaller and have more biface thinning platforms and worn bits; tundra hafts are more ground (Tables 6.38a-c). Spurred Earliest phase scraper KkLn-4:369 is depicted in Fig. 6.7 center.

Difference	Forest scrapers	Tundra scrapers	Remarks
distribution	only in KeNi-4	in KkLn-4 & KjNb-7	Taltheilei pioneers are few, as expected
colour	red (unlike other phases)	beige and purple	locally available material
plan and section	rhomboid and tabular^	1/3 are triangular and tabular^	seasonally different hafting
basally ground	almost all are ground*	2/3 are ground*	winter hand or binding sinew protection
bit wear	worn^	worn/very worn^	more tundra wear
biface platform	many thinning flakes	1/6 are thinning flakes	more large biface reduction flakes in forest
size	smaller	larger	more forest retouch or sharpening

Table 6.38c. Comparing Earliest Taltheilei forest and tundra scrapers (^like & *unlike Middle and Early phases).

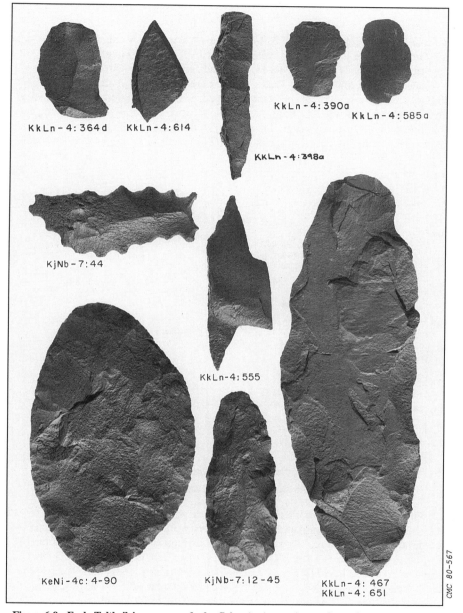

KkLn-4:364d KkLn-4:614

KkLn-4:390a

KkLn-4:585a

KkLn-4:398a

KjNb-7:44

KkLn-4:555

KeNi-4c:4-90

KjNb-7:12-45

KkLn-4:467
KkLn-4:651

CMC 80-567

Figure 6.9. Early Taltheilei scrapers and adze flakes (top), art piece and core fragment (middle) and bifacial knives (bottom).

Analysis of Early phase knives

Of 347 knives in 74 sites (171 F & 176 T), tundra site clusters are at Mantic-Sid-Mary Lakes, Wardens's Grove and the lower Thelon, with finds at Eyeberry and Grant Lakes (Fig. 6.10). Forest clusters are at Athabasca, Whitefish-Lynx-Howard and Jarvis-Damant-Firedrake Lakes, with isolated finds at Nonacho and south Artillery Lakes. Knives are unrecorded at Black and Cree Lakes and Churchill and Cree Rivers, although points were found. Knife distribution suggests hunters followed the Thelon and Dubawnt Rivers, favouring the Thelon. Most knives are quartzite with more diverse minerals in forest sites. Forest knives are mainly gray; tundra ones are beige. Most knives are bifacial, with twice as many tundra bases and tips, and five times as many edge fragments (Tables 6.39a-c).

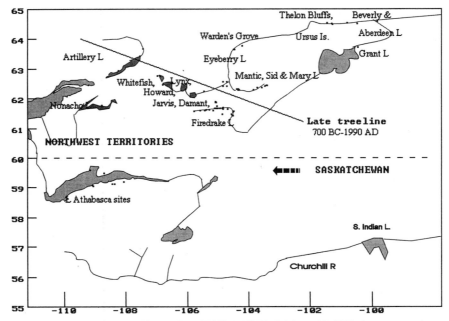

Figure 6.10. Distribution of 74 Early Taltheilei sites with 347 knives.

A fourth of knives are ovoid, a fifth are lanceolate and a fourth of forest knives are shouldered. Most are biconvex and about a third each have unworn or worn bifacially retouched edges. More forest knives are serrated or have unground or ground, bifacially retouched bases or midsections. Worn round forest tips imply special use, and knife KkLn-4:614 at Grant Lake is even striated. Tundra knives have more transverse breakage. Like other phases, more bases are tapered on tundra and square in forest. No backs are blunted for hand hafting, but more forest platforms are removed or ground and facetted for hafting. Except for two huge forest choppers (331 & 342 g), forest knives are smaller (Tables 6.42-6.54c).

Difference	Forest knives	Tundra knives	Remarks
stone and colour	gray mottled quartzite*	beige banded quartzite*	locally available material
complete	less than 1/2. More bases*	1/4. More tips. Many edge fragments*	much breakage on surface tundra rock
haft	some are shouldered	some are stemmed	retaining forest sinew or tundra socket
biface base-midsection	more*	less*	forest conservation; base retention for retouch
serration	more *	less *	cutting frozen forest meat?
tip wear	more*	less*	more forest knife conservation
transverse breaks	less*	more*	more tundra rock breakage at water crossings
platform	more ground or removed*	less ground or removed*	more forest retouch for wood or hand hafting
size	smaller*	larger*	more forest retouch, sharpening & conservation

Table 6.54c. Comparing Early Taltheilei forest and tundra knives (*like Late and Middle phases).

Analysis of Earliest phase knives

None of the four KkLn-4 bifacial knives (Gordon 1976:96,181; 3 buried) have striae, backs or cortex. Knife #380, the only full knife, is unworn beige quartzite, biconvex, semilunar, and basally round and unground (Fig. 6.7 bottom). It is 103.6x69.2x8.3mm/62 g with a retouched platform. Ovoid red quartzite base-midsection #382 (undepicted) is worn, biconvex and 50x36x5.3mm, with a tapered unground round base and unground unfacetted platform. Banded, worn, beige quartzite base-midsection #397 (Fig. 6.7 bottom) is fragmentery and uni-shouldered, with a pointed ground base and ground facetted platform. Tip #47 (undepicted) is red quartzite, ovoid, unworn and round.

Analysis of Early phase chithos

Forty-three buried and 29 surface chithos (54 F & 18 T) are dispersed on the Thelon River, Warden's Grove and Mary and Grant Lakes, with forest finds at Lynx-Whitefish and Athabasca Lakes (Fig. 6.11). At Warden's Grove, sandstone is ample, but some chithos are quartzite. Most forest and three-fourths of tundra edges are worked bifacially. Half of chithos are halved, quartered or spalled. Most forest and half of tundra chithos have cortex. Tundra ones tend to be ovoid, unworn, flat and smaller (Tables 6.55a-6.62c). KkLn-4:605 from Grant Lake is depicted in Fig. 6.12 top left.

Difference	Forest chithos	Tundra chithos	Remarks
stone and colour	beige sandstone*	some gray quartzite*	locally available material
bifaciality and cortex	more*	less*	sharpening confined to edge. More conservation
plan and section	less ovoid and tabular*	more ovoid and tabular*	locally available material
wear	more^	less^	greater forest conservation
size	smaller^	larger^	more forest retouch, use and conservation

Table 6.62c. Comparing Early Taltheilei forest and tundra chithos (*like Middle ^and Late phase).

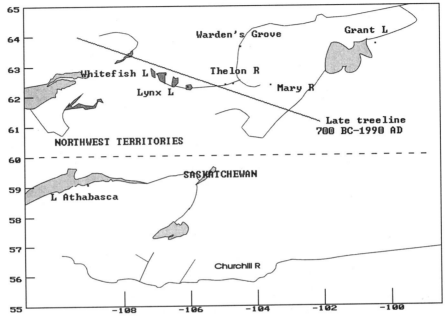

Figure 6.11. Distribution of 10 Early Taltheilei sites with 77 chithos.

Analysis of Earliest phase chithos

One chitho occurs, KkLn-4:363a at Grant Lake (Gordon 1976:96), its breakage preventing size estimate. Made of brown sandstone, it is round, bifacial, tabular, unworn and free of cortex.

Analysis of Early phase wedges

Twenty-one sites with 24 buried and 31 surface wedges (48 F & 7 T) are in forest at Nonacho, Whitefish, Rennie-Damant-Jarvis, Athabasca and Black Lakes, and Pipestone River, a Cree tributary, and on tundra on the upper Thelon, Warden's Grove and Mary and Grant Lakes. Flakelike wedges at Cree Lake and Churchill River likely went unrecognized in the field (Fig. 6.13). Most wedges are quartzite; white or gray on tundra, and beige or orange in forest, with some of chert and taconite. Most wedges are biconvex and 4-sided, with some 3-sided in the forest. A third of flake scars are amorphous or channelled columnar, with a rise in flat and channelled types in tundra and forest wedges, respectively. Two-thirds of forest and all tundra types are bipolarly struck, with more variety in forest wedges. Forest wedges are smaller (Tables 6.63a-68c). KkLn-4:532, KeNi-4C:4a-12 and KeNi-4C:4-5 are struck on all four sides; i.e., double bipolar percussion. Rectangular or square KkLn-4:511 and KeNi-4:493 on lanceheads are bipolarly percussed (Figs. 6.4 second row, and Fig 6.14 bottom right).

JiNc-1:37

KkLn-4:605

KeNi-4c:4-257

KeNi-4c:2-103

KeNi-4c:4-257

KjNb-6:62-3

KeNi-4c:419-72

CMC 80-572

Figure 6.12. Early Taltheilei chitho, notched whetstone fragments, adze, hammerstone and copper fragments

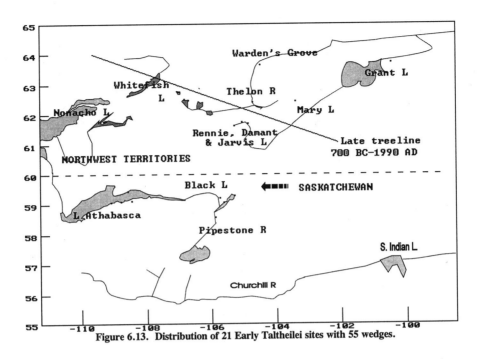

Figure 6.13. Distribution of 21 Early Taltheilei sites with 55 wedges.

Difference	Forest wedges	Tundra wedges	Remarks
quartzite colour	beige, white and orange^	white or gray^	locally available material
flake scars	more channelled columnar*; unlike Middle phase	more flat columnar	splitting forest wood versus tundra antler
percussion	mixed^	all bipolar	splitting forest wood versus tundra antler
plan	more rhomboid like Middle phase	rectangular or ovoid	
size	smaller#	larger#	opposite other traditions and phases

Table 6.68c. Comparing Early Taltheilei forest and tundra wedges (*like Late ^and Middle phases; # unlike both)

Analysis of Earliest phase wedges

Four Earliest Taltheilei quartzite wedges are identified using buried wedges. They include KkLn-4:378 (Fig. 6.7 top right), a bipolarly split pebble, and three undepicted ones in Aberdeen Lake site LdLl-2: #27a is rhomboid, biconvex, discoidally percussed with amorphous flake scars and 29.3x28x11.3mm & 8.8g; #27b is rhomboid, planoconvex, discoidally percussed with channel-grooved/columnar flake scars and 25.9x27.5x9.5mm & 8.3g; and #28 is rectangular, biconvex and bipolarly struck with channelled-columnar flake scars and 25x19.5x8.5mm & 4g.

KgLo – 1:1

KiNc – 6:1

JkNf – 5:105

KbNo – 1:1

KeNi – 4:616

KeNi – 4:1527

KeNi – 4:493

CMC 80-587

Figure 6.14. Ground stone tools by culture (clockwise from top). Early Taltheilei adze, two General phase axes, Early phase wedge (bottom right), Early phase whetstone, Late phase bar whetstone (left) and Shield Archaic whetstone (center)

Analysis of Early phase adzelike artifacts

Eight surface and 55 buried adzelike artifacts are thinly dispersed on tundra at Warden's Grove-Grassy Island, Slow River and Grant Lake, and in forest sites at Whitefish and Damant Lakes. None are recorded in Saskatchewan (Fig. 6.15). Adzelike artifacts include four forest and 47 tundra adze flakes and 12 tools (7 adzes, 3 chisels, a gouge and a pick; Table 6.77c-d). Three adzes, three chisels and the gouge are complete; four adzes, the pick and 50 adze flakes were stratified. Two adzes were in forest sites; five in tundra sites. The three forest chisels, gouge and pick infer intensive woodworking. Like Middle phase, tundra adzelike artifacts include many adze sharpening flakes, but no Middle phase adzes are reported.

Most tundra artifacts are shock-resistant basalt, due to 40 KkLn-4 adze sharpening flakes from the same adzes (Fig. 6.9 top right). Half of flakes are from adze sides; a fourth are from bits. Black silicious shale #398a is a ridge flake. Shale #390a and basalt #585a are from the sides of other adzes. Half of forest artifacts are weathered gray surface basalt; a fourth are quartzite. Buried tundra artifacts remain black. Most striae are transverse from bit sharpening, but a fifth of forest artifacts have this striae combined with diagonal use striae. Diverse tundra striae imply many unknown uses. Half of all grinding is restricted in surface area in forest flakes and widespread in tundra flakes. Grooved platforms implying careful sizing in adze sharpening are absent in forest and rare in tundra flakes. Forest flakes are larger, like those of other phases (Tables 6.70a-6.77d).

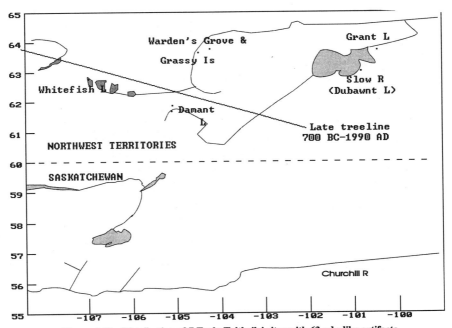

Figure 6.15. Distribution of 7 Early Taltheilei sites with 63 adzelike artifacts.

Difference	Forest types	Tundra types	Remarks
stone and colour	some quartzite#	more of black basalt#	locally available material
striae	more variable^	less variable^	special forest applications like Late Taltheilei
grinding and polish	heavy and localized@	heavy and widespread	used on soft forest wood, versus hard tundra antler
grooved platform	absent*	present*	controls adze sharpening limits for hard antler application
size	larger^	smaller^	less adze sharpening needed for soft forest wood

Table 6.77c. Comparing Early Taltheilei forest and tundra adzelike artifacts.
(*like Middle ^and Late phases; #like Late; and @heavy and widespread in both phases)

Measurements of 7 adzes, 3 chisels, a gouge and a pick are in Table 6.77d. Forest adzes are too broken to compare, but tundra adzes are alike, except KgLo-1:1 is wide (Fig. 6.14 top), KkLn-4:580-2b has a wide bit, and KjNb-6:1946 is keeled. They are larger but resemble KkNa-2:9. Forest and tundra bit angles and strial combinations overlap. Tundra platform angles (between base & side) vary 50-90 degrees. Adze #552 has a platform groove for controlled sharpening. Forest chisels JlNg-8:24 & 5 and JkNg-3:26 are alike, except the first is tabular and triangular. Gouge KeNi-4:291 has a large grooved bit chamfered to 70 degrees. Pick KeNi-4C:B48 is lanceolate with a tiny 20 degree piercing bit.

Number	R	L mm	W mm	T mm	Wt g	Plan	Section	Bit	Striae	SP
KeNi-4C4:A32	F	-34	-79	-7.8	-23	?	?	60	triangular/diagonal	?
KeNi-4 C4:A40	F	-63	-33	22.3	-51	lanceolate	keeled	?	longitudinal	?
KgLo-1:1 (Fig. 6.14 top)	T	159	65.6	39.2	465	ovoid	planoconvex	40	0	60
KkNa-2:9	T	119	79.8	36.3	380	ovoid	planoconvex	30	0	50
KkLn-4:552-2	T	-129	-58	-9.4	-63	lanceolate	keeled	?	triangular	90
KkLn-4:580-2b	T	181	44.4	39.2	399	lanceolate	planoconvex	80	longitudinal	90
KjNb-6:1946	T	172	42.5	? lost	473	lanceolate	keeled	?	?	?
JlNg-8:5	F	46.5	27.7	7.01	9.4	lanceolate	biconvex	50	0	0
JlNg-8:24	F	38.9	27.2	7.87	9.0	triangular	biplanar	40	0	0
JkNg-3:26	F	49.3	25.8	8.84	10.9	lanceolate	biconvex	40	0	0
KeNi-4:291	F	60.9	29.2	9.97	19.3	lanceolate	biconvex	70	0	0
KeNi-4C4:B48	F	-40	26.6	12.2	-13	lanceolate	biconvex	20	0	0

Table 6.77d. Early Taltheilei forest and tundra adzes (top), chisels, gouge and pick.
R=range; (-)=incomplete and broken; bit=bitangle; SP=striking platform

Analysis of Early phase cores

Eleven buried cores each are from a Whitefish Lake forest site and three Warden's Grove and Grant Lake tundra sites (Figs. 6.16 & 6.9, core frag. KkLn-4:555). Most cores are quartzite; white and beige in forest and beige and orange on tundra. Tundra cores are mainly 4-sided; forest cores, round cobbles. One-fourth of forest cores are bladelike with a straight platform; while 91% of tundra cores are flakelike with a curved platform. Ten per cent of forest cores are bipolar. Most cores are unworn and pocked at one end. A forest knife and two tundra pushplanes are also cores. Serration is only in forest cores, and twice as many are depleted or smaller (Tables 6.78a-6.92c).

Difference	Forest cores	Tundra cores	Remarks
stone and colour	beige or white quartzite	beige or orange quartzite	locally available material
plan and section	once were cobbles*	once were 4-sided slabs*	locally available cobbles or slabs
profile	more blocky	more conical	seasonal differences in reduction
flake scars and platform	more bladelike and single@	less bladelike and more curved@	forest blocky cores versus tundra conical cores
depleted	twice that of tundra cores^	half that of forest cores^	restricted forest material under snowcover
serration	present^	absent^	forest cores used in scraping frozen hides
size	smaller@	larger@	more forest reduction and conservation

Table 6.92c. Comparing Early phase forest and tundra cores (*like Middle ^and Early phases, or @but unlike Early).

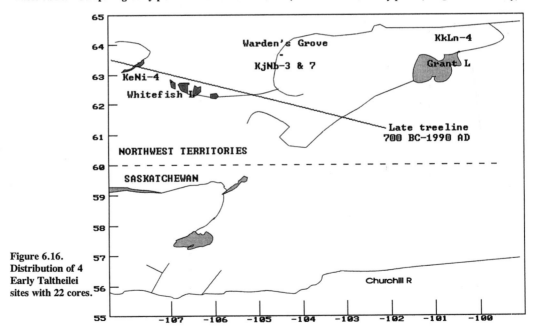

**Figure 6.16.
Distribution of 4
Early Taltheilei
sites with 22 cores.**

Analysis of Early phase flakes

Stratified detritus includes 6,638 unanalyzed flakes in 40 bags, 114 retouched flakes, 99 analyzed regular, randomly chosen flakes (52 F; 47 T) and 3 sharpening flakes. Regular and worked flake and core distributions are alike (Fig. 6.17), with 374 entries (114 worked & 260 regular flakes, flake bags and multiple flake entries [under one number]) from 11 sites (KjNb-3, 6 & 7 at Warden's Grove, KeNi-4 at Whitefish Lake, Lynx Lake, KkLn-4 at Grant Lake and 5 sites on Archibald and MacFarlane Rivers, and Yakow and Athabasca Lakes). Of 374 entries (31 surface; 343 buried), 158 are from forest sites and 216 from tundra sites. The total weight of flake bags and multiple flake entries is 84 kg, of which the forest component weighs 7 kg; the tundra component, 77 kg. Regular flakes are quartzite; white and gray and smaller in forest; beige and orange on tundra. Retouched flakes (52 F; 62 T) are mostly beige quartzite, but also smaller and pink in forest and orange on tundra (Tables 6.93a-6.95c). They include two wedges, two uniface knives, three sidescrapers and an endscraper.

Difference	Forest flakes	Tundra flakes	Remarks
stone and colour	white and gray mixed stone	beige and orange quartzite	locally available material
size	smaller	larger	greater forest core reduction and conservation
stone and colour	some pink mixed stone	some white quartzite	locally available material
size	smaller	larger	greater forest flake use and retouch

Table 6.95c. Comparing Early Taltheilei regular (top) and retouched forest and tundra flakes.

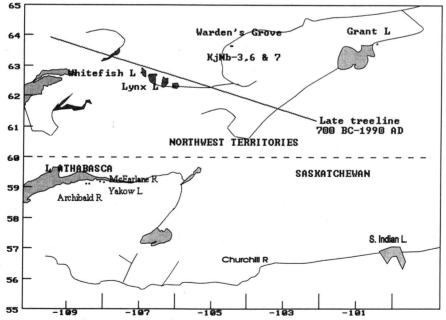

Figure 6.17. Distribution of 11 Early Taltheilei sites with 374 flakes.

Analysis of Earliest phase flakes

Mean measurements of 5 retouched tundra flakes are 36.6x8.8x7.2mm & 7.6g. This is midway between Early Taltheilei forest and tundra flakes, and suggests similar core reduction. Also included are 354 unanalyzed flakes in bags weighing 520g.

Analysis of Early phase hammerstones

Two surface and seven buried hammerstones (6 F & 3 T; e.g., KjNb-6:62-3, Fig. 6.12, lower left) are scattered on the tundra at Warden's Grove and Grant Lake, and in the forest at Athabasca and Whitefish Lakes (Fig. 6.18). Most forest ones are beige or gray quartzite; tundra ones are gray granite. Most plans and sections are 3 or 4-sided and end-pocked. Forest hammerstones are shorter, wider, thinner and heavier, with one each with bipolar and side-pocking (Tables 6.96-100c). One only Earliest phase hammerstone, KkLn-4:372-3 at Grant Lake, is very end-pocked. It is 4-sided, white and gray quartzite (123.2x69.57x64.94 mm & 794 g), and depicted in Gordon (1976:97).

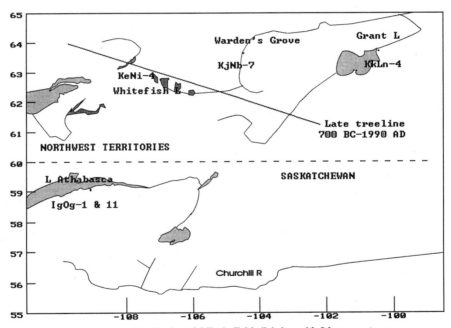

Figure 6.18. Distribution of 5 Early Taltheilei sites with 9 hammerstones.

Difference	Forest hammerstones	Tundra hammerstones	Remarks
stone and colour	beige or gray quartzite	gray granite	locally available material. More forest selection
pocking	diverse types	all unipolar	seasonally differing uses? Anvil use in forest, like other phases
size	short and wide	long and narrow	seasonally differing uses? Forest ones better for anvil use

Table 6.100c. Comparing Early Taltheilei forest and tundra hammerstones.

Analysis of Early phase forest whetstones

Five surface and 6 buried slate bar whetstones at Nonacho, Firedrake and Whitefish Lake forest sites are unmapped. Their lengthwise wear and grooves suggest use as sharpeners and for dulling point and knife bases and shaft smoothing. One is notched for suspension. Mean size is 71.4x27.8x9 mm & 46.2g (Tables 6.101-6.105b). KeNi-4C:4-257 and JiNc-1:37 fragments are seen in Fig. 6.12, and KbNo-1:1, JkNf-5:105 and KeNi-4:1527 whetstones are depicted in Fig. 6.14 (bottom left).

Analysis of Early phase pushplanes

Nine dispersed quartzite pushplanes (4 F; 10T) are at JhNe-2 and JiNc-2 at Firedrake Lake, JlNg-8 at Damant Lake, and KbNg-1 at Howard Lake in the forest; and at KcNc-16 on the upper Thelon, KjNb-6 & 7 at Warden's Grove (5), KkLn-4 at Grant Lake (1) and LdLl-2 at Aberdeen Lake on tundra (3; Fig. 6.19). Forest ones are rounded; half of tundra ones are keeled. Tundra ones are more abruptly retouched on their bits, sides and ventral midsection, leaving less cortex. Forest ones are larger with thinned hafts and platforms (Tables 6.106a-6.114c).

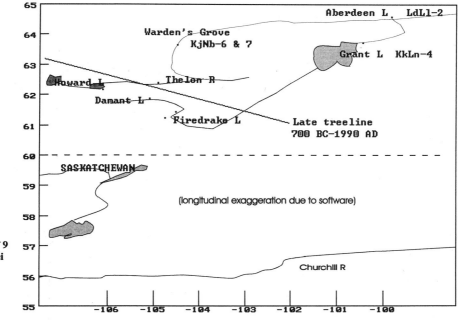

Figure 6.19. Distribution of 9 Early Taltheilei sites with 14 pushplanes.

Analysis of Early phase skin flexers

The four tundra and three forest skin flexers are from five sites at Whitefish and Mary Lakes, Eyeberry Esker and the junction of the Elk and Thelon Rivers (Fig. 6.20). The Whitefish forest flexers are larger but less serrated and more gently retouched than tundra flexers, but have thinned bashed hafts (Table 6.115a-b).

Difference	Forest pushplane	Tundra pushplane	Remarks
section	tortoise	keeled	opposite Middle Taltheilei sections*
serration	less	more	opposite Middle Taltheilei serration*
steep retouch	less abrupt	more abrupt	more exaggerated than that in Middle Taltheilei pushplanes
cortex	more	less	less forest retouch due to risky breakage and unavailable raw material
haft	bashed and thinned	normal	for forest hand hafting? Seasonally differing hafting and use
size	larger	smaller	opposite Middle Taltheilei size*

Table 6.114c. Comparing Early Taltheilei forest and tundra pushplanes. *tiny forest sample lowers significance.

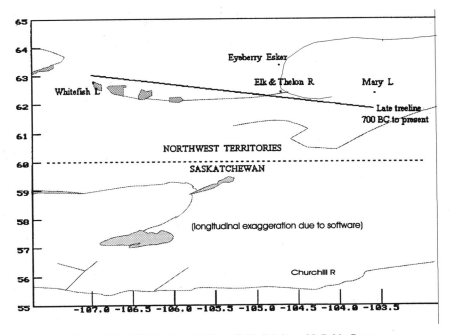

Figure 6.20. Distribution of 4 Early Taltheilei sites with 7 skin flexers.

Analysis of Early phase miscellaneous artifacts

Other tools are an edge grinder, two spokeshaves and a shaft polisher at forest site KeNi-4, four awls at tundra and forest sites KjNb-3 and KeNi-4 & KcNi-3, four gravers at forest sites KeNi-4 and JlNg-8, three saws at tundra sites KjNb-6 & 7, and four fire-split rocks at forest sites KeNi-4 and KbNg-6 (Table 6.116). Other items are a tundra art piece from KjNb-7, and a forest bone skin stretcher and tool and bone fragments from KeNi-4. Tundra wood includes three charcoal fragments (40 mg), a 30 mg burnt wood fragment at KkLn-4, and 14 wood fragments (74 mg; 13 charred) at KjNb-7 (untabled). Eight forest wood pieces weigh a total of 3 g. Drills or ochre nodules are unreported.

Artifact	Size (mm/g)	Description
KeNi-4:1527	102x39x8/57. Flat curved edge. Black shale	like KeNi-4C:4-257. 4 grooves.Long/transv.striated whetstone/edge grinder
KeNi-4:440	71x41x12/46. Beige quartzite	like KcNc-2:76. Flexer tip. Spokeshave
KeNi-4:4-240	45x20x14/12. Gray chert	on concave retouched flake. Spokeshave
KeNi-4:4-256	91x43x18/70. Gray sandstone	worn edge. Shaft polisher resembling a whetstone
KjNb-3:2-1-2	38x13x9/5. Gray basalt	keeled with worn tip. Awl
KeNi-4:1111	42x18x9/5. Red quartzite	long sharp bifacially retouched tip. Awl
KeNi-4:1097	104x19x9/21. Gray basalt	worn and keeled. Spatulate. Awl
KcNi-3:51	83x9x9/7. Gray basalt	keeled and worn, with longitudinal striae. Awl
KeNi-4:1147	21x12x5/1. Red taconite	no tip. Graver
KeNi-4:4-137	26x17x4/2. Beige chert	notched with very worn haft. Graver
JlNg-8:4	38x30x8/10. Gray quartzite	on shouldered Early Taltheilei point. Graver
KeNi-4:4-54	19x29x8/4. Green chert	in stratified level. Graver
KjNb-6:1937	42x37x8/9. White chert	saw with four unworn notches
KjNb-6:1936	47x33x8/9. White chert	saw with five unworn notches
KjNb-7:21-22a	36x31x6/6. Black quartzite	saw with thin unworn notches
fire-cracked rock includes beige quartzite KeNi-4C:4-195 (83x52x58mm & 320g) and gray sandstone KbNg-6:8-1; 10-1 & 25-1 (33x33x21mm & 21g, 21x19x8mm & 4g, and 23x14x6mm & 1g, respectively)		
KjNb-7:44 T	65x28x6/11. Gray quartzite	bent. Worn grooves. Art piece* (Fig.6.8)
bone skin stretcher KeNi-4C:4A-75 measures 100x20x5mm & 11g. Also bone unidentified tool fragments KeNi-4C:4A-69 & 71		
bone fragments (probably caribou long bone) include beige-brown KeNi-4C:4A-70 & 93 (44x21x5mm & 2g and 25x21x16mm & 4g)		

Table 6.116. Early phase miscellaneous forest artifacts *except tundra art piece.

Although 72 buried osteological entries (1355 g) include 11 long bone fragments in area D of KeNi-4, area C immediately above the crossing has cranial bones suggesting initial on-site butchering. Fifty-eight cranial entries (1189 g) include: (a) 81 beige-brown antler fragments; (b) 3 beige-brown bone tools (Table 6.117), (c) two caribou jaw fragments, one partial and one lower jaw with teeth, one lower jaw with four premolars and molars, and two teeth removed for determining seasonality, and six fragments of one tooth. In addition, there are 2,326 bone fragments (1021 g), including 2,090 calcined fragments (635 g), two caribou right astragali, a right calcaneum and a right distal tibia.

Tundra records are from two sites. KkLn-4 has 597 calcined bone fragments (105 g), including two caribou phalange and patellar fragments. KjNb-7 has 14 bone fragments (62 g), including a right cut-marked caribou astragalus, a rib and seven calcined fragments.

This section of miscellaneous artifacts finishes with six copper pot fragments (KeNi-4C:4-A72; 6 g) in a forest site (Fig. 6.12 bottom).

Conclusions on Early/Earliest Phase Artifacts

Dating and site distribution of the ancestral Dene Early and Earliest Taltheilei phases is similar in forest and tundra and confirms the practice of herd following from 2,500 years ago until disruption by the fur trade. Forest points, scrapers, knives, chithos, cores and flakes are smaller from sustained use and sharpening, likely due to inaccessible raw material under snowcover or faraway in the tundra. Many tundra point tips are on the rocky surface, but their parallel-sided midsections are evidence of less sharpening, while forest points have become pentagonal through sharpening into their midsections. More forest bases are square, more tundra bases are stemmed; suggesting wooden shaft binding in winter, and bone and antler socketting in summer. Tundra points are more transversely broken, burinated, and converted to other tools, but less eared than forest points. The few single shouldered Earliest phase tundra points reflect seasonally differing hafting from double shouldered forest points. Forest scrapers and knife bases are more rhomboid for hand hafting. Tundra ones are more triangular for bone or antler sockets. More forest scrapers and knives are serrated for scraping and cutting frozen hides. Forest scrapers with biface thinning platforms suggest a greater reduction of knives from which they came. Red taconite scrapers at Whitefish Lake are the only artifacts of this stone and infer a local source. Forest wedges are smaller, unlike other phases, but adze flakes are larger due to light wear on soft wood rather than antler. Forest hammerstones may be shorter and wider for anvil use in tool reduction. Forest pushplanes are rounder with thinned hafts for wood mounting. Smaller forest regular and retouched flakes suggest more use of stone resources, while larger retouched flakes at big tundra water-crossings suggest quick use and discard before herd migration south. Many caribou cranial fragments suggest heads were severed near the kill site for the extraction of the tongue and brains, while jaws and teeth were preserved. As most bone fragments are calcined, long bones were likely thrown into campfires. (Fig. 6.117a).

Trait	Forest range	Tundra range	Remarks
C14 dates	1545 to 2545 B.P.	1915 to 2440 B.P.	simultaneous herd following
points	167. Smaller. More unground bases	163. Larger. More ground bases	more forest retouch & sharpening
scrapers	200. 4-sided. More unground bases.Smaller	177. 3-sided. Ground worn haft. Larger	seasonal haft. More forest use
knives	171. 4-sided. More bases. Serrated. Smaller	176. 3-sided. More tips & wear. Larger	more forest retouch. Seasonal haft
chithos	54. Sandstone. Less ovoid. Worn. More cortex. Smaller	18. 1/3 quartzite. More ovoid. Unworn. Less cortex. Larger	locally available material. More forest use and conservation
wedges	48. Smaller (some surface ones ignored)	7. Larger	more forest retouch & conservation
adze flakes	4. Transverse and longitudinal striae. Larger	47. Multiple types of striae. More ground. Smaller	little wear from soft forest wood, versus much on hard tundra antler
cores	11. Cobbles. Blade-scars. Serrated. Smaller	11. 4-sided slabs. Flake-scars. Larger	slabs/cobbles. More forest reduction
flakes	Smaller regular and retouched flakes	Larger regular and retouched flakes	more forest core & flake reduction
hammer-stone	6 . Quartzite. Short and wide	2. Granite. Long and narrow	seasonally different uses. Use as anvils for reducing tools in forest
whetstone	11. Forest only. More than one-third have suspension notch. Heavily ground and worn		
pushplane	4. More ovoid. Less serrated. Larger	10. Less ovoid. More serrated. Smaller	forest wood, versus tundra antler
bone	high tooth and jaw frequency	higher long bone frequency	more tundra butchering

Table 6.117a. Comparing Early phase forest & tundra tools and bone.

Much less comparison is possible for Earliest Taltheilei forest and tundra artifacts because there are so few. Forest points are smaller, more parallel-sided, eared and tanged, while tundra points have burinated tips and unground square bases. Like Early phase, forest scrapers are rhomboid, unworn, unground and likely hand-hafted in winter. Tundra ones are worn and ground, with triangular hafts for fitting antler or bone sockets in summer (Table 6.117b).

Trait	Forest range	Tundra range	Remarks
Spread	limited	limited	beginning of Taltheilei herd following
C14 dates	2575 to 2600 B.P.	2485 to 2570 B.P.	contemporaneous herd following
points	3. Parallel sided. More tanged. Fewer ears. Smaller	20. Unground square bases. Larger	more forest sharpening and retouch. Seasonally different hafting
scrapers	2. Rhomboid. Unworn unground base	6. Triangular. Worn ground base	more wear in triangular tundra bone sockets

Table 6.117b. Comparing Earliest phase forest and tundra tools.

Chapter 7

General Taltheilei and Middle Plains Indian Phases

Tool allocation to a general Taltheilei phase is based more on excluding other traditions than the presence of culturally unique traits. As stated in the Introduction, surface sites are assumed to be culturally mixed because hunters of all traditions used the same water-crossings to hunt caribou. But most Taltheilei, Pre-Dorset, Shield Archaic and Northern Plano tools and even retouched chert flakes are assignable to their tradition. Except for rare quartzite knives of ovoid, tearshaped or triangular plan, Pre-Dorset artifacts are of finely retouched chert. If we accept Wright's (1972b) suggestion of cultural continuity, Shield Archaic and Northern Plano can be regarded as one tradition, leaving this combined tradition and that of Taltheilei to compare. Differences in points, scrapers, knives and chithos present little problem, but differences in highly specialized fully ground tools like adzes, axes and chisels are problematic because they rarely occur in stratified contexts and their traits are too general for assigning surface tools. As the few stratified Northern Plano and Shield Archaic ground tools do have unique traits, I am calling the others Taltheilei because they are generalized and were found near existing Dene settlements, rather than the distant tundra, where most Shield Archaic and Northern Plano sites occur.

This chapter discusses those generalized tools that are unassignable to Taltheilei phase, plus the Beverly component of the Middle Plains Indian phase which immediately precedes Taltheilei.

Analysis of General phase artifacts

A broken 30x17.8x5.2 mm white quartz point at IhNh-2 (#676-45) on the Chipman River above Black Lake is called General Taltheilei on its unground asymmetric side-notches. A 42.3x32.8x7.6 mm wedge at KeNi-4 (#1307) on Whitefish Lake is called Taltheilei on its large size, channelling and bipolar percussion. The adze category numbers 41, with rangewise comparison of 26 surface axes (21 F; 5 T), four chisels (3 F; 1 T), five picks (2 F; 3 T), and three flakes each from forest adzes and tundra axes (Table 7.1a). Four shaft polishers complete the inventory. Two surface axes are KiNc-6:1, a red basalt tundra axe at Eyeberry Lake on the upper Thelon River (Fig. 6.14 center), and KeNi-4:616, a black basalt forest axe at Whitefish Lake, about 80 km southwest (Fig. 6.14 bottom right).

Tundra adzelike artifacts are dispersed at Warden's Grove and Eyeberry, Mantic-Mary and Grant Lakes. Forest ones are at Sandy-Whitefish-Lynx, Damant-Jarvis and Hatchet Lakes and Fond du Lac on Lake Athabasca (Fig. 7.1). They are almost all black or gray basalt depending on weathering, plus minor quartzite and silicious shale. Transverse and diagonal grinding striae and longitudinal wear striae occur throughout the range. Half of tundra artifacts are axe and adze side and bit flakes. Forest ones also include haft and ridge flakes. Half are widely ground, with one in each range slightly ground. A third have heavy polish; a few have light polish. Grooved platforms are absent. Two forest and three tundra adze flakes are hinge-fractured. Forest flakes are smaller, but this may be irrelevant for comparing tool sharpening, as their numbers are too few for comparison (Tables 7.1b-7.8b).

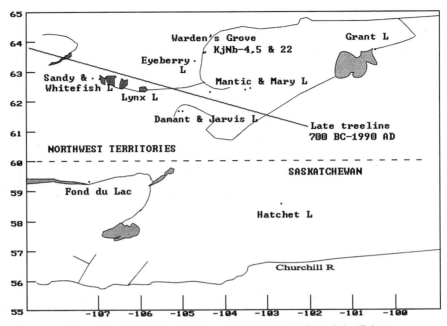

Figure 7.1. **Distribution of 41 General Taltheilei adzelike tools in 15 sites.**

Bit angles on 14 forest axes and five tundra axes range 30-80 and 30-70 degrees, with means of 46 and 45 degrees and standard deviations of 13 and 17 degrees. Seasonal differences in axe bits are dubious, but a long tundra chisel has a squared bit. Mean size of three forest chisels is 52.9x50.6x15.3 mm & 25.4 g. The snapped tundra chisel is 120x66.9+x28.2 mm & 223+ g (Table 7.8c). It has a bit angle of 90 degrees, while only one of three forest chisels had a measurable bit angle of 20 degrees. Bit angles in picks are similar, but forest picks are twice as long, the reverse of chisels. Mean size of two forest picks is 133x47x29 mm (no wt.). One has a bit angle of 20 degrees. Estimated mean size of three tundra picks is 56x40x26 mm, with a complete one weighing 31.4 g. One has a bit angle of 30 degrees (Tables 7.9a-b).

Tundra shaft polishers include one of red quartzite at KjNb-6; a forest one of red sandstone at JiNd-11, and a star-shaped one of pink quartzite at JkNf-2. The last has many concave surfaces for grinding and polishing various shaft diameters. Forest polishers are larger (Tables 7.10a-b).

Middle Plains Indian Phase Prior to Taltheilei

Middle Plains Indian points

Between Early Taltheilei and Shield Archaic, Oxbow hunters were on the Northern Plains at 5,000 to 2,000 B.P. (pers. comm., Ian Dyck). During Pre-Dorset and Taltheilei phases, Pelican Lake, Besant, Oxbow and Duncan points are deep in the Beverly range, without Plains hunters likely being present (Fig. 7.2). It is likely these points were carried north by Beverly hunters who had met over-wintering Plains hunters taking bison in the aspen parkland-forest transition.

Middle Plains artifacts include nine widely scattered Oxbow or Oxbow-like points, one McKean-Oxbow point from a 4,200 year old KeNi-4 level, five Pelican Lake points at Lake Athabasca and Lockhart River, and three Besant-Late Taltheilei-like points of the Artillery Lake complex (MacNeish 1951). All are quartzite, except white and beige chert IgOg-12:36 and quartz KeNi-4C:5-60 (Table 7.11). Most are beige, white or gray, except IgOg-2:1c which is red, and KiNk-8:66 (NMC Old system XI-C-6), which is green. Plains type points in the southern range demonstrate a degree of trade or communication between northern caribou hunters and more southerly bison hunters (Fig. 7.2).

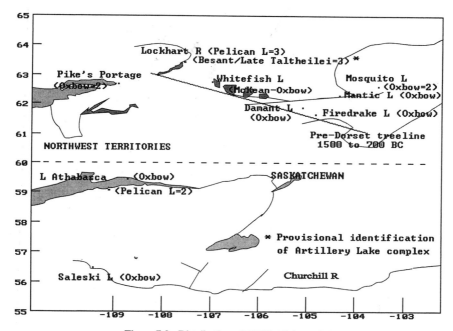

Figure 7.2. Distribution of Middle Plains points.

Middle Plains points are from both stratified levels and surface scatters (Fig. 7.3) in typical large sand blowouts at water-crossings (Fig. 7.4).

Number	R	L	W	T	Wt	Plan	Base	Reference
HcOi-2:401	F	19	21	20	5	spadelike S-N	concave	Meyer (1979). Saleski Lake
IiOe-2:1	F	43	24	7	8	spadelike S-N	concave ground	Wright (1975: 110). Lake Athabasca
JjNe-6:19	F	44	23	6	6	triangular S-N	concave unground	identified by Dyck. Firedrake Lake
JlNg-8:25	T	35	18	7	5	lanceolate eared	flat ground	identified by Dyck. Damant Lake
KbNa-20:4	T	23	18	5	2	triangular S-N	flat unground	identified by Dyck. Mantic Lake
KdLw-1:45	T	35	27	7	7	triangular S-N	concave ground	see point preform in Dyck (1977:Fig 19f)
KdLw-1:67	T	25	18	6	3	triangular S-N	concave ground	identified by Dyck. Mosquito Lake
KeNo-30	F	48	18	?	?	spadelike S-N	concave ground	Noble 1971:4c. Pike's Portage
KeNo-36	F	40	27	?	?	spadelike S-N	concave ground	Noble 1971:4b. Pike's Portage
KeNi-4C:5-60	T	33	16	8	4	triangular S-N	concave unground	C14 date of 4200 years B.P. at Whitefish Lake
IgOg-2:1c	F	63	27	7	?	spadelike C-N	flat unground	Wilson 1981:301. Lake Athabasca
IgOg-12:36	F	48	24	4	?	spadelike C-N	flat unground	Wright 1976. Lake Athabasca
KiNk-9:80a XI-C8(ASC)	T	58	28	8	12	spadelike C-N	flat ground	tentative identification. Lockhart River
KiNk-9:80b	T	51	23	8	?	spadelike	concave	tentative identification. Lockhart River
KiNk-9:80c	T	37	20	6	5	spadelike	concave	tentative identification. Lockhart River
KiNk-8:66a	T	64	25	8	?	spadelike S-N	flat unground	mixed Besant and Late Taltheilei on Lockhart River
KiNk-8:66b	T	57	26	9	?	spadelike	flat	mixed Besant and Late Taltheilei on Lockhart River
KiNk-8:66c	T	56	24	10	?	spadelike	flat	mixed Besant and Late Taltheilei on Lockhart River

Table 7.11. Middle Plains points of the Beverly Range.
From top: 9 Oxbow, 1 McKean, 5 Pelican & 3 Besant points. Measurements of broken points are estimated.
Besant identification is tentative. Length/width/thickness in mm; weight in g. T=tundra; F=forest during Pre-Dorset.
S/C-N=side/corner-notched. Tables 7.1 to 7.10 are in the Appendix.

Figure 7.3. Typical quartzite artifact scatter.

Figure 7.4. Typical large blowout sites surround caribou water-crossings.

Chapter 8

The Pre-Dorset Tradition

Dating and Distribution

Most Pre-Dorset tools are distinctive from Taltheilei, Shield Archaic and Plano tradition tools in manufacture, material and in the presence of some tools unique to a Pre-Inuit people. Tools are tiny, finely retouched and made of fine-grained, banded gray chert. They include endblades and sideblades (concave or flat-based triangular or semilunar tips and sides in harpoons, arrows or spears to facilitate wound penetration), microcores and blades, scrapers, quartzite knives (few more than 10 cm), many slotting and planing burins and their spalls, chithos, wedges, adzelike tools, hammerstones and gravers. Many tools are depicted and analyzed in Gordon (1975).

Pre-Dorset is the Canadian component of Arctic Small Tool, a tradition traceable to the Siberian Neolithic (Irving 1970:341). It is well-known in the High Arctic, where it began over 4,000 years ago. Originally, Pre-Dorsets lived on the coast, moving inland 500 years later when maritime hunting was adversely affected by prolonged cold. In their quest for meat, these arctic-adapted people were forced further south, ultimately linking with migrating caribou herds. As only a tenth of caribou winter on the tundra, Pre-Dorset hunters adapted to spending their winters in the forests, like later Taltheilei Indians. With treeline retreat in this cold period, they even reached Alberta, Saskatchewan and Manitoba, but not as far south as the Churchill River, due to their unique tundra adaptation or the presence of Middle period Plains Indians wintering in the forest while hunting bison and caribou.

I doubt if a claustrophobic fear of the forest often attributed to Inuit was a factor in limiting southern expansion, as they adapted to living hundreds of km south of treeline (Fig. 8.1). Tundra site distribution is wide and dense like that of Taltheilei, with clusters at Warden's Grove, the middle Thelon, and Dubawnt and north Artillery, Whitefish-Lynx-Howard, Sid-Mary-Mosquito, Damant-Jarvis, east Firedrake and Grant Lakes. Forest sites are limited to Pike's Portage-south Artillery, Rennie-west Firedrake, Athabasca and Black Lakes. Many hunters stayed in the range until 2,650 years ago when climate warmed. Many returned to the coast to merge with Dorset. Others vanished.

The Pre-Dorset tradition lasted 3,450-2,650 years ago. Its sites are mostly small surface tool scatters, but a dozen dated buried levels, two with profuse tools, allow dating and inclusion of many similar surface artifacts (Table 8.1). Far northwest are Ekalluk River tools at NiNg-1, 7 and 10 on Victoria Island, their Late and Early phases dating 2,600-2,910 and 2,980-3,180 B.P. (Taylor 1967, 1972). Near the Mackenzie River, the Hyndman Lake Early phase site extends the Early period to 3,390 and 3,470 B.P., but Pilon (pers. comm., 1992) thinks this site has western rather than eastern affiliation, based on his bipointed points (I have only one). East of the Beverly range, Nash's (1972:15) Late phase Seahorse Gully site at Churchill, Manitoba in the Kaminuriak range dates 2,900 B.P.

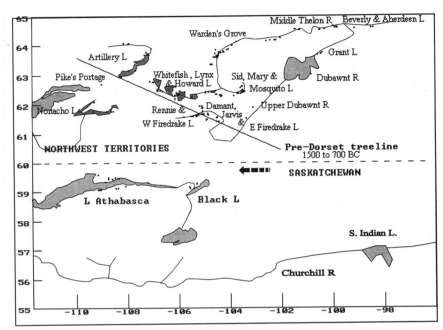

Figure 8.1. Distribution of 246 ASTt Pre-Dorset sites.

In the Beverly range, Late and Early phases are dated using 2-3 sublevels each in KjNb-6 and 7. No dates occur for forest sites. The Late phase dates 2,785-2,890 B.P. in tundra sites and 2,745-2,800 in areas forested before and after Pre-Dorset. The Early phase dates 3,085-3,550 B.P., the earliest estimate dating only KdLw-1 bottom level flakes, but with many Pre-Dorset surface artifacts. The northern Late phase Pre-Dorset sites of KkLn-4 at Grant Lake and KjNb-6 at Warden's Grove complement southern dates at Mary and Mosquito Lakes. Combining and rounding all Barrenland estimates, the Late and Early phases date 2,650-2,950 and 2,950-3,450 years ago.

An understanding of treeline shift under rapidly cooling climate is needed to appreciate human adaptation, as represented in Pre-Dorset tools. With treeline retreat came an accumulation of dead trees and buried stumps which could be used as fuel, but not for making handles, sledges or tent poles. Campfire remains occur, but any wooden tools originating in the shrunken northern forest were not preserved. In spite of this, wood-working tools were found in the south of the range in permanent forest that persisted throughout the Pre-Dorset. Stone tools showed modifications to forest living similar to those in other Barrenland traditions. Thus, the question of where the treeline existed is not only of botanical interest, but it also demarcates past human and caribou seasonal adaptations.

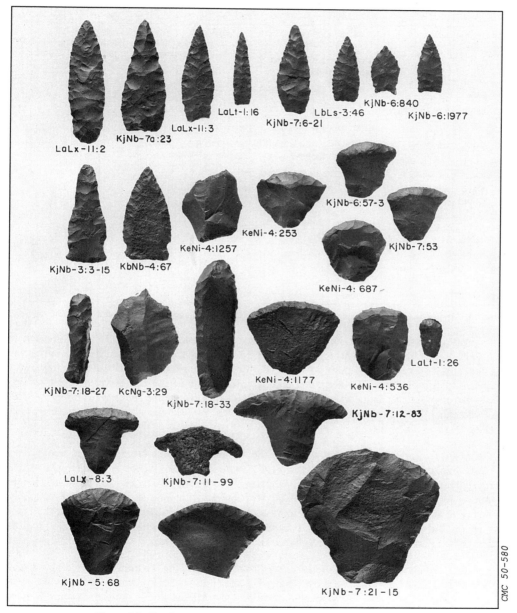

Figure 8.2. Pre-Dorset points, scrapers, knife, graver and microblade.

N.W.T. (WEST)	BEVERLY TUNDRA	BEVERLY TUNDRA	N.W.T. (EAST)
2600±130 B.P. (GSC-656) in NiNg-1 on Victoria Island, Franklin District (Taylor 1967 and 1972)	2785±85B.P. (S-978) in KkLn-4 at Migod site on Grant Lake	2745±250 B.P. (S-2224) in KcLw-2 at river exit from Mary to Mosquito Lakes, Dubawnt R .	2900±100 B.P (S-521) in Seahorse Gully, Manitoba (Nash 1972:15)
2880±105 B.P. (I-2058) in nearby NiNg-10	2840±95 B.P. (I-5975 in KjNb-6 on the upper Thelon River	2800±110 B.P. (S-2192) in KdLw-1 at north Mosquito Lake. Upper Dubawnt River quartzite flakes	
2910±105B.P. (I-2053) in NiNg-1	2890±125B.P. (S-632) at KjNb-6		

Late Pre-Dorset period 2650-2950 years ago

2980150 B.P. (GSC-713) and	3085±70 B.P. (S-664) at KjNb-7 on upper Thelon River	3550±125 B.P. (S-2193) in KdLw-1, north Mosquito Lake Upper Dubawnt River quartzite chips with ASTt artifacts on surface.	
2990±125 B.P. (I-2054) in NiNg-10 & 1, Victoria Island	3160±95 B.P.(I-5978) at KjNb-6 on upper Thelon River		
3180±120B.P. (I-2057) at NiNg-7 (Taylor 1967 and 1972)	3280±80 B.P. (S-1006) at KkLn-13 on Migod Island at Grant Lake, Dubawnt River		
3390±255 B.P. (S-3000) in NbTj-8 at Hyndman Lake near Great Bear Lake, N.W.T., and			
3470±430(S-3377) in NbTj-9 at Hyndman Lake (Pilon, (pers. comm. 1992)			

Early Pre-Dorset period 2950-3450 years ago

Table 8.1. Barrenland Pre-Dorset radiocarbon dates. * Forested in other traditions. Unreferenced dates are the author's

East of the study area in the Kaminuriak range, treeline retreated 50 to 75 km (Sorenson et al. 1971:471). Relief here is low and rolling like the Beverly range. Extrapolating treeline retreat in the east end of the Beverly range during Pre-Dorset, the Firedrake Lake cluster had to be divided into forest and tundra portions. The northwest and southwest arms of the lake were in forest, while the middle narrows and east shore were on tundra. In the interior, where the range was flatter, the treeline retreated farther than in areas of varied relief. Transposing from Sorenson's data, the treeline probably retreated 59 to 75 km or more.

At Pike's Portage and Artillery Lake in the western part of the Beverly range, treeline retreat was altitudinal rather than southerly (Larsen (1971), with only sheltered valley trees remaining. Using nearby palynology and macrofossil data, Nichols (1976:66) suggests a 28 km retreat at Thompson Landing west of Pike's Portage. As elevation at Thompson Landing is half that at Pike's Portage (Timoney et al. 1992:Fig.2), and slightly more than half that at Artillery Lake, retreat at the latter of only 14 km, but many meters vertically, is expected, and places all Artillery Lake Pre-Dorset sites on tundra, and all Pike's Portage and Fort Reliance sites barely in the forest.

As the treeline retreated, the forest moved south 100 km onto the prairie, expanding the area of protection for Plains bison that were over-wintering and spring calving. Middle Plains Indian hunters, therefore, came close to Pre-Dorset peoples. Some of the Middle Plains projectile points were even carried north into the Beverly caribou range and are described in the previous chapter under General Taltheilei.

Analysis of Pre-Dorset points

Stone points (33 excavated; 110 surface) are in only 46 of 246 Pre-Dorset sites, 136 in tundra sites at Thanakoie-Caribou Narrows, Grassy Island, Thelon Bluffs, Slow River, and Artillery, Lynx-Whitefish, Grant, Eyeberry, Barlow, Mosquito and Aberdeen Lakes. Seven points were in forest sites at Pikes's Portage, Fond du Lac and Rennie, Firedrake, Black and Athabasca Lakes (Fig. 8.3).

Points are long symmetric endblades in a variety of bases. They are uniquely tiny, biconvex, lanceolate and finely retouched, with unground stem (Fig. 8.2 top). Many tundra points are tipless. Bases are unground square (LaLt-1:16, KjNb-6:1977 and LbLs-3:46), tapered flat (KjNb-7a:23, LaLx-11:3, KjNb-7:6-21/18-34) or round (LaLx-11:2). Some points are side-notched, unground and bipointed, or fishtailed. Basal edges are unground concave or flat. Forest points are end-thinned. Some tundra points are eared (KjNb-6:840) and lightly notched. Most tundra points are of banded gray chert. Most forest ones are of beige quartzite. Breakage is transverse or diagonal, with four tundra points accidentally burinated on a side or face.

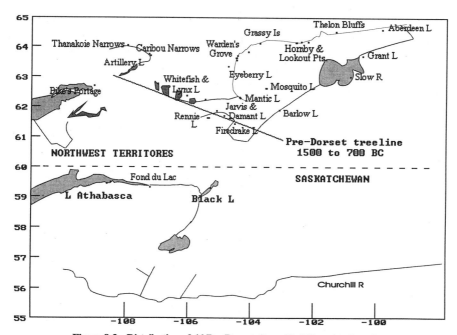

Figure 8.3. Distribution of 46 Pre-Dorset sites with 143 projectile points.

Four points are multi-purpose: spokeshave LdLp1:53 with a retouched concave tip; and knives KdLw-1:854 and 980 (only known Beverly bipoint), and KjNb-6:39-7 with wide thick tip like those in Middle Taltheilei. Point length:width ratio is 2.5:1, with tundra points averaging 31.2x13.6x3.6mm & 1.3g. Two forest points average 27.3x11.7x4mm (weight unknown; Tables 8.2-8.15c).

Difference	Forest points	Tundra points	Remarks
stone and colour	some beige quartzite	gray or white chert	locally available material
plan	lancelate; one side-notched	lancelate; one triangular	Middle phase Plains Indian influence in the forest?
accidentally burinated	none	four	falling points were split on exposed tundra rock at water crossings
basally thinned	more	much less	seasonally differing hafting?
multiple use	1 spokeshave	3 knives	seasonally differing multiple use?
size	smaller	larger	greater forest sharpening, conservation and use

Table 8.15c. Comparing Pre-Dorset forest and tundra points.

Analysis of Pre-Dorset sideblades and sideblade-like knives

Sideblades are in tundra sites at Artillery, Whitefish, Boyd and Grant Lakes, Hornby and Lookout Points, Thelon Bluffs, and in clusters at Mantic-Jim-Mosquito-Mary, Damant-Jarvis-Firedrake and Beverly-Aberdeen Lakes and Warden's Grove. Isolated forest finds are at Gray, Athabasca and Rennie Lakes (Fig. 8.4). Plans are triangular (Fig. 8.6 top; KjNb-6:55-34), ovoid (KjNb-6:185 and KcLw-10:1) or semilunar (LaLx-11:7 and KjNb-6:1642 and 183; Fig. 8.7 bottom right). Forty buried sideblades were used to culturally assign 154 surface ones (6 F; 188 T).

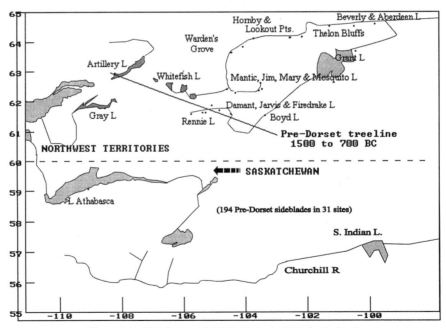

Figure 8.4. Distribution of 194 Pre-Dorset sideblades in 31 sites.

Most sideblades are semilunar with biconvex section, ideal for mounting in the sides of spears, harpoons and arrows. Most have a straight unground edge for insetting, a curved sharpened edge for cutting, and removed platforms for easy insetting. One sideblade is lanceolate, 11 are notched and 13 are ovoid (e.g.s, KjNb-6:185 and KcLw-10:1). All are gray banded chert (mean=29x17x5mm & 2.3g), and three are striated (KjNb-6:146, 186 and 1644; undepicted). Plan, striae and square or round tips of KjNb-6:146 and 186 suggest later use as knives. Six triangular blades (e.g., KjNb-6:55-34, Fig. 8.6 top) may be whittling knives, as they are too large to mount in harpoon sides, but readily socketted or hafted. Unfortunately, they have no striae as proof. Like points, most tundra sideblades are gray banded chert. Most forest ones are white quartzite (some mottled). Forest ones are larger, with mean dimension ratios in 69 of: length=2.1x width, width=3.6x thickness & weight = 1.8 g (Tables 8.16a-8.31b).

The use of harpoons by the Beverly Pre-Dorset

In the absence of large stone lanceheads as well as bone and antler arrowheads, the Beverly Pre-Dorset may have used harpoons inset with endblades and sideblades, as both are serrated for piercing, with an unworn base for insetting. As maritime hunters traditionally and historically used them, inland people might have taken caribou in water or on land by attaching harpoons to brush-catching caribou racks similar to, but larger than, those used by Inuit as sledge foot brakes. Such cumbersome drags may have slowed animals on land, freeing hunters for attaching new heads to lances. After fall hunts, either cranially-attached full racks or naturally shed winter half racks are numerous. In winter, the Pre-Dorset likely used caribou corrals and snares modified after the techniques described by Hearne (1958:49-50).

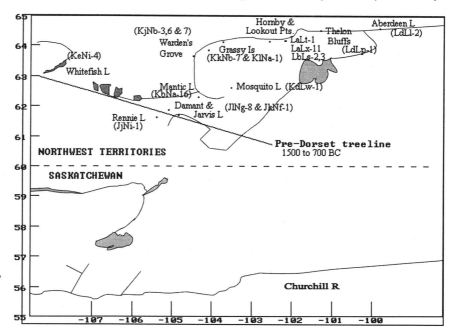

Figure 8.5. Distribution of 17 Pre-Dorset sites with points and sideblades.

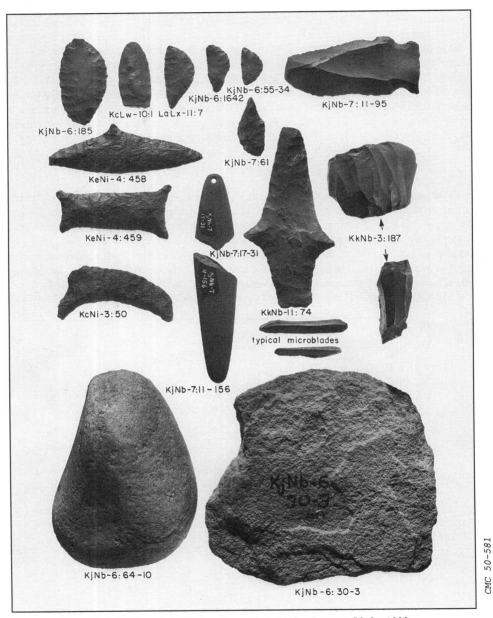

KjNb-6:55-34

KjNb-6:1642

KcLw-10:1 LaLx-11:7

KjNb-7:11-95

KjNb-6:185

KeNi-4:458

KjNb-7:61

KeNi-4:459

KjNb-7:17-31

KkNb-3:187

KcNi-3:50

KjNb-7:11-156

KkNb-11:74

typical microblades

KjNb-7:11-156

KjNb-6:64-10

KjNb-6:30-3

CMC 50-581

Figure 8.6. Pre-Dorset sideblades, side-notched chisel, microcores/blades, chitho, hammerstone, art objects and graver (clockwise).

Figure 8.7. Pre-Dorset ovate, side-notched, symmetric, asymmetric and left-leaning knives and sideblades (clockwise).

CMC 50-582

If antler harpoons were used and since decomposed in acid soils, their endblades and sideblades are the only remains. In addition to having overlapping distribution (Fig. 8.5), I looked for similar size, stone and retouch in both (like High Arctic harpoons) to suggest their association in Beverly harpoons.

Endblades and sideblades co-exist in 17 caribou water-crossings (Figs. 8.4 and 8.5). They include a forest site at Rennie Lake, and tundra sites at Whitefish, Mantic, Damant-Jarvis, Mosquito and Aberdeen Lakes, Warden's Grove, Grassy Island, Hornby and Lookout Points, and Thelon Bluffs. I compared endblades and sideblades from sites with four or more of each. Six large samples (19-67 of each) and 11 small samples (4-8 of each) are compared (Tables 8.32a and 8.32b).

Difference	Forest	Tundra	Remarks
stone and colour	white quartzite	gray banded chert	locally available material
plan and breakage	fewer semilunar. More breaks	more semilunar. Fewer breaks	fewer forest harpoons due to more corrals or snares?
wear and serration	less of both	more of both	more tundra use of harpoons?
transverse breaks	multi-transverse	transversely halved	harpoon sideblades apt to be halved in hitting bone*
striae and cortex	none of either	rare in both	slightly greater tundra use
base	1/3 are ground and round	1/3 are unground and pointed	sideblades apt to have unground bases for mounting
size	larger	smaller	forest quartzite harder to thin than tundra chert

Table 8.31c. Comparing Pre-Dorset forest and tundra sideblades. (* with flat half or base retained in harpoon slot).

Borden	Artifact	No.	L	W	T	Wt	L/W	Mineral	Colour	End-/sideblade ratio*
KdLw-1	endblade	21	31	12	3	1.2	2.58	chert	gray and pink	1.15
"	sideblade	33	27	12	3	0.6	2.25	chert	multi-coloured	
KeNi-4	endblade	4	39	16	5	3.6	2.44	quartzite	multi-coloured	1.15
"	sideblade	4	34	16	5	3.2	2.13	quartzite	gray	
KjNb-3	endblade	5	38	15	4	inc.	2.53	chert	beige and gray	1.18
"	sideblade	8	30	14	3	1.9	2.14	chert	gray	
KjNb-6	endblade	24	29	13	4	3.5	2.23	chert	gray	1.12
"	sideblade	67	26	13	3	1.1	2.00	chert	gray	
KjNb-7	endblade	19	35	16	4	1.7	2.19	chert	beige and gray	1.10
"	sideblade	33	26	13	3	0.9	2.00	chert	grey and white	
LdLp-1	endblade	4	42	16	5	2.6	2.63	chert	white	1.09
"	sideblade	10	41	17	4	3.6	2.41	chert	white	

Table 8.32a. Comparing side- and endblades (points) in major sites.
L, W, T & Wt=mean length, width, thickness (mm) & weight (g). Inc.=incomplete. * L/W(point)//L/W(sideblade) or ratio of L/W for points to L/W for sideblades for comparing paired sideblades and endblades in specific sites.

Length:width ratio varies from 2.2:1 to 2.6:1 (mean=2.4:1). Sideblade length to width ratio is 2:1 to 2.4:1 (mean=2.2:1). As their sizes in a harpoon should correspond, I compared their length to width ratios, obtaining a 1.1-1.2 range (mean=1.13; right column). With the reasons stated above, the correspondence of endblade and sideblade metrics does not prove that Pre-Dorset caribou hunters used harpoons, but it favours their use.(Table 8.32a).

Even endblades and sideblades in minor sites, with less than four of each, have ratios similar to those in Table 8.32a; e.g.s, JjNi-1, JkNf-1, JlNg-8, LaLt-1 and LbLs-3 (Table 8.32b). The other ratios in KbNa-16, KkNb-7, KlNa-1, LaLx-11, LbLs-2 and LdLl-2 are too high or low to imply they were in the same harpoon head, and may have been separate points or knives.

Borden	Artifact	No.	L	W	T	Wt	L/W	Stone	Colour	Endblade/sideblade ratio*
JjNi-1	endblade	1	36	16	4	2.3	2.25	quartzite	beige	1.09
"	sideblade	1	35	17	6	inc.	2.06	chert	white	
JkNf-1	endblade	1	48	17	5	5	2.82	quartzite	beige, pink and white	1.18
"	sideblade	2	30	12	3	inc.	2.40	chert	gray and white	
JlNg-8	endblade	1	35	15	5	2.5	2.33	quartzite	beige	1.32
"	sideblade	1	30	17	4	inc.	1.76	chert	white	
KbNa-16	endblade	4	48	15	6	6	3.20	quartzite	multicoloured	1.45
"	sideblade	3	42	19	6	inc.	2.21	chert	pink and gray	
KkNb-7	endblade	1	43	11	4	inc.	3.9	chert	white	2.29
"	sideblade	2	26	15	5	2.3	1.7	chert	gray	
KlNa-1	endblade	2	30	15	3	inc.	2.0	quartzite	white	0.76
"	sideblade	1	34	13	4	inc.	2.62	chert	orange and gray	
LaLt-1	endblade	8	29	10	3	inc.	2.9	chert	white and gray	1.22
"	sideblade	2	25	11	3	inc.	2.37	chert	gray	
LaLx-11	endblade	2	40	13	4	1.7	3.08	chert	white and gray	2.13
"	sideblade	2	29	14	4	0.8	2.07	chert	gray and white	
LbLs-2	endblade	5	28	16	5	2.0	1.75	chert	gray and pink	0.69
"	sideblade	2	33	13	3	0.5	2.54	chert	gray	
LbLs-3	endblade	6	34	14	4	1.4	2.43	chert	white and pink	1.39
"	sideblade	1	35	20	4	inc.	1.75	chert	beige	
LdLl-2	endblade	2	30	17	3	1.9	1.76	quartzite	white and gray	0.52
"	sideblade	1	27	8	3	0.6	3.38	chert	white	

Table 8.32b. Comparing points and sideblades in minor sites. (* see Table 8.32a. Inc.=incomplete)

Analysis of Pre-Dorset scrapers

For assigning 452 surface scrapers, 123 excavated ones were used (34F; 541T in 99 sites). Half are beige quartzite or gray and white chert, plus spurred bifacial flexer KjNb-7:11:99 of copper (Fig. 8.2 bottom center). A fifth of all scrapers are spurred; dual spurs on tundra scrapers suggesting special use. A third of forest scrapers are tearshaped. Fine craftsmanship is more characteristic than shape in Pre-Dorset scrapers, but plans vary: bifacial (2F; 78T), end (16F; 327T), side (1F; 32T), side and end (9F; 97T) and discoid (6F; 7T; Fig. 8.8). Of 541 tundra scrapers, a fifth each are rhomboid, tearshaped or dual ulu-like and spurred (Fig. 8.2 LaLx-8.3, KjNb-7:11-99 and 12-83 and KbNa-16:232 bottom left). Other shapes depicted are single spurred KeNi-4:253, KjNb-6:57-3 and KjNb-7:53 (mid-right), blade KjNb-7:18-27 and 18:33 (mid-left), discoid KeNi-4:536 (mid-right), ovoid KeNi-4:1177 center), big triangular KjNb-7:21-15, small triangular KJNb-5:68 (bottom) and tiny LaLt-1:26 (mid-right).

Serration and striae in tundra scrapers infer heavy use, while cortex in forest scrapers suggests an attempt at reducing breakage risk. More bifacial and dorsal retouch in forest scrapers hint at special applications. Compared to forest scrapers, tundra ones are larger due to less sharpening and plentiful chert, especially from farther northwest. Abundant chert allowed more biface knife manufacture, from which sharpening flakes with bifacial platforms were selected for tundra scrapers (Tables 8.3-8.44c).

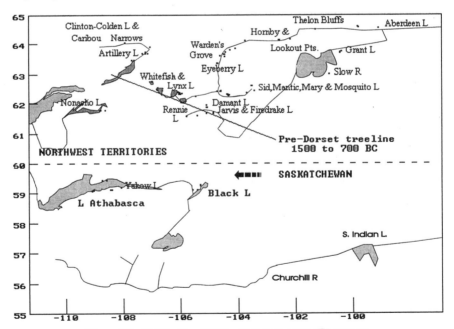

Figure 8.8. Distribution of 99 Pre-Dorset sites with 575 scrapers.

KjNb-7:44-12a
KjNb-7:44-12b

KkNa-5:103

KeNi-4:651

KeNi-4:1009

KjNb-6:1306

KeNi-4c:2

KeNi-4:16

LbLs-3:9

KjNb-6:227   LaLt-1:14

CMC 50-583

Figure 8.9. Pre-Dorset ovoid, tearshaped, semilunar and asymmetric knives.

Difference	Forest scrapers	Tundra scrapers	Remarks
stone and colour	more gray quartzite	more gray and white chert	locally available stone
plan and section	tearshaped and tortoise	rhomboid and tabular	seasonally differing hafting
serration	half that of tundra	twice forest; unlike other traditions	serration common throughout Pre-Dorset
basal retouch & grinding	most are dorsally retouched. 1/5 are bifacially retouched	40% are dorsally retouched. 1/5 are unretouched or ventrally retouched	seasonal hafts and applications. More forest basal retouch and grinding
cortex	twice that of tundra	half that of forest (plentiful chert)	more cortex lowers forest breakage risk
striae and wear	half that of tundra	twice that of forest	sand grit striae suggests more tundra use
bifac. retouched platform	half that of tundra	twice that of forest	tundra biface knife thinning (much chert)
spurring	less	more	more tundra engraving
size	smaller	larger	more forest sharpening, use, conservation

Table 8.44c. Comparing Pre-Dorset forest and tundra scrapers.

Analysis of Pre-Dorset knives

Knives and scrapers not only have have distinct craftmanship, but similar distribution, in keeping with joint butchering and hide preparation (Fig. 8.10). Two-thirds of knives are quartzite and a fourth are chert, with some of quartz in the forest. They are lanceolate: e.g.s, KjNb-6:148/500, KjNb-7:142 and LbLt-2:1; tearshaped KeNi-4:44 & 1009, KcNf-1:1, KkNa-5:103 and KjNb-7:44-12a-b; symmetric KjNb-6:30-2 & 196, KeNi-4:263 & 651 and asymmetric ovoid KjNb-6:1306, KjNb-7:17-34 & 12-125; semilunar KeNi-4:16, KjNb-6:227, KjNb-7:10-37, KbNa-16:62 and LaLt-1:14; left-leaning KjNb-7:21-21 and LbLs-3:9; lozenge-shaped KeNi-4:1255, and corner-notched KdNi-5:5 and KjNb-3:3-15 (Figs. 8.7, 8.9 & 8.2 left). Although forest knives are smaller, unifacial and more complete, with retouched platforms, like other traditions; their differences with tundra knives are distinctly Pre-Dorset. More forest knives are semilunar or 3-4-sided, with alternately retouched midsections and round or square bases. In contrast, half of tundra knives are broken transversely, leaving worn bifacial bases or tip-midsections. More tundra knives are lanceolate preforms with serrated edges. Five have blunted, ground or cortex backs, perhaps for hand-hafting from one side (Tables 8.45a-8.60c).

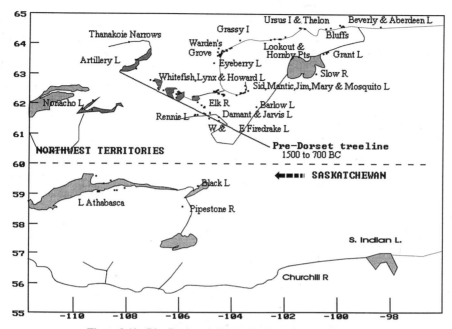

Figure 8.10. Distribution of 136 Pre-Dorset sites with 532 knives.

Analysis of Pre-Dorset chithos

Chithos are worn flat unifacial sandstone with cortex faces and include unworn flat, squarish KjNb-6:30-3 (Fig. 8.6 bottom), KjNb-6:46-9, and KjNb-6:55-24 (Gordon 1975:Plate 38a; Tables 8.61-8.64). All eleven chithos are in tundra areas and equi-distributed in KdLw-1, KeNi-4 and KjNb-6. Half are complete; half are round.

Difference	Forest knives	Tundra knives	Remarks
stone and colour	more quartz. Less gray chert	more quartzite. More multi-coloured chert	locally available stone
plan and faciality	more ovoid and unifacial	more lanceolate and bifacial	seasonally differing haft and use?
complete	more	less	breakage on exposed tundra rock
wear & grinding	less	more	tundra striae also infers more use
midsection	1/3 have alternate retouch	no alternate retouch	special forest cutting applications?
breakage	more diverse	1/4 are transversely broken	breakage on exposed tundra rock
cortex	on base and midsection	more widespread on knife	forest emphasis on cutting tip?
basal plan	1/5 are unground and square	1/10 are tapered or round	seasonally differing hafting
blunted back	none	five	tundra hand-hafting from one side
platform	more retouched	less retouched	more forest retouch & conservation
size	smaller	larger	more forest retouch & conservation

Table 8.60c. Comparing Pre-Dorset forest and tundra knives.

Analysis of Pre-Dorset wedges

Twenty-five surface wedges from 21 sites were culturally assigned using seven buried ones (Fig. 8.11). Tundra wedges are at Thanakoie Narrows, Warden's Grove, Hornby-Lookout Points and Whitefish-Lynx, Eyeberry, Jarvis-Damant, Mantic-Mary-Mosquito and Grant Lakes and Slow River; forest ones at Lake Athabasca. Wedges KeNi-4:1257, KjNb-6:56-7, KjNb-7:11-142 and KkLn-4:408a are in Fig. 8.2 (middle) and Gordon (1975:Plate 38 and 1976:82). Most wedges are quartzite struck at both ends, but a seventh of tundra ones are chert, with some peripherally struck. Forest wedges are larger, their colour, plan and section varying; tundra ones are mainly beige or clear biconvex or planoconvex rectangles. Most forest wedges have flat columnar scars, but variable tundra scars suggest multi-tasking (Tables 8.66a-8.71c).

Difference	Forest wedges	Tundra wedges	Remarks
stone and colour	varied quartzite	some white chert	locally available stone
plan and section	varied	both discoid	disc periphery disperses shock points from hard antler
flake scars	flat columnar	varied	flat columnar flake scars common in wood splitting
percussion	unipolarly struck	discoidally struck	disc periphery disperses shock points from hard antler
size	larger	smaller	discs are smaller. Forest wedges wear less on soft wood

Table 8.71c. Comparing Pre-Dorset (ASTt) forest and tundra wedges.

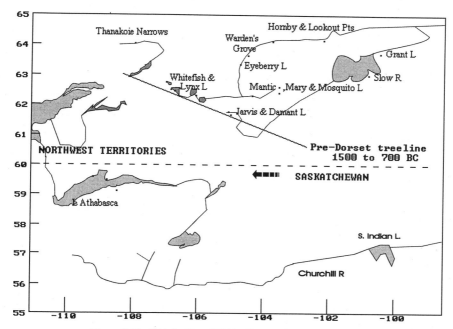

Figure 8.11. Distribution of 21 Pre-Dorset sites with 32 wedges.

Analysis of Pre-Dorset adzelike artifacts

All adzelike artifacts are in 12 tundra sites in Pre-Dorset; Warden's Grove sites KjNb-6, 7, 16 and 18, with separate finds at Sandy Island, Whitefish-Lynx, Mary-Mosquito, Damant and Grant Lakes (Fig. 8.12). They are 9 adzes, 11 adze flakes, 10 chisels and a gouge; 12 buried ones used to assign 19 surface ones (Table 8.72a). Unifacial chert side-notched chisel KjNb-7:11-95 is in Fig. 8.6 (top right), while long keeled, unground preform adze KeNi-4C:2-103 with perpendicular sides and 50 degree bit angle, was placed in Late Taltheilei Fig. 4.14 (right) because it came from a disturbed level.

Most adzelike artifacts are black or weathered gray basalt, then chert and shale. A third of flakes are from adze sides and some from bits. Most are heavily ground and half have striae. A tenth each have diagonal, longitudinal or transverse-longitudinal striae. A few have hinge fractures, but grooved platforms are absent (Tables 8.72a-8.74). Tundra adze measurements are in Table 8.75.

Artifact number, length, width, thickness, weight, plan, section, bit angle, type of striae and platform angle of 20 tools are in Table 8.76. Lines lines are used to separate nine adzes, ten chisels and a gouge. Table 8.77 contrasts Pre-Dorset and Taltheilei tundra adze flakes.

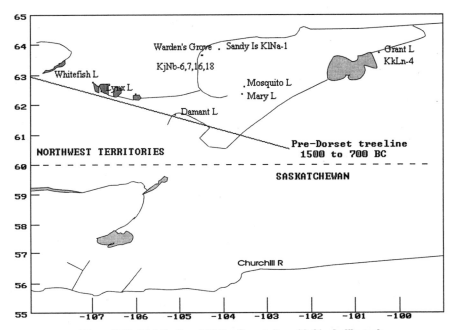

Figure 8.12. Distribution of 12 Pre-Dorset sites with 31 adzelike tools.

Artifact	L	W	T	Wt	Plan	Section	Bit	Type of striae	Platform angle
KcLw-26:7	180	66	45	439	triangular	keeled	?	none	80
KcLw-26:63	135	33	38	195	rectangular	keeled	60	diagonal	90
KcNf-3:6	83	39	13	42	unknown	keeled	?	none	80
KcNi-3:2	154	43	38	339	lanceolate	keeled	40	longitudinal	90
KdLw-1:90	130	32	41	135	lanceolate	keeled	0	none	80
KdLw-1:1217	135	50	49	302	lanceolate	keeled	0	none	80
KeNi-4C2:103	183	49	31	333	lanceolate	keeled	50	none	90
KjNb-18:21	137	43	38	281	rectangular	keeled	45	all types	90
KlNa-1:28	144	51	39	334	rectangular	round	45	tranverse	70
KjNb-6A:111	21	7.7	2.5	0.4	rectangular	biplanar	40	diagonal and longitudinal	unknown
KjNb-6A:1488	31	21	5.6	2.8	rhomboid	planoconvex	0	longitudinal	unknown
KjNb-6A:1914	30	24	6.6	3.9	rhomboid	planoconvex	30	none	unknown
KjNb-6a:2005	17	6.5	2.6	0.3	rectangular	biplanar	15	all types	unknown
KjNb-6A:2020	-25	-13	5.7	-2	triangular	planconvex	40	transverse and longitudinal	unknown
KjNb-7 11-95 (Fig. 6.6)	53	24	7.9	8.7	side-notched	keeled	70	double diagonal	unknown
KjNb-7:11-152	30	20	6.1	3.5	ovoid	planconvex	80	diagonal	unknown
KjNb-7:18-43	28	18	5.9	3.2	triangular	planconvex	70	tranverse	unknown
KjNb-7:27-37	-16	6	1.6	-.1	rectangular	biplanar	90	diagonal	unknown
KjNb-7:31-1	35	23	8.2	5.6	rhomboid	planoconvex	40	diagonal	unknown
KeNi-4E-2	-30	24	9.4	-9	ovoid	biconvex	45	none	unknown

Table 8.76. Comparing Pre-Dorset tundra adzes, chisels and gouge. (-)= break

Trait	Tundra Pre-Dorset	Tundra Talthellei	Remarks
flakes	many lateral	mixed lateral and bit	Pre-Dorset sizing versus mixed Taltheilei applications
polish	2/3 heavily polished	common heavy polish	similar heavy range use
hinging	6%	Late & Early Taltheilei; none in Middle	a general Pre-Dorset tundra chert trait
grooved platform	none	one in Middle phase; 3 in Early phase	a minor Taltheilei tundra quartzite trait
size(mean)	40x25x5 and 9.2g	smaller in forest sites	forest adze sharpening and conservation

Table 8.77. Comparing Pre-Dorset and Taltheilei tundra adze flakes.

Analysis of Pre-Dorset cores and microcores

Forty cores, 7 core fragments, 51 microcores and one microcore fragment in 20 sites (8 F; 91 T; 82 surface) were identified by way of their blade scars and distinct Pre-Dorset chert. Microblades have parallel edges. So do their scars left on microcores. A cylindrical microcore looks like a section of fluted Greek column. A conical microcore is cylindrical and tapered. A boatshaped microcore resembles a ship's hull. Bipolarly percussed and depleted microcores KkNb-3:187 (boatshaped) and JjNh-2:23 (conical) have curved platforms (Fig. 8.6 right).

Tundra cores cluster at Warden's Grove, Hornby-Lookout Points and east Firedrake-Jarvis, Mantic-Sid-Mosquito and Sandy-Whitefish-Lynx Lakes. Isolated finds are at Artillery, Clinton-Colden and Grant Lakes (Fig. 8.13). Forest cores are at Athabasca, Rennie, Damant and west Firedrake Lakes.

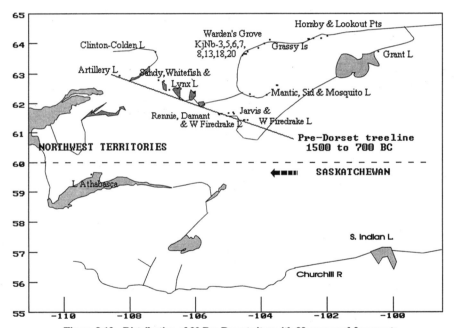

Figure 8.13. Distribution of 20 Pre-Dorset sites with 99 cores and fragments.

Tundra (micro)cores are mainly banded-gray, boatshaped or blocky chert of round, biconvex or triangular section. Forest cores are absent, but forest microcores are conical or ovoid, quartzite or white quartz of planoconvex section. Forest microcores are more worn and depleted than tundra microcores, with fewer hinge fractures on their blade scars emerging from a curved platform. One forest microcore is a pushplane. Tundra core tools are mainly wedges, plus a knife. Over a sixth of all cores are serrated from blade or flake removal. Forest microcores are larger, but tundra cores average 55x44x26mm/131g (Tables 8.78a-8.93b).

Difference	Forest microcores	Tundra (micro)cores	Remarks (no forest cores)
stone and colour	white quartzite & quartz	gray banded chert	locally available material
plan and section	fewer 4-sided	more 4-sided	no parallel cleavage in forest quartz
profile	conical	blocky or boatshaped	greater forest reduction and use
blade scars	more	fewer*	skewed for reason below*
platform	more curved	more linear and flat	due to more forest conical cores
wear and battering	more	less	more forest use and unavailable raw material
depleted	more	less	more forest use and unavailable raw material
use wear & multi-tools	1 pushplane	a pushplane, 5 knives and wedge	varied tundra tool uses, like Taltheilei
hinge fractures	less	more*	skewed for reason below*
size	larger (quartz)	smaller (chert)	difficultly reducible forest quartzite

Table 8.93d. Pre-Dorset forest and tundra (micro)cores. *half are hinge-fractured macrocores without blade scars.

Analysis of Pre-Dorset flakes and microblades

Just as Pre-Dorset tools are mainly banded gray chert, so is flaking detritus resulting from their manufacture. This class of 606 surface and 587 buried entries (24 F; 1169 T) in 11 forest and 55 tundra sites (Fig. 8.14) includes flakes (431 unretouched; 182 retouched), blades (85 unretouched; 5 retouched), 258 microblades, 8 microtools, 8 sharpening flakes and many unanalyzed flakes (146 bags of counted flakes and 70 weighed bags; each bag counted as an entry) - for a total of 1193 entries.

Tundra finds are at Warden's Grove-Grassy Island, Hornby-Lookout Point and Whitefish-Sandy-Lynx, Jarvis-Damant, Mantic-Mary-Mosquito and Beverly-Aberdeen Lakes. Isolated finds are at Thanakoie Narrows, and Artillery and Grant Lakes. Forest finds are at Athabasca, Middle and west Firedrake-Rennie-Jarvis Lakes (Fig. 8.15).

The 70 bags of mainly chert flakes from KjNb-3, 5, 6 and 7 (17 surface; 53 buried; 15.5kg) are impressive in a culture noted for its micro-technology and conservation of material. They indicate most knapping occurred in late summer at Warden's Grove. Bags (4 F; 142 T) with counted and weighed flakes contain 1,386 of chert (1.3kg), 1,397 of quartzite (618 g), and 162 of mixed material (262 g). All bags with counted and uncounted flakes weigh 17.7kg. Some unretouched flakes, but all retouched and sharpening flakes, and unretouched and retouched blades and microblades, were measured separately. Unretouched, retouched and sharpening flakes (8 F; 612 T) are combined for material, colour and metric analysis (Table 8.94a-e). Of 182 retouched flakes, four have abrupt scraping edges (KlNa-1:129, KjNb-6:39-5 and KjNb-7:44-13 & 33-83), two have sharp knife edges (LaLt-5:3a and KjNb-6:55-18), one is a graver (KjNb-6:50-29) and two are serrated as saws (KjNb-7:24 & 27-61).

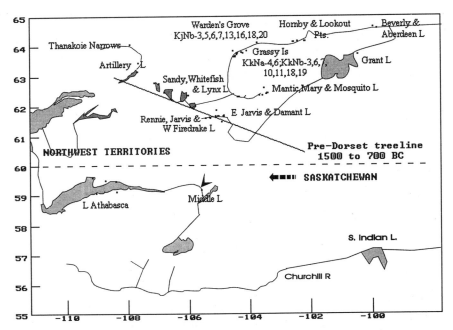

Figure 8.14. Distribution of 66 Pre-Dorset sites with 1193 flake records.

Some flakes and microblades of mainly gray chert, with some quartzite, were made into scrapers, knives, saws, gravers and flexers. Mean blade size is 46x18x5mm & 7g (Table 8.97).

Item	Flakes	Blades	Microblades
stone and colour	gray chert	half are gray quartzite	gray chert
mean size	26x19x5mm & 4g	46x18x5mm & 7g	23x6x2 mm & 0.3 g
size	forest flakes are bigger despite absnce of macrocores	1 forest blade	less reducible forest quartzite flakes
retouched tools	182, comprising 4 scrapers, 2 knives, 2 saws, 1 graver, etc.	4 with retouched edges	8, comprising 1 scraper, 3 knives, 3 gravers, and a skin flexer

Table 8.97. Comparing Pre-Dorset flake, blade and microblade tools.

Blades or parallel-sided flakes with length greater than width, are not the dominant flake type. Half of blades are chert; half are quartzite. Excluding quartz, taconite and shale, only one forest and 89 tundra chert blades remain. Care was taken to select fine grained chert to make the strong, flexible and thin blades which were struck or pressed from a (micro)core with an antler billet (Tables 8.95a-d).

Microblades (10 F; 256 T) resemble blades in shape and fabrication, but are smaller (Figs. 8.6 center and 8.22; KjNb-6:1987 bottom right). As only one forest blade occurs, IjOg-2:35 at Lake Athabasca, it is included in Table 8.95d. They average 46x18x5 mm & 7 g. Big microblades may be tools, like blade tools JkNf-2:244, KdLw-1:858 and 859, and KjNb-7:12-98. Forest microblades are longer (1.4X), wider (1.9X), thicker (1.7X) and heavier (3X) than tundra ones, the opposite of Taltheilei flakes (Tables 8.96a-e). Of eight microblades, one is a sidescraper (KjNb-7:100), three are knives (KjNb-7:96 & 11-80 and KkNb-3:236), three are gravers (KjNb-6:1245 & 50-4 and KjNb-7:167), and one is a skin flexer (KjNb-7:116).

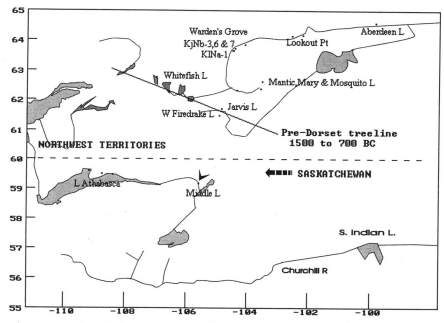

Figure 8.15. Distribution of 18 Pre-Dorset sites with 266 microblades.

Analysis of Pre-Dorset hammerstones

Sites with hammerstones are dispersed, but sufficient to compare ranges (Fig. 8.16). Three forest ones are at two Lake Athabasca sites; four tundra ones at Mary Lake, KjNb-6 at Warden's Grove and LbLs-2 and 3 at Lookout Point. KjNb-6:64-10 is in Fig. 8.6 and Gordon (1975:Plate 38). Mostly quartzite; forest ones are mainly ovoid. Half of tundra ones are round, a form common in river cobbles. Forest ones are smaller and pocked at both ends. Tundra ones have variable pocking (Tables 8.98a-e).

Difference	Forest	Tundra	Remarks
stone and colour	varied quarzite	white quartzite	locally available material. More forest selection
plan and section	ovoid and mixed	round and ovoid	locally available material. More forest selection
pocking	most are bipolar	half are equatorial	many tundra hammerstone used as anvils for flaking, unlike all traditions
size	smaller	larger	size like Shield Archaic, but tundra anvils have increased width and size

Table 8.102c. Pre-Dorest forest and tundra hammerstone comparison.

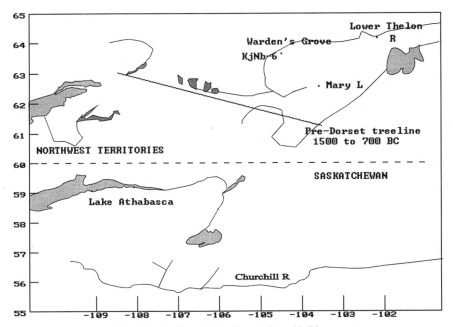

Figure 8.16. Distribution of 6 Pre-Dorset sites with 7 hammerstones.

Analysis of Pre-Dorset gravers

Fourteen tundra gravers, mostly banded gray chert, are from sites KcNg-3 and KiNc-10 at Lynx and Eyeberry Lakes, and KjNb-6 and 7 at Warden's Grove (Fig. 8.17). One gray shale forest graver is from Lake Athabasca forest site IiOb-1. Mean size is 28.6x14.7x4.7 mm & 2.37 g (Tables 6.103a-c). The forest graver is 59.5x25.3x10 mm & 10.62 g. Depicted typical gravers are KcNg-3:29 (Fig. 8.2 mid-left) and KjNb-7:61 of orange chert, with a unifacial tip (Fig. 8.6 top).

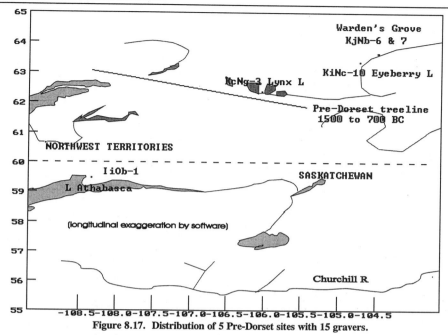

Figure 8.17. Distribution of 5 Pre-Dorset sites with 15 gravers.

Analysis of Pre-Dorset miscellaneous artifacts

Except edge grinder LdLp-1:24, grinding tools like whetstones or shaft polishers are absent, although they likely were used (Table 8.104). Tundra spokeshaves are LdLp-1:53 on a collaterally worked point from Thelon Bluffs, and KcNi-4:12 at Lynx Lake. They are assigned to Pre-Dorset on their similarity to excavated KkLn-4:416 and KjNb-6:55-9 at Grant Lake and Warden's Grove (Gordon 1976:82). All are chert except the last, and all except LdLp-1:53 are also scrapers. KcNi-4:12 has a scraper opposite its spokeshave. KjNb-6:55-9 is crude, unstriated and hafted, while KkLn-4:416 is worn but unstriated, tortoise-backed and ovoid. They average 39.7x23.5x91.2 mm & 8.5 g.

Tundra pushplanes include excavated KjNb-7:49-9 at Warden's Grove. It was used to assign LbLs-1:4, LbLs-3:55 and LbLt-2:5 at Lookout Point and LdLl-2:20 at Aberdeen Lake. All have gradual end and side retouch, no striae and tortoise-backs, except #4. Half have cortex, except KjNb-7:49-9 and LbLt-2:5. #4 is keeled, ovoid and worn; #55 is tearshaped, serrated and hafted; #5 is left-leaning, serrated and hafted; #20 is tearshaped, serrated and hafted by face and edge thinning; and #9 (bit only) is ovoid, worn and unhafted. Mean size is 59.2x32.6x13.8 mm & 24.3 g.

Piercing tools include awls and drills. Tundra awls are stratified. KjNb-7:32-33 was used to assign KcLw-23:7 (Mary Lake), KjNb-6:1616 (Warden's Grove) and LaLt-3:19 (Lookout Point). Mean width and thickness are 14.9 & 7.1 mm, but an unbroken awl is 45.4 mm long and weighs 2.3 g. Awls #'s 7 and 33 are very striated over or along their edge, while #1616 is ground like a pendant. Drills are excavated KeNi-4D:5A-5 at Whitefish Lake, used to assign KbNb-5:12 at Mantic Lake, and KjNb-6:1644a & 2023 (also a worn sideblade) at Warden's Grove. Mean width and thickness are 14.9 & 7.14

mm, but an unbroken drill is 51.8 mm long and weighs 6 g. The tip of KjNb-6:1644a has worn concentric striae, while keeled KeNi-4D:5A-5 is a thick, alternately retouched blade.

Other miscellaneous artifacts include fire-cracked cobbles, red ochre nodules, two skin flexers, two skin burnishers, a flaking tool and a nodule of unknown function (Table 8.104).

Artifact	Size (mm/g)	Description
LdLp-1:24	42.9x16x5.32/3.6	symmetric ovoid sideblade with midgroove for blunting tundra tool edges. In the Pingawalook site on the middle Thelon River
KdLw-1:987	55.2x45.8x31.4/105	fire-cracked tundra cobble
KdLw-1:386	27.9x13.8x3.8/1.3	buried ochre tundra nodule
KdLw-1:387	25.1x17.2x5.7/2.5	buried ochre tundra nodule
KjNb-7:40-8	36.9x18.5x5.8/3.1	bifacial 70-115 degree striae on side 1 and 70-90 degree striae on side 2, suggest tilting of tip when used. Buried tundra skin flexer
LdLp-1:40	40.14x19.8x9.2/6.8	skin flexer on tundra surface. Very worn but unstriated. Thelon Bluffs on middle Thelon R.
KdLw-1:566	48.12x23.3x6.3/7.1	buried skin burnisher that is worn transversely like a burin, but there are no spall scars
KjNb-3:3-122	fragment	surface skin burnisher. Dual transverse and longitudinal striae indicate scraping and burnishing function
KdLw-1:437	68x16.66x14.3/22.7	flaking tool for retouching edges. Long thin rod with worn tip.
KdLw:286	11 mm 2.4g	nodules of unknown function

Table 8.104. Pre-Dorset miscellaneous artifacts.

Analysis of Pre-Dorset art pieces

Some artifacts are unassignable except as art. All are from tundra sites, tiny, bifacial, finely retouched and exquisitely crafted (even quartzite), and smoothed from long handling. Two fragments excavated between Eyeberry Esker and Warden's Grove are used to assign six from Whitefish and Lynx Lakes on the above criteria, but differ sufficiently to suggest different knappers moving as herd followers between these areas (Fig. 8.18).

Excavated fully ground striated slate pendant KjNb-7:11-156 & 17-31 has a drilled suspension hole and an estimated length of 90 mm (Fig. 8.6). This pendant suggests Pre-Dorset artisans used bow drills, likely with hardened copper drill bits. They may also have used a bow drill with a dull spindle inserted in a tinder depression for starting fires. Red quartzite crosslike KkNb-11:74 at Grassy Island is asymmetric, its side projections pointed, its base snapped, and its plan and absence of wear or striae negating any knife use. Other depicted pieces are quartzite baluga whalelike KeNi-4:458 and spool-like but flattened pink and brown quartzite KeNi-4:459 at Whitefish Lake, and scimitar-like quartzite KcNi-3:50 at Lynx Lake. Undepicted are lozenge-shaped KlNb-1:1 of pink and beige mottled quartzite measuring 48x31.7x7.8mm & 15.2g, and sock-like KiNc-15:1 of orange and white mottled chert measuring 40.6x20.3x5.1mm & 4.8g. Pieces of indeterminate shape, but finely crafted are KkNb-11:74 (Grassy Island), KlNb-1:1 (Warden's Grove) and KiNc-15:1 (Eyeberry Lake).

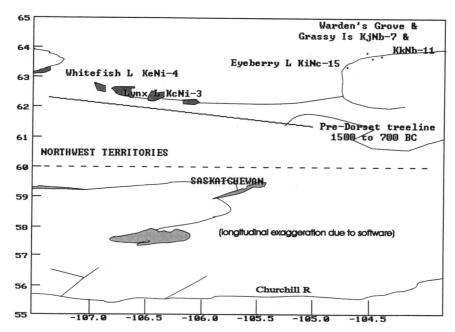

Figure 8.18. Distribution of 6 Pre-Dorset sites with 8 art pieces.

Analysis of Pre-Dorset burin-related artifacts

Ice-Age Magdalenian artifacts of bone, antler and mammoth ivory are world-renowned and fashioned into needles, harpoon heads and artwork. Likewise, these materials were used by arctic Inuit, Siberians and Dene, but the Inuit used walrus ivory, and the Dene used bone and antler. Some Dene still make and use bone and antler beamers and fleshers to remove hair and flesh from hides. As summer bull antler is too soft and bloody, and cow antler is too small and spindly; strong, thick and flexible autumn bull antler is preferred, and was used by all northern and glacial peoples.

Magdalenian, Inuit, and Siberian tools are somewhat similar due to their bull antler medium. Magdalenian and Pre-Dorset antler tools were also trimmed, grooved and incised with burins. Pre-Dorset burins vary in type, but possess a common trait in being sharpened by deliberately pressing edge spalls off mitlike blanks using an antler tine placed at the tip, and pressed down and in towards the base of the "thumb". Spalls can also be made accidentally, when stone lanceheads and arrowheads split their tip face or edge by hitting rock. But they show little preparation and are called "burin-like" primary spalls. If antler or bone is sand-contaminated, striae cut by sharp granules form on the chert burin face, only to reappear later on the detached spall. They are measured to elicit burin use, but antler or bone striae are to similar to differentiate.

While Pre-Dorsets are like other arctic peoples in using bone and antler harpoons, needles, awls and art, these are unpreserved in the Beverly range, just like the previously suggested harpoons. But burins themselves indicate bone and antler working, and four forest and 565 burin-related artifacts are distributed like points, knives and scrapers. This suggests hunting, butchering, hide processing and bone and antler tool-making were joint activities at these camps (Fig. 8.19). Burin-related artifacts are burin blanks, burin planes (109) and their spalls (39 primary and 145 secondary), burin slotters (114) and their spalls (11 primary and 48 secondary), and unburinated planes (109).

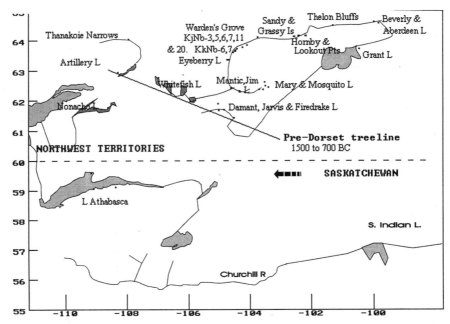

Figure 8.19. Distribution of 49 Pre-Dorset sites with 569 burin-related artifacts.

The natural environment provided a means to interpret how burins and spalls were used. In a land of dunes, eskers and beaches where sand is common, granules invariably became caught between the antler or bone being worked and the burin used to work it. The sand grains scratching both worked piece and burin face created striae which remained on detached spalls and may be used to elicit burin function and the order of spall removal.

A spall has uni- or bifacially retouched sides, remnants of the original blank. If the blank was unifacial it became a burin plane and its spalls, plane type; if the blank was bifacial it became a burin slotter; its spalls, slotter type. Burin planes have ventral face and edge striae if the worked object is sand-contaminated (Enlargement 8.1), a pattern duplicated and analyzable on the spall and separating it from slotter spalls. Burin slotters and spalls have identical striae on both faces showing slotter depth, direction and pressure (Enlargement 8.2). A new burin is drawn perpendicularly towards the user (Gordon 1975:Fig. 19). As burins are sharpened by spalling, the tip tilts increasingly back, making striae oblique, especially in depleted burins. Development of striae angles on spalls may be visualized using the hand as a model for the burin, and fingers as models for the spalls. Joint wrinkles are seen as striae perpendicular to the fingers. Opening the fingers slightly mimics distal spall thickening, and bending each to the palm simulates spall removal. Wrinkles angle back in the same way as striae. As each spall removal leaves a hinge scar at the facet bottom, the scar count shows the number of burin sharpenings. Sometimes, the spall face is interrupted by new scarring areas or scar groups closer to the tip.

Enlargement 8.1. Striae on a burin plane.   Enlargement 8.2. Striae on a slotter burin.

Burin planes and their spalls

The production of burin planes from simple bifaces, sideblades (lateral insets) and discs is seen in Fig. 8.20. One edge of a simple biface is retouched to a mitlike plan, from which spalls are detached inward from and parallel to the 'thumb'. As spalls taper, much spalling causes the spall face to lean inwards, producing a pointed or "left-leaning" burin. Non-mitlike sideblades and discs also show this lean when heavily spalled. A mitlike unburinated plane (to be discussed) is at lower left. A double or dihedral burinated plane, where both spall faces lean inward to converge at the tip, is at upper right. If a mitlike uniface is spalled, it becomes a burin plane and its spalls are called plane spalls

Except for slotter KjNb-7:11-112 (Fig. 8.21 second row), burin planes are in the top three rows, with plane spall KjNb-7:27-90 in Fig. 8.22 at bottom right. From left to right and top to bottom, burin planes include KjNb-7:19-17, a left-leaning, unground and unbacked burin with striae from tip to basal edge, but with most distally. KkNb-6:1 has heavy 100 degree striae from its facet to its ground back. Notched KjNb-7:11-114 has rotational striae on its adjoining right dual facets, inferring use as a drill. KjNb-7:11-152 has 45 degree striae suggesting chiselling. KjNb-6:567 resembles an endscraper, but has characteristic burinlike striae completely across its expanded tip. Lozenge-shaped KjNb-6:62-6 (Fig. 8.21 row three) has a striated and worn spall face edge, indicating high pressure use. LbLs-2:38

with snapped tip has 90 and 110 degree cross-striae, denoting rotation. KjNb-3:3-47 is a discoidal scraper with one spall scar. Like hafted endscrapers, burin planes are thick to withstand heavy oblique application. Unlike thinner burin slotters that are used 'in line" rather than obliquely, the retouched bases of some thick burin planes are heavily worn by these applications; e.g. KjNb-7:19-77.

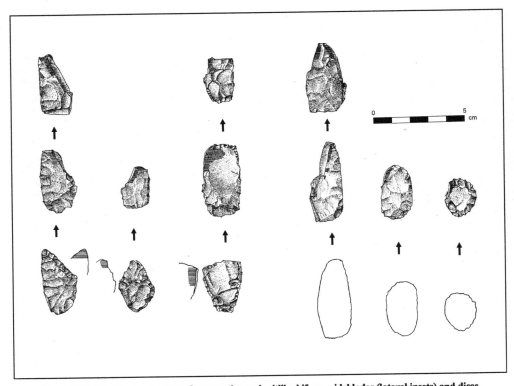

Figure 8.20. Making burin planes from regular and mitlike bifaces, sideblades (lateral insets) and discs.

Burin planes (109) are scattered in 24 sites at Warden's Grove-Sandy Island in KjNb-3, 6, 7 and 20, Eyeberry Lake in KiNc-1, 12 and 13, and at Hornby-Lookout Point and Thelon Bluffs. Others are at Thanakoie Narrows and Artillery, Mantic-Jim, Whitefish, Jarvis and Mary-Mosquito Lakes (Fig. 8.23). As there is only one forest plane, IjOg-2:54b at Lake Athabasca (22x14x5mm & 1.5g), it is included with tundra planes. All have a mean size of 30.6x17x 6mm & 3.4g (Table 8.106; support data in Tables 8.105a-c).

Table 8.107 arranges 108 tundra burin planes by: (1) spalling or carination; (2) spall face, unless smashed away; (3) retouch to scrapers and gravers; (4) pressure backing, except unbacked bidirectional burins; and (5) multiple use as another tool.

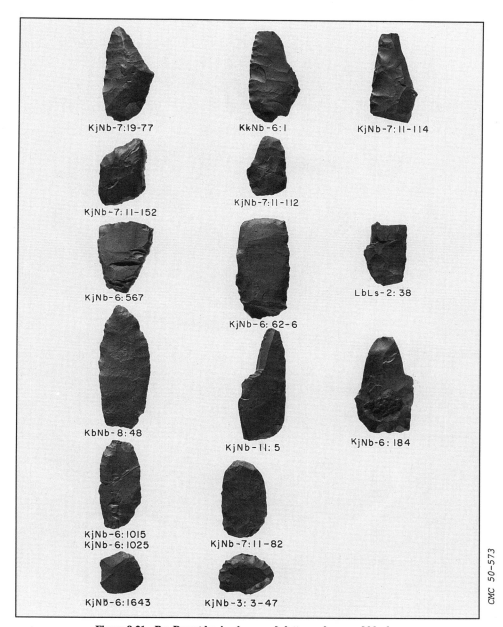

KjNb-7:19-77

KkNb-6:1

KjNb-7:11-114

KjNb-7:11-152

KjNb-7:11-112

KjNb-6:567

KjNb-6:62-6

LbLs-2:38

KbNb-8:48

KjNb-11:5

KjNb-6:184

KjNb-6:1015
KjNb-6:1025

KjNb-7:11-82

KjNb-6:1643

KjNb-3:3-47

CMC 50-573

Figure 8.21. Pre-Dorset burin planes and slotters, planes and blanks.

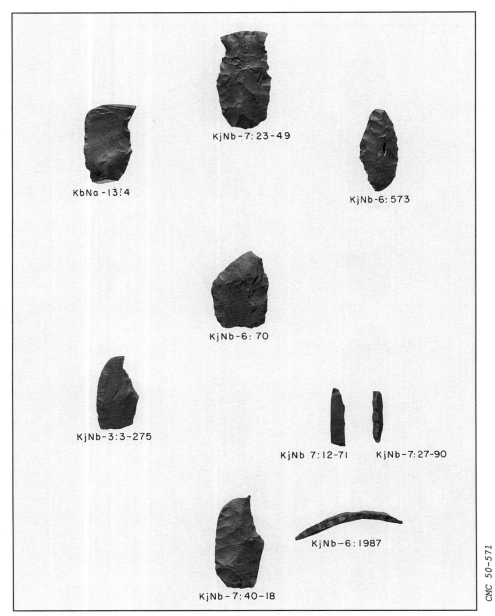

KjNb-7: 23-49

KbNa-13:4

KjNb-6: 573

KjNb-6: 70

KjNb-3:3-275

KjNb 7:12-71

KjNb-7: 27-90

KjNb-6:1987

KjNb-7: 40-18

CMC 50-571

Figure 8.22. Pre-Dorset carinated, dihedral slotters, spalls and microblade.

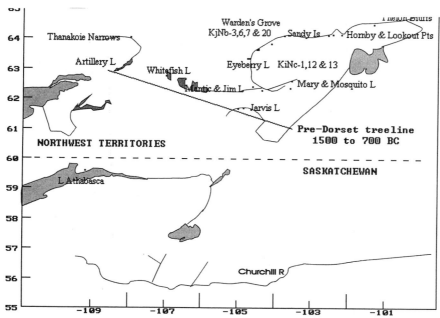

Figure 8.23. Distribution of 24 Pre-Dorset sites with 109 burin planes.

Attribute	Yes (no. and %)	Absent (no. and %)	Unknown (no. and %)	Conclusion
carinated (parrot-beaked)	3(03)	96(89)	9(08)	few burin tips overhang for special uses
spall face present	99(92)	8(07)	1(01)	some burins are destroyed by pressure
retouch	9(08)	83(77)	16(15)	one-tenth of planes are made into other tools
ground haft	74(69)	23(21)	11(10)	2/3 have worn sockets from high pressure
backed	80(74)	18(17)	10(09)	3/4 adapted with back for high pressure
back wear	81(75)	17(16)	10(09)	3/4 are worn from bone pressure backing
back retouch & blunting	84(78)	14(13)	10(09)	3/4 have blunted backs to take pressure
multiple use	4(04)	104(96)		1 endscraper, 1 discoidal scraper and 2 sideblades

Table 8.107. Comparing Pre-Dorset tundra burin plane attributes.

Burin plane spall scars and their groups, and the internal angle of the converging tip (tip angle) were measured in 108 burin planes (Table 8.108). Eighty-five have 1-12 spall scars from one edge (mean =3.45; S.D.=2.4); 23 are unscarred. Ten dihedral planes have 1-4 spall scars from the other edge (mean=2; S.D.=1.05. Scar groups are in 19 burins; almost all as one group, but some with three separate groups along the spall face. Of 24 burins with pointed tips, tip angle is 30-135 degrees (mean= 64.2; S.D.=28).

Analysis of striae in burin planes and their spalls

Just as shallow wide striae over scraper bits are from sand-contaminated hide, deep narrow striae on burin faces are caused by grit adhering to worked antler. Striae orientation and size replicate the pressure and direction of tool application. As windblown sand also removes striae, as seen in glossy surface tools, most striated tools are from buried blowout levels, even those outside the Beverly range at Victoria Island and the Coppermine (pers. comms., W. E. Taylor 1989; R. McGhee 1977). Striae is heavy or light, widespread or confined, unifacial or bifacial, or crossed when the burin is tilted.

The longitudinal axis of a burin plane is the main reference for strial measurements because it follows the midline, even in depleted or split burins and midsection-hafts (Fig. 8.24). As spalls widen at their platforms upon removal at the burin tip, the spall face tilts back and angle L between the midline and striae increases (top right). To keep angle F at an effective perpendicular cutting edge, the burin is tilted obliquely. Angle F between striae and spall face is equal to angle F^1 between striae and midline in spalls. This common angle, plus patterned cross-striae in inner spalls, produced when burins are tilted, are used to recreate the spall sequence (right bottom). Often-broken spalls are oriented for study using their bulb of percussion, platform, facet edge wear or hinge scar.

Angle L between striae and the longitudinal burin axis is L1 in regular, and L1 and L2 in both edges of dihedral burins. Angles L1 & L2 approach 90 degrees because dihedral burins are used bi-directionally, their spall faces finally joining at the tip. Half of burin planes and their spalls have L1 & F^1 strial angles of 90 degrees, followed by equal numbers that are smaller (80-85 degrees) or larger (95-105 and 105-115 degrees; Table 8.109a). Three with 70 degree striae are little-spalled new burins. Eight with 115-125 degree striae are depleted. Carinated burins may have angles greater than 90 degrees, as their noselike tips jut over the midline.

Angle F^1 varies considerably in 31 burin planes (strial range=85-94 degrees) because the spall face was tilted as it entered and left a groove, and after spalling when the burin was tilted. New to depleted plane and slotter burins were tilted at all phases of spall removal. Deep strial signs of high pressure are in two-thirds of all burins, a significant sign that they were heavily used on hard bull antler.

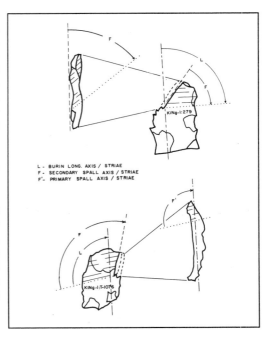

L - BURIN LONG. AXIS / STRIAE
F - SECONDARY SPALL AXIS / STRIAE
F'- PRIMARY SPALL AXIS / STRIAE

Figure 8.24. Measuring burin and spall striae.

High or low pressure signs occur as variable striae on a spall side; with bifacial striae $F^{1a \& b}$ of a burin slotter spall in Enlargements 8.3 and 8.4 and Table 8.109b. Angles L1, L2 and F^1 in Table 8.109a suggests most burin planes were heavily applied, independently of the angle of application.

Degrees	No	Angle L1	Angle L2	Angle F^1	X	Pressure	Strial type
65-74	3	all are 70 deg.	110(1)		0	high (1); low(2)	rotational like drill
75-84	7	80(4), 85(3)	0	60(1), 70(3), 80(1) and 90(2)	0	high (3); low(4)	regular use
85-94	31	all are 90 deg.	0	45(3), 50(1), 70(5), 75(1), 80(6), 85(1), 90(8), 100(1), 110(1), 130(1), & 135(1)	(1)	high (20); low (11)	most common type for regular use
95-104	6	all are 100 deg.	0	70(1), 80(3) and 90(2)	0	high (5); low (1)	heavy
105-114	6	110(5), 115(1)	90(1)	50(1), 80(2) and 90(3)	(1)	all high	heavy and rotation
115-124	8	115(1),120(7)	120(1)	45(1), 70(1), 90(5) and 35(1)	(1)	high (5); low (3)	heavy and rotation

Table 8.109a. 10 degree Angle L increments between striae and midline in 61 burin planes.
Angles L1 & L2 refer to dihedral planes. X=cross-striae. Bracketted numbers are counts of burins with specific striae

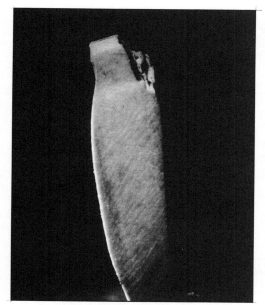

Enlargement 8.3. Angle F^{1a} in dorsal spall striae.

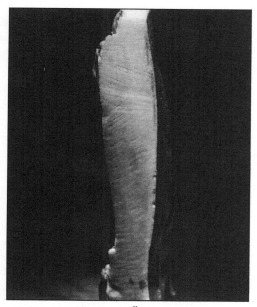

Enlargement 8.4. Angle F^{1b} in ventral spall striae.

Angle L becomes La in unburinated unifacial planes. Here, ten degree increments to the midline show most striae are perpendicular (29 where La=84-104 degrees; Table 8.109b). Other angles suggest some form of oblique use for left-leaning burins. High pressure does not relate to tilting, but seems to be higher in chisels.

Degrees	No	Angle La	Angle F	Cross-striae	Pressure	Striae type
55-64	1	60	40	0	high (1)	chisel end use, rather than lateral edge
65-74	4	70(4)	45	0	high(2); low(2)	highly left-leaning
75-84	3	80(2) & 85(1)	50(1)	0	high (3)	chisel use. Highly left-leaning
85-94	15	80(2), 85(1) and 90(12)	50(1)	0	high (8); low (7)	chisel use. Highly left-leaning
95-104	14	85(1), 90(12) and 100(1)	50(1)	(1)	high (7); low (7)	Highly left-leaning
105-114	1	100	0	0	high (1)	chisel use from opposite edge, rather than top
115-124	1	120	0	0	low (1)	
130-134	1	135	120	0	low (1)	

Table 8.109b. Ten degree increments between striae and midline in 40 unburinated unifacial planes.

Ten degree increments to the midline in 134 plane spalls show most striae are perpendicular (57 at 85-94 degrees), followed by many that are less (34 at 75-84; 9 at 65-74 degrees) or more (13 at 95-104; 12 at 105-114 degrees). A few with small (3 at 54-64 degrees) or large angles (3 at 115-124, 2 at 135-144, and 1 at 145-154 degrees) infer heavy inner or outer tilting of new or depleted planes. Briefly, the spall sequence is recreated by comparing spall striae, which show burin tilt. Initial spalls may show an inward tilt, mid-sequence spalls a perpendicular application, and very late spalls a heavy outward tilt (see Table 8.109c, Remarks). Pressure is independent of tilt. Six spalls are cross-striated.

Degrees	No	Angle F^{1a} in degress (no.)	Cross-striae	Pressure	Spall type. Burin type. Tilt
54-64	3	59(1), 60(1) and 64(1)		high (3)	very early. Burin tilted ininward
65-74	9	65,70(8)		high (9)	early. Light burin inner tilt
75-84	34	75(2), 77(1), 80(26),82(1),83(3) and 84(1)	75(1)	high(18);low(16)	used perpendicularly to work
85-94	57	85(4),86(1),87(1),89(3),90(44),91(2) & 92(2)	90(3)	high(33);low (24)	used perpendicularly to work
95-104	13	95(1), 99(1) & 100(11)	100(2)	high(7); low(6)	late. Light outer burin tilt
105-114	12	108(2), 110(7), 111(1),112(1) and114(1)		high(6); low(6)	late. Light outer burin tilt
115-124	3	120(3)		low (3)	very late. Heavy outer burin tilt
135-144	2	135(2)		high(1); low(1)	very late. Depleted burin. Heavy tilt
145-154	1	148(1)		low (1)	very late. Depleted burin. Heavy tilt

Table 8.109c. Ten degree angle increments between striae and midline in 134 plane spalls.

The finding of 183 tiny burin plane spalls (38 primary, 145 secondary - all tundra and mainly gray or white chert) is due to their proximity in stratified levels (Figs. 8.23 and 8.25). Spalls are at Grassy Island and Warden's Grove, but absent at Thanakoie Narrows, Thelon Bluffs, and Artillery, Whitefish, Jim-Mantic and Eyeberry Lakes. Correspondingly, these are also areas of burin planes. The six unworn and two worn primary spalls are from burin blanks, but are untabled because they are unstriated. Mean size of plane spalls is 18.9x4.8x2mm & 0.21g (Table 8.115a). The converging tip angle in 69 of 83 spalls has a range of 45-120 degrees and a mean of 88.8 degrees.

Slotter burins and their spalls

Like plane spalls, 59 slotter spalls are more confined than their parent slotters which were taken elsewhere for added use (Figs. 8.26 & 8.28). Slotter spalls converge at Warden's Grove sites KjNb-3, 4 and 7, with findspots at Mosquito Lake and Hornby Point. Most were in a 1-meter diameter KjNb-7 hearth, implying most harpoon and shaft grooving was done in one tiny workshop by a few specialists who threw discarded spalls into the fire. After excluding seven striated slotter blank spalls, 52 secondary spalls are compared, with mean size of 18.5x1.3x0.6mm & 0.1g (Table 8.115b). As plane spall mean size is 18.9x4.8x2.12mm & 0.21g, slotter spalls are similar in length, but much narrower for cutting deep grooves, and much thinner for more extensive spalling before burin discard.

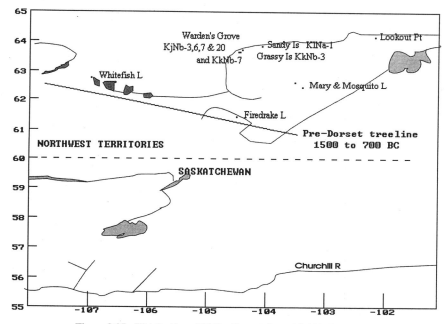

Figure 8.25. Distribution of 12 Pre-Dorset sites with 183 plane spalls.

If a bifacial burin blank is spalled, it becomes a slotter, and its spalls are worn on both sides. Slotters are made from knives, gravers, skin flexers and sideblades (e.g.s, KjNb-6:1015/1025 and KjNb-7:11-82; Fig. 8.21 row 5 and KjNb-6:573; Fig. 8.22 upper right). KjNb-7:11-82 has deep bifacial striae perpendicular to its major axis. Unlike burin planes, slotters are thin and snap easily like hacksaw blades, but are very strong when properly used. Similar depth and direction of striae on both faces of burins and spalls infer balanced slotter use and groove depth.

Spalling sometimes leaves no scar, particularly when the tips of parrot-beaked and dihedral burins are sharpened by removing spalls joining opposite facets (Fig 8.27; burins are identified in Fig. 8.22). KjNb-6:184 is a bidirectionally-used, unstriated dihedral burin with converging spall faces (Fig. 8.21 row 4). KjNb-7:23-49 is a dihedral, bidirectionally-used burin, but with expanding tip (Fig. 8.22

top middle). Parrot-beaked and dihedral burins may be bifacially thinned with tip spalled away (KjNb-7:40-18; Fig 8.22 bottom, in which spalling has destroyed its tip). This in turn creates new striae which gradually obliterate the bifacial retouch. Other examples of tip-spalled parrot-beaked or carinated slotters are KbNa-13:4 (Fig. 8.22 top left) and KjNb-3:3-275 (bottom left). Bifacial striae and heavy tip wear from dragging through a slot identifiy these as slotters. Almost four-fifths of the 114 slotter burins are carinated, a ratio much higher than for burin planes (3%). This high amount of carination indicates that slotter tips were used in deep grooves.

Distribution of equal numbers of burin planes and slotters (114 in 27 sites) is alike, suggesting sequential use in tool-making (Fig. 8.26). Perhaps burin planes were used to shape shafts and harpoon heads, while slotters were used in the final work of insetting points and sideblades. Almost four-tenths of slotters are carinated, a ratio much higher than planes (3%) and reinforcing the above suggestion that slotters were used in deep grooves. Of 114 slotters, 85 have 1-12 spall scars on side 1 (mean = 2.6; S.D. = 2); six have 1-7 scars on side 2 (mean = 2.38; S.D. = 2.34; Table 8.111). This high bifacial spalling infers slotters were more bidirectionally used than burin planes, an efficient back and forward motion for deep grooves. Of 87 slotters with scar groups, few have more than one; the rest, retouched or crushed. As almost half (31) have tip angles of 30-110 degrees (mean = 76.4; S.D. = 20.5), they were used in a variety of grooving motions. Slotters average 29.4x16.2x4.7mm & 2.5 g (Table 8.112).

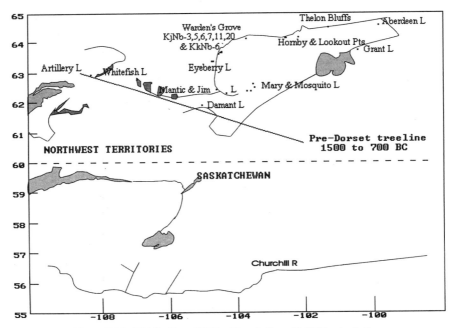

Figure 8.26. Distribution of 27 Pre-Dorset sites with 114 burin slotters.

An example of scar grouping is KjNb-11:5 with two scar groups: one with four, the other with seven scars showing interrupted spalling (Fig. 8.21 row 4). Of 87 slotters with scar groups, few have more than one. Multiple scarring has been obliterated by retouch or crushing. That half (31) of slotters with scar groups have tip angles of 30-110 degrees (mean=76.4; S.D.=20.5), shows various tilting motions as the slotter enters and leaves its slot. Slotters in Table 8.109d are arranged by carination, spall face, spall scars and groups, retouch, backing, back wear and retouch, tip angle and multiple use.

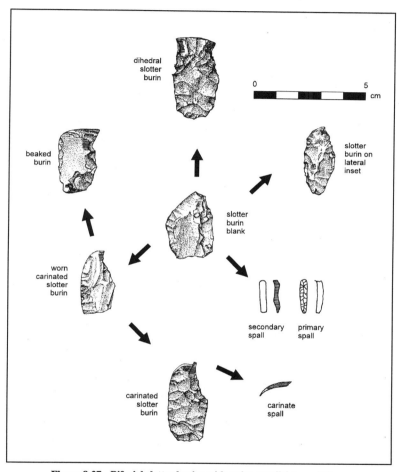

Figure 8.27. Bifacial slotter burins with striae parallel to spall face.

Carinated burins at top of Table 8.109d include KdLw-1:1207, KjNb-6:76 and LbLs-2:36. Worn retouched hafts and backs indicate four-fifths of planes are very used. Forest plane IjOg-2:64b (not shown) is uncarinated, spalled and unbacked, with an unground unretouched round haft. It has six spall scars in one group, no striae, and converges at its tip at 80 degrees. Of nine converted burins, four are identified as endscrapers and discoid scrapers, and two as sideblades.

Attribute	Yes	Absent	Unknown	Remarks
carinated	42(37)	68(60)	4(04)	many burins are beaked
spall face	102(89)	11(10)	1(01)	one-tenth of burins are destroyed
retouch	13(11)	82(72)	1 9(17)	one-tenth of slotters are retouched into other tools
ground haft	86(75)	37(32)	11(10)	3/4 are socket worn from high pressure application
backed	88(77)	19(17)	7(06)	3/4 were under high pressure application
back wear	88(77)	19(17)	7(06)	3/4 were under high pressure application
back retouch	100(88)	10(09)	4(04)	9/10 were under high pressure application
multiple use	7(06)	107(94)		knife, graver, four side-blades and a skin flexer

Table 8.109d. Comparing Pre-Dorset tundra burin slotter attributes.

Analysis of striae in slotters and their spalls

Most striae are perpendicular in bifacial slotters; followed by equal numbers of three 10 degree increment ranges on either side (Angles La-b; Table 8.109e). As slotters tilt when entering and leaving slots, their strial angles vary more than planes (45-120 degrees) and result in cross-striae, especially in six with with perpendicular striae. Carinated burins and spalls have angles less than 90 degrees, as their beaked tips overhang the facet.

Degrees	No	Angle La	Angle Lb	Angle F	X	Pressure	Striae type
?	1	?= broken	90	0	0	high (1)	tip only
45-55	1	45(1)	135(1)	0	0	high (1)	rotational type like awl
65-75	2	70(2)	80(1)	70(1) & 90(1)	0	high (2)	half depleted burin
75-85	10	80(9) and 82(1)	80(5)	30(1), 70(4), 77(1), 90(2) & 120(1)	1	high (8); low (2)	parallel slotter striae. Rotated and carinated multi-use burin
85-95	31	90(26), 93(1) and 95(4)	45(2), 80(1), 85(1) and 90(20)	60(1), 70(2), 75(1), 80(3), 9 0(19) and 110(2)	6	high (22); low (9)	parallel striae of slotter.
95-105	6	95(4) & 100(2)	45(1), 80(1), 85(1), 90(2) and 100(1)	75(2), 80(2), 85(1) and 90(2)	3	high (6)	rotation and carination. Multiple use
105-115	5	110(4) & 113(1)	110(2) and 113(1)	70(1), 90(2) and 120(1)	3	high (5)	parallel striae of slotter. Rotated, multi-use carinate
115-125	6	120(6)	90(1) & 120(1)	70(1), 75(1), 90(2), 120(1) and 135(1)	2	high (4); low (2)	parallel striae of slotter

Table 8.109e. Ten degrees increments between striae and midline in 62 slotters.
Angles La and Lb refer to uni- and bifacial striae. Angle F between striae and facet in burins is equivalent to F^{1a} and F^{1b} in regular and dihedral spalls for finding spall order. X=cross-striae. Brackets enclose burin counts of particular strial ranges

Increments between striae and midline in blanks and primary spalls show burin blanks were used before spalling (Angles La-b; Table 8.109f). Most have 90 degree striae but a primary spall with heavy bifacial striae $\geq$ 90 degrees shows it is from a slotter blank.

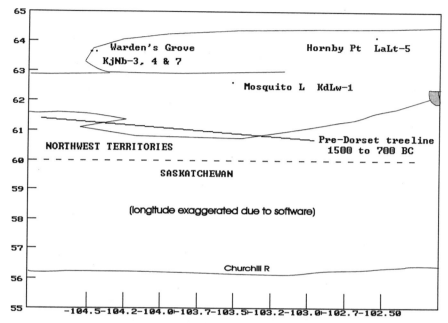

Figure 8.28. Distribution of 5 Pre-Dorset sites with 59 slotter spalls.

Degrees	No.	Angle La	Angle Lb	Angle F	X	Pressure	Remarks
75-85	1	80	worn	0	0	high (1)	slotter blank
85-95	3	90 (3)	90 (1)	80, 90	0	high(1); low(2)	slotter blank with parallel striae
105-115	1	110	100	90	1	high (1)	slotter blank with parallel striae

Table 8.109f. Ten degree increments between striae and midline in 5 blanks and primary spalls.
(worn unstriated blanks and primary spalls are untabled)

Degrees	No	Angle F^{1a} in deg (no.)	Angle F^{1b} in deg(no.)	Pressure	Place in spall sequence. Remarks
55-60	3	60(3)	60,120(2)	high(2); low(1)	very early spall; parallel striae
65-70	2	70(2)	worn	high(1); low(1)	early spall. Parallel striae. One tilted
75-84	8	76(1) & 80(7)	80,104	high(5); low(3)	early spall. Parallel striae. One tilted
85-94	22	85(5), 88(1) and 90(16)	80(1), 90(6), 95(1), 118(1)	high(11); low(6)	used perpendicularly. Parallel striae
95-105	7	95(3), 100(3) and 104(1)	78(1), 90(1) and 95(1)	high(3); low(1)	used perpendicularly. Parallel striae
105-110	1	110(1)	worn	high (1)	tilted carinate (parrot-beaked) burin
115-125	1	120(1)	80(1)	low (1)	not parallel=not slotter. One tilted
125-135	1	130(1)	worn	high (1)	made from depleted scraper

Table 8.109g. Bifacial grooving strial angles F^{1a-b} in 45 slotter spalls. Total slotter spalls=134

Ten degree increments to midline in 45 slotter spalls show most striae (22) are perpendicular, followed by equal numbers with lower (8 at 75-84 degrees) or higher angles (7 at 95-105 degrees) showing early or late use (Angles F^{1a-b}; Table 8.109g). Many spalls infer burin tilting. Like slotter burins, slotter spalls show heavy burin use independent of tilt.

Unburinated planes and burin blanks and their striae

Unspalled tools with unifacial striae are planes rather than burin planes, as their retouched but unspalled edge was used to plane bone or antler. More dispersed than other burin-related tools, three are at Athabasca and Whitefish Lake forest sites, and 100 at Warden's Grove and Hornby-Lookout Points. Other unburinated planes are at Whitefish, Mary, Mantic, Mosquito and Beverly Lakes (Fig. 8.29).

Unlike burin planes, unburinated planes are pointed, larger, curved over their length, and have a serrated planing edge. Perhaps the curved serrated edge was used for quickly removing round antler cortex softened in water, while the curved pointed tip was used for finer rounding. Later, the straight edge of the spall face in burin planes was used to shape decortexed antler into tools (Tables 8.113a-b).

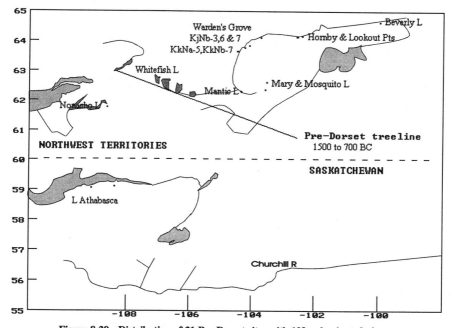

Figure 8.29. Distribution of 21 Pre-Dorset sites with 103 unburinated planes.

Of three forest unburinated planes, one is made from another tool, one leans left, two have similar tip taper, and all are unstriated but worn on haft and back. Two-thirds of tundra unburinated planes (100) also lean left, suggesting rangewide use by right-handers pulling them towards themselves for removing cortex from antler, or trimming curved shafts. This is sunstantiated by 25 unburinated planes with a striated concave ventral face (Tables 8.113c-d).

Attribute	Presence (frequency)	Absent or unknown	Remarks
left-leaning	1(33)	2(67)	1/3 are left-leaning planes
striae		3(100)	destroyed by surface exposure
retouch	1(33)	2(67)	made from another tool
round haft	3(100)		all worn by socket use
backed	2(67)	1(33)	2/3 indicate high pressure use
back wear	3(100)		all indicate high pressure use
back retouch	3(100)		all indicate high pressure use
tip angle	2(67); both 50 degrees	1(33)	fine rounding of bone or antler
multiple use		3(100)	used only as plane

Table 8.113c. Pre-Dorset unburinated forest plane attributes.

While surface exposure quickly destroys striae, a fourth of unspalled planes (17 surface; 8 stratified) have striae, 14 densely. Retouch suggests seven tundra planes were used as a sidescraper, two knives, three chisels and a sideblade. Light back and haft wear show less than half were used heavily (Table 8.113d). Burin blanks and unburinated planes are unspalled, but burin blanks are like sideblades with bifacial striae. Mitlike left-leaning planes have a steeply retouched serrated edge with unifacial striae. When spalled, most burin blanks become slotters; most planes become burin planes.

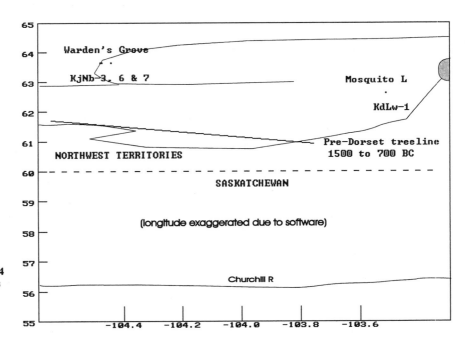

Figure 8.30. Distribution of 4 Pre-Dorset sites with 28 burin blanks.

Primary spall striae infer burin blanks. The blank class (all tundra) includes a burin plane, 5 slotters, 21 primary burin plane spalls and 6 primary slotter burin spalls. Their distribution centers on Warden's Grove sites KjNb-3, 6 and 7, with one spall at KdLw-1, Mosquito Lake, and a slotter blank at Mary Lake (unmapped; Fig. 8.30).

The single burin plane blank is untabled, but KjNb-7:7-48 is 33.7x-17.6(split)x6.6 mm & 3.6g, with heavy perpendicular striae. Five slotter blanks, all gray chert except quartzite KdLw-1:13, are from KdLw-1 and KjNb-6 (2 each; KjNb-6:48-16 excavated) and one from Mary Lake (Table 8.114a). As they are unspalled, they are larger than slotters (means=32.8x17.3x5mm/6.3g & 29.4x16.2x4.7mm/ 2.5g; Table 8.112). The tiny 0.3 mm thickness difference is expected because slotter and blank tips are uniformly thin over their length for cutting deep even-sided grooves.

Of five slotter blanks, three are striated; two heavily. One blank is made from a sideblade. Sixty per cent are worn, as seen in worn hafts and backs (Table 8.114b). A mean tip angle of 63 degrees and wide range of 45-80 degrees, suggests tundra slotter blanks have wider applications than forest planes.

Attribute	Presence (frequency)	Absence or unknown	Remarks
left-leaning	66 (66)	34 (34)	2/3 are left-leaning planes
striae	25 (11 light; 14 heavy)	75 (75)	3/4 destroyed by wind exposure on sand surface
retouch	3 (03)	97 (97)	3 used as other tools
ground haft	29 (29)	71 (71)	about 1/3 are socket worn
backed	44 (44)	56 (56)	less than 1/4 show high pressure application
back wear	42 (42)	58 (58)	less than 1/4 show high pressure application
back retouch	76 (76)	24 (24)	3/4 show high pressure application
tip angle	32(32) Range=40-120 deg.; mean=66.6 deg.	68 (68)	more expanding than forest ones; wider uses
multiple use	7(07)	93 (93)	1 sidescraper, 2 knives, 1 sideblade and 3 chisels

Table 8.113d. Pre-Dorset unspalled tundra plane attributes.

Attribute	Yes (frequency)	Absence or unknown	Remarks
striae	3(60) 1 light and 2 heavy	2 (40)	40% destroyed by sand abrasion, or never created
retouch	1 (20)	4 (80)	one used as other tool
ground haft	3 (60)	2 (40)	about 3/5 were worn in their sockets
backed	3 (60)	2 (40)	3/5 are backed for high pressure use
back wear	3 (60)	2 (40)	3/5 are backed for high pressure use
back retouch	4 (80)	1 (20)	4/5 are backed for high pressure use
tip angle	2 (40) Range=45-80deg.; mean=63 deg.	3 (60)	more expanding than forest planes. Wider uses
multiple use	1 (20)	4 (80)	one made from sideblade

Table 8.114b. Comparing Pre-Dorset tundra slotter blank attributes.

All 38 burin plane primary spalls are from Warden's Grove sites KjNb-3, 6, 7 and 20; except 7 from KdLw-1 at Mosquito Lake. All are white or gray chert, except one of orange; 17 have broken lengths and weights, and 15 are stratified (Table 8.114c). Mean =19x3.9x2.7mm & 0.18g.

Six chert primary slotter spalls are from KjNb-3, 6 & 7. Both KjNb-7 spalls are stratified, with mean size of 20.7x4x2.74mm & 0.2g (Table 8.114d). Primary plane spalls are slightly longer, thicker and heavier than primary slotter spalls, but the latter are wider, because slotters were selected from thicker bifacially retouched flakes, and artifacts such as sideblades and discoids.

Conclusions on burin-related artifacts

While rare in forest sites, most burin-related artifacts are banded gray or white chert from unknown tundra quarries. Their location, wear and spalling suggest use on antler portions carried north from fall-killed bulls by herd followers in spring. Smaller, repeatedly used forest burin planes, slotters, blanks and unburinated planes, suggest winter chert conservation in a snow-covered area, where new material was unavailable. Small thin slotters used as groovers for insetting end and sideblades contrast with larger thick burin planes that were heavily used obliquely for trimming antler into heads for lances and possibly harpoons, and handles for knives, awls and scrapers. Forest burins are rare because they would not be needed to make lanceheads and harpoons, as they are useless in thick ice. Rather, most winter caribou were likely snared or corralled as they were for the Dene, with limited need for lances.

A small tip angle between converging sides (1 & 2; Table 8.116) suggests depletion in slotters or burin planes as their spall faces join, and piercing or engraving in unburinated planes. It varies from 50 degrees in slimly pointed, partly depleted forest planes to a much wider 63-67 degrees in little used blanks, burin planes and tundra planes, to 76 degrees in perpendicularly used carinated slotters.

Type of burin-related artifact	Size mm/g Mean tip angle	Mean number of spalls at edge (range)		Mean number of scar groups	Haftworn (ratio)	Backworn (ratio)	Dual tool use and remarks
		Side 1	Side 2				
burin plane	31x17x6/3.4 65 degrees	3.45 (1-12)	2	1.13	3/4	4/5	2 scrapers
slotter burin Many carinated	29x16x5/2.2 76 degrees	2.6 (1-12)	2.4 (1-7)	1.09	3/4	3/4	3 (knife, graver and flexer)
forest plane (unburinated)	31x13x6/2.6 50 degrees	none	none	none	1/3	1/4	2/3 are left-leaning
tundra plane (unburinated)	33x17x6/4 67 degrees	none	none	none	under low pressure	under low pressure	2 knives, side-scraper & 3 chisels
blank (unburinated)	33x17x5/6.3 63 degrees	none	none	none	3/4	3/4	one made from side-blade

Table 8.116. Comparison of burin-related artifact tip angles.

Compared to slotters, an extra spall from burin plane sharpening (Side 1;Table 8.116) is expected, because they are heavily, obliquely applied single-sided tools, while paired slotter sides share the task of grooving, and are applied in line with the groove. A sixth of burins (62) have one sequence of spall scars, 9 have two sequences, and one has three. Multi-sequences suggest intended angular change to make a multi-purpose tool, or failed attempts at removing a full length spall due to a poorly angled pressing tool at the burin tip. A degree of intention is favoured by the greater number of scar groups in burin planes. This allows different planing angles, while angular change in slotters is limited to entering and leaving grooves. Dihedral slotters are more spalled on side 2 than dihedral planes with doubly-paired cutting edges (ratio of 2.4:2) because back and forth grooving requires sharpening via spall removal from both sides. Very worn hafts and backs on burin planes and slotters infer good back and socket support for heavy use.

Burins had other uses: scrapers from planes; and knives, gravers and skin flexers from slotters; and microscrapers from spalls (Gordon 1975:Plate 6). Striae on the working bit of skin flexer KjNb-7:12-129 are magnified in Enlargement 8.5. They originated from sand-contaminated hide (e.g., Fig. 8.31). Unburinated planes are lightly worn on haft and back, left-leaning and pointed, suggesting light whittling, cortex removal from softened antler, and the planing or rounding of spear shafts. They were also used as knives, sidescrapers and chisels. Blanks are heavily worn in haft and back in accordance with their burin role prior to spalling.

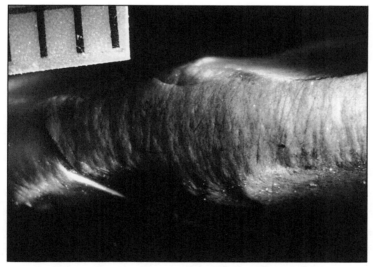

Enlargement 8.5. Cross-striae on chert skin flexer KjNb-7:12-129 caused by sand-contaminated hide indicate motion across rather than along the bit.

Primary plane and slotter spalls are longer, narrower and thicker than secondary spalls because they retain their original burin side (Table 8.117; Gordon 1975:Plates 9c-d). Secondary spalls from the interior of the burin retain a smaller cross-section, but shorten as scars gather on the spall face. Except for four tiny primary slotter spalls, most slotter spalls have perpendicular striae. Secondary spalls have a wider range of strial angles than primary spalls because secondary striae are added to initial striae as the burin is spalled and used. Secondary spalls with very oblique striae infer burin chisel use. Ignoring the small primary slotter sample, secondary spalls with parallel striae infer grooving. About one primary plane spall was found for every five secondary spalls, a suggestion perhaps that burin planes and slotters were considered depleted or useless after a half dozen sharpenings.

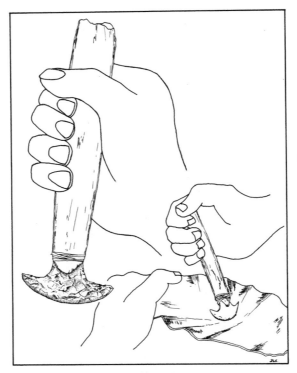

Figure 8.31. Hafted skin flexer KjNb-7:12-29 in use.

Type	Size mm (mean)	No.	Angle F^{1a} mean, range & deviation	No.	Angle F^{1b} mean, range & deviation
primary plane spall	21x4x3/0.22 g	24	87.33 (59-114) S.D. = 12.49		none in unifacial planes
secondary plane spall	19x5x2/0.21 g	106	90.33 (60-148) S.D. =1 4.63		none in unifacial planes
primary slotter spall	21x4x3/0.20 g	4	82.75 (70-95) S.D. = 11.70	2	100 (95-104) S.D. = 6.36
secondary slotter spall	19x5x2/0.20 g	40	89.18 (60-130) S.D. = 12.86	15	90.07 (60-120) S.D. = 15.01

Table 8.117. Primary and secondary spalls in striated plane and slotter burins.

Of 251 striated tools, 66 surface ones have heavy striae, 34 have light striae, 107 buried ones have heavy striae, and 44 have light striae. More buried tools have striae because they are protected from wind-blown sand and weather. Most burins have striae over their face (69 of 84), but 15 have striae in certain areas suggesting light or special use. That more slotters than burin planes have cross-striae (20 of 79, versus 18 of 153; including spalls), implies some degree of tilting while grooving. Slotters and their spalls conform, as do planes and their spalls. Planes have wider use; slotters are mainly perpendicular groovers.

Conclusions Regarding Site Distribution and Artifacts

Unlike southern Indian traditions, many widespread tundra tools reflect Pre-Dorset origin and adaptation, but contemporary forest tools infer a rapid adjustment to herd following that began from the north rather than south (Table 8.118). Like other traditions, the choice of tool material in the forest was greater, while tundra stone was mainly chert, due to source and long familiarity with it elsewhere in the north. Chert forest points, knives, scrapers and planes are smaller from resharpening because new chert was unavailable. The banded gray chert source may be in the Bathurst caribou range, as chert along Beverly and Kaminuriak rivers is multi-coloured and poor. Good chert is rare, highly valued and conserved for its superior knapping. In the forest, inferior chert, quartzite and silicious shale was substituted. Quartzite forest flakes, blades and cores are larger because they are less reducible than chert. Forest wedges may be larger because their use on soft wood rather than bone or antler entailed less smashing and retouch. Forest sideblades are larger perhaps because they were used as whittling knives. As large stone lanceheads and bone and antler arrowheads are absent, I suggest caribou were snared in winter using corrals described by Hearne (1958:49,50). In summer, they could have been harpooned in water or on land. Unlike Taltheilei, tundra tools are more worn and retouched because Pre-Dorset people lived more of the year on the tundra. They have less cortex because trimming and breakage risk were unimportant when chert was plentiful. Like Taltheilei, breakage was higher from striking surface rock. Haft, 3-4-sided plan, serration, grinding, striae, wear and spurring differ and may relate to cold, versus warm weather handling, cutting and scraping. Similar point and scraper distributions suggest hides were scraped right after caribou were killed. More ulu-like scraper wear implies summer skin-softening. More forest cortex implies less forest tool preparation. The midsection of tundra hammerstones have areas of deep pocking from anvil use in reducing or sharpening tools. More than 15 kg of mainly tiny chert flakes from KjNb-3, 5, 6 and 7 infer intensive knapping at late summer tundra water-crossings.

Trait	Forest range	Tundra range	Remarks
spread	concentrated; e.g, Lake Athabasca	very widespread	Pre-Dorset tundra origin
dating	2745 to 3550 years B.P.	2785 to 3280 years B.P.	fast herd-following adjustment
points	7 Quartzite. End-thinned. Smaller	136 Chert. Burinated. Bigger	more forest retouch. Local stone
sideblade	6 Quartzite. Less semilunar. Bigger	188 Chert. More semilunar. Smaller	bone/antler insets would be small
scrapers	34 More 3-sided, tortoise-backed and ground bases. More cortex. Smaller	541 More 4-sided, tabular & serrated. More striae. Bigger due to thinning flakes	more forest retouch but seasonally different applications
knives	28 More semilunar or triangular unfaces More cortex, alternate ret. & tips. Smaller	504 More lanceolate bifaces, transverse breaks, wear and ground tapered bases. Bigger	more forest retouch, versus more tundra wear and breaks
wedges	3 More flat columnar scars. Variable plan. Bigger. Used on soft wood?	29 Rectangular, round and ovoid. Smaller. Used on hard antler and bone	seasonally different use and hardness of material
cores	8 Quartzite. More conical. Larger	91 Chert. More blocky and bladelike	quartzite, versus chert reduction
flakes	9 Bigger	612 Smaller	quartzite, versus chert reduction
micro-blades	10 Bigger	256 Smaller	quartzite, versus chert reduction
hammer-stones	3 Ovoid and bipolarly pocked. Smaller	4 Round and used as anvils. Bigger	more forest tool reduction
planes	smaller	larger	more forest tool reduction

Table 8.118. Comparing Pre-Dorset forest and tundra tools.
(unlisted data similar in both ranges. Number of tools listed at left of data. Chithos are found only in tundra sites. No whetstones are reported)

Chapter 9

The Shield Archaic Tradition

Dating and Distribution

The Shield Archaic tradition occupied the northern boreal forest and tundra during the "Climatic Optimum" or Hypsithermal, beginning about 6,500 years ago. Indian sites are as widespread in this warm period as Pre-Dorset sites would be in the following colder period. Shield Archaic tundra sites are divided into Early, Middle and Late phases using point change, and eleven dates as a criterion for the evolution of the tradition (Table 9.1) The 5,450 to 6,450 B.P. Early phase is associated only with a small notched point from KjNb-7 at Warden's Grove. The 4,450 to 5,450 B.P. Middle phase has eight dates, five from KkLn-4 (Migod) at Grant Lake, and three from Warden's Grove sites. The 3,500 to 4,450 B.P. Late phase is dated from as far north as Aberdeen and Grant Lakes, as far south as Whitefish Lake, and southeast into Manitoba. A 4,040 B.P. (S-1435) date from level 5 at Whitefish Lake, is associated with a Plains Archaic McKean-Duncan point (Fig. 9.2 bottom).

Several tundra sites are at Hornby-Lookout Points, Ursus Island-Thelon Bluffs, and Grant and Beverly-Aberdeen Lakes. Forested sites cluster the way they would when tundra-covered during Pre-Dorset; e.g.s, Warden's Grove, Eyeberry Lake and Grassy Island on the Thelon River (Fig. 9.1). Remote forest sites are at Thanakoie Narrows, Artillery Lake, and Boyd Lake on the upper Dubawnt River, and Black and Athabasca Lakes and Pipestone River in Saskatchewan.

Post-glacial temperatures rose 2 degrees C or more in summer, fall and winter (Foley et al. 1994). As forest extended farther north due to higher temperature and precipitation, it itself caused a temperature rise of 4 degrees C in spring and about 1 degree C in other seasons. *Sphagnum* peaks along with spruce and other pollens indicate the mean July temperature was 4 degrees C higher than present. Pollen suggests tree growth 120 km northwest of Grant Lake 5,000 to 6,000 years ago (Terasmae and Craig 1958). Treeline advance from Ennadai to Dubawnt Lakes (Nichols 1967a) is verified by 5,000 year-old spruce micro-fossils in upper Thelon River sites (Mott, pers. comm., 1975). The treeline in Fig. 9.1 is based on Nichols' (1976) "Arctic frontal mean position and forest-tundra boundary at the time of maximum Holocene summer warmth". This in turn is based on research by Rowe (1972), Larsen (1974), Nichols (1976 and others. Nichols' Holocene treeline applies to both Shield Archaic and Plano traditions, but summers were warmest 4,800-5,200 years ago in the Middle phase, and 3,800-4,000 years ago in the Late phase (Nichols 1967a, 1967b). These were periods when Shield Archaic people fully occupied the range, and when higher rainfall was balanced by evaporation. This resulted in constant river levels, a constancy similar to that of today, as seen in Migod's three Shield Archaic strata. They are less than a meter above the present level of the Dubawnt River and would have been washed out if river levels were higher (Gordon 1976).

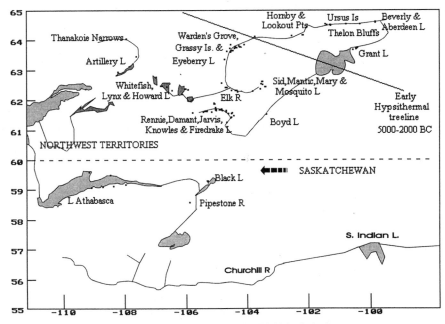

Figure 9.1. Distribution of 121 Shield Archaic sites.

   All Beverly people hunted caribou during its late summer and early autumn migration, but Shield Archaic people exploited the northerly expanding forest by pushing their hunting and habitation into areas that would become tundra in Pre-Dorset (Fig. 8.1). They were able to hunt at open river-crossings in spring because higher temperatures brought earlier ice break-up. Indeed, an examination of caribou teeth increments from a jaw associated with the oldest Shield Archaic radiocarbon date (Table 9.1) reveal a May kill (Gordon 1985). Likewise, a later freeze-up not only extended hunting at water crossings, but shortened winter. Later cultures, and especially Pre-Dorset, had to master short summers and long range tundra hunting to approach the caribou calving ground.

West N.W.T.	BEVERLY TUNDRA	BEVERLY FOREST	East N.W.T.
		6120±110B.P. (S-1258) KjNb-7 at Warden's Grove (spring hunting on tooth increments)	(all from Manitoba)

Early Phase at 5,450 to 6,450 years ago

none due to limited and sporadic seasonal hunting excursions from the east	4770±170B.P. (S-979) in level 4a of KkLn-4 at Grant Lake, Dubawnt River	4515±140B.P. (I-5976) in KjNb-6 at Warden's Grove, Thelon River	
	4770±170B.P. (S-980) in level 4a of KkLn-4	5010±235B.P. (S-735) KjNb-7 at Warden's Grove, Thelon River	
	4950±85B.P. (S-1005) in level 4b of KkLn-4	5060±310B.P. (S-710) in KjNb-7 at Warden's Grove, Thelon River	
	5070±75B.P. (S-981) in level 4b of KkLn-4		
	5485±95B.P. (S-1026) in level 4c of KkLn-4		

Middle Phase 4,450 to 5,450 years ago

	3025±95B.P. (S-506) in LdLl-2 at Aberdeen Lake, lower Thelon River #	2935±205B.P. (S-1434) in level 5 of KeNi-5 at Whitefish Lake, Thelon River	2760±240 B.P. (Gak-1860) at Elk Island in God's Lake@
	3680±155B.P. (S-982) in level 4 of KkLn-4 at Grant Lake	3620±125B.P. (S-1261) in testpit bottom of KeNi-4 at Whitefish Lake	2830±210 B.P. (Gak-1861), Elk Island@
		4040±125B.P. (S-1435) in level 5 of KeNi-4 at Grant Lake (Plains Archaic McKean-Duncan point)	3170±70 B.P. (S-780) in the Kame Hills site on South Indian Lake^
			3340±65 B.P. (S-967), Kame Hills site^

Late Phase 3,500 to 4,450 years ago in N.W.T.; later in Manitoba.

Table 9.1. Barrenland Shield Archaic radiocarbon dates.
probable error. Wright 1972a:78-9 originally attributed this date to Late Shield Archaic, but additional research since his publication suggest it is Pre-Dorset. @ Wright 1972b:31. ^ Dickson 1980. Blakeslee (1994:205) cautions against the use of Gakushuin dates for constructing archaeological chronologies. The two Kaminuriak dates fit the regional chronology, but their large standard deviations limit their usefulness.

Analysis of Shield Archaic Material Culture

Analysis of projectile points

Wright (1976:91-3) infers that Shield Archaic evolved from Northern Plano on the basis of a change from long lanceolate to side-notched points, similar types and ratios of burinated points, and unifacial knife ratios. But his Grant, Aberdeen and Schultz Lake sites where Plano points occur, do not have Early Shield Archaic components, according to my data. Warden's Grove site KjNb-7 does, but its 6,120 year-old stratified point is short, crude and side-notched, instead of refined and lanceolate (Gordon 1985). One might think that the earliest Shield Archaic points would retain Plano length and fineness, and shorten with time as Wright suggests, but the opposite occurs. Hindsight and radiocarbon dates show his long notched points are really Middle and Late phases. Excusing the pun, Wright may be right, as it is safer to accept rapid point change, than add a new culture to an area as vast and rugged as the Barrenlands. Buried dated tools are also reviewed in Gordon (1976).

Points (117), instrumental in assigning 35 sites to Shield Archaic, are distributed like that of Shield Archaic sites generally (Fig. 9.3). While almost all are quartzite, they are distinct from those in other traditions in being side-notched lanceheads with ground, rocker bases. However, some very small points may resemble arrowheads (JiNc-1:6 and LdLl-2:114 in Fig. 9.2).

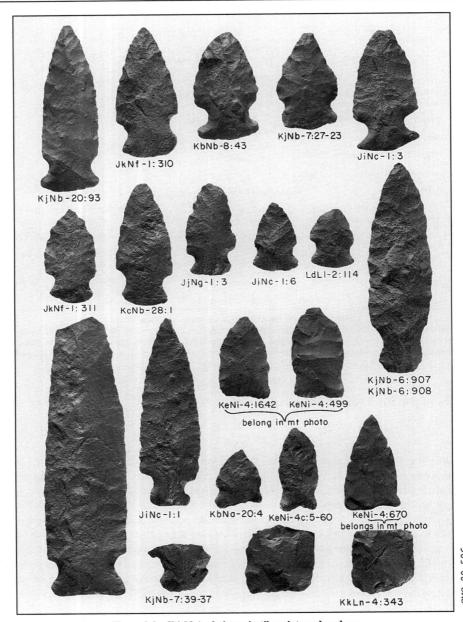

KjNb-20:93

JkNf-1: 310

KbNb-8:43

KjNb-7:27-23

JiNc-1: 3

JkNf-1: 311

KcNb-28: 1

JjNg-1: 3

JiNc-1: 6

LdL1-2:114

KjNb-6:907
KjNb-6:908

KeNi-4:1642   KeNi-4:499
belong in mt photo

JiNc-1:1

KbNa-20:4   KeNi-4c:5-60

KeNi-4:670
belongs in mt photo

KjNb-7:39-37

KkLn-4:343

CMC 80-586

Figure 9.2. Shield Archaic projectile points and wedges.

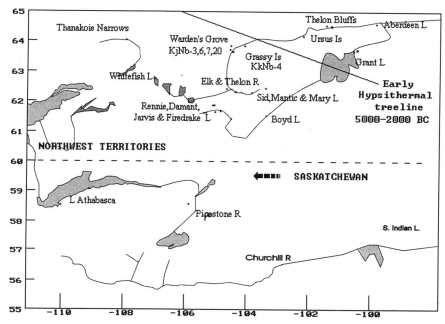

Figure 9.3. Distribution of 36 Shield Archaic sites with 117 points.

        About 80% of all points are medium length and notched or spadelike, and two-thirds are eared
(Fig. 9.2 top half). Most are biconvex, with some planoconvex points in tundra sites. Most have
pointed tips, but forest point tips may also be rounded (JjNg-1:3 center). Some are short, like KjNb-
7:39-37, the 6,120 year-old side-notched point mentioned earlier (bottom), while a few have flat bases
like JiNc-1:1 (just above). Large lancehead KkLn-4:147-4 may also be a knife (bottom left). One forest
point (not illustrated) has stepwise spalling on the edge and face, and is transitional from Northern
Plano, based on its intentional burination (Wright 1976). Tundra breakage is higher from hitting
exposed or submerged rock after being thrown or thrust. Notching, basal edges and shortness show
more complex forest preparation on a winter haft than those of ancestral Northern Plano, which have
more rangewide homogeneity. About half of tundra points are white from plentiful quartzite at
Aberdeen and Grant Lakes. A few are red from Aberdeen Lake cobbles. A forest point is also a bifacial
scraper, and one forest and one tundra point are chisels (Tables 9.2-9.14d). Several surface Hanna and
Oxbow points (KbNa-20:4 bottom center) in the southwest range, and the Mckean-Duncan point in the
Shield Archaic level at Whitefish Lake, suggest contact with Plains Archaic hunters (Table 9.1 & Fig.
9.2 KeNi-4C:5-60 bottom center).

KkLn-4:240

KjNb-7:24-12

KjNb-6:39-3

KeNi-4:1460

KkLn-4:278

KkLn-4:239

KjNb-7:24-13

KeNi-4:721

KjNb-7:39-29
KjNb-7:39-30

KjNb-7:42:9

KjNb-7:39-39

Figure 9.4. Shield Archaic 'bent' knives and scrapers.

Difference	Forest range	Tundra range	Remarks
distribution	highly dispersed in expanded forest*	confined to migration routes*	primarily forest-adapted people
stone and colour	beige quartzite	white quartzite	locally available material
section	almost all are biconvex*	some are planoconvex*	more forest retouch
ground base	fewer	more	to protect split wooden shaft on tundra
ground notch	more	fewer	to protect sinew on forest shafts
broken or burinated	less*	more*	hitting exposed rock on tundra
multiple use	1/10 are burins, scraper and chisel	1/5 are burins and a chisel	for slotting and shaping bone and antler
size	shorter^	longer^	more forest resharpening

Table 9.14d. Comparing Shield Archaic forest and tundra points *like or ^unlike Northern Plano.

Analysis of scrapers

Four typical scrapers are in Fig. 9.4. KkLn-4:239 is stemmed, asymmetric, tearshaped and tortoise-backed. Above are KjNb-6:39-3, an ovoid tanged tortoise-back with a spokeshave side and a large platform; KjNb-7:24-12, a tanged, flat tearshape with a bifacially ground socketted base and bashed platform; and KkLn-4:240, a worn and striated tortoise-backed ovoid. Many tundra scrapers cluster at Aberdeen and Grant Lakes, with a few at Lookout Point (Fig. 9.5). Forest clusters resemble those of points, with findspots on the upper Thelon, Caribou Narrows, and Black and Athabasca Lakes.

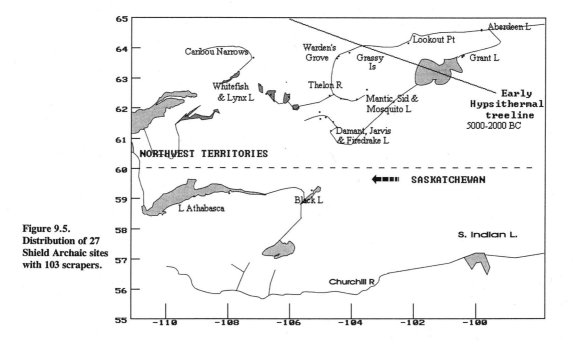

Figure 9.5. Distribution of 27 Shield Archaic sites with 103 scrapers.

More tundra scrapers are 3-sided and flat, with less cortex for socketting. Forest scrapers are round or ulu-like in plan, keeled or planoconvex in section, and serrated for hand-hafting on frozen hides. More tundra scrapers have worn bits and ground dorsally retouched bases from working bone or antler, but a fourth of forest bits are very worn. A tenth of all bits have striae. A seventh of all scrapers are made from biface thinning flakes. Common forest spurs suggest winter engraving. Unlike most tools, forest scrapers are larger (Tables 9.15a-9.26c).

Difference	Forest scrapers	Tundra scrapers	Remarks
distribution	widespread*	confined to migration routes*	more forest sites; treeline farthest north*
stone and colour	some gray chert and quartz	beige quartzite	locally available material
plan and section	more 4-sided, but less tabular*	more 3-sided and tabular*	hand vs. tundra sockets, like other traditions
serration and cortex	more*	less*	for scraping frozen hides, like other traditions
basal retouch/wear	less*	more*	heavy scraper socket wear, like other traditions
ground base	less	more	heavy scraper socket wear, like other traditions
single spur	more^	less^	more engraving in winter forest^
size	bigger^	smaller^	opposite most tools of all traditions^

Table 9.26c. Comparing Shield Archaic forest and tundra scrapers *like and ^unlike Northern Plano.

Analysis of knives

Most knives are linear (KjNb-6a:16-10, KjNb-3:4-49, KkNb-3:40 and 4-48/50; Fig. 9.6 top) or ovoid (KjNb-6:5-4 and KjNb-7:35-14 bottom), but a few are uniquely sinuous and thick (KjNb-7:29/30 and 39-39; Fig. 9.4 bottom). KjNb-7:42-9 (bottom center) is a planoconvex, ribbon-flaked uniface with unground base; others are KkLn-4:278 and KjNb-7:24-13 (center). Of 364 knives in 88 sites (234 F; 130 T; 114 buried), distribution resembles that of points except for isolated forest finds at Artillery, Lynx-Howard, Mosquito and Black Lakes, and isolated tundra finds at Hornby-Lookout Points, Ursus Island, Thelon Bluffs and Beverly Lake (Fig. 9.7).

Knives are beige or white quartzite, except for some of chert, quartz and shale in forest sites, and a red quartzite knife from the Aberdeen Lake tundra cobbles. Unifaces are slightly more common in tundra sites and may relate to quick manufacture, use and discard by herd followers. More tundra knives are broken, most being bases and midsection-bases. This suggests a return to camp of the hafted base for knife replacement. Plans are alike in both ranges. Basally thinned, sinuous, uni-shouldered or triangular knives of planoconvex and tortoise-backed section are only in forest sites. Keeled and bi-shouldered knives are on tundra sites. Unlike Taltheilei, more tundra knives are serrated with square tips, but some might be odd unretouched blanks. One forest knife is retouched alternately. Lengthwise breaks are more common in forest knives; semi-transverse breaks on tundra ones. Striated scrapers with hand-hafted square bases or side-notches with missing platforms are in forest sites, but unraised lateral platforms are in three forest knives. Unlike Taltheiei, forest knives are larger than tundra ones (Tables 9.27a-9.41c).

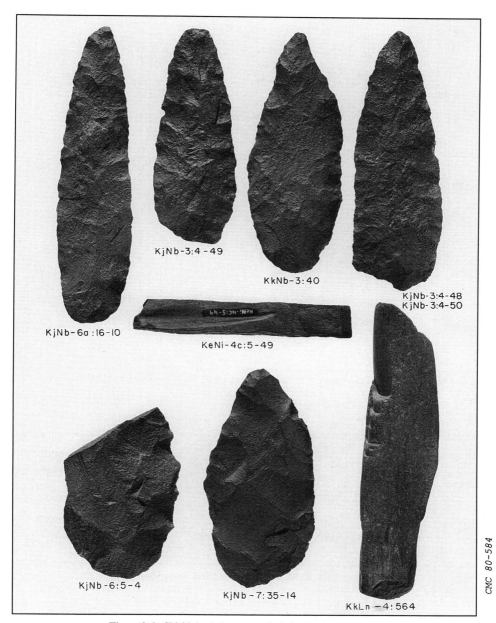

KjNb-3:4-49

KkNb-3:40

KjNb-3:4-48
KjNb-3:4-50

KjNb-6a:16-10

KeNi-4c:5-49

KjNb-6:5-4

KjNb-7:35-14

KkLn-4:564

CMC 80-584

Figure 9.6. Shield Archaic symmetric knives and whetstones.

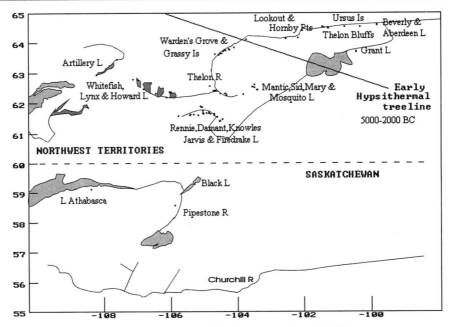

Figure 9.7. Distribution of 88 Shield Archaic sites with 364 knives.

Trait	Forest knives	Tundra knives	Remarks
stone and colour	more variable than tundra	quartzite; some are red	local stone, including Aberdeen Lake red cobbles
faciality	mostly bifacial	12% are unifacial*	quick tundra manufacture, use and discard
complete	more. More tips	less. More bases	base returned to tundra camp, like other traditions
plan and section	more 3-sided and planoconvex	more bishouldered and notched	different seasonal hafts, but unlike other traditions
wear and serration	less	more	more tundra serration, unlike other traditions
retouched base and midsection	more	less	more forest preparation, like other traditions
cortex	more	less	lowers forest breakage risk, like other traditions
ground base	more	less	opposite to Taltheilei knife bases
platform	more retouched and on side	more ground and on base	seasonally differing preparation
size	bigger	smaller	opposite Taltheilei and other tools

Table 9.41c. Comparing Shield Archaic forest and tundra knives.
*Wright (1976:91-3) claims Shield Archaic knife unifaciality is a continuous trait from its Northern
Plano predecessor, with a uniface knife frequency of 18% (Table 10.28).

Analysis of chithos

Chitho confinement to five in Whitefish-Lynx Lake sites KcNf-3 and KeNi-4, and three in Warden's Grove sites KjNb-6 and 7, and their absence at normally rich Firedrake Lake may be due to a better selection of prime autumn hides in a more northerly part of the range due to climatic warming. Thus, I could compare only forest ones to see if 250 km of separation affect their size and material. Most chithos are sandstone bifaces, with rising unifaciality and decreasing size to the south. Most are complete worn ovoids having uneven faces with cortex. Southern chithos are more unifacial and worn (Tables 9.42a-9.46b).

Analysis of wedges

Of 20 wedges in 9 scattered sites, two were in a Grant Lake tundra site, and 18 in widespread forest sites at Whitefish-Lynx, Jarvis-Firedrake, Mantic, Athabasca and Black Lakes (Fig. 9.8). While most are biconvex, white quartzite rectangles, their flatter unipolarly created flake scars and larger forest size suggest their use on soft wood with an antler hammer (Tables 9.47a-9.51d). An identical situation exists in Northern Plano.

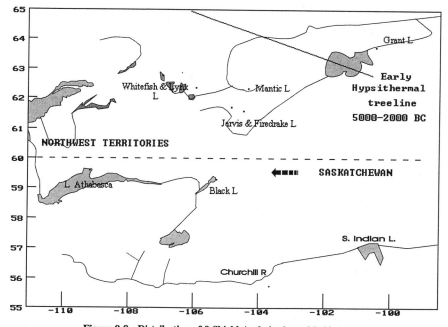

Figure 9.8. Distribution of 9 Shield Archaic sites with 20 wedges.

Difference	Forest wedges	Tundra wedges	Remarks
distribution	greater*	less*	like Early Taltheilei wedges. Very expanded forest in Shield Archaic
stone & colour	some white quartz*	both are quartzite*	locally available material
plan & section	both mixed^	3-4-sided/biconvex^	more flexible choice of types of wedges for woodworking
flake scars	fewer flat columnar	more flat columnar	like other traditions. Soft forest wood, versus hard tundra antler or bone
percussion	half are unipolar*	all are bipolar	unipolar marks by hammer; bipolar from wedge between antler & hammer
size	bigger*	smaller*	like other traditions. Soft forest wood, versus hard tundra antler or bone*

Table 9.51d. Comparing Shield Archaic forest and tundra wedges *like or ^unlike Northern Plano.

Analysis of adzelike artifacts

One tundra and all forest chisels are alike in shape, grinding and bit angle (45 degrees), with an absent grooved platform. White quartz forest chisel JlNg-6:1 is 39.1x27.5x10mm & 11.3g, and gray chert tundra chisel LdLq-2:7 is 49.7x23x8mm & 10g. Beige-gray chert forest flake KeNi-4C:5-11 is 21.3x16.9x6.9mm & 1.15g, its deeply ground, tranversely striated curved face showing it came from the ventral side of an adze bit. Highly keeled and polished, black basalt tundra adze flake KkLn-4:25-4a came from the side of an adze and is 27.7x28.5x2 mm & 1.7g.

Analysis of cores

Curved platform KkLn-4 tundra cores (8) vary less than KeNi-4 and KjNb-7 forest ones (21) in material and plan, and are smaller with less cortex and bipolar battering. Almost all are reduced from quartzite river cobbles and retain their roundness, but some tundra cores become cones with curved platforms, while forest ones become blocky with straight platforms. While few cores are blade-scarred, a fifth each of forest cores are wedges or choppers, and a tundra core is a wedge. More forest than tundra cores are serrated, suggesting use as frozen hide scrapers (Tables 9.52a-9.65c).

Difference	Forest	Tundra	Remarks
stone and colour	gray quartzite and basalt	white quartzite	locally available material. More forest selection
plan, section & profile	round, then blocky	round, then conical	tundra reduction via a round cone platform, like other traditions
platform and battering	straight and unipolar	curved and bipolar	bashed top & bottom of tundra cone; top only in forest block
wear/serration/cortex	more	less	more forest use on frozen hide and lower breakage risk
wedge use	more, plus 4 choppers	less	more forest uses as other tools; i.e., tool conservation
size and depletion	larger and less	smaller and more	unlike Taltheilei cores. Only one Northern Plano core occurs

Table 9.65c. Comparing Shield Archaic forest and tundra cores.

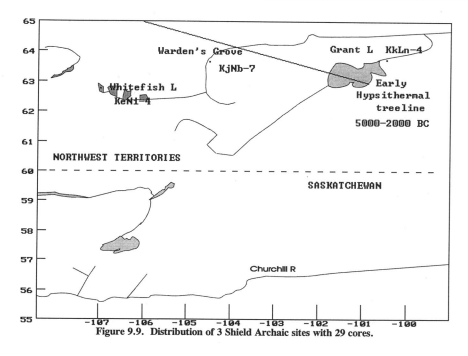

Figure 9.9. Distribution of 3 Shield Archaic sites with 29 cores.

Analysis of flakes

As surface flakes are unassignable to culture (1241 F; 2846 T in KeNi-4, KjNb-7 and KkLn-4), 126 stratified entries are compared. They are a biface sharpening flake, 73 unretouched flakes, 37 flake tools, three blades, 11 split or worked pebbles, and one entry of 49 KjNb-6 & 7 level 3 & 5 flake bags. The bags (39.7 kg), range from 250 mg to 10 kg (mean= 810 g). As expected, worked and regular flake distribution resembles that of cores, as do larger size and choice of material in the forest (Fig. 9.10). Four forest knives and a sidescraper were made from biface thinning flakes. Eleven gray quartzite pebbles associated with cores (9 split), flakes and wedges from KeNi-4C level 4, have a mean size of 32.8x23.3x15.6mm & 13.3g. Three blades from KjNb-7 level 5 are beige or purple quartzite: #39-3 is 64.1x20x6.2mm & 8.5g; #39-6 is 36.4x 22.6x7mm & 6g; and #39-14 is -31.6x-28.3x4.8mm & -4.0 g (- indicates incompleteness; Tables 9.66a-9.70).

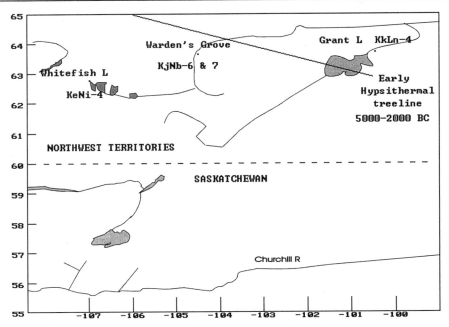

Figure 9.10. Distribution of 4 Shield Archaic sites with 126 flake class entries.

Difference	Forest range	Tundra range	Remarks
stone and colour	varied	white quartzite	locally available material
blades	none	all from KjNb-7	no blade tradition, but bladelike in KjNb-7 conical cores
biface sharpening flakes	all	none	from forest biface knife and scraper manufacture and sharpening
unretouched flakes	46x35x11mm & 23g	37x31x7mm & 9g	larger forest blocky cores, versus smaller tundra conical cores*
retouched flakes	53x39x13mm & 33g	39x36x9mm & 16g	larger forest blocky cores, versus smaller tundra conical cores*
pebbles	33x23x16mm & 13g	none	forest pebble use
unanalyzed	1241; mostly in KeNi-4	2846; all in KkLn-4	more reduction in tundra conical cores
flake bags	39 kg in 49 bags	none	heavier flakes from forest blocky cores

Table 9.70. Comparing Shield Archaic forest and tundra flakes and pebbles *Northern Plano retouched flakes are also larger.

Analysis of hammerstones

One hammerstone was in tundra site KkLn-4 at Grant Lake, and four were in three forest sites (Whitefish and Mantic Lakes KeNi-4 and KbNb-8, and Warden's Grove KjNb-7; Fig. 9.11). Most are white quartzite, and KbNb-8:123 is a surface find. Forest hammerstones are smaller, with oval plan and 4-sided ends. The tundra hammerstone is tearshaped (Tables 9.71-9.75c).

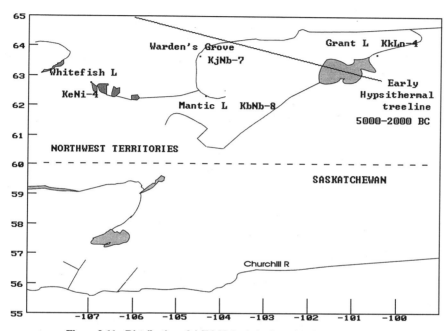

Figure 9.11. Distribution of 4 Shield Archaic sites with 5 hammerstones.

Difference	Forest	Tundra	Remarks
distribution	dispersed	one site only	much greater forest expansion due to post-glacial warmth
stone and colour	white quartzite	gray quartzite	locally available material
plan and section	ovoid, with 4-sided end	both are 3-sided	like all Taltheilei phases and Pre-Dorset
size and pocking	smaller; one anvil	larger; unipolar^	forest use as flaking anvils, like all Taltheilei phases^

Table 9.75c. Comparing Shield Archaic forest and tundra hammerstones ^but unlike Northern Plano with many anvils.

Analysis of whetstones

Gray slate whetstone KeNi-4C:5-49 (Fig. 9.6 center) has a wide shallow, edge-grinding groove opposite a flat ground face. Like hammerstones, whetstones are at Grant Lake (e.g., buried KkLn-4:564 in Fig. 9.6 right) and dispersed forest sites IdNh-2, KeNi-4 & JkNf-5 at Black, Whitefish and Jarvis Lakes (Fig. 9.12). Whetstone JkNf-5:105 is with general ground tools in Fig. 6.14 bottom center).

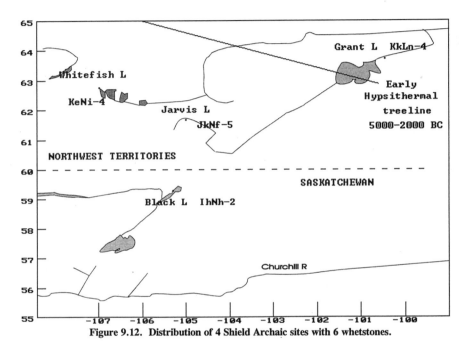

Figure 9.12. Distribution of 4 Shield Archaic sites with 6 whetstones.

Most forest whetstones are gray barlike slate; a tundra one is schist. One of each was suspended, but are now broken at their notches. All are worn and polished on their edges and faces, with three forest and a tundra whetstone striated lengthwise. A fifth each of forest whetstones have grinding groove striae, edge abrasion or both. The tundra whetstone has only edge abrasion. The tundra one is much bigger than the mean forest size of 65x20x9mm & 15g (Tables 9.76a-9.79c).

Trait	Forest range	Tundra range	Remarks
stone and colour	varied	gray schist	locally available material
multiple use tool*	as groovers	as edge abrader	seasonally differing uses
size and notches	65x20x9mmx16g. Notched	one only (larger)* Notched	suspension notches used throughout the year

Table 9.79c. Comparing Shield Archaic forest and tundra whetstones *like Northern Plano, but not as groovers.

Analysis of pushplanes

All three pushplanes for planing wood, bone or antler are quartzite, tearshaped, serrated, haft-thinned, unstriated and at forest sites at Athabasca and Lynx Lakes and Warden's Grove. IgOe-6:25 (Lake Athabasca) is 75x43.8x21.5mm & 60.7g, round-backed, abruptly retouched on sides and ends, retouched on the ventral bit, and thinned on the dorsal haft. KcNi-1 at Lynx Lake is 87.1x51.8x23mm & 92.8 g, round-backed, gently retouched on sides and ends, fully ventrally retouched, and thinned on sides and faces. KjNb-7:56-1, the buried pushplane from Warden's Grove used to assign surface ones, is 99.7x55.6x28.5mm & 128g, keeled and gently retouched on sides and ends with full ventral retouch.

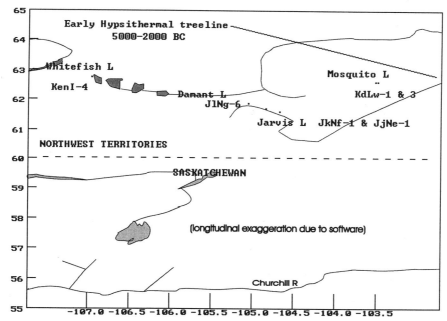

Figure 9.13. Distribution of 6 Shield Archaic sites with 7 skin flexers.

Analysis of skin flexers

Six skin flexers, all quartzite except one of quartz, are from Jarvis, Damant, Whitefish and Mosquito Lake forest sites (Fig. 9.13). Five are made from long thick Shield Archaic knives (one striated), and one is from a side-notched point. Mean size is 54.5x28.2x12.2mm & 23.2g (Table 9.80).

Wood and bone analysis

The only wood is Whitefish Lake fragment KeNi-4C:5-52 (1.5g). The bone category is limited to Whitefish and Grant Lakes and Warden's Grove (Fig. 9.14). Forest bone includes 142 bone pieces (65.6g). Some are calcined, others are crushed for grease extraction, and a left caribou mandible was sectioned for assessing spring season of death. Two only tundra bone fragments weigh 0.3g.

Conclusions on Shield Archaic artifacts

A more widespread forest than that in later traditions results in imbalanced tool comparison, but certain generalizations follow. Forest points, sandstone chithos, wedges, hammerstones and slate whetstones are smaller. Forest scrapers, knives and flakes are larger because their readily available quartzite at Warden's Grove renders a ready castoff of half-used tools and blanks. Like other traditions, more types of forest tools are 4-sided for winter hand gripping; more summer tundra tools are 3-sided for bone or antler socketting. Forest tools also have a greater range of materials like other phases.

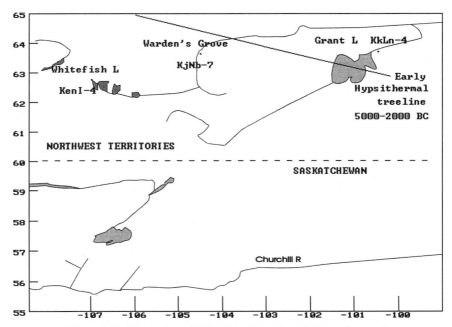

Figure 9.14. Distribution of 3 Shield Archaic sites with 9 bone fragments.

A number of traits in Shield Archaic follow trends seen in Northern Plano. Forest scrapers are more spurred for engraving, and serrated for scraping frozen hide. Tundra knives are more unifacial, and forest wedges are larger, presumably due to less need for sharpening (soft forest wood versus hard tundra antler. Unlike Northern Plano, forest chithos are more unifacial. Shield Archaic hammerstones are 4-sided in the forest and 3-sided on the tundra, while rangewide Northern Plano ones are ovoid.

Trait	Forest range	Tundra range	Remarks
distribution	numerous and very widespread*	few and close to calving grounds*	post-glacial treeline farther north*
dating	4,000 to 3,200 B.P.	6,450 to 3,500 B.P.	earlier tundra Northern Plano origins
points	52 Most quartzite. Beige. Shorter@ Notching. At many small crossings	65 All quartzite. White. Longer@^. At few large crossings*. More broken*	local stone. More forest ret./notching Seasonally different haft/hunting unit
scrapers	103 4-sided*. Spurs^. Serrated* and unground. Larger^	63 3-sided and flat.* More worn bits and ground bases.* Smaller^	winter hand-haft, versus tundra socket More tundra use*. Forest engraving*
knives	364 Bifacial. More grinding/cortex and 3-sided. Larger*. Fewer bases	234 Some unifacial*/notched/shouldered More serrated and unground. Smaller*.	seasonal haft. More forest use. More tundra prep'n./breakage/replacement
chithos	3 Smaller* and more unifacial^	5 Larger* and more bifacial^	more use and retouch from forest hides
wedges	20 Larger*. Half are unipolar	18 Smaller*. Bipolar. More columnar	soft forest wood, vs. hard tundra antler
adze category	chisel and ventral adze bit flake	similar chisel, but lateral adze flake	heavy wood-working in both areas
cores	29 Gray. Reduction to blocks	21 White. Reduction to cones	block core/flakes,vs. conical core/flakes
flake category	Larger*.Beige.Few from sharpening	Smaller*. White	seasonally different reduction
hammerstones	5 Smaller*. More 4-sided^	4 Larger*. More 3-sided^	like other phases. Forest flaking anvils
whetstones	5 Varied stone. Smaller*	1 Schist. Larger*	available rock. Notching in both ranges
pushplane	gently retouched on ends and sides	abruptly retouched on ends and sides	forest wood, vs. tundra antler working
skin flexers	mean=55x28x12mm/23g	none	more use on southern autumn hides

Table 9.81. Comparing Shield Archaic forest and tundra tools
*like or ^unlike Northern Plano. @ too many Northern Plano tundra points are burinated for accurate rangewide comparison of length.

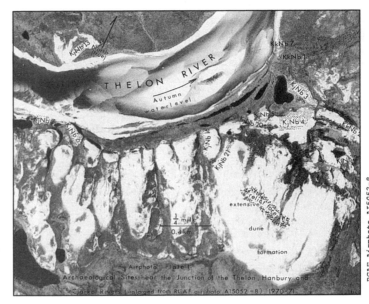

Figure 9.15.
Shield Archaic sites at Warden's Grove were forested. Later, cold Pre-Dorset climate left relict stumps and roots (bottom left).

Figure 9.16.
Shield Archaic site KjNb-13 was found near the relict forest depicted in Fig. 9.15.

Chapter 10

The Northern Plano Tradition

Dating and Distribution

The oldest Beverly archaeological tradition is Northern Plano, identified mainly from Agate Basin points. In their Wyoming type site they are 9-10,000 years old; midway in the Prairie provinces, they are 8-9,000 years, and in the Barrenlands only 7-8,000.[7] A thin distribution of bison hunting camps extends northeast from Wyoming to northern Saskatchewan. At Athabasca and Black Lakes, the prey changed to caribou, with some overlap of both animal ranges in the Beverly forest.

Newly growing lichen, grass and trees gradually followed the glaciers receding northeast of the range. Two arboreal pollen dates near Cree Lake of 8,640±240 and 8,770±250 years ago (GSC-1446 and 1466; Mott 1971) are not even from the bottom of their cores and indicate deglaciation was earlier. Farther north, pollen profiles and a 8,000 year old Northern Plano date from KkLn-4 at Grant Lake infer nearby trees (Wright 1976:82-84; Gordon 1976:39-43). Precipitation and runoff were also similar to that of today because Plano levels at KkLn-2 and 4 are only a meter above the Dubawnt River. The dates and water level indicate Glacial Lakes Dubawnt and Thelon drained earlier, probably about 9,500 years ago. This allowed 1,000-2,000 years for lichen to cover the range sufficiently to provide caribou forage, plus several centuries for humans to adapt to caribou herd following.

If Northern Plano evolved to Shield Archaic, as Wright (1972b:85-86) suggests, Northern Plano sites should be fewer and concentrated, which is the case. Northern Plano alone is on the Taltson River, but it and Shield Archaic are on Lake Athabasca and the Thelon River where most (35) sites occur. Despite a poorly surveyed Dubawnt River, the heavy concentration of Grant Lake material suggests the Dubawnt and Thelon Rivers were major Plano caribou migration corridors (Fig.10.1).

Northern Plano has four radiocarbon dates, the oldest at 7,930±500 years (S-834) in KkLn-4 at Grant Lake (Wright 1976, Gordon 1976; Table 10.1). A km away at KkLn-2, dates are 7,220±850 (S-1056) and 5,545±120 years (S-813), the latter on shallow subsurface bone contaminated by humic acid. A date of 6,720±140 years (S-2191) in the deepest level of KdLw-1 at Mosquito Lake was associated with only quartzite chips, but is likely Northern Plano.

---

[7]Agate Basin points at the type site, at Grant Lake and elsewhere in the Northwest Territories are compared in Wright (1976:74-81).

East N.W.T.	BEVERLY TUNDRA	BEVERLY FOREST	East N.W.T.
6850±150 B.P. (Gak-3277) and 6970±360 B.P. (I-3957) in LiPk-1 at Acasta (dates contemporaneous Kamut points Lake near Great Bear Lake. See Noble 1971)	7220±850 B.P. (S-1056) and 5545±120 B.P. (S-813; humic acid contaminated) from KkLn-2 on Grant Lake, Dubawnt River. 7930±500 B.P. (S-834) at KkLn-4 on Grant Lake (Wright 1976 and Gordon 1976)	6720±140 B.P. (S-2191) at KdLw-1 on Mosquito Lake, upper Dubawnt River (no culturally diagnostic tools. Quartzite flakes only in this level below the Pre-Dorset chert level)	no estimates

Table 10.1. Beverly 7,000-8,000 year old Northern Plano radiocarbon dates.

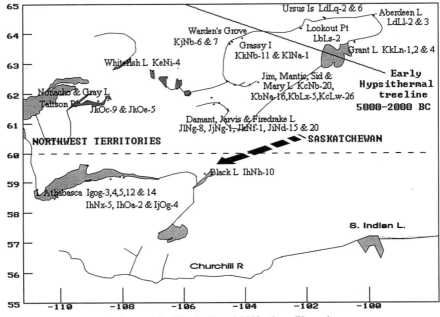

Figure 10.1. Distribution of 34 Northern Plano sites.

Analysis of Northern Plano Material Culture

Analysis of projectile points

Northern Plano points (Agate Basin lanceolates) are basally-tapered, biconvex quartzite lanceolates with ground, stemmed bases. They have shallow collateral flaking and their ground base is thinned by removing 3-4 tapering flakes in a triangular area that is too narrow and shallow to be called fluted or channelled. Lanceolates vary from long KkLn-2:277/301 and 114 (Fig. 10.4 upper left), medium, almost ovoid KkLn-2:51/101 (middle), to short KkLn-2:263 (left bottom). More ovoid KkLn-2:216 and 132 (bottom center) have fine collateral retouch.

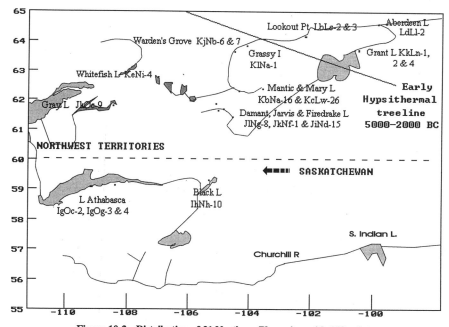

Figure 10.2. Distribution of 21 Northern Plano sites with 158 points.

Compared to later traditions, points, especially in tundra sites, have fewer tips due to conversion to burins and gravers, a trait rare in Southern Plano. They include KkLn-2:263 (Fig. 10.4 left bottom), a channel-flaked graver shortened to a pentagonal by double tip burination. Other doubly burinated gravers are KkLn-2:298 and KeNi-4:299 (Fig 10.4 center). Burins include KkLn-2:114 and KeNi-4:302 (top) with burinated sides, KjNb-6:776 and KeNi-4:596 (top) that are doubly-burinated so that little original shape remains, and collaterally retouched KjNb-7:169 with snapped tip and burinated side (bottom). Of 158 points (19F; 149 T), KkLn-2 at Grant Lake has all 135 buried points (Fig. 10.2).

Most points are quartzite, but a tenth each of forest and tundra points are chert or basalt. More tundra points are broken and two are also a knife and end scraper. One tundra point is dual-shouldered, two are eared. Compared with forest points, tundra ones are shorter, of similar width and thickness, but heavier. Shorter length in tundra sites has to do with their reduction into burins (Tables 10.2a-10.13c).

Difference	Forest points	Tundra points	Remarks
distribution	highly dispersed*	confined to migration route*	post-glacial treeline was furthest north*
stone and colour	some are gray chert	beige quartzite	locally available material
section and sides	biconvex and parallel*	mixed and tapered*	many tundra points heavily altered to burins
tapered base and edge	flatter	rounder	seasonally different hafting
breakage	mixed types*	heavy and transverse*	breakage from exposed tundra rock
burinated into gravers	less*	more*	ratio of tundra to forest burination is 3:1
thinned channelled base	more	less	more forest retouch and a different haft
size	longer and lighter^	shorter and heavier^	more tundra burination to other tools

Table 10.13c. Comparing Northern Plano forest and tundra points *like or ^unlike Shield Archaic.

Figure 10.3. Migod site KkLn-4 at Grant Lake.
This site has radiocarbon-dated levels for all Beverly
traditions and phases, including Northern Plano.

KjNb-6:776

KeNi-4:596

KeNi-4:302

KkLn-2:114

KkLn-2:277/301

KkLn-2:298

KeNi-4:299

JjNg-1:1

KkLn-2:51/101

KkLn-2:76

KkLn-2:216

JiNd-15:1

LbLs-2:24

KkLn-2:263

KjNb-7:169

KkLn-2:132

KeNi-4:259

CMC 80-569

Figure 10.4. Northern Plano projectile points.
Including single (left) and double burinated points (right).

KkLn-2:55

KkLn-2:237

KkLn-2:142

KkLn-3:73/106

KkLn-2:243

KkLn-2:65

KkLn-2:233

KkLn-2:80

Figure 10.5. Northern Plano wedge, scrapers, knives, chitho and adze.

Analysis of scrapers

Most scrapers are beige quartzite. A tendency to rhomboid shape in forest scrapers occurs, as it does in all traditions and phases, and may relate to improved gripping with winter mittens. Triangular summer tundra scrapers are compatible with socketted bone or antler hafts. Most are flat and worn with bases dorsally retouched, so cortex is uncommon. Forest scrapers are smaller due to sharpening and wear. Ground bases and serrated bits infer heavy frozen skin scraping. More tundra scrapers are on biface knife thinning flakes, two have striae, and three have single or double graver spurs (Tables 10.14a-10.25c). Two scrapers in a KkLn-2 buried level at Grant Lake are in Fig. 10.4: #237 (top) is a collaterally flaked, unstriated but very worn big triangular side-endscraper with bifacially retouched base; #142 (right) is a smaller endscraper with unifacially retouched base and platform facets. Four forest and 39 tundra scrapers are from sites on lakes: IhNx-5 at Athabasca, KeNi-4 at Whitefish, JkNf-1 at Jarvis, KcNb-20 at Jim and KkLn-2 at Grant (Fig. 10.5). KkLn-2 has all 13 buried and most of the 30 surface scrapers.

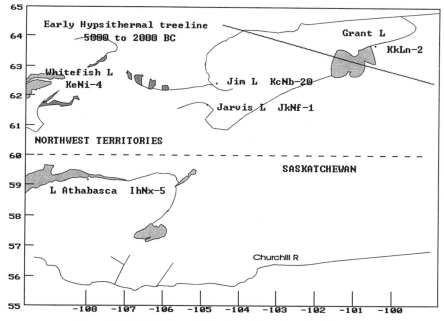

Figure 10.6. Distribution of 5 Northern Plano sites with 43 scrapers.

Difference	Forest scrapers	Tundra scrapers	Remarks
distribution	widespread*	confined to migration paths*	more forest sites; treeline farthest north*
material and colour	more beige quartzite	less beige quartzite	locally available material
plan and section	more 4-sided, but less tabular*	more 3-sided and tabular*	hafted by hand in forest and socket on tundra
serrated and worn	more*	less*	heavy wear on frozen forest caribou hides?
basal retouch & grinding	less*	more*	more preparation for tundra antler sockets*
striae and spurring	less^	more^	tundra engraving and sand strial replication^
size	smaller^	larger^	conserving and sharpening forest material^

Table 10.25c. Comparing Northern Plano forest and tundra scrapers *like and ^unlike Shield Archaic.

Analysis of knives

Undiagnostic traits limit Northern Plano surface knife assignment to LdLq-6:1, but their humus location, just above the single KkLn-2 level with 22 buried ones, add 17 more surface ones. Most are biconvex quartzite bifaces (mean=67x40x9mm & 25g). Half of knives are worn, but striae are absent. Most breaks are transverse. More tips than bases occur, due to selective surface collecting of easily seen bases by earlier visitors, which skews knife proportions (Wright 1976:51,69).

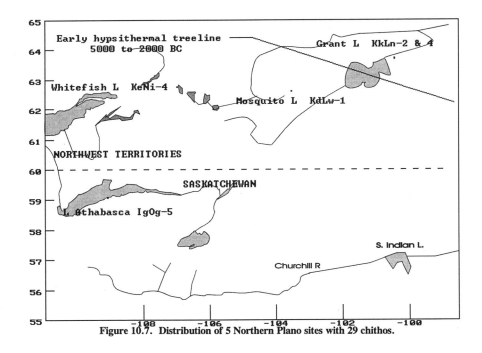

Figure 10.7. Distribution of 5 Northern Plano sites with 29 chithos.

KkLn-3:73/106 and KkLn-2:243 are thin, worn, unstriated, finely retouched biconvex bifaces (Fig. 10.5). One is semilunar; the other is ovoid. Basal plans vary, but a tenth are unground and square. Knives are unbacked and a fourth have no platforms (Tables 10.26-10.33).

Analysis of chithos

Of 29 chithos, 11 were in forest sites IgOg-5 and KdLw-1 at Athabasca and Mosquito Lakes. The rest are in tundra sites KkLn-2 and 4 at Grant Lake (Fig. 10.7). Almost all are sandstone; forest ones are beige; tundra ones are red. Half are unifacial, most forest ones are complete; tundra ones are fragmentary. Most forest chithos are flat worn cortexed discs, versus larger wavy tundra discs (Tables 10.34a-10.41b). KkLn-2:65 is a typical round, thin, wavy and worn biface (Fig. 10.5 bottom left).

Analysis of wedges

Most wedges are beige quartzite, but a third of forest ones are white quartz. Forest ones are larger biconvex or flat rectangles or squares. Tundra ones include some planoconvex rhomboids. More forest scars are channelled by unipolar hammer striking; tundra ones are discoidal like later phases (Tables 10.42a-10.47c). KkLn-2:55 is dual bipolarly struck between hammer and antler, with all edges used in splitting (Fig. 10.5 top left). Of 33 wedges, seven were in six forest sites at Athabasca (IjOg-4), Firedrake (JiNd-20), Sid (KbLx-5), Jim (KcNb-20), Lynx (KcNf-3) and Whitefish (KeNi-4) Lakes, and 26 are from tundra sites at Aberdeen (LdLl-2) and Grant Lakes (24 in KkLn-2; six buried: Fig. 10.8).

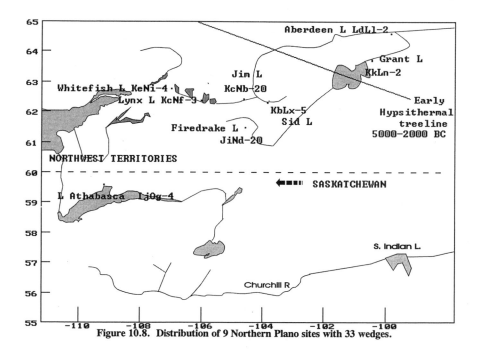

Figure 10.8. Distribution of 9 Northern Plano sites with 33 wedges.

Difference	Forest wedges	Tundra wedges	Remarks
stone and colour	few of white quartz*	mostly beige quartzite*	locally available material
plan and section	rectangular or square & biconvex^	rhomboid/planoconvex^	seasonally different wood or antler splitting?
channelled flake scars	more	less	channels caused by unipolar hammering
percussion	about 1/2 are unipolar*	1/10 are discoidal*	disc spreads shock points for splitting antler
size	larger*	smaller*	tundra wedges are circular rather than elongated

Table 10.47c. Comparing Northern Plano forest and tundra wedges *like or ^unlike Shield Archaic.

Analysis of adzelike artifacts

Twenty-nine of 30 adzelike artifacts from Grant Lake are black basalt. Four were in the KkLn-2 buried level. Adzelike artifacts include an adze fragment, equal numbers of side and bit flakes, and two full tools. Adze KkLn-2:80 has a bifacially ground bit and thinned haft (Fig. 10.4 bottom). Long surface chisel KkLn-2:383, a former adze, has a 30 degree ventrally ground bit (Table 10.50b; Wright 1976:103, 110). Neither have platforms. A seventh each of all flakes have transverse or diagonal striae from sharpening, while the adze, 13 bit flakes, 13 side flakes and chisel have longitudinal striae from use. Four-fifths of all are polished, a fourth are somewhat ground, and two-thirds are widely ground. Mean flake measurements are 27x20.9x4.1mm & 3.2g (Tables 10.48-10.50a).

Tool	Length	Width	Thickness	Weight	Plan	Section	Bit angle (degrees)	Striae
KkLn-2:80	98.4	37.0	30.3	151	rectangular	keeled	70	longitudinal
KkLn-2:383	49.4	28.2	7.5	12.6	lanceolate	planoconvex	30	none

Table 10.50b. Comparing the Northern Plano tundra adze and chisel (mm/g) .

Analysis of flakes and cores

Buried material includes four regular and one worked flake, a flake bag, and 107 unmeasured bagged flakes. Surface items include six regular and three worked flakes, four flake bags (3773g), and 3111 bagged flakes (5776g). Items studied are half beige, or half white or gray quartzite. A beige quartzite split round cobble core is 98.6x73.8x41.6mm & 373g. Mean regular flake size is 31x25x7.7mm & 7.3g, while mean retouched flake size is 45x29x8.6mm & 16.4g. Obviously, large flakes were chosen for conversion to tools (Tables 10.51-10.52b), as they were for Shield Archaic.

Description	Tundra total	Colour	Tundra total (frequency)
flake bags	4; weight=3772.9 g	beige	7(50)
unmeasured flakes	3111: weight=5775.9 g	white	6(43)
worked flakes	4; weight=65.76 g	gray	1(07)
regular flakes	10; weight=73.18 g	Total	14(100)
Total	weight=9687.8 g		

Table 10.51. Northern Plano flake type and colour One flake bag with 5 unmeasured flakes is omitted.

Analysis of hammerstones

One hammerstones each is at Lake Athabasca forest sites IgOg-12 and 14 and IhOa-2, while tundra ones are confined to the lower Thelon and Dubawnt Rivers at Ursus Island LdLq-2, and Grant Lake KkLn-2 (Fig. 10.8). Two-thirds of forest hammerstones are quartzite, versus granite tundra ones from a Grant Lake source. Two-thirds of tundra ones are beige; each forest one is beige, white or gray. Most are round with ovoid section. Most are bipolarly pocked. Seven tundra and one forest hammerstones have a middle pocking cluster for use as anvils for flaking. Forest ones are smaller (Tables 10.53-10.58c).

Difference	Forest hammerstones	Tundra hammerstones	Remarks
stone and colour	mixed coloured quartzite	beige granite	locally available material
plan and section	both views are ovoid	ovoid and mixed	locally available material
pocking	mostly bipolar; one anvil	bipolar and mixed; many anvils^	much flaking using KkLn-2 tundra anvils
size	smaller*	larger*	wider tundra hammerstones for use as anvils

Table 10.58c. Comparing Northern Plano forest and tundra hammerstones *like or ^unlike Shield Archaic.

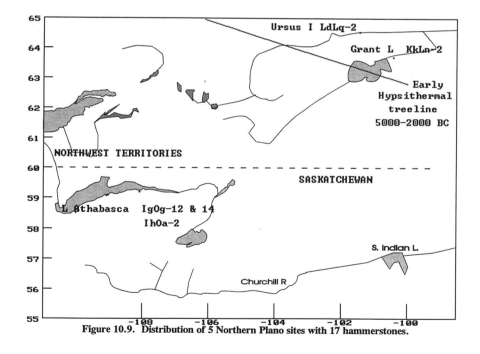

Figure 10.9. Distribution of 5 Northern Plano sites with 17 hammerstones.

Analysis of whetstones

All whetstones are unnotched polished bars. None are made into other tools. The forest one is gray shale; three tundra ones are red and brown sandstone or beige slate. The Nonacho Lake forest whetstone and tundra ones at Grant Lake are worn or ground on edges and faces (Fig. 10.9; Tables 10.59a-10.62c). One tundra whetstone has longitudinal striae from sharpening, while a Nonacho forest one has the same, plus transverse striae. It is shorter and wider, but heavier, than the tundra whetstones.

Trait	Forest range	Tundra range	Remarks
stone and colour	shale	mixed/mixed	locally available material
plan and section	both are barlike	both are barlike	typical, but some whetstones in other traditions have round or triangular plans
striae	longitudinal*	mixed	greater diversity of tundra grinding tasks, but sample is too small
size	smaller	larger*	plentiful tundra sandstone slabs, versus smaller, less common forest shale

Table 10.62c. Comparing Northern Plano forest and tundra whetstones *like Shield Archaic but theirs were groovers.

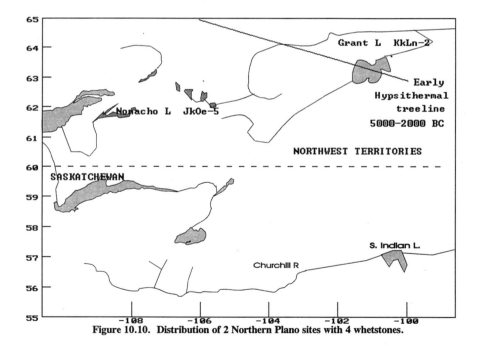

Figure 10.10. Distribution of 2 Northern Plano sites with 4 whetstones.

Analysis of saws

Five triangular quartzite saws are widely scattered at KkNb-11 and KlNa-1 at Warden's Grove and Grassy Island in the forest, and KkLn-2 at Grant Lake on the tundra (Table 10.63; Fig. 10.11).

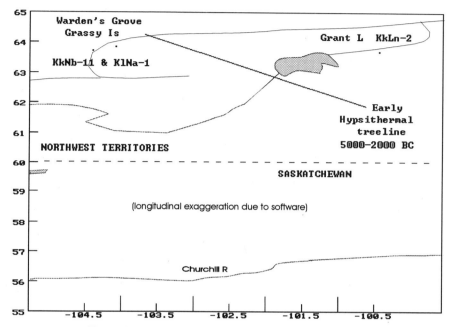

Figure 10.11. Distribution of 3 Northern Plano sites with 5 saws.

Saw or denticulate	Length	Width	Thickness	Weight	Quartzite colour
KkNb-11:142	-47.12	55.37	11.33	-31.41	beige-orange
KlNa-1:126	-40.22	-55.3	13.25	-21.30	orange-beige-purple
KkNb-11:178	38.95	25.07	5.18	5.60	orange
KkLn-2:44*	-26.24	-13.1	4.51	-1.55	beige
KkLn-2:48M	-62.76	55.02	9.45	-39.28	beige-pink

Table 10.63. Northern Plano forest (top) and tundra (bottom) denticulates and saws (mm & g).
*Denticulates are more sharply serrated than saws. Saws have deep, worn, thick, unilateral notches.(-)=broken.

Analysis of burins

Of 45 burins, 10 forest ones are from JiNd-15 at Firedrake, JjNg-1 at Jarvis, JlNg-1 at Damant, JkOc-9 at Gray, KeNi-4 at Whitefish (3) and KbNa-1 at Mantic Lakes, and KjNb-6 and 7 at Warden's Grove. Thirty-three tundra burins are from KkLn-2 at Grant Lake and two are from LlLl-2 at Aberdeen Lake. All are on Agate Basin points, spalled to make a planing or slotting facet (see Points). All retain their original ground point base, none are striated, backed or carinated, and tundra burins are smaller. Of the total, 31 were suitable for estimating spalling (Fig. 10.12).

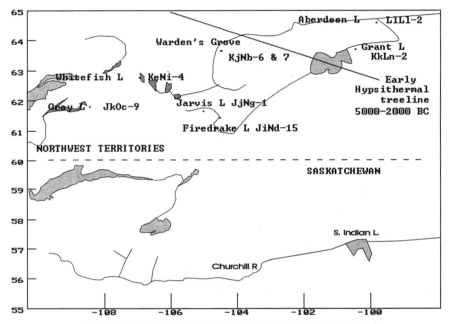

Figure 10.12. Distribution of 8 Northern Plano sites with 31 burins.

The dominant Grant Lake burins are spalled most heavily from antler and bone working, yet they have the same mean number of spall groups as forest burins. As most are quartzite, the creation of new spall groups seems to relate to new and similar uses in both ranges, with heavy use on the tundra. Tundra burins have square ends versus 80 degree ends (or tip angle) in forest burins, suggesting an added tundra use as a chisel (Tables 10.64a-10.66b).

Estimated	No.	Min	Max	Mean	S.D.	Particulars
Edge 1 scars	7	1	2	1.29	0.49	fewer scars than tundra burins
Edge 2 scars	2	1	2	1.50	0.71	more scars than tundra burins
Scar groups	7	1	2	1.29	0.49	forest mean identical to tundra mean
Tip angle	7	35	90	80.71	20.50	less tip flattening than tundra burins

Table 10.66a. Comparing Northern Plano forest burin spalling and tip angle.

Estimated	No.	Min	Max	Mean	S.D.	Particulars
Edge 1 scars	24	1	4	1.71	1.00	more scars than forest burins
Edge 2 scars	7	1	2	1.14	0.38	fewer scars than forest burins
Scar groups	24	1	2	1.29	0.46	forest mean identical to tundra mean
Tip angle	24	40	110	86.88	12.32	added tundra use as a chisel

Table 10.66b. Comparing Northern Plano tundra burin spalling and tip angle.

Analysis of drills and gravers

Three forest drills and a graver are from Whitefish (KeNi-4), Damant (JlNg-8) and Sid (KbNa-6) Lakes, and at Grant Lake in a KkLn-2 buried tundra level (Table 10.67 & Fig. 10.13). Gravers on altered points are in Wright (1976:107 #25 & 108 #'s 21 & 36). Gravers KbNa-16:264, JlNg-8:28 and KeNi-4:299 are also on altered points. Gravers KkLn-2:320b & c are untabled.

Artifact	Length	Width	Thickness	Weight	Remarks
JlNg-8:28	88.00	21.53	6.99	12.10	on fine collaterally retouched point tip
KbNa-16:264	-33.6	21.62	7.63	-6.16	on bilaterally retouched point tip
KeNi-4:299	54.16	22.43	8.07	10.64	on point tip
KkLn-2:187	-38.0	19.79	8.88	-6.97	on truncated point tip
KkLn-2:263	32.33	21.38	6.03	5.12	on channel flaked point base
KkLn-2:298	46.00	22.60	7.90	9.30	on bilaterally retouched point tip
KkLn-2:211	44.53	12.54	5.45	2.48	on longitudinally split graver with wear and striae

Table 10.67. Northern Plano drills and graver.
(mm & g; minus (-)=broken)

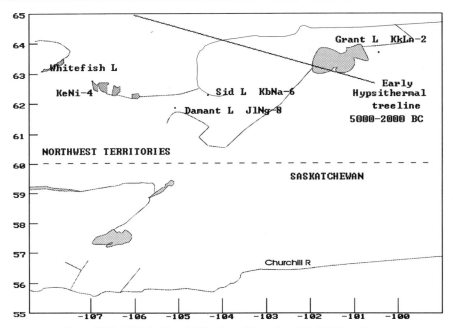

Figure 10.13. Distribution of 5 Northern Plano sites with 6 drills and gravers.

Analysis of bone

Of 18 unidentified calcined bone pieces (49.2 g), four were in a KkLn-2 level, and 14 above on the surface. Buried identified caribou bone was destroyed in the process of radiocarbon dating.

Conclusions on Northern Plano Artifacts

Plano forest artifacts are widespread because the treeline extended farther north than later times, due to the warm post-glacial (Table 10.68). Tundra sites are radiocarbon-dated, but forest sites are older because Plano peoples came from the south. Tundra points are shorter from heavy burination into gravers, drills and chisels. Rangewide scraper hafts differ and relate to warm, versus cold weather use on either wood or antler and bone hafts. As forest scrapers have more serrated bits and wear, heavy frozen skin scraping is suggested. Like most tools of all traditions, forest scrapers are smaller due to more sharpening and stone conservation in snow-covered terrain. More tundra scrapers are on biface sharpening flakes, and more are spurred for bone and antler engraving. As knife bases are usually returned to camp for knife replacement, a surplus of tundra tips and midsections seems due to selective surface collecting of more easily identified bases by earlier visitors, which skews knife proportions (Wright 1976:51,69). That more tundra chithos are unworn and wavy, while forest ones are worn and flat, reflects the large number of unique wavy sandstone disks from KkLn-2, plus heavier forest use. Like later phases, forest wedges are larger and unipolarly hit with a soft hammer for use on wood. Tundra wedges are smaller and discoidally struck, dispersing hard blows on antler or bone at their periphery. Different material in forest and tundra hammerstones and whetstones is due to local source, but some tundra hammerstones have concentrated midshaft pocking from their use as anvils for manufacturing other tools. Larger tundra whetstones are due to plentiful, easily replacible sandstone slabs, versus smaller and scattered forest shale. Tundra gravers are half the size of forest ones. Tundra burins and gravers are shorter due to heavy use on antler and bone.

Trait	Forest range	Tundra range	Remarks
distribution	very wide*	very limited*	farthest north treeline*
dating	from 7,000 B.P., but estimated earlier	8,000-5,550 B.P. on radiocarbon	6 tundra radiocarbon dates
points	19 Gray. Some chert. Longer@ Complete	139 Quartzite. Beige. Shorter@ More broken*	shortening from tundra burination
scrapers	4 4-sided* and serrated* ,but ground^ Less retouch, wear, striae, spurring. Smaller^	39 3-sided*; 1/5 each are bifacial or on bifacial thinning flakes. 1/2 have dorsal retouch. Larger^	tundra socket vs. forest haft & frozen hide. Tundra engraving^. More forest sharpening^
knives	none reported	40 Mostly worn tips and midsections. Bifacially retouched base. Tranverse and diagonal breaks. Unbacked	selective collecting by many past visitors to Grant Lake has distorted tip and base ratios
chithos	29 Beige. Complete worn flat discs. 4/5 have cortex. Smaller*	11 Mostly worn, wavy, red-brown unifacial disc fragments^. 1/2 have cortex. Larger*	more forest usage, but chitho preparation differs. Wavy due to Grant Lake tundra source
wedges	7 12% quartz. 4-sided. White. Larger*	26 1/3 quartz. 3/4 are 4-sided. Beige. Smaller*	local source. Wedges long for wood, or disc for tundra antler*
adze flakes	none	27 black basalt. Mean=27x21x4mm\3g	shaping of antler or transported wood at Grant Lake
cores	none	1.99x74x21mm\373g	Grant Lake stone tool production
flakes	none	Mean=31x25x8mm\7g	Grant Lake stone tool production
hammerstones	3 Quartzite.Ovoid^.Midshaft pocking*	14 Granite. Ovoid^	local stone source. Tundra anvils
whetstones	1 Silicious shale. Longitudinal and transverse striae. Long^, narrow, light	3 Sandstone and slate. Longitudinal striae. Shorter^, thick, heavy	local stone source and similar use
burins	7 Longer	24 Shorter. Flat tip.	more tundra burin use & spalling
gravers	Mean=71x22x8mm;11g	Mean=39x21x8mm;7g	forest=twice tundra size

Table 10.68. Northern Plano forest and tundra tools
*like or ^unlike Shield Archaic. @ too many tundra points are burinated for accurate estimation of length. Number of tools listed. Unlisted data alike in both ranges.

Figure 10.14. Beginning excavations at KjNb-6 near Warden's Grove in 1971.
Northern Plano tools were on the surface (Brian Yorga at tripod, Bob Janes and Priscilla
Bickel measuring, Steve Burger taking notes, and author at right).

**Figure 10.15. Many stratified sites occur in windblown dunes formed from the sand of glacial
lakes. This area at Warden's Grove has several Northern Plano sites.**

Chapter 11

Conclusions and Related Research

Archaeological Sequence

Indigenous peoples of the Canadian Sub-arctic have left a rich archaeological legacy since they first adapted their annual cycle to that of the caribou 8,000 years ago. Within the winter range, migration corridor and calving grounds of the Beverly caribou are 1,002 hunting camps, representing all traditions and their phases. Site distribution affirms that all peoples except the Caribou Inuit followed the herd along its migration route. Summer camps at water crossings accumulated layers of cultural refuse separated by layers of sterile sand. These stratified sites illustrate that year after year, one culture after another hunted the massed herds. Small sites within the past and present forest are compatible with the distribution of the herd in winter, and human dependence upon them in that season.

Four major cultural traditions from deglaciation to the historic period left 6,385 excavated artifacts and 6,715 surface artifacts. The cultural affiliation of surface artifacts was determined from stratified artifacts using large data bases. These were analyzed in terms of type and attributes to develop the cultural sequence, and to elucidate specific adaptations to forest and tundra environments.

Beverly prehistory (Table 11.2) began when Northern Plano people entered the caribou range 8,000 years ago. They came from the south, changing their prey from southern bison to caribou, which came from the west to graze on patchy new post-glacial vegetation. In spring, Northern Plano people tracked the herd northeast to its calving ground near the last Keewatin ice remnants. In autumn, they followed the herd south to the winter forest. Small family groups are identified by sites with Northern Plano/Agate Basin points, along with small round chithos of a distinct local red sandstone, and large triangular endscrapers. Agate Basin points are biconvex quartzite lanceolates with tapered ground stemmed bases. Collateral flaking is shallow, and the base is thinned by removing 3-4 tapered flakes in a triangular area too shallow to be called channelled or fluted. Northern Plano hunters transformed their broken point tips into burins and gravers, a trait rare in Southern Plano.

Culture	Forest	Mixed	Tundra	Total	Origin, adaptation or movement
Caribou Inuit	0	0	53	53	tundra adaptation
Dene Indian	135	34	34	203	retraction to forest because of tundra epidemics and southern fur trad
General Taltheilei	5	8	8	21	too general to assign to Taltheilei phase
Late Plains	1	1	0	2	Late Plains forest points carried north to treeline by herd followers
Late Taltheilei	117	64	66	247	southern retreat by effects of Little Ice Age. Mainly forest-adapted
Middle Taltheilei	125	87	144	356	greatest forest and tundra adaptation seen in most widespread sites
Early Taltheilei	76	56	58	190	forest origin in northwest British Columbia or adjacent Alaska
ASTt Pre-Dorset	24	99	123	246	move from northwest possible through tundra origin and adaptation
Middle Plains	10	5	2	17	Middle Plains forest points carried north to tundra by herd followers
Shield Archaic	40	60	21	121	treeline origin and primarily forest adaptation
Northern Plano	14	12	8	34	plains origin and primarily forest adaptation
Total	547	426	517	1490	

Table 11.1. Cultural components by range, tradition and phase.

Tradition	Years ago	Significant cultural traits
Caribou Inuit	50-175	kayak, harpoon, soapstone lamp and vessel, copper staple, compound bow and distinct clothing
Taltheilei (originated in northwestern British Columbia or southeastern Alaska)		
Historic	present-200	snowshoes, canoes, birchbark, simple bow, and distinct clothing
Late	200-1300	crude asymmetric side and corner-notched points
Middle	1300-1800	long thin stemmed lanceolate points and large triangular endscrapers
Early	1800-2450	long thin wide shouldered points
Earliest	2450-2600	long thick stemmed lanceolate points
Pre-Dorset (tundra dwellers with microlithic end- & sideblades (set in harpoons?), burins, microblade tools & ulu-like skin flexers)		
Late	2650-2950	maximum southerly penetration into forest of primarily tundra-adapted culture
Early	2950-3450	the only successful Beverly culture to enter the range from the north
Shield Archaic (mainly forest dwellers near northernmost post-glacial treeline)		
Late	3500-4450	long narrow rocker-based, side-notched points and sinuous knives
Middle	4450-5450	long thin lanceolate bifacial knives
Early	5500-6500	small crude side-notched points
Northern Plano	7000-8000	burinated Agate Basin points and small wavy discoid chithos

Table 11.2. Beverly traditions and range occupancy.

The Northern Plano proved their adaptability to the north when they changed their herd following from southern bison to northern caribou. But their tundra adaptation was tested for only a few summer weeks over a 100 km wide belt of open ground between the calving ground and the treeline. It was at the furthest advance of the post-glacial treeline that they likely developed into Shield Archaic forest hunters, under a generally warm climate. During the 6,500 year-old Climatic Optimum, hunting families multiplied when they remained longer at northern river crossings than families of later traditions. This was possible because the water was ice-free earlier in spring and later in fall, as deduced from caribou tooth sectioning. Many medium length notched points and linear or ovoid knives were used in lancing and butchering, and tortoise-backed scrapers were used for hide preparation.

During the early part of a prolonged cold period about 3,500 ago, Shield Archaic peoples moved into the Manitoba forest, while Pre-Dorset peoples spread into Saskatchewan, some as far south as Reindeer Lake. The Pre-Dorset also traced the migrating caribou into the winter forest, but not far south of the retreating treeline, where they left small surface tool scatters. Theirs is an Asiatic tradition, distinct in its finely retouched, tiny chert endblades and sideblades, microblades, microcores and burin-related tools. They used these tools centuries earlier while maritime hunting, and may have used them at river crossings, as there are equal numbers and types of endblades and sideblades for harpoons. The PreDorsets adapted partly to forest, adopting some wood-working tools in the south part of their range. About 2,700 years ago, they disappeared, probably moving to the coast under warming climate to become part of the martime Dorset tradition.

Hard on their heels were Taltheilei peoples. Earliest and Early Taltheilei were forest-adapted, reinforcing my belief that they originated in northwest British Columbia, moved down the Peace and Slave Rivers, and entered the range north of Lake Athabasca. Finely stratified levels with slowly changing projectile points allow their tracing to the modern Dene. Like the Northern Plano and Shield Archaic Indian traditions, quartzite tools dominate. From Earliest to Early phases, lanceheads widen, thin and become shouldered, knives are crude and temporary, and there is evidence of copper trade with the ancestors of the neighbouring Yellowknife (or copper knife) Dene occupying the Coppermine River valley. Trade between the two continued as they merged into Middle Taltheilei.

Middle Taltheilei expansion was dramatic 1,800 years ago, when the complete range was fully exploited. This is observed in a similar large number of forest and tundra archaeological components. Sites at water crossings are compatible with gathering for mass hunts during southern summer caribou migration, as seen in symmetrical ground stem lanceheads, the greatest number and variety of butchering knives, and triangular scrapers thicker than previous ones. They also had an eyeless copper needle, the earliest found on the Barrenlands, although the Pre-Dorsets probably had bone needles.

The Little Ice Age of 300 to 700 years ago forced Late Taltheilei peoples towards the forest. They are the last herd followers because their Dene descendents were ravaged by epidemics, and enticed south by the fur trade. Sites are numerous in the center of the range, but tools are now more poorly made. Asymmetric lanceheads have squared, stemmed, flared or wide expanding bases, while ovoid knives are crude with less retouch. Small side and corner-notched arrowheads show the influence of overwintering Plains Indians. The bow and arrow gave Taltheilei peoples greater freedom to kill animals from piled slab hunting blinds on the open tundra and from the forested sides of frozen lakes.

European cloth, metal and glass trade goods mark Dene emergence from prehistoric Late Taltheilei. They occur among collapsed tent poles, or mixed with crude quartzite surface tools on archaeological sites. Hearne mentions the everyday use of bows, tents, canoes and snowshoes near brush-enclosed corrals, plus games and practises surrounding birth and death. He remarks on the few needs of the Dene and the difficulty of the Hudson Bay Company in luring them into the fur trade. Eventually, they did participate, depending less on caribou and more on imported flour and local moose, birds and fish from the forest. In so doing, they relinquished the freedom of herd following for the dubious security of the trading post.

The empty tundra was quickly claimed by historic Caribou Inuit who pushed south to the treeline about 1825 to 1850 A.D. Unlike other peoples, they did not follow the caribou through their cycle, as they were prevented from living in the winter range by Dene fur trappers.

Seasonal Variations in Tools

All Beverly people adapted to both forest and tundra except the historic Caribou Inuit. All older summer sites are on tundra, while late winter sites extend north from Churchill River to Cree, Black and Athabasca Lakes. Small lake and river camps continue north along Nonacho, Firedrake, Whitefish and south Artillery Lakes, grow in size at Thelon and Dubawnt water-crossings, and shrink near the calving ground. In every tradition, lance and arrowheads, knives and scrapers indicate the killing, butchering and processing of caribou. The paucity of hooks, lack of net weights or other fishing tools imply fishing was not of major importance. The paucity of art objects is in keeping with people who travel far on foot in a harsh land.

Except for Pre-Dorset burins and harpoons, all Beverly people used similar tools for similar tasks. Points are the most easily identified, but knives and scrapers are the most common. Chithos and flexers infer hide working, and awls attest to sewing from earliest times. In a harsh environment for most of the year, tailored clothing was crucial, and probably existed from the start of human occupation. Pushplanes, wedges and adzes suggest wood and bone working. Quartzite cores and flakes, the by-products of tool production, occur in all phases, changing to chert microcores and microblades in Pre-Dorset.

Non-Pre-Dorset points, scrapers, knives, cores, flakes, hammerstones, pushplanes and wedges are quartzite. Throughout all phases, chithos are mainly sandstone, whetstones are mostly sandstone or shale, and adzes, axes and chisels are mainly basalt.

That knife and point bases normally outnumber tips in all phases has to do with the mechanics of breakage on surface rock. A tip breaks off and is lost away from camp in sand, water or flesh. While the haft is returned to camp and attached to a new knife, the discarded base becomes trampled underfoot, only to be later excavated by an archaeologist.

While tool types and materials are similar, material and tool alterations are specific to site location and season (Table 11.3). Tundra tools are mainly confined to major caribou route water crossings, while forest tools are dispersed over the winter range like caribou. In response to many small forest camps over a large area, lithics are more varied, with more non-quartzite tools in the forest than on the tundra.

Trait	Winter forest	Summer tundra	Exceptions to nine phases and possible reason
Points (1,544)	smaller	larger	16 of 19 NP tundra points are incomplete, altering normal patte
Scrapers (2,360)	smaller	larger	LT and Dene. There are only two Dene tundra scrapers
sides and serration	4-sided. More	3-sided. Less	ASTt. Serration is normal in this non-Indian culture
basal grinding	more	less	ASTt and NP. Many ASTt endblades are inset in harpoons
wear	less	more	ET and NP are equal exceptions
striae	less	more	ET and ASTt. Almost all ASTt sites are on tundra
spurring	less	more	MT and SA. SA forest much greater than that of later cultures
biface thinning flakes	fewer	more	MT and ET. Taltheilei people made tundra preforms for winter
Knives (3,164)	smaller	larger	SA. Plentiful tundra stone with quick knife making and discard
serration	more	less	ASTt and SA. Serration is normal in ASTt. For SA, see above*
bifaces=2X unifaces	normal	normal	SA has 12% tundra unifacial knives. See above*
more bases than tips	normal & 4-sided	normal & 3-sided	
cortex/wear/breakage	more/less/less	less/more/more	
Chithos (353)	smaller	larger	
Cores (278)	smaller	larger	ASTt, SA (on weight). Almost all ASTt quarries are on tundra
Flake category (3,116)	smaller	larger	ASTt and SA; ASTt quarries are on tundra. For SA, see above*
Whetstones (40)	smaller	larger	
Pushplanes, flexers, wood (145, 45 and 164)	smaller	larger	
Hammerstones (75)	larger	smaller	ASTt and NP
Wedges (225)	larger	smaller	ET
Adze category (242)	larger	smaller	LT

Table 11.3. Comparing tool attributes by season and environment.
Wedges and adze sizes oppose usual trend due to material. LT, MT, ET, ASTt, SA and NP are Late, Middle and
Early Taltheilei, Pre-Dorset, Shield Archaic and Northern Plano. Parentheses surround artifact counts.

Cortex was measured wherever possible on scrapers, knives, cores and pushplanes. Where the amount of cortex remaining on a tool differed between forest and tundra tools, it is higher in forest. Perhaps people were unwilling to assume the greater breakage risk associated with finer finishing, when supplies of raw material were limited by snowcover or distant tundra quarries used in summer.

Forest points, scrapers, knives, chithos, cores, flakes, whetstones, flexers and pushplanes are smaller than those from tundra sites. Undoubtedly, this was due to careful resharpening in the winter when local new stone was inaccessible. Exceptions to the smaller forest tools are hammerstones, wedges and adzes. They may reflect use on wood as opposed to bone and antler on the tundra. Wood is softer than bone and antler, and less sharpening reduction is needed. Forest hammerstones are larger because many were also used as anvils for tool retouch. Shield Archaic forest knives, cores and flakes are larger than tundra ones, in opposition to the general trend, but they were made from easily available large cobbles at Warden's Grove (which became tundra during later traditions and phases). Too many burinated points or fragments (16 of 19) made it impossible to prove whether the Northern Plano tradition followed the general trend as to size differences. Pre-Dorset has the most seasonal trait exceptions, due to its heritage of common edge serration, and tundra sources of high quality chert.

Except Pre-Dorset, more forest scrapers and knives are serrated, an advantage for working and cutting frozen hides and meat in winter. A tendency for four-sided winter scraper and knife hafts may be due to the parallel fit of wooden handles or better hand gripping. A prevalence of exposed ground bases in the forest environment may also have to do with hand hafting. Three-sided scrapers common on tundra sites were probably hafted in bone or antler sockets. For such hafts, the tapering base is more advantageous. Fewer forest scrapers are spurred, except for Middle Taltheilei and Shield Archaic, where spurs on tundra scrapers may have been used for bone engraving.

Scrapers were made on fewer knife thinning flakes in the forest, because the large flakes needed would have quickly depleted knife material which was not easily replaced, due to snowcover or distant quarries. Forest knives and scrapers are less worn or striated, probably due to the absence of sand, which gets caught between the tool and its application. Sand pervades most tundra sites in their ground cover and from adjacent dunes.

Family Units

Men's and women's tools appear together over the range. Survival depended upon a cooperative venture, with men hunting and women preparing meat and hides. Men's tools include knives, points, cores, wedges, adzes and spokeshaves; i.e., those relating to hunting or tool making. Women's tools include knives, scrapers, chithos, perforators, flexers, awls and needles; i.e., those tools used to process carcasses and hides.

Knives used by both men and women are endemic at large K-site water crossings like KjNb-6 and 7 on the Thelon, and KkLn-2 and 4 on the Dubawnt (Fig. 11.1a). Numbers fall quickly north to the calving ground and south to the forest, reflecting the decreasing size of hunting groups, which are in concert with herd size.

Cores, chithos, points and scrapers are also abundant at the K-sites, suggesting contemporaneity in tool making, hunting and hide processing (Fig. 11.1b-c). While men speared caribou in the water, women and older daughters were downriver, dragging carcasses ashore and up the bank to camp, where their hide was removed and their muscles delaminated with stone knives to hasten drying in the warm sunshine. After hunting and butchering, people congregated at hearths where men reduced cores and flakes to tools, while women and girls scraped and softened new hides for carrying south. Cores, flakes, scrapers and chithos near hearths suggest a certain degree of mutual protection from clouds of black flies and mosquitoes, using smoke. Chithos for hide softening are most numerous in the K-sites near treeline (e.g. KeNi-4; Fig. 11.1b), because winter clothing was made at the end of summer or the beginning of fall, when hides were prime and caribou crossed the treeline going into the forest, and again when they returned to the tundra to rut.

a. Knife distribution; non-gender related; all cultures

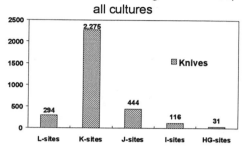

b. Male micro(cores) vs. Female chithos; all cultures

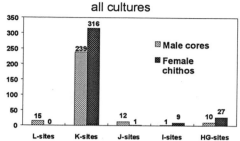

c. Male points vs. Female scrapers; all cultures

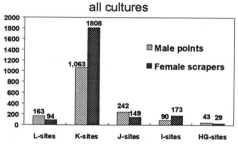

d. Male points vs. Female scrapers; Dene

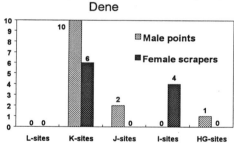

Figure 11.1. Comparing knives, chithos, points and scrapers by latitudinally oriented Borden blocks.
(north Borden block L on left, through intermediate range blocks K, J and I to combined south Borden blocks H-G on right. The latitudinally oriented Borden site designation system is used throughout Canada).

e. Male points vs. Female scrapers;
Late Taltheilei

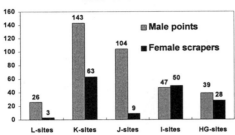

f. Male points vs. Female scrapers;
Middle Taltheilei

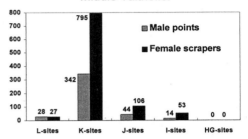

g. Male points vs. Female scrapers;
Early Taltheilei

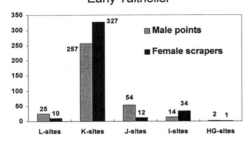

h. Male points vs. Female scrapers;
Pre-Dorset

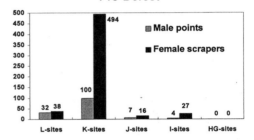

i. Male points vs. Female scrapers;
Shield Archaic

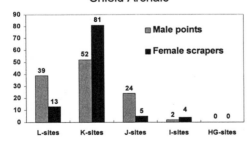

j. Male points vs. Female scrapers;
Northern Plano

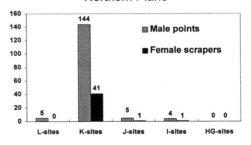

Figure 11.1 (cont'd).

Very many points and scrapers at K-site crossings (Fig. 11.1c-j) suggest the largest number of men and women for mass hunting, butchering, meat-drying and hide processing at 62-64 degrees latitude (Figs. 11.2 and 11.4). Scrapers usually outnumber points because one point can kill an animal, but many scrapers are needed to process a hide. Scrapers are also more readily discarded because heavy wear and reduction through sharpening quickly render them unusable. Where scrapers are few, the site surface often has more scrapers, but they are too general to be assigned to a specific phase or tradition.

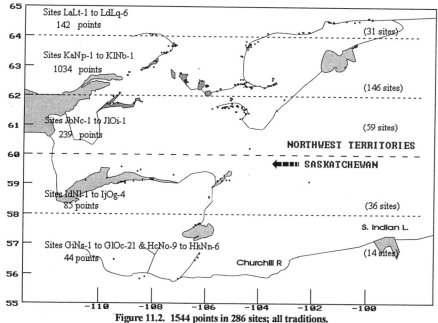

Figure 11.2. 1544 points in 286 sites; all traditions.
Capital letters denote 2 degree Borden blocks (see Fig. 11.1); small letters denote internal 4km blocks.

Uneven distribution of too few Dene and Northern Plano points and scrapers, plus an inability to assign general surface scrapers to culture, create a false impression that points outnumber scrapers in these cultures (Fig. 11.1d and Fig. 11.1j). A more accurate impression is that of easily identified Middle Taltheilei scrapers (Fig. 11.1f), which slightly outnumber points.

Of the thousand Beverly sites, the best for hypothesizing a single family are small Pre-Dorset camps JkNf-1 and JlNg-8 with point and scraper ratios like that of the range at 1:1.5. These sites represent several days of processing at most. In contrast, remains at large crossings may represent as many as 250 family gatherings over a few decades. Equating tools with events is not realistic, but does demonstrate that human groups came together and split in response to herd behavior.

Children joined their parents in the long trek across the Beverly range. Hearne (1958: 201) reported that it was rare to see a woman with more than 5-6 children. Birth spacing was 2-3 years due to suppression of fertility and nutritional deficits caused by breast feeding of children to ages 3-4. Due to the nature of herd migration and following, human conception and birth seasonality would have been similar in all Beverly people (Fig. 11.5). Pregnancies were most likely to occur during the maximum nutrition of extensive harvesting of summer migration. Children were least likely to be conceived at times of chronic malnutrition in late winter. Ethnographically and historically, the Dene had most babies in late winter around Black and Athabasca Lakes. Ancient peoples likely were similar, and during herd following, may even have carried their 3-4 month old babies north towards the treeline in moss bags like the Dene. As human conception occurred during late summer band aggregation at the major Thelon and Dubawnt water-crossings, I suggest young men and women from different sub-bands met and coupled there, rather than during winter activities that were traditional in many northern societies.

Burial signs exist mainly in Dene culture after the missionaries introduced Christianity, although I have seen what I believe are log-outlined, pre-Christian graves deep in the forest. Earlier observers like Hearne noted that the Dene did not bury their dead, but left them where they lay (Hearne 1958:218) or placed them in trees. Surface and buried bone has since dissolved in the acid soil.

Culture	L-sites		K-sites		J-sites		I-sites		HG-sites	
Tool	scrapers	points	scrapers	points	scrapers	points	scrapers	points	scrapers	points
Dene	0	0	7	10	0	2	4	0	0	1
Late Taltheilei	3	24	64	166	9	105	50	46	28	41
Middle Taltheilei	27	21	900	299	106	44	45	14	0	0
Early Taltheilei	10	24	324	280	11	52	33	15	1	2
Pre-Dorset	37	29	516	103	16	7	24	4	0	0
Shield Archaic	13	39	83	52	4	24	4	2	0	0
Northern Plano	0	5	40	124	0	5	1	4	0	0
Total	90	142	1934	1034	146	239	161	85	29	44

Table 11.4. Ratio of 2360 scrapers in 230 sites to 1544 points in 2864 sites by culture and 2 degree latitude Borden block, from north (left) to south (right). L -sites to HG-sites are in major Borden site blocks.

Figure 11.3. Caribou bull migrating south in August.

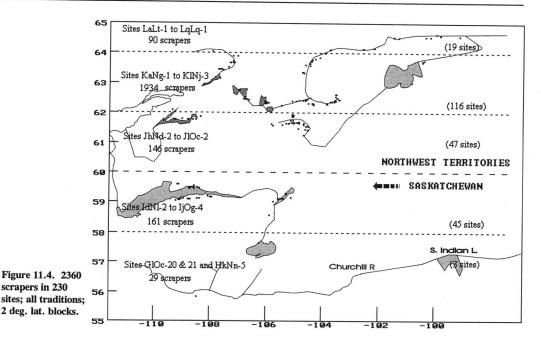

Figure 11.4. 2360
scrapers in 230
sites; all traditions;
2 deg. lat. blocks.

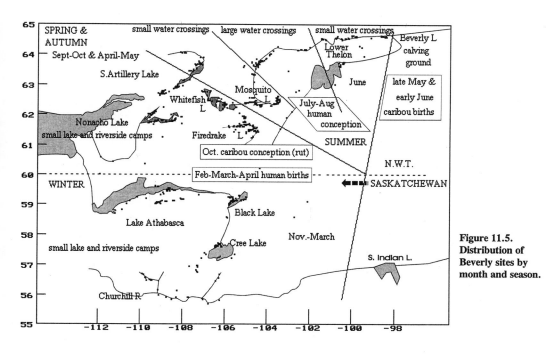

Figure 11.5.
Distribution of
Beverly sites by
month and season.

Figure 11.6. The first snow on the tundra is a signal to the herd to move towards the forest.

Figure 11.7. Packing artifacts and equipment on the last day of fieldwork.

ADZELIKE TOOLS adzes and their flakes, axes, chisels, gouges and picks are included under one class because all are ground tools analyzed using similar traits. **ADZES** are long asymmetric unifacial tools with retouched hafts for wood and antler sockets. Their asymmetry arises from flaking and grinding on the dorsal face of the tip and sides of their bits, using the flat ventral bottom of the adze as a platform. Sometimes, a small groove was cut here parallel to the sides. This groove served as a limit for flake removal when the adze was sharpened. Sharpening **FLAKES** from the cutting edge or bit may be identified from the orientation of their striae or use lines and the curved platform. Lateral adze flakes have straight platforms. **AXES** are bifacial symmetric tools also with retouched hafts, their symmetry coming from equal flake removal and grinding of both lateral faces, with the cutting edge parallel to the long axis. **CHISELS** with unifacially or bifacially retouched bits are smaller than adzes unless hand-hafted, where they are larger. **GOUGES** are channel-ground for grooving wood while **PICKS** are crude pointed earth-diggers.

ARTIFACT usually refers to tools, but includes samples of soil, wood, antler, etc., from a cultural context, plus unworked flakes and blades.

ATTRIBUTE a trait used in assigning an artifact to a phase or tradition. In this work, they include: material, colour, plan, section, metric data, location, type of base, retouch, wear, platform and breakage. Non-tool cores, blades, flakes and soil samples do not use all traits, while special burins, pushplanes and skin flexers have added traits. Most are self-explanatory but some, such as TORTOISE section, refer to an inverted dish-shaped face.

AWL a copper or bone hide-piercing tool.

AXE see under adzelike tools

BURINATION results from accidental longitudinal splitting of a point tip after striking a stone or bone, or intentional removal of spalls from one or both edges of a flake or artifact to form the sharp edges of a burin. The degree of spalling in burins is counted as the number of step-wise hinge fractures at the base of the spall face.

COLOUR mixed or blended colours in the text are simplified; e.g., beige-gray or beige and minor gray are called beige. Stone was selected for knapping quality and perhaps for visibility against snow or sand when tools were dropped.

CORE a round, cubic, flat, keeled, pyramidal, cylindrical, conical or amorphous stone mass used as a source of flakes or blades for making tools. Flakes and blades are removed by striking a platform, resulting in a scar on the core face. Flake scars along the periphery of a core usually diverge, while bladescars along a prepared curved platform resemble fluted Greek columns. The only true **BLADE CORES** are Pre-Dorset, but rare Taltheilei quartzite cores may look bladelike. A core itself may be a tool, e.g., **PUSHPLANE** if its platform series was deliberatly serrated, then worn by planing wood, bone or antler.

CULTURE prehistorically, a way of life defined through artifacts of phase and tradition.

DRILL stone or copper parallel-sided tool used to make and enlarge holes in antler, bone or wood. May have rotational striae.

EDGE GRINDER tool, usually sandstone, used for dulling point and knife basal edges to protect haft sinew from shredding.

FLAKES   flakes are waste material resulting from core reduction; tiny flakes or shatter from tool sharpening. Those with part of the original cutting edge of a knife on their platform are SHARPENING FLAKES. Their size may infer original knife size or its conservation due to scarce raw material. WORKED FLAKES were used as awls, scrapers, gravers and knives. BLADELIKE FLAKES resemble blades in the absence of a blade tradition.

FLEXER   identified by striae over their round ends, indicating skin bending for softening as in chitho edges. They occur in all Beverly traditions and phases on elongated tools such as points, knives, spokeshaves and the ends of bar whetstones. Similar to burnisher.

GOUGE   see under adzelike tools

GRAVER   a flake with retouched corners for engraving wood or bone, its multi-directional or rotational use not forming strial patterns.

HAMMERSTONE   a round or long symmetric pock-marked cobble or pebble of shock-resistant granite, quartzite or basalt. End or polar- pocked ones were likely used directly on cores; side or equatorially-pocked ones as anvils or via a striker. As simple castoffs, many surface examples are too uniform for cultural assignment. Dene hammerstones were replaced by historic metal axes.

PHASE   a time period with a distinctive collection of tools from many archaeological sites which identify a group of people over their seasonal round and within a given tradition. Phase can be conceived as an archaeological culture in a time period.

PICK   see under adzelike tools.

PLATFORM AND BULB OF PERCUSSION   PLATFORM is the area on a flake struck using a hammerstone or billet when it was part of a core. The shock wave generated by the blow resulted in a convex or positive BULB OF PERCUSSION on the flake, and a corresponding concave or negative bulb on the core. As bulb or platform remain on some tools, they are used as orientation in measuring and describing attributes. Some PLATFORMS are facetted, indicating careful core preparation to control flake or blade removal.

PUSHPLANE   stone with abruptly or gently serrated tip and sides for planing wood, bone or antler. Not ground like an adze.

SHAFT POLISHER   an abrasive sandstone block with a deep groove for smoothing arrow and lance shafts.

SKIN FLEXER   a smooth rounded copper, bone or antler tool for shaping or burnishing hides.

SPATULA   a long antler, bone or wood spoon for extracting marrow.

SPOKESHAVE   a concave scraper for rounding arrow and spear shafts.

SPUR   either a sharp unretouched but used corner on a flake or an retouched barb or apex on the end or side of an intentionally-made tool such as a graver or endscraper.

STRIAE AND POLISH   microscopic parallel lines made through tool use or manufacture. Visible use STRIAE form when scrapers and knives are used on sand-contaminated skin and flesh; on burins while planing or slotting wood, bone or antler objects. Striae size typify pressures needed; striae orientation their angle of application. POLISH lines are much smaller than striae and differ from wind abrasion because they may also be linear.

TALTHEILEI   name given to ancestral Dene and taken from the Taltheilei Narrows which separates the main body of Great Slave Lake and its East Arm.

TOOLS AND THEIR DIVISION   artifacts for performing specific tasks and analyzed by use wear and retouch on their tip (bit in scrapers and ground tools), midsection and base. Divisions may not be obvious. Reworked projectile points may have round or flat tips. Bases of knives and points may be pointed and sharp, or their midsections may merge into base or tip, leaving side and basal edge fragments identifiable on use wear and blunting. If a retouched edge fragment has some base, it is classed as retouched. If the retouch ends before the break, it is classed as unretouched.

TRADITION a series of phases depicting consistently changing toolkits of a group, its ancestors and descendants living a similar lifestyle. The Beverly range has four traditions: Taltheilei (historic through 2,600 B.P.), Pre-Dorset (2,650 to 3,450 B.P.), Shield Archaic (3,500 to 6,450 B.P.) and Northern Plano (7,000 to 8,000 B.P.)

WEDGE bashed stone tool for splitting soft wood, hard antler or bone. May be hit unipolarly or bipolarly (one or both ends), double bipolarly, or discoidally. Wood splitting results in unipolar percussion and channel flakes from the hammerstone; the opposite end is seldom smashed due to softer wood. Wedges used on antler or bone are often discoidally-hit because bashing around the periphery disperses hammerstone blows and prolongs the life of the wedge.

WHETSTONE a long symmetric bifacial tool of abrasive sandstone or schist for sharpening stone and copper tool edges, or smoothing their faces. Mainly barlike in plan, some have suspension notches, while round or ovoid ones may have been carried in pouches, as they were not easily replaced. All have flat tops and bottoms. Some are retouched, most are plain, and some are striated and very worn. Commercial whetstones of carborundum and Arkansas sandstone were imported and used by the Dene in the 19th century.

List of Abbreviations

ASTt = Arctic Small Tool tradition or Canadian Pre-Dorset. See relevant chapter for more information.

ET = Early & Earliest Taltheilei phase.

LT = Late Taltheilei phase.

MT = Middle Taltheilei phase.

SA = Shield Archaic.

SP or **pltfrm** = striking platform.

// = parallel, as in striae or tool sides.

> (used extensively in Tables due to confined space) = greater or more than (or in). E.g., quartzite is <forest; but >tundra.

< = less than.

Est. = estimated measurement.

T=tundra;

F=forest

No. = Number of full measurements used in a table. As some tools are broken, number of length, width measurements, etc., in columns vary.

Back, Captain (Sir George)

1836   Narrative of the Arctic Land Expedition to the mouth of the Great Fish River, in the Years 1833, 1834, and 1835. London.

Banfield, A.W.F.

1961   A revision of the reindeer and caribou, Genus Rangifer. National Museums of Canada, Bulletin 77. Ottawa.

Bergerud, A.T.

1974   The role of the environment in the aggregation, movement and disturbance behavior of caribou. In: The behavior of ungulates and its relation to management (V. Geist & F. Walthers, eds.). IUCN Publication 24, International Union of Conservation, National and Natural Resources, Morges, Switzerland.

Bielowski, Ellen

1984   Tsu Lake archaeology, 1984 interim report. Manuscript on file (no. 2589), Document collection, Library, Canadian Museum of Civilization, Hull (18 pp).

Birket-Smith, Kaj.

1929   The Caribou Eskimo. Report of the Fifth Thule Expedition, 1921-4, vol.3.

Blakeslee, Donald J.

1994   Reassessment of some radiocarbon dates from the Central Plains. Plains Anthropologist 39:148:203-210.

Blanchet, G.M.

1928   Manuscript 1018.1/B17P2. Department of Mines, Geological Survey of Canada Archives, Division of Anthropology. Written in March and accessioned April 8.

Burch, Ernest S., Jr.

1972   The caribou/wild reindeer as a human resource. American Antiquity 37:339-68.

1978   Caribou Eskimo origins: an old problem reconsidered. Arctic Anthropology, 15:1:1-35.

1991   Herd following reconsidered. Current Anthropology 32:4:439-444.

Calef, George W. and Douglas C. Heard

1980   The status of three tundra wintering caribou herds in north-eastern mainland Northwest Territories. Arctic Islands Pipeline Project Escom Report A1-44.

Condon, Richard G.

1991   Birth seasonality, photoperiod, and social change in the central Canadian Arctic. Human Ecology, 19:3:292.

Cook, Frederick

1894a   Dr. Cook among the Esquimaux: Editorial New York Journal of Gynecology and Obstetrics IV:287.

1894b   Gynecology and obstetrics among the Ekimos. Brooklyn Medical Journal 8:154.

1897   Some physical effects of arctic cold, darkness and light. Medical Record 51:833-836.

Craig, Bruce G.

1964   Surficial geology of east-central District of Mackenzie. Geological Survey of Canada, Bulletin 99, Ottawa.

Dennis, John

1970   Preliminary ecology survey within the Thelon Game Sanctuary. Progress Report. Upper Thelon River Archaeological-Botanical Project.

Dickson, Gary A.

1972   An archaeological appraisal of Southern Indian Lake, northern Manitoba. Technical Report 6, Churchill River Diversion Project. University of Winnipeg, Manitoba.

Foley, Jonathan A., John E. Kutzbach, Michael T. Coe & Samuel Levis

1994   Feedbacks between climate and boreal forests during the Holocene epoch. Nature, vol. 371, Sept. 1.

Frisch, Rose E.

1988   Fatness and fertility. Scientific American, March.

Gordon, Bryan C.

1975   Of men and herds in Barrenland prehistory. Archaeological Survey of Canada, Mercury Series 28, National Museum of Man, Ottawa.

1976   Migod - 8,000 years of Barrenland prehistory. Archaeological Series of Canada, Mercury Series 56, National Museum of Man, Ottawa.

1977   Chipewyan prehistory. In: Prehistory of the North American sub-arctic: the Athapaskan Question, p. 73. Chacmool, Archaeological Association of the University of Calgary, Alberta.

1985   Shield Archaic origins and the Barrenland climatic optimum. 17th Annual Chacmool Conference, Archaeological Association of the University of Calgary, Alberta. 10 pp.

1988   Nadlok and its unusual antler dwellings. Arctic, Journal of Arctic Institute of North America, 42(2):161-162.

1990   More on the herd-following hypothesis. Current Anthropology 31:4:399-400.

Hanbury, David T

1904   Sport and travel in the northland of Canada. MacMillan Co., New York

Harp, Elmer Jr.

1958   Prehistory in the Dismal Lake area. Arctic (2)4:219-249.

1959   The Moffatt archaeological collection from the Dubawnt country, Canada. American Antiquity 24(4):412-422

1961   The archaeology of the lower and middle Thelon, Northwest Territories. Arctic Institute of North America, Technical Paper 8.

Heard, D. C. and Calef, G. W.

1986   Population dynamics of the Kaminuriak caribou herd, 1968 - 1985. *Rangifer,* Special Issue No. 1, 1986.

Hearne, Samuel

1958   A journey from Prince of Wales' Fort in Hudson's Bay to the Northern Ocean 1769˙ 1770, 1771˙ 1772 (ed. with introduction by Richard Glover). Macmillan Company of Canada Ltd., Toronto.

Heitzman, Rod

1980   Slave River Hydro feasability study. Task area 5. Archaeological studies, phase 1. Interim report. Manuscript on file (no. 1883), Document collection, Library, Canadian Museum of Civilization, Hull 154 pp.

Hoare, W.H.B.

1990   Journal of a Barrenlander. W.H.B. Hoare, 1928-1929 (ed. by Sheila C. Thomson). MOM Printing, Ottawa.

Irving, William N.

1968   The Barren Grounds. In: Science, History and Hudson Bay. Dept. of Energy, Mines and Resources, Ottawa.

1970   The Arctic Small Tool tradition. Eighth Conference of Anthropological and Ethnological Sciences 3:340-342. Tokyo.

Jarvenpa, Robert and Hetty Jo Blumbach

1988   Socio-spatial organization and decision-making processes: observations from the Chipewyan. American Anthropologist 90(3):598-618

Jenness, Diamond

1955   Indians of Canada. National Museums of Canada, Bulletin 65, Anthropological Series 15. Ottawa.

1956   Chipewyan Indians: an account by an early explorer. Anthropologica , vol. 3. Ottawa.

Kalinka, Hans

1978   1975 correspondence and 1972-1978 sketch maps of a survey of Grant and Dubawnt Lakes, N.W.T. Manuscript on file (no. 2125), Document collection, Library, Canadian Museum of Civilization, Hull (17 pp).

Kelsey, Henry

1929   The Kelsey Papers (A.G. Doughty & C. Martin, eds.) Public Archives of Canada, Ottawa.

Larsen, James A.

1971   Vegetation of Fort Reliance, Northwest Territories.   Canadian Field-Naturalist 85:2:147-178. Ottawa.

1974   Ecology of the northern continental forest border. In: Arctic and alpine environments (Ives, J.D., and R.G. Barry, ed.). London. Methuen. pp. 341-369.

Linnamae, Urve, and Brenda L. Clarke

1976   Archaeology of Rankin Inlet, N.W.T. The Muskox, 19:37-73.

McEwan, E.H. and P.E. Whitehead

1970   Seasonal changes in the energy and nitrogen intake in reindeer and caribou. Canadian Journal of Zoology 48(5):905-913.

McGhee, Robert

1970   Excavations at Bloody Falls, N.W.T., Canada. Arctic Anthropology 6(2):53-72

Mackenzie, Alexander

1801   Voyages from Montreal on the river St. Lawrence, through the continent of North America to the frozen Pacific Ocean. London.

MacNeish, Richard S.

1951   An archaeological reconnaissance in the Northwest Territories. National Museum of Canada, Bulletin 123:24-41, Ottawa.

Mallet, Thierry Capt.

    1930   Glimpses of the Barren Lands. Revillon Frères, New York.

Mary-Roussellière, Guy

    1970   Importance du voyage du Père Gasté. Eskimo 57:3-17.

Meyer, David

    1979   Archaeology. In: Key Lake project environmental impact statement. Beak Consultants Ltd., Calgary.

    1983   The prehistory of northern Saskatchewan, Chapter 11. In: Tracking ancient hunters: prehistoric archaeology in Saskatchewan (H.T. Epp & Ian Dyck, ed.), Saskatchewan Archaeological Society, Regina.

Millar, James F.V.

    1968   Archaeology of Fisherman Lake, western District of Mackenzie, N.W.T. Unpub. Ph.D. thesis, University of Calgary.

    1983   The Chartier sites: two stratified campsites on Kisis channel near Buffalo Narrows, Saskatchewan. Northern Heritage Limited, Consulting Archaeologists. Manuscript on file (no. 2599), Document collection, Library, Canadian Museum of Civilization, Hull, Quebec.

Miller, Frank

    1974   Biology of the Kaminuriak population of barren-ground caribou, Part 2, Canadian Wildlife Service Report, Series 31. Ottawa.

    1976   Biology of the Kaminuriak population of barren-ground caribou, Part 3, Canadian Wildlife Service Report, Series 36. Ottawa.

Miller, Frank L. and E. Broughton

    1974   Calf mortality on the calving ground of the Kaminuriak herd. Canadian Wildlife Service, Report Series 26. Ottawa.

Minni, Sheila Joan

    1976   The prehistoric occupations of Black Lake, northern Saskatchewan. Archaeological Survey of Canada, Mercury Paper 53, Ottawa.

Morrison, David

    1981   Chipewyan drift fences and shooting-blinds in the central Barren Grounds. In: Megaliths to medicine wheels: boulder structures in archaeology (M. Wilson, K. Roads & K. Hardy, ed.). pp. 171-185, U. of Calgary Archaeological Association.

    1982   Report on an archaeological survey of the middle Lockhart River system, N.W.T. Manuscript on file (no. 2109), Document collection, Library, Canadian Museum of Civilization, Hull, Quebec (82 pp).

Mott, Robert J.

    1971   Radiocarbon dates from Saskatchewan: In: Report of Activities, Geological Survey of Canada Paper 71-1b.

Murdoch, W.W. and A. Oaten

    1975   Predation and population stability. Advances in Ecological Research (ed. by A. MacFadyen), vol. 9, 385 pp. Academic Press.

Nash, Ronald J.

    1972   Dorset culture in northeastern Manitoba, Canada. Arctic Anthropology 9:1:10-16. Madison.

    1975   Archaeological investigations in the transitional forest zone: northern Manitoba, southern Keewatin, N.W.T. Manitoba Museum of Man and Nature, Winnipeg

Nichols, Harvey

    1967a   The post glacial history of vegetation and climate at Ennadai Lake, Keewatin and Lynn Lake, Manitoba, Canada. Eiszeitalter und Gegenwart 18:176-197. Ohringen.

1967b   Pollen diagrams from sub-arctic central
         Canada. Science 155:1665-1668.
         Washington.

1976   Historical aspects of the northern Canadian
         treeline. Arctic 29(1)38-47.

Noble, William C.

1971   Archaeological surveys and sequences in
         the central District of Mackenzie, N.W.T.
         Arctic Anthropology 3:102-135.

Parker, Gerry R.

1972a   Biology of the Kaminuriak population of
         barren-ground caribou, Part 1, Canadian
         Wildlife Service Report Series 20. Ottawa.
         95 pp.

1972b   Distribution of Barren-Ground caribou
         harvest in north-central Canada from ear-
         tag returns. Canadian Wildlife Service,
         Occasional paper 15. Ottawa. 20 pp.

Rosetta, L.

1992   The relation between chronic malnutrition
         and fertility. Coll. Antropol. 1:83-88. UDC
         Scientific Paper.

Rowe, J. S.

1972   Forest regions of Canada. Canadian Forest
         Service, Department of the Environment
         Publication 1300. 172 pp.

Sharp, Henry S.

1988a   The transformation of Bigfoot. Maleness,
         Power and Belief among the Chipewyan.
         Smithsonian Institution Press.

1988b   Untitled 1977 tentative report - Appendices
         II and IV. Firedrake Lake archaeological
         survey. Manuscript on file (no. 2479),
         Document collection, Library, Canadian
         Museum of Civilization. 80 pp.

Smith, J.G.E.

1970   The Chipewyan hunting group in a village
         context. Western Canadian Journal of
         Anthropology, vol. 2, no. 1.

1975   The ecological basis of Chipewyan socio-
         territorial organization. In: Proceedings:
         Northern Athapascan Conference, 1971,
         (ed. by Annette McFadyen Clark), Mercury
         Series, National Museum of Man, Ottawa.
         pp. 390-461.

1978   Economic uncertainty in an "Original
         Affluent Society": Caribou and Caribou-
         Eater Chipewyan adaptive strategies. Arctic
         Anthropology 15:68-88.

Smith, J.G.E. and Ernest S. Burch, Jr.

1979   Chipewyan and Inuit in the central
         Canadian arctic. Arctic Anthropology
         16(2)76-101.

Sorenson, Curtis J., James C. Knox, James A. Larsen,
and Reid A. Bryson

1971   Paleosols and the forest border in
         Keewatin, N.W.T. Quaternary Research
         1:468-473.

Stefansson, V.

1919   The Stafansson-Anderson Arctic expedition:
         preliminary ethnological report.
         Anthropological Paper 14, American
         Museum of Natural History.

Taylor, William E., Jr.

1967   Summary of archaeological field work on Banks and Victoria Islands, Arctic Canada, 1965. Arctic Anthropology 4:1:221-243.

1968   Prehistory of Hudson Bay: Part 1. Eskimos of the north and east shores. In: Science, History and Hudson Bay, vol.1, pp. 1-26. Department of Energy, Mines and Resources, Ottawa.

1972   An archaeological survey between Cape Perry and Cambridge Bay, N.W.T., Canada in 1963. Archaeological Survey of Canada, Mercury Paper 1, National Museum of Man, Ottawa.

Terasmae, J. and Bruce G. Craig

1958   The discovery of fossil *Ceratophyllum demersum* L. in N.W.T., Canada. Canadian Journal of Botany 36:567-569.

Terasmae, J.

1961   Notes on Late Quaternary climatic changes in Canada. Annals of the New York Academy of Sciences 96(1)658-675).

Thompson, David

1916   David Thompson's Narrative of His Explorations in Western America, 1784-1812. (J.B. Tyrrell, ed.). The Chaplain Society, vol. 12, Toronto.

Timoney, K.P., G.H. La Roi, S.C. Zoltai, and A.L. Robinson

1992   The high subarctic forest-tundra of northwestern Canada: position, width, and vegetation gradients in relation to climate. Arctic. Arctic Institute of North America,

Tyrrell, J.B.

1898   Report on the Doobaunt, Kazan, and Ferguson Rivers, and the northwest coast of Hudson Bay and on two overland routes from Hudson Bay to Lake Winnipeg. Geological Survey of Canada, Annual Report for 1896 (n.s.), vol. 9, report F, pp. 1-218. Ottawa.

1911   A journey from Prince of Wales' Fort in Hudson's Bay to the Northern Ocean in the years 1769, 1770, 1771 and 1772, by Samuel Hearne. The Chaplain Society, Toronto. Vol. 6.

Tyrrell, James W.

1902   Report on an exploratory survey between Great Slave Lake and Hudson Bay. Department of the Interior, Bulletin 12. Ottawa. 62 pp.

Wilson, James S.

1981   Archaeology, Chapter VIII. In: Athabasca Sand Dunes in Saskatchewan (Z.M. Abouguendia, ed.). Mackenzie River Basin Study, supplement 7.

van Kirk, Sylvia

1974   Thanadelthur. The Beaver. Spring, pp.40-45.

Whalley, George

1962   The Legend of John Hornby. MacMillan Company of Canada, Toronto.

Wright, G.M.

1967   Geology of the southeastern barren grounds, parts of the Districts of Mackenzie and Keewatin. Geological Survey of Canada, Memoir 350, Ottawa.

Wright, J.V.

   1972a   The Aberdeen site, Keewatin District,
             N.W.T. Archaeological Survey of Canada,
             Mercury Series 2, National Museum of
             Man, Ottawa.

   1972b   The Shield Archaic. Publications in
             Archaeology 3, National Museums of
             Canada.

   1975   The prehistory of Lake Athabasca: an initial
             statement. Archaeological Survey of
             Canada, Mercury Paper 9, National
             Museum of Man, Ottawa.

   1976   The Grant Lake site, Keewatin District,
             N.W.T. Archaeological Survey of Canada,
             Mercury Paper 47, Ottawa.

Y

List of Figures and Tables

Figures

Tables *(Tables not listed below are in the Appendix)*

Tables not included below are in the text

Material	Range total	Forest total	Tundra total
quartzite	293(82)	169(74)	124(95)
chert	28(08)	24(11)	4(03)
quartz	10(03)	9(04)	1(01)
silicious shale	8(02)	6(03)	2(01)
basalt	1(00)	1(00)	
schist	1(00)	1(00)	
sandstone	16(04)	16(07)	
felsite	1(00)	1(00)	
siltstone	1(00)	1(00)	
Total	359(99)	228(99)	131(100)

Table 4.3a. Late phase point material.

Colour	Range total	Forest total	Tundra total
beige	84(23)	53(23)	31(24)
white	110(31)	59(26)	51(39)
orange	14(04)	6(03)	8(06)
gray	102(28)	84(37)	18(14)
pink	16(04)	4(02)	12(09)
red	8(02)	3(01)	5(04)
brown	9(03)	6(03)	3(02)
green	3(01)	3(01)	
purple	4(01)	2(01)	2(02)
clear	1(00)	1(00)	
black	6(02)	5(02)	1(01)
other	2(01)	2(01)	
Total	359(100)	228(100)	131(101)

Table 4.3b. Late phase point colour.

Plan	Range total	Forest total	Tundra total
lanceolate	129(36)	49(25)	80(49)
triangular	1(00)	1(01)	
spadelike	226(63)	144(73)	82(51)
pentagonal	1(00)	1(01)	
Total	357(99)	195(100)	162(100)

Table 4.4. Late phase point plan.

Cross-section	Range total	Forest total	Tundra total
biconvex	322(90)	199(87)	123(94)
planoconvex	33(09)	27(12)	6(05)
biplanar	4(01)	2(01)	2(02)
Total	359(100)	228(100)	131(101)

Table 4.5. Late phase point section.

Type of tip	Range total	Forest total	Tundra total
none/unknown	148(41)	80(35)	68(52)
pointed tip	170(47)	121(53)	49(37)
round	30(08)	22(10)	8(06)
serrated	1(00)	1(00)	
square	3(01)	2(01)	1(01)
burinated	7(02)	2(01)	5(04)
Total	359(99)	228(100)	131(100)

Table 4.6. Late phase point tips.

Type of taper	Range total	Forest total	Tundra total
unknown fragment	35(10)	21(09)	14(11)
tapered to tip	164(46)	117(51)	47(36)
tapered to base	25(07)	12(05)	13(10)
parallel sided	135(38)	78(34)	57(44)
Total	359(99)	228(99)	131(101)

Table 4.7. Late phase point taper.

Type of base	Range total	Forest total	Tundra total
unknown fragment	12(03)	10(04)	2(02)
unground square	11(03)	9(04)	3(03)
ground square	1(00)	1(00)	
unground stem	15(04)	12(05)	3(03)
ground stem	7(02)	3(01)	4(03)
unground flare	1(00)	1(00)	
parallel tang	55(15)	41(18)	14(11)
tapered tang	21(06)	10(04)	11(09)
unground side-notch	170(47)	104(45)	66(51)
ground side-notch	42(12)	19(08)	23(18)
unground corner-notch	19(05)	18(08)	1(01)
ground corner-notch	1(00)	1(00)	
fishtail	4(01)	2(01)	2(02)
Total	359(98)	230(98)	129(103)

Table 4.8. Late phase point bases.

Basal edge	Range total	Forest total	Tundra total
unknown fragment	42(12)	31(14)	11(08)
unground flat	156(43)	103(45)	53(40)
ground flat	56(16)	34(15)	22(17)
unground round	54(15)	28(12)	26(20)
ground round	19(5)	12(05)	7(05)
unground concave	19(5)	10(04)	9(07)
ground concave	6(02)	4(02)	2(02)
unground pointed	7(02)	6(03)	1(01)
Total	359(100)	228(100)	131(100)

Table 4.9. Late phase point basal edges.

Shoulder type	Range total	Forest total	Tundra total
none/unknown	282(79)	170(71)	112(93)
ungroundsingle	9(03)	7(03)	2(02)
ground single	3(01)	3(01)	
unground double	35(10)	29(12)	6(05)
ground double	30(08)	29(12)	1(01)
Total	359(101)	238(99)	121(101)

Table 4.10. Late phase point shoulders.

Breakage	Range total	Forest total	Tundra total
none	170(47)	125(55)	45(34)
transverse	121(33)	65(29)	56(43)
diagonal	24(07)	13(06)	11(08)
semi-diagonal	22(06)	12(06)	10(08)
double diagonal	3(01)	2(01)	1(01)
transverse-diagonal	5(01)	4(02)	1(01)
double transverse	7(02)	5(02)	2(02)
longitudinal/transverse	7(02)	2(01)	5(04)
Total	359(99)	228(102)	131(101)

Table 4.11. Late phase point breakage.

Burination	Range total	Forest total	Tundra total
none/unknown	349(97)	225(98)	124(96)
1 side or face	8(02)	3(01)	5(04)
2 sides/faces	2(01)	2(01)	
Total	359(100)	230(100)	129(100)

Table 4.12. Late phase point burination.

Special traits	Range total	Forest total	Tundra total
none/unknown	161(45)	97(42)	64(49)
eared	134(37)	88(38)	46(35)
almost notched	15(04)	11(05)	4(03)
burnt	1(00)	1(00)	
patinated	5(01)	3(01)	2(02)
single side-notch	6(02)	5(02)	1(01)
channel-flaked	4(01)	1(00)	3(02)
almost tanged	31(09)	21(09)	10(08)
thinned base	2(01)	2(01)	
Total	359(100)	229(98)	130(100)

Table 4.13. Special traits in Late phase points.

Other usage	Range total	Forest total	Tundra total
none/unknown	345(96)	218(96)	127(97)
wedge	1(00)		1(01)
knife	9(03)	7(03)	2(02)
graver	2(01)	2(01)	
bifacial scraper	1(00)		1(01)
endscraper	1(00)	1(00)	
Total	359(100)	228(100)	131(101)

Table 4.14. Late phase points with other functions.

Est.	No.	Min.	Max.	Mean	S.D.	Exclude
L	204	18.00	90.00	44.42	12.68	24 frag.
W	217	12.48	38.91	21.05	4.46	11 frag.
T	218	00.16	11.00	6.74	1.52	10 frag.
Wt	103	1.00	60.00	6.47	6.46	125 frag.

Table 4.15a. Late phase forest point data (mm and g).

Est.	No.	Min.	Max.	Mean	S.D.	Exclude
L	120	19.48	90.00	47.79	13.10	11 frag.
W	126	14.10	35.98	21.28	3.83	5 frag.
T	129	3.60	11.18	7.28	1.54	2 frag.
Wt	47	1.40	47	7.72	4.60	84 frag.

Table 4.15b. Late phase tundra point data (mm and g).

Material	Range total	Forest total	Tundra total
quartzite	96(63)	54(52)	42(86)
chert	26(17)	21(20)	5(10)
quartz	24(16)	22(21)	2(04)
silicious shale	1(01)	1(01)	
sandstone	5(03)	5(05)	
basalt	1(01)	1(01)	
Total	153(101)	104(100)	49(100)

Table 4.16a. Late phase scraper material.

Colour	Range total	Forest total	Tundra total
beige	31(20)	21(20)	10(20)
white	45(29)	33(32)	12(24)
orange	11(07)	1(01)	10(20)
gray	36(24)	29(28)	7(14)
pink	10(07)	8(08)	2(04)
red	1(01)		1(02)
brown	6(04)	5(05)	1(02)
green	3(02)		3(06)
purple	2(01)		2(04)
other	8(05)	7(07)	1(02)
Total	153(100)	104(101)	49(98)

Table 4.16b. Late phase scraper colour.

Plan	Range total	Forest total	Tundra total
unknown fragment	2(01)	1(01)	1(02)
rhomboid	34(22)	26(25)	8(16)
tearshape	26(17)	15(14)	11(22)
triangular	14(09)	4(04)	10(20)
ovoid	23(15)	16(15)	7(14)
rectangular/bladelike	32(21)	24(23)	8(16)
square	16(10)	13(13)	3(06)
ululike	1(01)	1(01)	
discoid	5(03)	4(04)	1(02)
Total	153(99)	104(100)	49(98)

Table 4.17a. Late phase scraper plan.

Plan	Forest	Tundra	Overall
rhomboid	31.55	23.80	33.28 for 4-sided
rectangle	35.15	41.73	
tearshaped	36.24	35.81	43.00 for 3-sided
triangular	68.35	30.55	

Table 4.17b. Mean lengths (mm) of 3 and 4-sided Late scrapers

Cross-section	Range total	Forest total	Tundra total
tabular	76(50)	50(48)	26(53)
keeled	31(20)	23(22)	8(16)
tortoise	30(20)	18(17)	12(24)
biconvex	1(01)		1(02)
planoconvex	14(09)	12(12)	2(04)
concavoconvex	1(01)	1(01)	
Total	153(101)	104(100)	49(99)

Table 4.18. Late phase scraper section.

Edge type	Range total	Forest total	Tundra total
serrated	25(16)	20(20)	5(10)
unserrated	128(84)	84(80)	44(90)
Total	153(100)	104(100)	49(100)

Table 4.19. Late phase scraper edge type.

Base	Range total	Forest total	Tundra total
unknown fragment	2(01)	1(01)	1(02)
unretouched/unground	61(40)	55(53)	6(12)
unretouched/ground	26(17)	7(07)	19(39)
dorsal retouch	58(38)	38(37)	20(41)
bifacial retouch	4(03)	2(02)	2(04)
double bitted	2(01)	1(01)	1(02)
Total	153(100)	104(101)	49(100)

Table 4.20a. Late phase scraper basal configuration

Basal grinding	Range total	Forest total	Tundra total
none/unknown	2(01)	1(01)	1(02)
ground	77(50)	42(40)	35(71)
very ground	4(03)	3(03)	1(02)
unground	70(46)	58(56)	12(24)
Total	153(100)	103(100)	49(100)

Table 4.20b. Late phase scraper basal grinding.

Cortex	Range total	Forest total	Tundra total
none	117(76)	77(74)	40(82)
present	36(24)	27(26)	9(18)
Total	153(100)	104(100)	49(100)

Table 4.21. Late phase scraper cortex.

Bit wear	Range total	Forest total	Tundra total
worn	83(54)	49(47)	34(69)
very worn	10(07)	4(04)	6(12)
unworn	60(39)	51(49)	9(18)
Total	153(100)	104(100)	49(99)

Table 4.22. Late phase scraper bit wear.

Striae	Range total	Forest total	Tundra total
none/unknown	147(96)	104(100)	43(88)
over the edge	6(04)		6(12)
Total	153(100)	104(100)	49(100)

Table 4.23. Late phase scraper striae.

Bifac. platform	Range total	Forest total	Tundra total
unknown	131(86)	90(87)	41(84)
present	22(14)	14(13)	8(16)
Total	153(100)	104(100)	49(100)

Table 4.24. Late phase scrapers made from thinning flakes.

Spurring	Range total	Forest total	Tundra total
unspurred	133(87)	93(89)	40(82)
single spur	17(11)	10(09)	7(14)
double spur	3(02)	1(01)	2(04)
Total	153(100)	104(99)	49(100)

Table 4.25. Late phase scraper spurring.

Est.	No.	Min.	Max.	Mean	S.D.	Exclude
L	103	12.00	100.0	35.64	17.49	1 frag.
W	104	10.00	68.12	26.63	9.74	none
T	104	3.02	24.04	9.29	4.22	none
Wt	67	0.60	190.4	19.80	27.92	37 frag.

Table 4.26a. Late phase forest scraper data (mm and g).

Est.	No.	Min.	Max.	Mean	S.D.	Exclude
L	47	14.04	50.60	32.87	9.25	2 frag.
W	47	14.06	38.26	27.21	5.52	2 frag.
T	49	2.87	12.42	7.60	2.52	none
Wt	35	0.90	21.40	8.08	4.97	4 frag.

Table 4.26b. Late phase tundra scraper data (mm and g).

Material	Range total	Forest total	Tundra total
quartzite	255(85)	70(67)	185(95)
chert	15(05)	9(09)	6(03)
quartz	17(05)	16(15)	1(01)
silicious shale	6(02)	4(04)	2(01)
sandstone	3(01)	2(02)	1(01)
greenstone	2(01)	2(02)	
gneiss	1(00)	1(01)	
schist	1(00)	1(01)	
Total	300(99)	105(101)	195(101)

Table 4.27a. Late phase knife material.

Colour	Range total	Forest total	Tundra total
beige	91(30)	17(16)	74(37)
white	42(14)	21(20)	21(11)
orange	27(09)	4(04)	23(12)
gray	63(21)	35(33)	28(14)
pink	24(08)	8(08)	16(08)
red	10(03)	2(02)	8(04)
green	4(01)	1(01)	3(02)
brown	16(05)	5(05)	11(06)
purple	12(04)	3(03)	9(05)
clear	2(01)	2(02)	
unknown	1(00)		1(00)
other	8(03)	7(07)	1(00)
Total	300(99)	105(97)	195(99)

Table 4.27b. Late phase knife colour.

Faciality	Range total	Forest total	Tundra total
unifacial	65(22)	27(26)	38(19)
bifacial	235(78)	78(74)	157(81)
Total	300(100)	105(100)	195(100)

Table 4.28. Late phase knife faciality.

Completeness	Range total	Forest total	Tundra total
base only	30(10)	6(06)	24(12)
midsection	31(10)	5(05)	26(13)
tip only	4(01)		4(02)
base-midsection	46(15)	9(09)	37(18)
tip and midsection	28(09)	9(09)	19(10)
edge fragment	27(09)	1(01)	26(13)
complete	124(41)	72(69)	53(27)
longitudinally split	1(00)		1(00)
light chipping	9(03)	3(03)	6(03)
Total	300(98)	105(102)	195(98)

Table 4.29. Late phase knife completeness.

Plan	Range total	Forest total	Tundra total
unknown	52(17)	3(03)	49(25)
lanceolate	43(14)	14(13)	29(15)
ovoid	100(33)	30(29)	70(36)
semilunar	11(04)	6(06)	5(03)
rectangular/square	21(07)	13(12)	8(04)
triangular	18(06)	9(09)	9(05)
pentagonal	3(01)	3(03)	
asymmetrically ovoid	7(02)	1(01)	6(03)
discoidal	27(09)	17(16)	10(05)
unishoulder	6(02)	2(02)	4(02)
bishoulder	4(01)	1(01)	3(02)
notched	2(01)	1(01)	1(01)
spadelike	2(01)	2(02)	
bladelike	2(01)	1(01)	1(01)
rhomboid	2(01)	2(02)	
Total	300(100)	105(101)	195(100)

Table 4.30. Late phase knife plan.

Section	Range total	Forest total	Tundra total
unknown	2(01)		2(01)
biconvex	166(55)	54(51)	112(57)
planoconvex	107(36)	45(43)	62(32)
tabular	5(02)	3(03)	2(01)
concavoconvx	3(01)		3(02)
keeled	12(04)	3(03)	9(05)
sinuous	5(02)		5(03)
Total	300(101)	105(100)	192(101)

Table 4.31. Late phase knife section.

Type of edge	Range total	Forest total	Tundra total
unknown	11(04)	1(01)	10(05)
serrated preform	63(21)	26(25)	37(19)
unworn bifacial retouch	78(26)	25(24)	53(27)
unworn unifacial retouch	31(10)	16(16)	15(08)
worn bifacial retouch	91(30)	31(30)	60(30)
worn unifacial retouch	20(07)	5(02)	15(08)
worn flake edge	1(00)		1(00)
serrated and worn	5(02)	1(01)	4(02)
Total	300(100)	105(99)	195(99)

Tables 4.32. Late phase knife edge type

Base	Range total	Forest total	Tundra total
unknown	80(27)	8(08)	72(36)
unground unretouched	14(05)	8(08)	6(03)
unground dorsal retouch	45(15)	19(18)	26(13)
unground ventral retouch	1(00)		1(01)
unground bifacial retouch	113(38)	54(51)	59(30)
ground dorsal retouch	5(02)	2(01)	3(02)
ground ventral retouch	1(00)		1(01)
ground bifacial retouch	37(12)	13(12)	24(12)
ground alternate retouch	2(01)	1(01)	1(01)
bifacial thinning	2(01)		2(01)
Total	300(101)	105(99)	195(100)

Table 4.33. Late phase knife base.

Midsection	Range total	Forest total	Tundra total
unknown	50(17)	5(05)	45(23)
unifacial retouch	40(13)	17(16)	23(12)
bifacial retouch	136(45)	49(47)	87(44)
serrated	74(25)	34(32)	40(20)
Total	300(100)	105(100)	195(99)

Table 4.34. Late phase knife midsection.

Type of tip	Range total	Forest total	Tundra total
unknown	130(43)	20(19)	110(55)
unworn and pointed	37(12)	16(15)	21(11)
worn and round	37(12)	22(21)	15(08)
worn point	19(08)	10(10)	9(05)
unworn round	51(17)	25(24)	26(13)
serrated	12(04)	5(05)	7(04)
square	14(05)	7(07)	7(04)
Total	300(101)	105(101)	195(100)

Tables 4.35 . Late phase knife tips.

Striae	Range total	Forest total	Tundra total
none	299	104	195
bifacial; parallel to edge	1	1	
Total	300	105	195

Table 4.37. Late phase knife striae.

Basal plan	Range total	Forest total	Tundra total
unknown	87(29)	13(12)	74(38)
tapered, flat and ground	7(02)	3(03)	4(02)
tapered, round and ground	6(02)	3(03)	3(02)
tapered, flat & unground	10(03)	3(03)	7(04)
tapered, round, unground	40(13)	20(19)	20(10)
round and ground	19(06)	5(05)	14(07)
round and unground	48(16)	25(24)	23(12)
ground pointed	9(03)		9(05)
unground pointed	27(09)	9(09)	18(09)
concave and ground	2(01)	1(01)	1(01)
concave and unground	1(00)		1(01)
square and ground	4(01)	1(01)	3(02)
square and unground	22(07)	13(12)	9(05)
ground side-notch	1(00)	1(01)	
unground side-notch	3(01)	2(02)	1(01)
unground corner-notch	1(00)		1(01)
ground tang	2(01)	2(02)	
unground tang	7(02)	4(04)	3(02)
serrated	4(01)		4(02)
Total	300(99)	105(101)	195(104)

Tables 4.39. Late phase knife basal plan.

Type of back	Range total	Forest total	Tundra total
unknown	83(28)	11(10)	72(37)
like opposite edge	213(71)	90(86)	123(63)
blunted	4(01)	4(04)	
Total	300(100)	105(100)	195(100)

Table 4.40. Late phase knife backing.

Cortex	Range total	Forest total	Tundra total
unknown	245(82)	79(75)	166(85)
dorsal face	21(07)	12(11)	9(05)
tip face	5(02)	1(01)	4(02)
midsection face	5(02)	2(02)	3(02)
midsection edge	2(01)		2(01)
basal edge	5(02)	4(04)	1(01)
striking platform	17(06)	7(07)	10(05)
Total	300(102)	105(100)	195(101)

Table 4.38. Late phase knife cortex.

Type of break	Range total	Forest total	Tundra total
unknown	115(38)	68(65)	47(24)
transverse	47(16)	11(10)	36(18)
diagonal	32(11)	7(07)	25(13)
transverse-diagonal	15(05)	3(03)	12(06)
longitudinal	20(07)	1(01)	19(10)
semi-transverse	24(08)	6(06)	18(09)
multi-transverse	6(02)	2(02)	4(02)
transverse/longitud.	13(04)	1(01)	12(06)
multi-diagonal	11(04)	2(02)	9(05)
diag. & longitudinal	8(03)	2(02)	6(03)
lightly chipped	4(01)		4(02)
transversely halved	2(01)	2(02)	
longitud. halved	3(01)		3(02)
Total	300(101)	105(101)	195(100)

Table 4.36. Late phase knife breakage.

Striking platform	Range total	Forest total	Tundra total
unknown	85(28)	14(13)	71(36)
ground & unfacetted	7(02)	2(02)	5(03)
unground/unfacetted	32(11)	11(10)	21(11)
ground and facetted	7(02)	4(04)	3(02)
unground & facetted	19(06)	9(09)	10(05)
on raised side	8(03)	2(02)	6(03)
on unraised side	2(01)	2(02)	
retouched away	139(46)	61(58)	78(40)
on raised base	1(00)		1(01)
Total	300(99)	105(100)	195(99)

Table 4.41. Late phase knife striking platform.

Est.	No.	Min.	Max.	Mean	S.D.	Exclude
L	92	19.00	150.0	63.22	30.89	13 frag.
W	99	13.00	107.0	38.46	18.13	6 frag.
T	104	3.66	45.06	12.61	5.90	1 frag.
Wt	45	1.52	421.3	63.17	92.82	60 frag.

Table 4.42a. Late phase forest knife data (mm and g).

Est.	No.	Min.	Max.	Mean	S.D.	Exclude
L	98	33.00	140.0	76.89	25.20	97 frag.
W	126	11.00	116.0	43.35	17.39	69 frag.
T	182	3.80	27.83	12.70	4.40	13 frag.
Wt	53	3.20	478.7	52.36	73.12	142 frag.

Table 4.42b. Late phase tundra knife data (mm and g).

Material	Range total	Forest total	Tundra total
sandstone	80(75)	61(72)	19(86)
quartzite	7(07)	4(05)	3(14)
schist	11(10)	11(13)	
gneiss	6(06)	6(07)	
granite	2(02)	2(02)	
phyllite	1(01)	1(01)	
basalt	1(01)	1(01)	
Total	107(102)	85(101)	22(100)

Table 4.44a. Late phase chitho material.

Colour	Range total	Forest total	Tundra total
beige	55(51)	47(55)	8(36)
white	4(04)	2(02)	2(09)
orange	3(03)	1(01)	2(09)
gray	12(11)	6(07)	6(27)
pink	3(03)		3(14)
red	3(03)	3(03)	
brown	2(02)	1(01)	1(05)
green	1(01)	1(01)	
purple	3(03)	3(03)	
black	1(01)	1(01)	
unknown	20(19)	20(24)	
Total	107(101)	85(98)	22(100)

Table 4.45. Late phase chitho colour.

Faciality	Range total	Forest total	Tundra total
bifacial	79(74)	65(76)	14(64)
unifacial	28(26)	20(24)	8(36)
Total	107(100)	85(100)	22(100)

Table 4.44b. Late phase chitho facilaity.

Completeness	Range total	Forest total	Tundra total
complete	92(85)	76(89)	16(73)
edge fragment	2(02)		2(09)
halved	3(03)	1(01)	2(09)
quartered	2(02)		2(09)
some spalling	8(07)	8(08)	
Total	107(99)	85(98)	22(100)

Table 4.46. Late phase chitho completeness.

Plan	Range total	Forest total	Tundra total
ovoid	36(34)	30(35)	6(27)
round	32(30)	27(32)	5(23)
rectangular/square	26(24)	17(20)	9(41)
lanceolate	4(04)	3(04)	1(05)
bell-shaped	1(01)		1(05)
pentagonal	2(02)	2(02)	
D-shaped	6(06)	6(07)	
Total	107(101)	85(100)	22(101)

Table 4.47. Late phase chitho plan.

Section	Range total	Forest total	Tundra total
flat/parallel	79(74)	65(76)	14(64)
uneven/wavy	28(26)	20(24)	8(36)
Total	107(100)	85(100)	22(100)

Table 4.48. Late phase chitho section.

Edge wear	Range total	Forest total	Tundra total
worn	98(92)	79(93)	19(86)
unworn	9(08)	6(07)	3(14)
Total	107(100)	85(100)	22(100)

Table 4.49. Late phase chitho wear.

Cortex	Range total	Forest total	Tundra total
unknown	23(21)	23(27)	
present	67(63)	55(65)	12(55)
none	17(16)	7(08)	10(45)
Total	107(100)	85(100)	22(100)

Table 4.50. Late phase chitho cortex.

Est.	No.	Min.	Max.	Mean	S.D.	Exclude
L	81	29.00	153.0	85.19	22.57	4 frag.
W	78	26.00	101.0	63.13	15.77	7 frag.
T	85	4.96	31.00	12.85	5.47	nonw
Wt	56	29.22	260.8	95.46	50.07	29 frag.

Table 4.51a. Late phase forest chitho data (mm and g).

Est.	No.	Min.	Max.	Mean	S.D.	Exclude
L	17	71.19	121.7	92.84	15.13	5 frag.
W	18	40.01	103.0	70.76	13.20	4 frag.
T	22	5.41	20.44	12.01	4.26	none
Wt	16	42.83	254.8	102.2	55.33	6 frag.

Table 4.51c. Late phase tundra chitho data (mm and g).

Material	Range total	Forest total	Tundra total
quartzite	15(48)	4(21)	11(92)
quartz	13(42)	13(68)	
chert	3(10)	2(11)	1(08)
Total	31(100)	19(100)	12(100)

Table 4.53a. Late phase wedge material.Table 4.53b.

Colour	Range total	Forest total	Tundra total
beige	3(10)		3(25)
white	11(35)	10(53)	1(08)
orange	1(03)		1(08)
gray	7(23)	2(11)	5(42)
pink	1(03)		1(08)
green	1(03)		1(08)
clear	6(19)	6(32)	
black	1(03)	1(05)	
Total	31(99)	19(101)	12(99)

Fig. 4.53b. Late phase wedge colour.

Plan	Range total	Forest total	Tundra total
unknown	1(03)		1(08)
rectangular	6(19)	4(21)	2(17)
square	4(13)	1(05)	3(25)
rhomboid	5(16)	3(16)	2(17)
parallelogram	6(19)	5(26)	1(08)
tearshape/triangle	4(13)	4(21)	
biconvex/ovoid	4(13)	2(11)	2(17)
round	1(03)		1(08)
Total	31(99)	19(99)	12(100)

Table 4.54. Late phase wedge plan.

Section	Range total	Forest total	Tundra total
unknown	1(03)		1(08)
biplanar	1(03)	1(05)	
biconvex	7(23)	4(21)	3(25)
plnocnvx	7(23)	3(16)	4(33)
triangle	6(19)	2(11)	4(33)
concavoconvex	2(06)	2(11)	
rhomboid	6(19)	6(32)	
parallellogram	1(03)	1(05)	
Total	31(99)	19(101)	12(99)

Table 4.55. Late phase wedge section.

Flake scar type	Range total	Forest total	Tundra total
unknown	1(03)		1(08)
amorphous	6(19)	3(16)	3(25)
flat column	7(23)	5(26)	2(17)
channelled	3(10)	2(11)	1(08)
" columnar	14(45)	9(47)	5(42)
Total	31(100)	19(100)	12(100)

Table 4.56. Late phase wedge flake scars.

Percussion	Range total	Forest total	Tundra total
unknown	1(03)		1(08)
bipolar	20(65)	13(38)	7(57)
double bipolar	5(16)	3(16)	2(17)
unipolar	2(06)	2(11)	
discoidal	3(10)	19(100)	12(100)

Table 4.57. Late phase wedge percussion.

Est.	No.	Min.	Max.	Mean	S.D.	Exclude
L	19	18.67	42.83	33.29	7.25	none
W	19	11.37	34.06	24.01	5.69	none
T	19	6.06	17.52	11.44	3.08	none
Wt	18	1.76	21.87	11.23	5.77	1 frag.

Table 4.58a. Late phase forest wedge data (mm and g).

Est.	No.	Min.	Max.	Mean	S.D.	Exclude
L	10	24.87	50.17	32.41	8.86	2 frag.
W	11	7.36	43.02	23.08	9.69	1 frag.
T	12	5.89	16.30	8.76	2.65	none
Wt	10	1.20	42.20	9.54	11.86	2 frag.

Table 4.58a. Late phase forest wedge data (mm and g).

Material	Range total	Forest total	Tundra total
basalt	9(43)	5(36)	4(58)
chert	2(10)	1(07)	1(14)
quartzite	3(14)	2(14)	1(14)
silicious shale	7(33)	6(43)	1(14)
Total	21(100)	14(100)	7(100)

Table 4.61. Late phase adze tool material.

Colour	Range total	Forest total	Tundra total
white	1(05)	1(07)	
orange	1(05)		1(14)
gray	12(57)	10(71)	2(29)
green	2(10)	2(14)	
brown	2(10)	1(07)	1(14)
black	3(14)		3(43)
Total	21(101)	14(99)	7(100)

Table 4.62. Late phase adze tool colour.

Striae type	Range total	Forest total	Tundra total
none	15(71)	9(64)	6(86)
transverse	1(05)	1(07)	
diagonal	2(10)	2(14)	
longitudinal	2(10)	2(14)	
transverse-diagonal	1(05)		1(14)
Total	7(101)	14(99)	7(100)

Table 4.63. Late phase adze striae relative to longitudinal axis.

Flake type	Range total	Forest total	Tundra total
lateral	15(71)	9(64)	5(71)
bit	2(10)	1(07)	
complete tool	4(19)	4(29)	2(29)
Total	21(100)	14(100)	7(100)

Table 4.64. Late phase adzelike tool flake type.

Area	Range total	Forest total	Tundra total
none	9(43)	4(29)	5(71)
restricted	2(10)	2(14)	
widespread	10(48)	8(57)	2(29)
Total	21(101)	14(100)	7(100)

Table 4.65. Late phase adzelike tool grinding.

Polish	Range total	Forest total	Tundra total
none	10(48)	4(29)	6(86)
light	1(05)	1(07)	
heavy	10(48)	9(64)	1(14)
Total	21(101)	14(100)	7(100)

Table 4.66. Late phase adzelike tool polish.

Grooved platform	Range total	Forest total	Tundra total
unknown	5(24)	2(14)	3(43)
none	16(76)	12(86)	4(57)
Total	21(100)	14(100)	7(100)

Table 4.67. Late phase adzelike tool grooved platforms.

Hinge fracture	Range total	Forest total	Tundra total
unknown	16(76)	10(71)	6(86)
present	3(14)	3(21)	
none	2(10)	1(07)	1(14)
Total	21(100)	14(99)	7(100)

Table 4.68. Late phase adzelike tool hinge fractures.

Est.	No.	Min.	Max.	Mean	S.D.	Exclude
L	9	12.65	44.13	26.52	9.85	none
W	9	16.30	59.68	30.86	15.29	"
T	9	1.78	8.64	4.62	2.03	"
Wt	9	0.59	12.05	4.11	3.73	"

Table 4.69a. Late phase forest adze flake data (mm and g).

Est.	No.	Min.	Max.	Mean	S.D.	Exclude
L	5	10.95	40.53	18.27	12.61	none
W	5	10.52	45.54	18.90	15.04	"
T	5	1.06	7.12	2.80	2.47	"
Wt	5	0.18	10.57	2.37	4.59	"

Table 4.69b. Late phase tundra adze flake data (mm and g).

Material	Range total	Forest total	Tundra total
quartzite	45(79)	12(57)	33(92)
chert	2(04)		2(06)
quartz	9(16)	8(38)	1(03)
sandstone	1(02)	1(05)	
Total	57(101)	21(100)	36(101)

Table 4.70a. Late phase core material.

Colour	Range total	Forest total	Tundra total
beige	15(26)	1(05)	14(39)
white	17(30)	10(48)	7(19)
orange	8(14)	1(05)	7(19)
gray	9(16)	7(33)	2(06)
pink	2(04)	1(05)	1(03)
brown	2(04)		2(06)
green	1(02)	1(05)	
purple	3(06)		3(09)
Total	57(102)	21(101)	36(101)

Table 4.70b. Late phase core colour.

Plan	Range total	Forest total	Tundra total
unknown	5(09)		5(14)
round cobble	20(35)	4(19)	16(44)
rectangular/square	17(30)	7(33)	10(28)
ovoid	10(18)	5(24)	5(14)
triangular	5(09)	5(24)	
Total	57(101)	21(100)	36(100)

Table 4.71. Late phase core plan.

Texture	Range total	Forest total	Tundra total
normal	43(75)	16(76)	27(75)
banded	10(18)	1(05)	9(25)
mottled	1(02)	1(05)	
veined	3(06)	3(14)	
Total	57(101)	21(100)	36(100)

Table 4.70c. Late phase core texture.

Section	Range total	Forest total	Tundra total
unknown	5(09)		5(14)
round	17(30)	2(10)	15(42)
rectang./rhomb/square	14(25)	3(14)	11(31)
triangular	5(09)	3(14)	2(06)
planoconvex	8(14)	6(29)	2(06)
biconvex	8(14)	7(33)	1(03)
Total	57(101)	21(100)	36(102)

Table 4.72. Late phase core section.

Profile	Range total	Forest total	Tundra total
blocky	30(53)	11(52)	19(53)
conical	18(32)	3(14)	15(42)
spherical	3(05)	1(05)	2(06)
boatshaped	1(02)	1(05)	
lenticular	5(09)	5(24)	
Total	57(101)	21(100)	36(101)

Table 4.73. Late phase core profile.

Flake removal	Range total	Forest total	Tundra total
blade/bladelike	5(09)	4(19)	1(03)
flakelike	52(91)	17(81)	35(97)
Total	57(100)	21(100)	36(100)

Table 4.74. Late phase core flake removal.

Platform	Range total	Forest total	Tundra total
single	13(23)	7(33)	6(17)
crescentic	37(65)	11(52)	26(72)
bipolar	7(12)	3(14)	4(11)
Total	57(100)	21(99)	36(100)

Table 4.75. Late phase core striking platform.

Cortex	Range total	Forest total	Tundra total
present	40(70)	10(48)	30(83)
none/unknown	17(30)	11(52)	6(17)
Total	57(100)	21(100)	36(100)

Table 4.76. Late phase core cortex.

Battering	Range total	Forest total	Tundra total
none/unknown	3(05)	2(10)	1(03)
unipolar	42(74)	13(62)	29(81)
bipolar	12(21)	6(29)	6(17)
Total	57(100)	21(101)	36(101)

Table 4.77. Late phase core battering.

Edge wear	Range total	Forest total	Tundra total
unknown	1(02)		1(03)
present	2(04)	2(10)	
none	54(95)	19(90)	35(97)
Total	57(101)	21(100)	36(100)

Table 4.78. Late phase core edge wear.

Depleted	Range total	Forest total	Tundra total
no	27(47)	1(05)	26(72)
yes	30(53)	20(95)	10(28)
Total	57(100)	21(100)	36(100)

Table 4.79. Late phase core depletion.

Multiple use	Range total	Forest total	Tundra total
none/unknown	51(89)	20(95)	31(86)
pushplane	2(04)		2(06)
wedge	1(02)	1(05)	
knife	2(04)		2(06)
hammerstone	1(02)		1(03)
Total	57(101)	21(100)	36(101)

Table 4.80. Late phase cores used as other tools.

Serrated	Range total	Forest total	Tundra total
no	42(74)	10(48)	32(89)
yes	15(26)	11(52)	4(11)
Total	57(100)	21(100)	36(100)

Table 4.81. Late phase core serration.

Hinging	Range total	Forest total	Tundra total
no	42(74)	10(48)	32(89)
yes	15(26)	11(52)	4(11)
Total	57(100)	21(100)	36(100)

Table 4.82. Late phase core hinge fractures.

Est.	No.	Min.	Max.	Mean	S.D.	Exclude
L	21	24.50	89.12	44.19	18.02	none
W	"	15.10	111.2	39.05	22.00	"
T	"	10.00	45.00	21.00	8.77	"
Wt	11	11.80	356.9	66.46	98.16	10 frag.

Table 4.83a. Late phase forest core data (mm and g).

Est.	No.	Min.	Max.	Mean	S.D.	Exclude
L	36	31.48	165.0	74.00	29.55	none
W	"	30.61	151.6	59.99	20.51	"
T	"	17.96	90.60	39.03	16.52	"
Wt	"	28.39	1600	233.8	319.5	"

Table 4.83b. Late phase tundra core data (mm and g).

Material	Range total	Forest total	Tundra total
quartzite	156(58)	43(32)	113(84)
chert	43(16)	26(19)	17(13)
quartz	61(23)	57(43)	4(03)
fossil wood	2(01)	2(01)	
mudstone	1(00)	1(00)	
sandstone	4(02)	4(03)	
silicious shale	1(00)	1(01)	
Total	268(100)	134(100)	134(100)

Table 4.84a. Late regular, worked, sharpening flake stone

Colour	Range total	Forest total	Tundra total
beige	55(21)	18(13)	37(28)
white	78(29)	52(39)	26(19)
orange	26(10)	10(07)	16(11)
gray	42(16)	24(18)	18(14)
pink	17(06)	7(05)	10(08)
red	10(04)	1(01)	9(07)
brown	17(06)	11(08)	6(05)
green	6(02)	1(01)	5(04)
purple	4(02)		4(03)
clear	1(00)	1(01)	
blue	2(01)	2(01)	
black	8(03)	7(05)	1(01)
assorted	2(01)		2(01)
Total	268(101)	134(99)	134(101)

Table 4.84b. Late phase regular, worked and sharpening flake colour

Est.	No.	Min.	Max.	Mean	S.D.	Exclude
L	55	9.47	83.16	30.83	14.46	none
W	55	6.00	67.51	22.33	12.46	"
T	55	2.05	23.75	7.58	4.35	"
Wt	34	0.30	124.6	11.90	23.96	21 frag.

Table 4.85a. Late phase regular forest flake data (mm and g)

Est.	No.	Min.	Max.	Mean	S.D.	Exclude
L	83	6.71	91.90	34.36	18.44	none
W	83	3.87	58.31	24.27	12.79	"
T	83	0.61	26.89	7.69	5.17	"
Wt	83	0.03	93.96	9.88	16.62	"

Table 4.85b. Late phase regular tundra flake data (mm and g)

Est.	No.	Min.	Max.	Mean	S.D.	Exclude
L	77	14.00	101.9	33.15	14.56	none
W	77	8.00	56.34	23.92	9.55	"
T	77	3.00	29.00	8.42	4.71	"
Wt	14	2.50	101.0	18.36	25.52	21 frag.

Table 4.86a. Late phase forest worked flake data (mm and g).

Est.	No.	Min.	Max.	Mean	S.D.	Exclude
L	47	18.11	149.8	50.19	25.89	none
W	47	13.06	125.6	40.82	24.58	"
T	47	4.10	29.10	10.53	5.23	"
Wt	47	1.28	443.7	35.88	72.28	"

Table 4.86b. Late phase tundra worked flake data (mm and g)

Material	Range total	Forest total	Tundra total
quartzite	19(86)	4(67)	15(94)
granite	2(09)	1(17)	1(06)
sandstone	1(05)	1(17)	
Total	22(100)	6(101)	16(100)

Table 4.87a. Late phase hammerstone material.

Colour	Range total	Forest total	Tundra total
beige	13(59)	3(50)	10(63)
white	4(15)	1(17)	3(19)
orange	1(05)		1(05)
pink	3(14)	1(17)	2(13)
brown	1(05)	1(17)	
Total	22(98)	6(101)	16(100)

Table 4.87b. Late phase hammerstone colour.

Texture	Range total	Forest total	Tundra total
none	19(86)	4(67)	15(94)
banded	2(09)	1(17)	1(06)
speckled	1(05)	1(17)	
Total	22(100)	6(101)	16(100)

Table 4.87c. Late phase hammerstone texture.

Plan	Range total	Forest total	Tundra total
round	4(18)		4(25)
square/rectangle	10(45)	2(33)	8(50)
tearshaped	3(14)		3(19)
triangular	1(05)	1(17)	
almost ovoid	4(18)	3(50)	1(06)
Total	22(100)	6(100)	16(100)

Table 4.88. Late phase hammerstone plan.

Section	Range total	Forest total	Tundra total
round	2(09)	1(17)	1(06)
ovoid	3(14)	2(33)	1(06)
square/rectangle	8(36)	1(17)	7(44)
biconvex	3(14)		3(19)
triangular	2(09)	2(33)	
planoconvex	4(18)		4(25)
Total	22(100)	6(100)	16(100)

Table 4.89. Late phase hammerstone section.

Pocking	Range total	Forest total	Tundra total
unipolar	10(45)	2(33)	8(50)
bipolar	9(41)	1(17)	8(50)
equatorial	2(09)	2(33)	
1 side only	1(05)	1(17)	
Total	22(100)	6(100)	16(100)

Table 4.90. Late phase hammerstone pocking.

Est.	No.	Min.	Max.	Mean	S.D.	Exclude
L	6	64.04	141.7	103.1	29.45	none
W	"	45.00	111.3	68.12	24.85	"
T	"	35.64	79.43	47.11	16.57	"
Wt	"	221.5	1700	577.9	559.3	"

Table 4.91a. Late phase forest hammerstone data (mm and g).

Est.	No.	Min.	Max.	Mean	S.D.	Exclude
L	16	45.10	170.4	86.72	31.49	none
W	"	37.10	75.70	58.14	12.84	"
T	"	23.50	70.22	40.49	14.12	"
Wt	"	74.10	754.4	302.2	215.1	"

Table 4.91b. Late phase tundra hammerstone data (mm and g)

Material	Range total	Forest total	Tundra total
sandstone	11(65)	9(69)	2(50)
schist	4(24)	2(15)	2(50)
quartzite	1(06)	1(08)	
slate	1(06)	1(08)	
Total	17(101)	13(100)	4(100)

Fig. 4.92a. Late phase whetstone material.

Colour	Range total	Forest total	Tundra total
beige	5(29)	5(38)	
gray	3(18)	2(15)	1(25)
pink	1(06)		1(25)
red	2(12)	1(08)	1(25)
brown	3(18)	3(23)	
green	2(12)	2(15)	
black	1(06)		1(25)
Total	17(101)	13(100)	4(100)

Table 4.92b. Late phase whetstone colour.

Plan	Range total	Forest total	Tundra total
unknown	2(12)	2(16)	
rectangular (bar)	12(71)	10(77)	2(50)
round/ovoid	2(12)	1(08)	1(25)
triangular	1(06)		1(25)
Total	17(101)	13(101)	4(100)

Table 4.93. Late phase whetstone plan.

Section	Range total	Forest total	Tundra total
unknown	2(12)	2(16)	
biplanar	15(88)	11(85)	4(100)
Total	17(100)	13(101)	4(100)

Table 4.94. Late phase whetstone section.

Suspension	Range total	Forest total	Tundra total
unknown	5(29)	4(31)	1(25)
none	12(71)	9(69)	3(75)
Total	17(100)	13(100)	4(100)

Table 4.95. Late phase whetstone suspension.

Edge wear	Range total	Forest total	Tundra total
unknown	3(18)	3(23)	
none	2(12)	2(15)	
worn/ground	12(71)	8(62)	4(100)
Total	17(101)	13(100)	4(100)

Table 4.96. Late phase whetstone edge wear.

Face wear	Range total	Forest total	Tundra total
unknown	2(12)	2(15)	
none	2(12)	1(08)	1(25)
present	13(76)	10(77)	3(75)

Table 4.97. Late phase whetstone facial wear.

Striae	Range total	Forest total	Tundra total
unknown/none	10(59)	8(62)	2(50)
longitudinal	5(30)	3(23)	2(50)
longitudinal/oblique	2(12)	2(15)	
Total	17(101)	13(100)	4(100)

Table 4.98. Late phase whetstone striae.

Polish	Range total	Forest total	Tundra total
unknown	2(12)	2(15)	
present	15(88)	11(85)	4(100)
Total	17(100)	13(100)	4(100)

Table 4.99. Late phase whetstone polish.

Other traits	Range total	Forest total	Tundra total
unknown	10(59)	7(54)	3(75)
wide groove *	1(06)	1(08)	
also chitho	3(18)	2(16)	1(25)
blocky	3(18)	3(24)	
Total	17(101)	13(102)	4(100)

Table 4.100. Late phase whetstones with odd traits.*striae.

Est.	No.	Min.	Max.	Mean	S.D.	Exclude
L	11	60.20	134.5	114.2	23.99	2 frag.
W	11	19.77	91.24	45.49	23.45	2 frag.
T	12	5.50	60.89	18.94	14.44	1 frag.
Wt	12	31.90	93.30	165.2	246.3	1 frag.

Table 4.101a. Late phase forest whetstone data (mm and g).

Est.	No.	Min.	Max.	Mean	S.D.	Exclude
L	2	56.33	108.8	82.56	37.09	2 frag.
W	4	22.64	55.88	40.98	16.72	none
T	4	7.00	15.70	12.05	4.26	none
Wt	2	17.40	78.71	48.06	43.35	2 frag.

Table 4.101b. Late phase tundra whetstone data (mm and g).

Est.	No.	Min.	Max.	Mean	S.D.	Exclude
L	11	31.28	129.5	67.98	29.20	2 frag.
W	13	16.73	60.44	39.69	12.80	none
T	13	4.91	21.46	13.69	4.07	none
Wt	11	2.80	96.00	46.85	29.45	2 frag.

Table 4.102a. Late phase forest skin flexer data (mm and g).

Est.	No.	Min.	Max.	Mean	S.D.	Exclude
L	3	42.39	101.4	69.90	29.71	none
W	3	25.51	43.24	31.47	10.28	"
T	3	8.86	14.69	12.13	2.98	"
Wt	3	9.80	49.30	31.20	19.99	"

Table 4.102b. Late phase tundra skin flexer data (mm and g).

Est.	No.	Min.	Max.	Mean	S.D.	Exclude
L	61	6.20	130.3	62.02	26.91	none
W	61	0.50	34.10	20.85	5.79	"
T	61	2.30	21.62	6.49	4.19	"
Wt	61	0.50	16.70	6.46	4.15	"

Table 4.103a. Late phase KeNi-4 forest bone fragmentdata (mm & g)

Est.	No.	Min.	Max.	Mean	S.D.	Exclude
L	4	19.7	69.4	48.00	21.2	none
W	4	2.68	20.7	14.87	8.46	none
T	4	2.50	6.9	5.18	1.89	none
Wt	4	0.26	9.2	4.59	3.79	none

Table 4.103b. Late KjNb-7 tundra bone fragment data (mm & g)

Est.	No.	Min.	Max.	Mean	S.D.	Exclude
L	3	8.14	36.79	24.04	14.58	none
W	3	3.94	16.50	11.62	6.73	none
T	3	2.10	8.39	4.71	3.28	none
Wt	3	0.05	1.58	0.93	0.79	none

Table 4.103c. Late phase KkLn-4 tundra bone fragmentdata (mm & g)

Material	Range total	Forest total	Tundra total
quartzite	367(86)	87(77)	280(89)
chert	29(07)	12(11)	17(05)
quartz	4(01)	4(04)	
silicious shale	22(05)	5(05)	17(05)
basalt	2(00)	1(01)	1(00)
copper	1(00)	1(01)	
slate	1(00)	1(01)	
felsite	1(00)	1(01)	
diorite	1(00)	1(01)	
Total	428(99)	113(102)	315(99)

Table 5.2a. Middle phase point material.

Colour	Range total	Forest total	Tundra total
beige	97(23)	24(21)	73(23)
white	100(23)	25(22)	75(24)
orange	36(08)	5(04)	31(10)
gray	90(21)	36(32)	54(17)
pink	36(08)	7(06)	29(09)
red	19(04)	5(04)	14(04)
brown	20(05)	1(01)	19(06)
green	9(02)	3(03)	6(02)
purple	4(01)	1(01)	3(01)
clear	3(01)	3(03)	
black	14(03)	3(03)	11(03)
Total	428(99)	113(100)	315(99)

Table 5.2b. Middle phase point colour.

Plan	Range total	Forest total	Tundra total
lanceolate	400(93)	96(85)	304(97)
rectangular	1(00)	1(01)	
triangular	2(00)	2(02)	
spadelike	1(00)	1(01)	
pentagonal	24(06)	13(12)	11(03)
Total	428(99)	113(101)	315(100)

Table 5.3. Middle phase point plan.

Cross-section	Range total	Forest total	Tundra total
biconvex	395(92)	100(88)	295(94)
planoconvex	20(07)	10(09)	19(06)
biplanar	3(01)	3(03)	
keeled	1(00)		1(00)
Total	428(100)	113(100)	315(100)

Table 5.4. Middle phase point section.

Type of tip	Range total	Forest total	Tundra total
none/unknown	212(50)	45(40)	167(53)
pointed tip	152(36)	48(42)	104(33)
round	26(06)	8(07)	18(06)
serrated	5(01)	2(02)	3(01)
flat	9(02)	1(01)	8(03)
intended burination	1(00)		1(00)
accidentally burinated	20(05)	6(05)	14(04)
other type of retouch	3(01)	3(03)	
Total	428(101)	113(100)	315(100)

Table 5.5. Middle phase point tips

Taper type	Range total	Forest total	Tundra total
unknown	74(17)	14(12)	60(19)
tip taper	97(23)	31(27)	66(21)
base taper	99(23)	22(19)	77(24)
parallel-sided	158(37)	46(41)	112(36)
Total	428(100)	113(99)	315(100)

Table 5.6. Middle phase point taper.

Base type	Range total	Forest total	Tundra total
unknown	15(04)		15(05)
unground square	10(02)	2(02)	8(03)
ground square	77(18)	32(28)	45(14)
unground stem	35(08)	8(07)	27(08)
ground stem	274(64)	66(58)	208(66)
unground flare	1(00)		1(00)
ground flare	6(01)		6(02)
parallel tang	1(00)	1(01)	
tapered tang	1(00)		1(00)
unground side-notch	1(00)	1(01)	
ground side-notch	1(00)		1(00)
unground round	1(00)		1(00)
fishtailed	5(01)	3(03)	2(01)
Total	428(98)	113(100)	315(99)

Table 5.7. Middle phase point bases.

Basal edge	Range total	Forest total	Tundra total
unknown	78(18)	21(19)	57(18)
unground flat	34(08)	8(07)	26(08)
ground flat	245(57)	70(62)	175(55)
unground round	15(04)	2(02)	13(04)
ground round	47(11)	9(08)	38(12)
unground concave	2(00)	1(01)	1(00)
ground concave	4(01)	1(01)	3(01)
unground pointed	1(00)		1(00)
ground pointed	2(00)	1(01)	1(00)
Total	428(99)	113(101)	315(98)

Table 5.8. Middle phase point basal edges.

Shoulder type	Range total	Forest total	Tundra total
none/unknown	396(93)	105(93)	291(92)
unground single	2(00)		2(01)
ground single	18(04)	5(04)	13(04)
unground double	1(00)		1(00)
ground double	11(03)	3(03)	8(03)
Total	438(100)	113(100)	315(100)

Table 5.9. Middle phase point shoulders.

Breakage type	Range total	Forest total	Tundra total
none	137(32)	44(39)	93(30)
transverse	164(38)	34(30)	130(41)
diagonal	34(08)	8(07)	26(08)
semi-diagonal	34(08)	5(04)	29(09)
double diagonal	6(01)	4(04)	2(01)
transverse-diagonal	18(04)	8(07)	10(03)
double transverse	26(06)	6(05)	20(06)
longitud./transverse	8(02)	4(04)	4(01)
burinated	1(00)		1(00)
Total	428(99)	113(100)	315(99)

Table 5.10. Middle phase point breakage.

Burination	Range total	Forest total	Tundra total
unknown	396(93)	105(93)	291(92)
1 side or face	19(04)	4(04)	15(05)
2 sides or faces	13(03)	4(04)	9(03)
Total	428(100)	113(100)	315(100)

Table 5.11. Middle phase point burination.

Spec. traits	Range total	Forest total	Tundra total
none/unkn	380(89)	97(86)	283(90)
eared base	11(03)	7(06)	7(02)
heat-treated?	5(01)		5(02)
end-thinned	13(03)	4(04)	9(03)
almost tanged	3(01)		3(01)
thinned base	3(01)	1(01)	2(01)
patinated	10(02)	4(04)	6(02)
Total	428(100)	113(99)	315(101)

Table 5.12. Middle phase point special traits.

Other usage	Range total	Forest total	Tundra total
unknown	380(89)	97(86)	283(90)
wedge	13(03)	5(04)	8(03)
knife	13(03)	5(04)	8(03)
burin	6(01)	1(01)	5(02)
graver	6(01)	3(03)	3(01)
bifacial scraper	1(00)	1(01)	
gouge	1(00)		1(00)
endscraper	1(00)	1(01)	
chisel	1(00)	1(01)	
Total	428(97)	113(101)	315(101)

Table 5.13. Middle phase points with other functions.

Est.	No.	Min.	Max.	Mean	S.D.	Exclude
L	102	21.20	100.0	58.82	17.43	11 frag.
W	108	11.37	52.21	25.60	5.80	5 frag.
T	111	1.41	14.49	8.32	1.90	2 frag.
Wt	48	3.41	44.30	12.12	8.24	65 frag.

Table 5.14a. Middle phase forest point data (mm and g).

Est.	No.	Min.	Max.	Mean	S.D.	Exclude
L	237	31.54	120.0	66.28	15.1	78 frag.
W	280	12.18	49.40	25.92	4.74	35 frag.
T	311	4.31	13.97	8.18	1.79	4 frag.
Wt	95	1.80	46.34	15.41	9.43	220 frag.

Table 5.14b. Middle phase tundra point data (mm and g).

Substance	Range Total	Forest Total	Tundra Total
quartzite	859(88)	376(85)	484(89)
chert	72(07)	33(07)	39(07)
quartz	38(04)	26(06)	12(02)
silicious shale	6(01)	2(00)	4(01)
basalt	6(01)	4(01)	2(00)
Total	981(101)	441(99)	540(99)

Table 5.15a. Middle phase scraper material.

Colour	Range Total	Forest Total	Tundra Total
beige	292(30)	123(28)	169(31)
white	137(14)	49(11)	88(16)
orange	87(09)	25(06)	62(11)
gray	209(21)	122(28)	87(16)
pink	119(12)	69(16)	50(09)
blue	1(00)		1(00)
red	22(02)	7(02)	15(03)
brown	37(04)	4(01)	33(06)
green	37(04)	20(05)	17(03)
purple	31(03)	17(04)	14(03)
black	7(01)	3(01)	4(01)
unknown	2(00)	2(00)	
Total	981(100)	441(102)	540(99)

Table 5.15b. Middle phase scraper colour.

Texture	Range Total	Forest Total	Tundra Total
banded	154(16)	100(23)	54(10)
mottled	30(03)	22(05)	8(01)
speckled	7(01)	1(00)	6(01)
solid	800(81)	318(72)	472(87)
Total	991(101)	441(100)	540(99)

Table 5.15c. Middle phase scraper texture.

Plan	Range Total	Forest Total	Tundra Total
unknown	7(01)	4(01)	3(00)
rhomboid	287(29)	153(35)	134(25)
tearshape	217(22)	93(21)	124(23)
triangular	195(20)	70(16)	125(23)
ovoid	98(10)	44(10)	54(10)
rectangle/bladelike	83(08)	32(07)	51(09)
square	72(07)	34(08)	38(07)
ululike	6(01)	5(01)	1(00)
discoid	12(01)	4(01)	8(01)
parallelogram	4(00)	2(00)	2(00)
Total	991(99)	441(100)	540(98)

Table 5.16. Middle phase scraper plan.

Cross-section	Range Total	Forest Total	Tundra Total
tabular	593(60)	257(58)	336(62)
keeled	195(20)	90(20)	105(19)
tortoise	165(17)	77(17)	88(16)
biconvex	6(01)	4(01)	2(00)
planoconvex	20(02)	11(02)	9(02)
concavoconvex	2(00)	2(00)	
Total	981(100)	441(98)	540(99)

Table 5.17. Middle phase scraper section.

Edge type	Range Total	Forest Total	Tundra Total
serrated	154(16)	67(15)	87(16)
unserrated	827(84)	374(84)	453(84)
Total	981(100)	441(99)	540(100)

Table 5.18. Middle phase scraper edge type.

Base	Range Total	Forest Total	Tundra Total
unknown	11(01)	4(01)	7(01)
unretouched/unground	203(20)	141(32)	62(11)
unretouched/ground	263(27)	86(20)	177(33)
dorsal retouch	418(43)	176(40)	242(45)
ventral retouch	53(05)	14(03)	39(07)
bifacial retouch	24(02)	14(03)	10(02)
discoidal	1(00)	1(00)	
double bitted	3(00)	3(01)	
alternate retouch	5(01)	2(00)	3(01)
Total	991(99)	441(100)	540(100)

Table 5.19. Middle phase scraper basal configuration.

Cortex	Range Total	Forest Total	Tundra Total
none	827(84)	374(84)	453(84)
present	154(16)	67(15)	87(16)
Total	981(100)	441(99)	540(100)

Table 5.20. Middle phase scraper cortex.

Bit wear	Range Total	Forest Total	Tundra Total
none/unknown	4(00)	3(01)	1(00)
worn	726(74)	329(75)	397(74)
very worn	86(09)	31(07)	55(10)
unworn	165(17)	78(18)	87(16)
Total	981(100)	441(101)	540(100)

Table 5.21. Middle phase scraper bit wear.

Basal grinding	Range Total	Forest Total	Tundra Total
none/unknown	10(01)	3(01)	7(01)
ground	649(66)	252(57)	397(74)
very ground	44(04)	29(07)	25(05)
unground	268(27)	157(36)	111(21)
Total	981(98)	441(101)	540(101)

Table 5.22. Middle phase scraper basal grinding.

Striae	Range Total	Forest Total	Tundra Total
none/unknown	922(94)	420(95)	502(93)
over edge	49(05)	21(05)	38(07)
Total	981(99)	441(100)	540(100)

Table 5.23. Middle phase scraper striae.

Bifac. platforms	Range Total	Forest Total	Tundra Total
unknown	709(72)	291(66)	418(77)
present	272(27)	150(34)	122(23)
Total	981(99)	441(100)	540(100)

Table 5.24. Middle phase scrapers made on thinning flakes.

Spurring	Range Total	Forest Total	Tundra Total
unspurred	791(81)	335(76)	456(84)
single spur	165(17)	90(20)	75(14)
double spur	25(03)	16(04)	9(02)
Total	9814(101)	441(100)	540(100)

Table 5.25. Middle phase scraper spurring.

Est.	No.	Min.	Max.	Mean	S.D.	Exclude
L	434	16.08	97.54	33.39	13.26	7 frag.
W	436	13.91	79.58	29.41	7.59	5 frag.
T	437	2.95	21.62	7.71	2.47	4 frag.
Wt	341	0.90	152.1	9.80	13.14	100 frag.

Table 5.26a. Middle phase forest scraper data (mm and g).

Est.	No.	Min.	Max.	Mean	S.D.	Exclude
L	529	11.98	99.00	34.28	12.58	12 frag.
W	534	13.93	73.51	29.40	7.01	7 frag.
T	540	2.64	20.42	7.52	2.64	1 frag.
Wt	428	1.20	107.0	9.77	10.47	113 frag.

Table 5.26b. Middle phase tundra scraper data (mm and g).

Material	Range total	Forest total	Tundra total
quartzite	1287(94)	384(93)	903(95)
chert	32(02)	4(01)	28(03)
quartz	10(01)	9(02)	1(00)
silicious shale	23(02)	9(02)	14(01)
sandstone	1(00)	1(00)	
basalt	5(00)	3(01)	2(00)
mudstone	6(00)		6(01)
schist	1(00)	1(00)	
Total	1365(99)	411(99)	954(100)

Table 5.27a. Middle phase knife material

Colour	Range total	Forest total	Tundra total
beige	434(32)	93(23)	341(36)
white	220(16)	76(18)	144(15)
orange	129(09)	22(05)	107(11)
gray	311(23)	147(36)	164(17)
pink	96(07)	43(10)	53(06)
red	27(02)	6(01)	21(02)
green	13(01)	4(01)	9(01)
brown	84(06)	5(01)	79(08)
purple	34(02)	6(01)	28(03)
clear	1(00)	1(00)	
black	16(01)	8(02)	8(01)
Total	1365(99)	411(98)	954(100)

Table 5.27b. Middle phase knife colour.

Texture	Range total	Forest total	Tundra total
burnt	29(13)	2(03)	27(08)
banded	161(72)	54(72)	107(72)
mottled	28(13)	16(21)	12(08)
speckled	5(02)	3(05)	2(01)
Total	223(100)	75(101)	148(99)

Table 5.27c. Middle phase knife texture.

Faciality	Range Total	Forest Total	Tundra Total
unifacial	198(15)	67(16)	131(14)
bifacial	1167(85)	344(84)	823(86)
Total	1365(100)	411(100)	954(100)

Table 5.28. Middle phase knife faciality.

Completeness	Range total	Forest total	Tundra total
base only	113(08)	28(07)	95(10)
midsection	70(05)	13(03)	57(06)
tip only	41(03)	2(00)	39(04)
base and midsection	374(27)	85(21)	289(30)
tip and midsection	134(10)	26(07)	108(11)
edge fragment	78(06)	1(00)	77(08)
complete	484(35)	241(59)	243(25)
longitudinally split	13(01)	2(00)	11(01)
light chipping	48(04)	13(03)	35(04)
Total	1365(99)	411(100)	954(99)

Table 5.29. Middle phase knife completeness.

Plan	Range total	Forest total	Tundra total
unknown fragment	192(14)	5(01)	187(20)
lanceolate	256(19)	74(18)	182(19)
ovoid	471(35)	152(37)	319(33)
semilunar	88(06)	50(12)	38(04)
rectangle/square	115(08)	42(10)	73(08)
triangular	76(06)	29(07)	47(05)
pentagonal	8(01)	4(01)	4(00)
asymmetrical ovoid	23(02)	6(01)	17(02)
discoidal	37(03)	17(04)	20(02)
unishouldered	54(04)	15(04)	39(04)
bishouldered	29(02)	7(02)	22(02)
notched	1(00)		1(00)
bladelike	12(01)	9(02)	3(00)
rhomboid	3(00)	1(00)	2(00)
Total	1365(101)	411(99)	954(99)

Table 5.30. Middle phase knife plan.

Section	Range total	Forest total	Tundra total
unknown fragment	5(00)		5(01)
biconvex	976(72)	288(70)	688(72)
planoconvex	267(20)	93(23)	174(18)
tabular	45(03)	10(02)	35(04)
concavoconvex	5(00)		5(01)
keeled	33(02)	12(03)	21(02)
tortoise	11(01)	5(01)	6(01)
sinuous	16(01)	1(00)	15(02)
biconvex C-F*	3(00)		3(00)
planoconvex C-F	3(00)	1(00)	2(00)
concavoconvex C-F	1(00)	1(00)	
Total	1365(99)	411(99)	954(101)

Table 5.31. Middle phase knife section *C-F=channel-flaked

Type of edge	Range total	Forest total	Tundra total
unknown fragment	39(03)	5(01)	34(04)
serrated preform	267(20)	108(26)	159(17)
unworn bifacial retouch	385(28)	107(26)	278(29)
unworn unifacial retouch	68(05)	13(03)	55(06)
worn bifacial retouch	512(38)	148(36)	364(38)
worn unifacial retouch	75(05)	27(07)	48(05)
worn flake edge	1(00)	1(00)	
serrated and worn	17(01)	2(00)	15(02)
alternate retouch & worn	1(00)		1(00)
Total	1365(100	411(99)	954(101)

Table 5.32. Middle phase knife edge.

Base	Range total	Forest total	Tundra total
unknown fragment	288(21)	33(08)	255(27)
unground/unretouched	31(02)	9(02)	22(02)
ground & unretouched	3(00)	3(01)	
unground dorsal ret.	113(08)	40(10)	73(08)
unground ventral ret.	7(01)	2(00)	5(01)
unground bif. retouch	478(35)	170(41)	308(32)
unground altern. ret.	1(00)		1(00)
ground dorsal ret.	26(02)	8(02)	18(02)
ground ventral retouch	6(00)	1(00)	5(07)
ground bifac. retouch	404(30)	144(35)	260(27)
knife biface thinning	5(00)		5(01)
full cortex base	3(00)	1(00)	2(00)
Total	1365(101)	411(100)	954(101)

Table 5.33. Middle phase knife bases.

Midsection	Range total	Forest total	Tundra total
unknown fragment	204(15)	20(05)	184(19)
unifacial retouch	104(08)	31(08)	73(08)
bifacial retouch	685(50)	202(49)	483(51)
alternate retouch	4(00)	4(01)	
serrated	368(27)	154(37)	214(22)
Total	1365(100	411(100)	954(100)

Table 5.34. Middle phase knife midsections.

Type of tip	Range total	Forest total	Tundra total
unknown fragment	633(46)	127(31)	506(53)
unworn and ptd	157(12)	49(12)	108(11)
worn and round	166(12)	73(18)	93(10)
worn and pointed	145(11)	52(13)	93(10)
unworn and round	156(11)	56(14)	100(10)
serrated	55(04)	25(06)	30(03)
square	53(04)	29(07)	24(03)
Total	1365(100)	411(101)	954(100)

Table 5.35. Middle phase knife tips.

Break type	Range total	Forest total	Tundra total
unknown/fragment	436(32)	222(54)	214(22)
transverse	312(23)	77(19)	235(25)
diagonal	166(12)	27(07)	139(15)
transverse and diagonal	57(04)	7(02)	50(05)
longitudinal	61(04)	3(01)	58(06)
semi-transverse	135(10)	46(11)	89(09)
multi-transverse	42(03)	8(02)	34(04)
transverse and longitudinal	46(03)	9(02)	37(04)
multi-diagonal	32(02)	10(02)	22(02)
diagonal & longitudinal	30(02)	2(00)	28(03)
lightly chipped	11(01)		11(01)
sharpening flakes	1(00)		1(00)
transversely halved	2(00)		2(00)
diagonally halved	3(00)		3(00)
longitudinally halved	31(02)		31(03)
Total	1365(98)	411(100)	954(99)

Table 5.36. Middle phase knife breakage.

Striae	Range total	Forest total	Tundra total
none	1362(100)	408(99)	954(100)
knife-like	1(00)	1(00)	
scraper-like	2(00)	2(00)	
Total	1365(100)	411(100)	954(100)

Table 5.37. Middle phase knife striae.

Cortex	Range total	Forest total	Tundra total
unknown/none	1174(86)	346(84)	828(87)
dorsal face	45(03)	16(04)	29(03)
most of edge	5(00)	2(00)	3(00)
tip face	6(00)	2(00)	4(00)
midsection face	9(01)	5(01)	4(00)
basal face	17(01)	5(01)	12(01)
midsection edge	6(00)	1(00)	5(01)
basal edge	12(01)	7(02)	5(01)
platform	88(06)	27(07)	61(06)
both ends	3(00)		3(00)
Total	1354(98)	411(99)	954(99)

Table 5.38. Middle phase knife cortex.

Basal plan	Range total	Forest total	Tundra total
unknown fragment	340(25)	50(12)	290(30)
taper, round & ground	60(04)	22(05)	38(04)
taper, flat & ground	148(11)	55(13)	93(10)
taper, round, unground	67(05)	18(04)	49(05)
tapered, flat & unground	145(11)	56(13)	89(09)
tapered. No basal edge	2(00)	1(00)	1(00)
round and ground	93(07)	33(08)	60(06)
round and unground	132(10)	47(11)	85(09)
pointed and ground	80(06)	24(06)	56(06)
pointed and unground	92(07)	32(08)	60(06)
concave and ground	5(00)	1(00)	4(00)
concave and unground	5(00)	1(00)	4(00)
square and ground	46(03)	19(05)	27(03)
square and unground	111(08)	38(09)	73(08)
unground side-notch	4(00)		4(00)
ground tang	9(01)	4(01)	5(01)
unground tang	17(01)	5(01)	12(01)
serrated	7(01)	4(01)	3(00)
cortex base	2(00)	1(00)	1(00)
Total	1365(100)	411(97)	954(98)

Table 5.39. Middle phase knife bases.

Platform	Range total	Forest total	Tundra total
unknown fragment	340(25)	50(12)	290(30)
ground/unfacetted	39(03)		39(04)
ground/facetted	47(03)	21(05)	26(03)
unground & unfacetted	111(08)	34(08)	77(08)
unground & facetted	67(05)	24(06)	43(05)
on raised side	4(00)		4(00)
on unraised side	12(01)	3(01)	9(01)
retouched away	742(54)	278(68)	464(49)
on raised base	1(00)		1(00)
arcuate facetted	2(00)	1(00)	1(00)
Total	1365(99)	411(100)	954(99)

Table 5.41. Middle phase knife striking platform.

Back type	Range total	Forest total	Tundra total
unknown fragment	331(24)	45(11)	276(29)
like opposite edge	1013(74)	343(83)	670(70)
dull cortex	10(01)	7(02)	3(00)
blunted retouch	11(01)	6(02)	5(01)
Total	1365(100)	411(98)	954(100)

Table 5.40. Middle phase knife backs.

Est.	No.	Min.	Max.	Mean	S.D.	Exclude
L	376	14.00	186.0	82.50	23.92	35 frag.
W	391	7.00	104.0	43.34	13.44	20 frag.
T	403	3.30	47.15	12.47	4.37	8 frag.
Wt	235	2.90	733.7	58.64	73.20	176 frag.

Table 5.42a. Middle phase forest knife data (mm and g).

Est.	No.	Min.	Max.	Mean	S.D.	Exclude
L	589	28.00	169.0	84.58	22.04	365 frag.
W	701	15.00	115.0	44.73	12.84	253 frag.
T	893	3.38	44.70	12.58	4.11	61 frag.
Wt	243	4.30	429.9	55.15	49.06	711 frag.

Table 5.42b. Middle phase tundra knife data (mm and g).

Material	Range total	Forest total	Tundra total
sandstone	102((89)	84(95)	18(67)
quartzite	11(10)	2(02)	9(33)
schist	1(01)	1(01)	
granite	1(01)	1(01)	
Total	115(101)	88(99)	27(100)

Table 5.43a. Middle phase chitho material.

Colour	Range total	Forest total	Tundra total
beige	77(67)	63(72)	14(52)
white	2(02)	2(02)	
gray	13(11)	8(09)	5(19)
pink	5(04)	3(03)	2(07)
red	4(03)	2(02)	2(07)
brown	5(04)	3(03)	2(07)
purple	9(08)	7(08)	2(07)
Total	115(99)	88(99)	27(101)

Table 5.43b. Middle phase chitho colour.

Faciality	Range total	Forest total	Tundra total
bifacial	105(91)	85(97)	20(74)
unifacial	10(09)	3(03)	7(26)
Total	115(100)	88(100)	27(100)

Table 5.44. Middle phase chitho faciality.

Completeness	Range total	Forest total	Tundra total
complete	56(49)	47(53)	9(33)
edge fragment	8(07)	5(06)	3(11)
halved	15(13)	7(08)	8(30)
quartered	5(04)	3(03)	2(07)
some spalling	31(27)	26(30)	5(19)
Total	115(100)	88(100)	27(100)

Table 5.45. Middle phase chitho completeness.

Plan	Range total	Forest total	Tundra total
unknown/fragment	5(04)	3(03)	2(07)
ovoid	36(31)	20(23)	16(59)
round	53(46)	49(56)	4(15)
rectangular/square	11(10)	11(13)	
triangular	3(03)	2(02)	1(04)
tearshaped	3(03)	1(01)	2(07)
bell-shaped	3(03)	2(02)	1(04)
pentagonal	1(01)		1(04)
Total	115(101)	88(100)	27(100)

Table 5.46. Middle phase chitho plan.

Section	Range total	Forest total	Tundra total
flat/parallel	89(77)	70(80)	19(70)
uneven/wavy	26(23)	18(20)	8(30)
Total	115(100)	88(100)	77(100)

Table 5.47. Middle phase chitho section.

Edge wear	Range total	Forest total	Tundra total
worn	98(85)	80(91)	18(67)
unworn	17(15)	8(09)	9(33)
Total	115(100)	88(100)	27(100)

Table 5.48. Middle phase chitho wear.

Cortex	Range total	Forest total	Tundra total
present	91(79)	74(84)	17(63)
none	24(21)	14(16)	10(37)
Total	115(100)	88(100)	27(100)

Table 5.49. Middle phase chitho cortex.

Est.	No.	Min.	Max.	Mean	S.D.	Exclude
L	71	60.04	155.9	87.79	15.18	17 frag.
W	58	49.71	120.8	73.35	11.77	30 frag.
T	87	3.86	21.87	11.27	3.49	1 frag.
Wt	49	38.88	196.8	100.8	39.85	39 frag.

Table 5.50a. Middle phase forest chitho data (mm and g).

Est.	No.	Min.	Max.	Mean	S.D.	Exclude
L	11	71.16	111.1	90.00	11.23	16 frag.
W	16	44.20	103.6	74.45	15.18	11 frag.
T	27	4.49	24.43	11.78	5.58	none
Wt	9	56.30	236.7	123.0	56.26	18 frag.

Table 5.50b. Middle phase tundra chitho data (mm and g).

Material	Range total	Forest total	Tundra total
quartzite	46(92)	19(86)	27(96)
quartz	2(04)	2(09)	
chert	2(04)	1(05)	1(04)
Total	50(100)	22(100)	28(100)

Table 5.51a. Middle phase wedge material.

Colour	Range total	Forest total	Tundra total
beige	20(40)	9(41)	11(39)
white	9(18)	2(09)	7(25)
orange	4(08)	3(14)	1(04)
gray	11(22)	5(23)	6(21)
pink	3(06)	1(05)	2(07)
red	1(02)		1(04)
brown	1(02)	1(05)	
clear	1(02)	1(05)	
Total	50(100)	22(102)	28(100)

Table 5.51b. Middle phase wedge colour.

Plan	Range total	Forest total	Tundra total
rectangular	10(20)	4(18)	6(21)
square	25(50)	11(50)	14(50)
rhomboid	9(18)	6(27)	3(11)
parallelogram	1(02)		1(04)
tearshape/triangular	1(02)		1(04)
biconvex/ovoid	3(06)	1(05)	2(07)
round	1(02)		1(04)
Total	50(100)	22(100)	28(101)

Table 5.52. Middle phase wedge plan.

Section	Range total	Forest total	Tundra total
biplanar	2(04)	1(05)	1(04)
biconvex	33(66)	15(68)	18(64)
planoconvex	10(20)	4(18)	6(21)
triangular	1(02)	1(05)	
concavoconvex	1(02)		1(04)
rhomboidal	2(04)	1(05)	1(04)
parallelogram	1(02)		1(04)
Total	50(100)	22(101)	28(101)

Table 5.53. Middle phase wedge section.

Flakescar type	Range total	Forest total	Tundra total
amorphous	27(54)	13(59)	14(50)
flat columnar	10(20)	4(18)	6(21)
channelled	3(06)	1(05)	2(10)
" columnar	10(20)	4(18)	6(21)
Total	50(100)	22(101)	28(102)

Table 5.54. Middle phase wedge flake scars.

Percussion	Range total	Forest total	Tundra total
bipolar	30(60)	13(59)	17(61)
double bipolar	7(14)	4(18)	3(11)
unipolar	9(37)	5(23)	4(14)
discoidal	4(08)		4(14)
Total	50(99)	22(100)	28(100)

Table 5.55. Middle phase wedge percussion.

Est.	No.	Min.	Max.	Mean	S.D.	Exclude
L	22	20.78	51.13	33.67	10.77	none
W	22	11.87	46.26	27.74	8.39	none
T	22	6.51	19.47	9.93	3.58	none
Wt	22	2.75	50.80	12.71	12.14	none

Table 5.56a. Middle phase forest wedge data (mm and g).

Est.	No.	Min.	Max.	Mean	S.D.	Exclude
L	23	17.59	48.81	32.09	8.33	5 frag.
W	27	18.73	41.03	27.49	5.99	1 frag.
T	28	5.88	13.48	9.27	2.20	none
Wt	23	2.39	27.11	10.63	6.97	5 frag.

Table 5.56b. Middle phase tundra wedge data (mm and g).

Type of tool	Range total	Forest total	Tundra total
adze flakes	47(92)	4(100)	43(91)
chisel	3(06)		3(06)
gouge	1(02)		1(02)
Total	51(100)	4(100)	47(99)

Table 5.57. Middle phase adzelike tools.

Material	Range total	Forest total	Tundra total
basalt	44(86)	4(100)	40(85)
chert	1(02)		1(02)
quartzite	2(04)		2(04)
silicious shale	4(08)		4(09)
Total	51(100)	4(100)	47(100)

Table 5.58. Middle phase adzelike material.

Colour	Range total	Forest total	Tundra total
beige	1(02)		1(02)
white	2(04)		2(04)
orange	1(02)		1(02)
gray	4(08)	4(100)	
pink	1(02)		1(02)
brown	1(02)		1(02)
black	41(80)		41(87)
Total	51(100)	4(100)	47(99)

Table 5.59. Middle phase adzelike colour.

Type of striae	Range total	Forest tota	Tundra total
none	31(61)	1(25)	30(64)
transverse	5(10)	1(25)	4(09)
diagonal	3(06)		3(06)
longitudinal	7(14)	1(25)	6(13)
transverse-diagonal	2(04)	1(25)	1(02)
transverse/diagonal/longitud.	1(02)		1(02)
unalligned. No platform	1(02)		1(02)
transverse/longitudinal	1(02)		1(02)
Total	51(101)	4(100)	47(100)

Table 5.60. Mid. adze flake striae in respect to main tool axis

Flake type	Range total	Forest total	Tundra total
bit	47(92)	4(100)	43(91)
ridge	1(02)		1(02)
complete tool	4(08)		4(09)
Total	51(102)	4(100)	47(102)

Table 5.61. Middle phase adze flake type.

Area	Range total	Forest total	Tundra total
none	10(20)	2(50)	8(17)
restricted	23(45)		23(49)
widespread	18(35)	2(50)	16(54)
Total	51(100)	4(100)	47(100)

Table 5.62. Middle phase adze flake grinding.

Type of polish	Range total	Forest total	Tundra total
none	25(49)	1(25)	24(51)
light	2(04)	1(25)	1(02)
heavy	6(12)	2(50)	4(09)
facial ridges	18(35)		18(38)
Total	51(100)	4(100)	47(100)

Table 5.63. Middle phase adze flake polish.

Grooved platform	Range total	Forest total	Tundra total
unknown fragment	8(16)	1(25)	7(15)
present	1(02)		1(02)
none	42(82)	3(75)	39(83)
Total	51(100)	4(100)	47(100)

Table 5.64. Middle phase adze flake grooved platforms.

Hinge fracture	Range total	Forest total	Tundra total
unknown fragment	50(98)	4(100)	46(98)
none	1(02)		1(02)
Total	51(100)	4(100)	47(100)

Table 5.65. Middle phase adzelike hinge fractures.

Est.	No.	Min.	Max.	Mean	S.D.	Exclude
L	4	20.57	41.95	33.27	9.47	none
W	4	16.37	46.22	35.29	13.24	"
T	4	2.97	6.48	4.58	1.45	"
Wt	4	0.95	9.41	5.78	3.61	"

Table 5.66a. Middle phase forest adzelike flake data (mm and g).

Est.	No.	Min.	Max.	Mean	S.D.	Exclude
L	43	8.46	55.27	22.06	9.67	none
W	43	7.97	54.56	21.35	10.43	"
T	43	1.23	6.22	3.47	1.20	"
Wt	43	0.21	10.82	1.84	2.12	"

Table 5.66b. Middle phase tundra adzelike flake data (mm and g).

Material	Range total	Forest total	Tundra total
quartzite	57(92)	4(100)	53(91)
chert	1(02)		1(02)
quartz	4(06)		4(07)
Total	62(100)	4(100)	58(100)

Table 5.67a. Middle phase core material.

Colour	Range total	Forest total	Tundra total
beige	27(44)	1(25)	26(45)
white	9(15)	2(50)	7(12)
orange	8(13)		8(14)
gray	3(05)		3(05)
pink	8(13)	1(25)	7(12)
brown	2(03)		2(03)
green	1(02)		1(02)
purple	4(06)		4(07)
Total	62(101)	4(100)	58(100)

Table 5.67b. Middle phase core colour.

Texture	Range total	Forest total	Tundra total
normal	49(79)	4(100)	45(78)
banded	12(19)		12(21)
mottled	1(02)		1(02)
Total	62(100)	4(100)	58(101)

Table 5.68. Middle phase core texture.

Section	Range total	Forest total	Tundra total
unknown	11(18)		11(19)
round	14(23)	1(25)	13(22)
rectang./rhomb./sq.	30(48)	2(50)	28(48)
triangular	2(03)		2(03)
planoconvex	2(03)	1(25)	1(02)
biconvex	3(05)		3(05)
Total	62(99)	4(100)	58(99)

Table 5.70. Middle phase core section.

Plan	Range total	Forest total	Tundra total
unknown fragment	12(19)		12(21)
round cobble	17(27)	2(50)	15(26)
rectangular/square	25(40)	1(25)	24(41)
ovoid	7(11)		7(12)
triangular	1(01)	1(25)	
Total	62(98)	4(100)	58(100)

Table 5.69. Middle phase core plan.

Profile	Range total	Forest total	Tundra total
blocky	47(76)	2(50)	45(78)
conical	5(08)		5(09)
spherical	3(05)	1(25)	2(03)
boatshaped	7(11)	1(25)	6(10)
Total	62(100)	4(100)	58(100)

Table 5.71. Middle phase core profile.

Flake removal	Range total	Forest total	Tundra total
blade/bladelike	5(08)		5(09)
flakelike	57(92)	4(100)	53(91)
Total	62(100)	4(100)	58(100)

Table 5.72. Middle phase core flake removal.

Platform	Range total	Forest total	Tundra total
single	15(24)	2(50)	13(22)
crescentic	43(69)	2(50)	41(71)
bipolar	4(06)		4(07)
Total	62(99)	4(100)	58(100)

Table 5.73. Middle phase core striking platform.

Cortex	Range total	Forest total	Tundra total
present	54(87)	4(100)	50(86)
none/unknown	8(13)		8(14)
Total	62(100)	4(100)	58(100)

Table 5.74. Middle phase core cortex.

Battering	Range total	Forest total	Tundra total
none/unknown	6(10)	2(50)	4(07)
unipolar	47(76)	2(50)	45(78)
bipolar	9(15)		9(16)
Total	62(101)	4(100)	58(101)

Table 5.75. Middle phase core battering.

Edgewear	Range total	Forest total	Tundra total
unknown	3(05)	2(50)	1(02)
present	4(06)		4(07)
none	55(89)	2(50)	53(91)
Total	62(100)	4(100)	58(100)

Table 5.76. Middle phase core edgewear.

Depleted	Range total	Forest total	Tundra total
no	48(77)	1(25)	47(81)
yes	14(23)	3(75)	11(19)
Total	62(100)	4(100)	58(100)

Table 5.77. Middle phase core depletion.

Multi-use	Range total	Forest total	Tundra total
none/unknown	56(90)	3(75)	53(91)
pushplane	2(03)		2(03)
hammerstone	1(01)	1(25)	
knife	2(03)		2(03)
cleaver	1(01)		1(02)
Total	62(98)	4(100)	58(99)

Table 5.78. Middle phase cores used as other tools.

Serrated	Range total	Forest total	Tundra total
no	56(90)	3(75)	53(91)
yes	6(10)	1(25)	5(09)
Total	62(100)	4(100)	58(100)

Table 5.79. Middle phase core serration.

Hinging	Range total	Forest total	Tundra total
no	61(98)	4(100)	57(98)
yes	1(02)		1(02)
Total	62(100)	4(100)	58(100)

Table 5.80. Middle phase core hinge fracturing.

Est.	No.	Min.	Max.	Mean	S.D.	Exclude
L	4	44.35	112.2	65.09	31.58	none
W	4	29.06	83.31	60.22	24.68	"
T	4	23.26	64.10	34.58	19.74	"
Wt	4	32.39	815.3	259.9	372.1	"

Table 5.81a. Middle phase forest core data (mm and g).

Est.	No.	Min.	Max.	Mean	S.D.	Exclude
L	58	25.19	167.2	80.43	33.50	none
W	58	28.77	142.6	63.19	23.37	"
T	58	11.56	74.61	37.18	14.30	"
Wt	58	8.10	1721	266.7	338.8	"

Table 5.81b. Middle phase tundra core data (mm and g).

Material	Range total	Forest total	Tundra total
quartzite	461(77)	62(67)	399(79)
chert	35(06)	1(01)	34(07)
quartz	4(01)	3(03)	1(00)
basalt	1(00)	1(01)	
mixed	87(15)	23(27)	64(13)
sandstone	6(01)	2(02)	4(01)
silicious shale	4(01)	1(01)	3(01)
Total	598(101)	93(102)	505(101)

Table 5.82a. Middle phase flake material.

Colour	Range total	Forest total	Tundra total
beige	126(21)	20(22)	106(21)
white	49(08)	5(05)	44(09)
orange	58(10)	1(01)	57(11)
gray	70(12)	20(22)	50(10)
pink	30(05)	7(08)	23(05)
red	4(01)	1(01)	3(01)
brown	29(05)	1(01)	28(06)
green	11(02)	1(01)	10(02)
purple	15(03)		15(03)
black	4(01)		4(01)
assorted	202(34)	37(40)	165(33)
Total	598(102)	93(101)	505(102)

Table 582b. Middle phase flake colour.

Est.	No.	Min.	Max.	Mean	S.D.	Exclude
L	7	11.62	33.14	24.92	7.81	none
W	"	8.56	35.60	20.64	9.26	"
T	"	2.09	10.65	5.35	3.34	"
Wt	"	0.21	6.73	2.86	2.35	"

Table 5.83a. Middle phase regular forest flake data (mm and g).

Est.	No.	Min.	Max.	Mean	S.D.	Exclude
L	160	6.03	150.1	44.17	21.62	none
W	"	3.40	94.88	32.60	15.42	"
T	"	0.81	26.07	9.60	5.07	"
Wt	"	0.02	291.4	18.24	29.16	"

Table 5.83b. Middle phase regular tundra flake data (mm and g).

Est.	No.	Min.	Max.	Mean	S.D.	Exclude
L	39	16.33	85.48	36.56	13.05	none
W	"	14.38	58.80	27.28	9.27	"
T	"	3.46	23.85	7.71	3.39	"
Wt	"	1.38	89.34	9.03	14.10	"

Table 5.84a. Middle phase forest worked flake data (mm and g).

Est.	No.	Min.	Max.	Mean	S.D.	Exclude
L	170	13.32	162.7	53.55	22.05	none
W	"	11.40	97.06	39.10	15.36	"
T	"	2.90	23.90	10.26	4.70	"
Wt	"	0.61	225.2	26.84	31.15	"

Table 5.84b. Middle phase tundra worked flake data (mm and g).

Est.	No.	Min.	Max.	Mean	S.D.	Exclude
L	4	29.14	74.80	53.00	19.00	none
W	"	26.37	50.76	40.17	10.24	"
T	"	6.38	9.36	8.08	1.28	"
Wt	"	2.61	20.80	14.81	8.29	"

Table 5.84c. Middle phase tundra sharpening flake data (mm and g).

Material	Range total	Forest total	Tundra total
quartzite	12(92)	4(80)	8(100)
sandstone	1(08)	1(20)	
Total	13(100)	5(100)	8(100)

Table 5.85a. Middle phase hammerstone material.

Colour	Range total	Forest total	Tundra total
beige	4(31)	1(20)	3(38)
white	2(15)		2(25)
gray	4(31)	1(20)	3(38)
pink	2(15)	2(40)	
red	1(08)	1(20)	
Total	13(100)	5(100)	8(101)

Table 5.85b. Middle phase hammerstone colour.

Texture	Range total	Forest total	Tundra total
none	12(92)	4(80)	8(100)
banded	1(08)	1(20)	
Total	13(100)	5(100)	8(100)

Table 5.85c. Middle phase hammerstone texture.

Plan	Range total	Forest total	Tundra total
square/rectangle	7(54)		7(88)
tearshaped	2(15)	2(40)	
almost ovoid	4(31)	3(60)	1(12)
Total	13(100)	5(100)	8(100)

Table 5.86. Middle phase hammerstone plan.

Section	Range total	Forest total	Tundra total
round	1(08)	1(20)	
ovoid	5(38)	3(60)	2(25)
square/rectangle	3(23)	1(20)	2(25)
biconvex	1(08)		1(13)
triangular	1(08)		1(13)
planoconvex	2(15)		2(25)
Total	13(100)	5(100)	8(100)

Table 5.87. Middle phase hammerstone section.

Pocking	Range total	Forest total	Tundra total
unipolar	6(46)	1(20)	5(63)
bipolar	1(08)		1(13)
bipolar equatorial	2(15)	1(20)	1(13)
unipolar equatorial	4(31)	3(60)	1(13)
Total	13(100)	5(100)	8(102)

Table 5.88. Middle phase hammerstone pocking.

Est.	No.	Min.	Max.	Mean	S.D.	Exclude
L	5	116.1	161.2	134.8	17.41	none
W	"	50.73	114.2	75.36	24.87	" "
T	"	41.62	71.12	58.70	12.64	" "
Wt	"	441.6	1337.	850.6	371.5	" "

Table 5.89a. Middle phase forest hammerstone (mm and g).

Est.	No.	Min.	Max.	Mean	S.D.	Exclude
L	8	81.89	154.0	116.5	24.24	none
W	"	45.82	71.05	58.34	9.08	"
T	"	31.93	52.82	41.35	8.38	"
Wt	"	180.5	650.5	399.2	162.6	"

Table 5.89b. Middle phase tundra hammerstone (mm and g).

Material	Range total	Forest total	Tundra total
quartzite	112(94)	30(100)	82(92)
chert	6(05)		6(07)
silicious shale	1(01)		1(01)
Total	119(100)	30(100)	89(100)

Table 5.90a. Middle phase pushplane material.

Colour	Range total	Forest total	Tundra total
beige	34(29)	4(13)	30(34)
white	13(11)	4(13)	9(10)
orange	20(17)	2(07)	18(20)
gray	29(24)	15(50)	14(16)
pink	7(06)	2(07)	5(06)
red	5(04)		5(06)
brown	5(04)	2(07)	3(03)
green	3(03)		3(03)
purple	3(03)	1(03)	2(02)
Total	119(101)	30(100)	89(100)

Table 5.90b. Middle phase pushplane colour.

Plan	Range total	Forest total	Tundra total
unknown	2(02)		2(02)
ovoid	72(61)	21(70)	51(57)
lanceolate	9(08)	1(03)	8(09)
rectangular	25(21)	8(27)	17(19)
tearshape/triangular	11(09)		11(12)
Total	119(101)	30(100)	89(99)

Table 5.91. Middle phase pushplane plan.

Section	Range total	Forest total	Tundra total
unknown fragment	3(03)		3(03)
keeled	30(25)	11(37)	19(21)
tortoise	82(69)	17(57)	65(73)
rectangular	4(03)	2(07)	2(02)
Total	119(100)	30(101)	89(99)

Table 5.92. Middle phase pushplane section.

Hafting	Range total	Forest total	Tundra total
unknown fragment	9(08)	1(03)	8(09)
thinned haft	87(73)	25(83)	62(70)
unstemmed haft	23(19)	4(13)	19(21)
Total	119(100)	30(99)	89(100)

Table 5.93. Middle phase pushplane hafting.

Edgewear	Range total	Forest total	Tundra total
unknown fragment	1(01)		1(01)
sharp and serrated	71(60)	25(83)	46(52)
worn and ground	47(39)	5(17)	42(47)
Total	119(100)	30(100)	89(100)

Table 5.94. Middle phase pushplane edgetype.

End retouch	Range total	Forest total	Tundra total
unknown	6(05)	1(03)	5(06)
abrupt	54(45)	13(43)	41(46)
gradual	59(50)	16(53)	43(48)
Total	119(100)	30(99)	89(100)

Table 5.95. Middle phase pushplane end retouch.

Side retouch	Range total	Forest total	Tundra total
unknown/none	1(01)		1(01)
abrupt	59(50)	15(50)	44(49)
gradual	59(50)	15(50)	44(49)
Total	119(101)	30(100)	89(99)

Table 5.96. Middle phase pushplane side retouch.

Ventral retouch	Range total	Forest total	Tundra total
unretouched overall	79(66)	15(50)	64(72)
retouched overall	21(18)	6(20)	15(17)
haft retouch	5(04)	3(10)	2(02)
midsection retouch	8(07)	1(03)	7(08)
bit retouch	6(05)	5(17)	1(01)
Total	119(100)	30(100)	89(100)

Table 5.97. Middle phase pushplane ventral retouch

Cortex	Range total	Forest total	Tundra total
none	68(57)	13(43)	55(62)
present	51(43)	17(57)	34(38)
Total	119(100)	30(100)	89(100)

Table 5.98. Middle phase pushplane cortex.

Platform	Range total	Forest total	Tundra total
normal/unidentified	70(59)	4(13)	66(74)
bashed or thinned	36(30)	18(60)	18(20)
unusually big	13(11)	8(27)	5(06)
Total	119(100)	30(100)	89(100)

Table 5.99. Middle phase pushplane platform.

Thinning	Range total	Forest total	Tundra total
unknown/none	65(55)	9(30)	56(63)
dorsal haft	25(21)	13(43)	12(13)
ventral haft	5(04)	2(07)	3(03)
both haft faces or edges	16(13)	3(10)	113(15)
bipolar and sides	8(06)	3(10)	5(06)
Total	119(99)	30(100)	89(100)

Table 5.100. Middle phase pushplane thinning.

Est.	No.	Min.	Max.	Mean	S.D.	Exclude
L	30	30.38	102.5	64.10	17.63	none
W	"	26.24	58.28	42.34	8.96	"
T	"	14.50	30.79	21.05	4.96	"
Wt	"	13.74	179.4	66.70	45.01	2 frag.

Table 5.101a. Middle phase forest pushplane data (mm and g).

Est.	No.	Min.	Max.	Mean	S.D.	Exclude
L	77	33.02	125.3	73.88	20.14	12 frag.
W	81	18.73	71.17	43.51	10.62	8 frag.
T	88	8.32	36.42	20.89	6.38	1 frag.
Wt	74	7.84	282.9	81.58	61.72	15 frag.

Table 5.101b. Middle phase tundra pushplane data (mm/g)

Est.	No.	Min.	Max.	Mean	S.D.	Exclude
L	3	35.76	53.90	42.15	10.19	1 frag.
W	4	18.66	27.63	23.46	4.75	none
T	4	6.14	9.57	7.43	1.54	"
Wt	3	4.30	14.60	8.23	5.56	2 frag.

Table 5.102a. Middle phase forest graver data (mm and g).

Est.	No.	Min.	Max.	Mean	S.D.	Exclude
L	6	33.61	65.63	51.37	137.0	none
W	6	22.56	25.10	24.14	0.89	"
T	4	5.01	12.15	8.55	2.38	"
Wt	5	5.19	16.99	9.29	4.81	1 frag.

Table 5.102b. Middle phase tundra graver data (mm and g).

Est.	No.	Min.	Max.	Mean	S.D.	Exclude
L	5	48.05	96.11	63.96	19.36	1 frag.
W	8	29.17	43.86	35.30	4.66	none
T	8	8.15	15.00	11.75	2.00	"
Wt	5	18.00	68.60	34.63	21.42	2 frag.

Table 5.103a. Middle phase forest skin flexer data (mm and g).

Est.	No.	Min.	Max.	Mean	S.D.	Exclude
L	4	59.57	85.63	75.15	11.20	1 frag.
W	5	20.64	50.24	38.09	11.61	none
T	5	5.28	23.67	14.26	7.39	"
Wt	4	3.60	104.2	55.30	48.27	1 frag.

Table 5.103b. Middle phase tundra skin flexer data (mm/g)

Material	Range total	Forest total	Tundra total
quartzite	275(83)	132(79)	143(88)
chert	30(09)	19(11)	11(07)
quartz	1(00)	1(01)	
silicious shale	21(06)	12(07)	9(06)
taconite	1(00)	1(01)	
basalt	2(01)	2(01)	
Total	330(99)	167(100)	163(101)

Table 6.2a. Early phase point material.

Colour	Range total	Forest total	Tundra total
unknown	2(01)	2(01)	
beige	90(27)	43(26)	47(28)
white	55(17)	22(13)	33(20)
orange	27(08)	14(08)	13(08)
gray	72(22)	45(27)	27(17)
pink	42(13)	23(14)	19(12)
red	7(02)	5(03)	2(01)
brown	10(03)	2(01)	8(05)
green	6(02)	3(02)	3(02)
purple	8(02)	3(02)	5(03)
black	11(03)	5(03)	6(04)
Total	330(100)	167(100)	163(100)

Table 6.2b. Early phase point colour.

Plan	Range total	Forest total	Tundra total
lanceolate	320(97)	158(95)	162(99)
rectangular	2(01)	2(01)	
side-notched	6(02)	5(03)	1(01)
pentagonal	2(01)	2(01)	
Total	330(101)	167(100)	163(100)

Table 6.3. Early phase point plan.

Cross-section	Range total	Forest total	Tundra total
biconvex	314(95)	159(95)	155(95)
planoconvex	16(05)	8(05)	8(05)
Total	330(100)	167(100)	163(100)

Table 6.4. Early phase point section.

Type of taper	Range total	Forest total	Tundra total
unknown fragment	89(27)	35(21)	54(33)
tapered to tip	125(38)	81(49)	44(27)
tapered to base	24(07)	10(06)	14(09)
parallel-sided	92(28)	41(25)	51(31)
Total	330(100)	167(101)	163(100)

Table 6.6. Early phase point taper.

Type of tip	Range total	Forest total	Tundra total
none/unknown	188(57)	76(46)	112(69)
pointed tip	100(30)	63(38)	37(22)
round	18(05)	11(07)	7(04)
serrated	2(01)	2(01)	
flat	3(01)	2(01)	1(01)
accidentally burinated	15(05)	10(06)	5(03)
other retouch	4(01)	3(02)	1(01)
TOTAL	330(100)	167(101)	163(100)

Table 6.5. Early phase point tip.

Type of base	Range total	Forest total	Tundra total
unknown fragment	21(06)	15(09)	6(04)
unground square	16(05)	12(07)	4(02)
ground square	190(58)	107(64)	83(51)
unground stem	6(02)		6(04)
ground stem	76(23)	26(16)	50(31)
unground flared	1(00)	1(01)	
ground flared	8(02)		8(05)
parallel tang	4(01)		4(02)
tapered tang	4(01)	3(02)	1(01)
unground side-notch	1(00)	1(01)	
fishtailed	3(01)	2(01)	1(01)
Total	330(100)	167(101)	163(101)

Table 6.7. Early phase point base

Basal edge	Range total	Forest total	Tundra total
unknown fragment	43(13)	23(14)	20(12)
unground flat	24(07)	15(09)	9(06)
ground flat	234(71)	122(73)	112(69)
unground round	1(00)		1(01)
ground round	23(07)	7(04)	16(10)
ground concave	3(01)		3(02)
ground pointed	2(01)		2(01)
Total	330(100)	167(100)	163(101)

Table 6.8. Early phase point basal edge.

Shoulder type	Range total	Forest total	Tundra total
none/unknown	104(32)	51(31)	53(33)
unground single	4(01)	1(01)	3(02)
ground single	29(09)	13(08)	16(10)
unground double	7(02)	4(02)	3(02)
ground double	186(56)	98(59)	88(54)
Total	330(100)	167(101)	163(101)

Table 6.9. Early phase point shoulder.

Breakage type	Range total	Forest total	Tundra total
none	81(24)	61(37)	30(18)
transverse	160(49)	69(41)	91(56)
diagonal	15(05)	7(04)	8(05)
semi-diagonal	26(08)	12(07)	14(09)
double diagonal	5(02)	2(01)	3(02)
transverse-diagonal	9(03)	5(03)	4(02)
double transverse	15(05)	6(04)	9(06)
longitudinal and transverse	9(03)	5(03)	4(02)
Total	330(99)	167(100)	163(100)

Table 6.10. Early phase point breakage.

Burination	Range total	Forest total	Tundra total
none/unknown	303(92)	150(90)	153(94)
1 side or face	13(04)	7(04)	6(04)
2 sides/faces	14(04)	10(06)	4(02)
Total	330(100)	167(100)	163(100)

Table 6.11. Early phase point burination.

Special traits	Range total	Forest total	Tundra total
none/unknown	262(79)	123(74)	139(85)
eared	42(13)	33(20)	9(06)
almost notched	8(02)	2(01)	6(04)
burnt	4(01)	3(02)	1(01)
fully ground	1(00)	1(01)	
patinated	3(01)	2(01)	1(01)
end-thinned	2(01)		2(01)
almost tanged	8(02)	3(02)	5(03)
Total	330(99)	167(101)	163(101)

Table 6.12. Early phase points with special traits.

Other usage	Range total	Forest total	Tundra total
none/unknown	305(92)	151(90)	154(94)
wedge	3(01)	2(01)	1(01)
knife	6(02)	2(01)	4(02)
burin	7(02)	3(02)	4(02)
graver	1(00)	1(01)	
gouge	1(00)	1(00)	
endscraper	4(01)	4(02)	
chisel	3(01)	3(02)	
Total	330(99)	167(100)	163(99)

Table 6.13. Early phase points with other functions.

Est.	No.	Min.	Max.	Mean	S.D.	Exclude
L	124	21.70	98.00	59.71	15.64	43 frag.
W	131	9.88	38.43	26.54	4.85	36 frag.
T	150	4.26	12.10	7.81	1.41	17 frag.
Wt	62	1.91	26.50	12.18	5.74	105 frag.

Table 6.14a. Early phase forest point data (mm and g).

Est.	No.	Min.	Max.	Mean	S.D.	Exclude
L	106	36.51	110.0	65.52	15.12	57 frag.
W	123	15.10	42.00	27.04	4.89	40 frag.
T	157	4.07	10.79	7.85	1.35	6 frag.
Wt	26	4.58	27.40	11.48	4.91	137 frag.

Table 6.14b. Early phase tundra point data (mm and g).

Colour	Range total	Forest total	Tundra total
beige	8(35)	1(33)	7(35)
white	5(22)		5(25)
orange	1(04)		1(05)
gray	2(09)	1(33)	1(05)
pink	2(09)	1(33)	1(05)
red	3(13)		3(15)
brown	2(09)		2(10)
Total	23(101)	3(99)	20(100)

Table 6.15. Earliest phase point colour.

Type of tip	Range total	Forest total	Tundra total
none/unknown	12(52)	1(33)	11(55)
pointed tip	7(30)	2(66)	5(25)
round	1(04)		1(05)
intended burinated	1(04)		1(05)
accidental burination	2(09)		2(10)
Total	23(99)	3(99)	20(100)

Table 6.16. Earliest phase point tips.

Taper type	Range total	Forest total	Tundra total
tip taper	6(26)		6(30)
base taper	1(04)		1(05)
parallel-sided	16(70)	3(100)	13(65)
Total	23(100)	3(100)	20(100)

Table 6.17. Earliest phase point taper.

Type of base	Range total	Forest total	Tundra total
unknown fragment	1(04)		1(05)
unground square	5(22)		5(25)
ground square	1(04)		1(05)
unground stem	1(04)		1(05)
parallel tang	13(57)	2(66)	11(55)
tapered tang	1(04)	1(33)	
fishtailed	1(04)		1(05)
Total	23(99)	3(99)	20(100)

Table 6.18. Earliest phase point basal sides.

Basal edge	Range total	Forest total	Tundra total
unknown fragment	2(09)		2(10)
unground flat	3(13)	1(33)	2(10)
ground flat	12(52)	2(66)	10(50)
unground and round	2(09)		2(10)
ground and round	4(17)		4(20)
Total	23(100)	3(99)	20(100)

Table 6.19. Earliest phase point basal edge.

Shoulder type	Range total	Forest total	Tundra total
none/unknown	2(09)		2(10)
ground single	6(26)		6(30)
ground double	15(65)	3(100)	12(60)
Total	23(100)	3(100)	20(100)

Table 6.20. Earliest phase point shoulder.

Break type	Range total	Forest total	Tundra total
none	6(26)	2(66)	4(20)
transverse	15(65)	1(33)	14(70)
semi-diagonal	1(04)		1(05)
intended burination	1(04)		1(05)
Total	23(99)	3(99)	20(100)

Table 6.21. Early phase point breakage.

Burination	Range total	Forest total	Tundra total
none/unknown	19(83)	3(100)	16(80)
1 side or face	3(13)		3(15)
2 sides/faces	1(04)		1(05)
Total	23(100)	3(100)	20(100)

Table 6.22. Earliest phase point burination.

Odd traits	Range total	Forest total	Tundra total
none/unknown	20(87)	2(66)	18(90)
eared	1(04)	1(33)	
almost notched	1(04)		1(05)
single side-notch	1(04)		1(05)
Total	23(99)	3(99)	20(100)

Table 6.23. Earliest phase point odd traits.

Other use	Range total	Forest total	Tundra total
none/unknown	21(91)	3(100)	18(90)
wedge	1(04)		1(05)
burin	1(05)		1(04)
Total	23(100)	3(100)	20(99)

Table 6.24. Earliest phase points with other functions.

Est.	No.	Min.	Max.	Mean	S.D.	Exclude
L	3	50.25	60.00	55.43	4.90	none
W	3	17.22	19.04	18.09	0.91	"
T	3	7.57	8.99	8.20	0.72	"
Wt	2	6.40	9.40	7.90	2.12	1 frag.

Table 6.25a. Earliest phase forest point data (mm and g).

Est.	No.	Min.	Max.	Mean	S.D.	Exclude
L	19	24.63	86.80	59.48	13.73	1 frag.
W	18	15.38	24.74	19.87	2.02	2 frag.
T	20	7.16	10.94	8.65	0.97	none
Wt	5	4.29	16.10	9.08	4.53	15 frag.

Table 6.25b. Earliest phase tundra point data (mm and g).

Substance	Range total	Forest total	Tundra total
quartzite	309(82)	142(71)	167(94)
chert	38(10)	33(17)	5(03)
quartz	17(05)	13(07)	4(02)
taconite	12(03)	12(06)	
basalt	1(00)		1(01)
Total	377(100)	200(101)	177(100)

Table 6.26a. Early phase scraper material.

Colour	Range total	Forest total	Tundra total
beige	100(27)	41(21)	59(33)
white	56(15)	24(12)	32(18)
orange	47(12)	23(12)	24(14)
gray	68(18)	46(23)	22(12)
pink	39(10)	28(14)	11(06)
red	26(07)	16(08)	10(06)
brown	18(05)	5(03)	13(07)
green	12(03)	9(05)	3(02)
purple	7(02)	5(03)	2(01)
black	4(01)	3(02)	1(01)
Total	377(100)	200(103)	177(100)

Table 6.26b. Early phase scraper colour.

Texture	Range total	Forest total	Tundra total
banded	40(67)	23(64)	17(71)
mottled	13(22)	11(31)	2(08)
speckled	6(10)	1(03)	5(21)
veined	1(01)	1(03)	
Total	60(100)	36(101)	24(100)

Table 6.26c. Early phase scraper texture.

Plan	Range total	Forest total	Tundra total
unknown fragment	6(02)	5(03)	1(01)
rhomboid	155(41)	91(46)	64(36)
tearshape	55(15)	26(13)	29(16)
triangular	72(19)	27(14)	45(25)
ovoid	32(08)	17(09)	15(08)
rectangular/bladelike	22(06)	12(06)	10(06)
square	21(06)	11(06)	10(06)
ululike	3(01)	3(02)	
discoid	9(02)	7(04)	2(01)
parallelogram	2(01)	1(01)	1(01)
Total	377(101)	200(104)	177(100)

Table 6.27. Early phase scraper plan.

Cross-section	Range total	Forest total	Tundra total
tabular	260(69)	123(62)	137(77)
keeled	54(14)	36(18)	18(10)
tortoise	57(15)	36(18)	21(12)
biconvex	3(01)	3(02)	
planoconvex	3(01)	2(01)	1(01)
Total	377(100)	200(101)	177(100)

Table 6.28. Early phase scraper section.

Edge type	Range total	Forest total	Tundra total
unknown fragment	1(00)	1(01)	
serrated	47(12)	28(14)	19(11)
unserrated	329(87)	171(86)	158(89)
Total	377(99)	200(101)	177(100)

Table 6.29. Early phase scraper edge type.

Base	Range total	Forest total	Tundra total
unknown fragment	6(02)	3(02)	3(02)
unretouched/unground	76(20)	58(29)	18(10)
unretouched/ground	80(21)	24(12)	66(37)
dorsal retouch	147(39)	78(39)	69(39)
ventral retouch	42(11)	25(13)	17(10)
bifacial retouch	12(03)	9(05)	3(02)
discoidal	1(00)	1(01)	
double bitted	1(00)		1(01)
alternate retouch	2(01)	2(01)	
Total	377(97)	200(102)	177(101)

Table 6.30. Early phase scraper basal configuration.

Cortex	Range total	Forest total	Tundra total
none	344(91)	181(91)	163(92)
present	33(09)	19(10)	14(08)
Total	377(100)	200(101)	177(100)

Table 6.31. Early phase scraper cortex.

Bit wear	Range total	Forest total	Tundra total
none/unknown	1(00)	1(01)	
worn	285(76)	148(74)	137(77)
very worn	17(05)	13(07)	4(02)
unworn	74(20)	38(19)	36(20)
Total	377(101)	200(101)	177(99)

Table 6.32. Early phase scraper bit wear.

Basal grinding	Range total	Forest total	Tundra total
none/unknown	6(02)	3(02)	3(02)
ground	244(64)	113(57)	131(74)
very ground	20(05)	14(07)	6(03)
unground	107(28)	70(35)	37(21)
Total	377(99)	200(101)	177(100)

Table 6.33. Early phase scraper basal grinding.

Striae	Range total	Forest total	Tundra total
none-unknown	359(95)	191(96)	168(95)
over the edge	18(04)	9(05)	9(05)
Total	377(99)	200(101)	177(100)

Table 6.34. Early phase scraper striae.

Bifacial platform	Range total	Forest total	Tundra total
unknown	277(73)	129(65)	148(84)
present	100(27)	71(36)	29(16)
Total	377(100)	200(101)	177(100)

Table 6.35 Early ph. scrapers made from thinning flakes

Spurring	Range total	Forest total	Tundra total
unspurred	266(71)	138(69)	128(72)
single spur	92(24)	51(26)	41(23)
double spur	19(05)	11(06)	8(05)
Total	377(100)	200(101)	177(100)

Table 6.36. Early phase scraper spurring.

Est.	No.	Min.	Max.	Mean	S.D.	Exclude
L	193	13.93	80.00	27.95	8.82	7 frag.
W	196	13.67	51.29	27.18	5.88	4 frag.
T	200	3.04	15.59	6.94	2.23	none
Wt	138	1.19	22.80	6.37	4.40	62 frag.

Table 6.37a. Early phase forest scraper data (mm and g).

Est.	No.	Min.	Max.	Mean	S.D.	Exclude
L	174	15.78	97.30	29.29	10.39	3 frag.
W	176	15.53	56.00	26.88	5.18	1 frag.
T	177	2.61	14.48	6.54	1.97	none
Wt	132	1.40	36.40	5.59	4.41	45 frag.

Table 6.37b. Early phase tundra scraper data (mm and g).

Est.	No.	Min.	Max.	Mean	S.D.	Exclude
L	3	21.38	45.21	32.80	11.95	3 frag.
W	4	22.54	44.00	35.40	9.92	2 frag.
T	5	5.81	8.50	7.09	1.15	1 frag.
Wt	2	2.86	10.00	6.43	5.05	4 frag.

Table 6.38a. Earliest phase forest scraper data (mm and g).

Est.	No.	Min.	Max.	Mean	S.D.	Exclude
L	2	19.78	25.29	22.54	3.90	none
W	2	24.50	26.30	25.40	1.27	"
T	2	4.24	4.55	4.40	0.22	"
Wt	2	2.40	4.10	3.25	1.20	"

Table 6.38b. Earliest phase tundra scraper data (mm and g).

Material	Range total	Forest total	Tundra total
quartzite	316(91)	151(88)	165(94)
chert	13(04)	8(05)	5(03)
taconite	2(01)	2(01)	
silicious shale	11(03)	6(04)	5(03)
sandstone	2(01)	2(01)	
basalt	2(01)	1(01)	1(01)
mudstone	1(00)	1(01)	
Total	347(101)	171(101)	176(101)

Table 6.39a. Early phase knife material.

Section	Range total	Forest total	Tundra total
biconvex	235(68)	122(71)	113(64)
planoconvex	71(21)	36(21)	35(20)
tabular	11(03)	4(02)	7(04)
keeled	20(06)	8(05)	12(07)
tortoise	3(01)		3(02)
sinuous	6(02)	1(01)	5(03)
biconvex C-F*	1(00)		1(01)
Total	347(101)	171(100)	176(101)

Table 6.43. Early phase knife section (*=channel-flaked).

Colour (main)	Range total	Forest total	Tundra total
beige	79(23)	31(18)	48(27)
white	40(12)	15(09)	25(14)
orange	44(13)	16(09)	28(16)
gray	110(32)	78(46)	32(18)
pink	23(07)	13(08)	10(06)
red	6(02)	2(01)	4(02)
green	3(01)	3(02)	
brown	20(06)	5(03)	15(09)
purple	18(05)	7(04)	11(06)
black	4(01)	1(01)	3(02)
Total	347(102)	171(101)	176(100)

Table 6.39b. Early phase knife colour.

Plan	Range total	Forest total	Tundra total
unknown fragment	68(20)	13(08)	55(31)
lanceolate	60(17)	25(15)	35(20)
ovoid	81(23)	39(23)	42(24)
semilunar	21(06)	17(10)	4(02)
rectangular or square	24(07)	15(09)	9(05)
triangular	3(01)	2(01)	1(01)
pentagonal	2(01)	1(01)	1(01)
asymmetrical ovoid	9(03)	3(02)	6(03)
discoidal	21(06)	11(06)	10(06)
unishouldered	32(09)	25(15)	7(04)
bishouldered	22(06)	17(10)	5(03)
notched	1(00)	1(01)	
bladelike	2(01)	2(01)	
rhomboid	1(00)		1(01)
Total	347(100)	171(102)	176(101)

Table 6.42. Early phase knife plan.

Texture	Range total	Forest total	Tundra total
banded	30(70)	10(50)	20(87)
mottled	12(28)	10(50)	2(09)
speckled	1(02)		1(04)
Total	43(100)	20(100)	23(100)

Table 6.39c. Early phase knife texture.

Faciality	Range total	Forest total	Tundra total
unifacial	63(18)	33(19)	30(17)
bifacial	284(82)	138(81)	146(83)
Total	347(100)	171(100)	176(100)

Table 6.40. Early phase knife faciality.

Type of edge	Range total	Forest total	Tundra total
unknown fragment	11(03)		11(06)
serrated preform	68(20)	37(22)	31(18)
unworn bifacial retouch	98(28)	53(31)	45(26)
unworn unifacial ret.	24(07)	11(06)	13(07)
worn bifacially retouch	116(33)	54(32)	62(35)
worn unifacial retouch	20(06)	11(06)	9(05)
ground and worn only	2(01)	1(01)	1(01)
serrated and worn	5(01)	2(01)	3(02)
altern. retouch & worn	1(00)	1(01)	
altern. retouch & unworn	1(00)	1(01)	
fully bifacially ground	1(00)	1(01)	
Total	347(99)	171(101)	176(101)

Table 6.44. Early phase knive edge.

Completeness	Range total	Forest total	Tundra total
base only	30(09)	11(06)	19(11)
midsection	34(10)	19(11)	15(09)
tip only	18(05)	6(04)	12(07)
base and midsect	83(24)	46(27)	37(21)
tip and midsection	26(07)	13(08)	13(07)
edge fragment	33(10)	5(03)	28(16)
complete	114(33)	68(40)	46(26)
longitudinally split	2(01)	1(01)	1(01)
light chipping	7(02)	2(02)	5(03)
Total	347(101)	171(102)	176(101)

Table 6.41. Early phase knife completeness.

Base	Range total	Forest total	Tundra total
unknown fragment	108(31)	38(22)	70(40)
unground-unretouched	10(03)	2(01)	8(05)
ground & unretouched	1(00)	1(01)	
unground-dorsal ret.	29(08)	17(10)	12(07)
unground-ventral ret.	4(01)	1(01)	3(02)
unground-bifacial ret.	108(31)	61(36)	47(27)
unground alternate ret.	1(00)	1(01)	
ground-dorsal retouch	6(02)	4(02)	2(01)
ground-ventral retouch	2(01)	1(01)	1(01)
ground bifacial retouch	72(21)	44(26)	28(16)
bifacial thinning	5(01)	1(01)	4(02)
full cortex base	1(00)		1(01)
Total	347(99)	171(102)	176(102)

Table 6.45. Early phase knife basal edge.

Midsection	Range total	Forest total	Tundra total
unknown fragment	70(20)	14(08)	56(32)
unifacial retouched	34(10)	17(10)	17(10)
bifacial retouch	156(45)	85(50)	71(40)
alternate retouch	1(00)	1(01)	
serrated	86(25)	54(32)	32(18)
Total	347(100)	171(101)	176(100)

Table 6.46. Early phase knife midsection.

Type of tip	Range total	Forest total	Tundra total
unknown fragment	173(50)	77(45)	96(55)
unworn pointed	31(09)	15(09)	16(09)
worn and round	36(10)	25(15)	11(06)
worn and pointed	30(09)	16(09)	14(08)
unworn and round	46(13)	19(11)	27(15)
serrated	15(04)	6(04)	9(05)
square	16(05)	13(08)	3(02)
Total	347(100)	171(101)	176(100)

Table 6.47. Early phase knife tip.

Type of break	Range total	Forest total	Tundra total
unknown/fragment	101(29)	65(38)	36(21)
transverse	74(21)	32(19)	42(24)
diagonal	37(11)	18(11)	19(11)
transverse-diagonal	22(06)	10(06)	12(07)
longitudinal	12(04)	2(01)	10(06)
semi-transverse	37(11)	18(11)	19(11)
multi-transverse	15(04)	9(05)	6(03)
transverse & longitudinal	17(05)	4(02)	13(07)
multi-diagonal	15(04)	5(03)	10(06)
diagonal and longitudinal	10(03)	6(04)	4(02)
light chipping	1(00)	1(01)	
sharpening flakes	1(00)	1(01)	
transversely halved	1(00)		1(01)
longitudinally halved	4(01)		4(02)
Total	347(99)	171(102)	176(101)

Table 6.48. Early phase knife breakage.

Striae	Range total	Forest total	Tundra total
none	346(100)	171(100)	175(99)
knifelike	1(00)		1(01)
Total	347(100)	171(100)	176(100)

Table 6.49. Early phase knife striae.

Cortex	Range total	Forest total	Tundra total
unknown/none	298(86)	144(84)	154(88)
most of dorsal face	17(05)	9(05)	8(05)
most of edge	2(01)	1(01)	1(01)
tip face	2(01)	1(01)	1(01)
midsection face	3(01)	3(02)	
basal face	4(01)	4(02)	
midsection edge	2(01)	1(01)	1(01)
basal edge	1(00)		1(01)
platform	18(05)	8(05)	10(06)
Total	347(101)	171(101)	176(103)

Table 6.50. Early phase knife striae.

Basal plan	Range total	Forest total	Tundra total
unknown fragment	120(35)	49(29)	71(40)
tapered, round, ground	13(04)	9(05)	4(02)
taper, flat & ground	22(06)	10(06)	12(07)
taper, round, unground	9(03)	5(03)	4(02)
taper, flat, unground	26(08)	9(05)	17(10)
round and ground	18(05)	14(08)	4(02)
round and unground	43(12)	22(13)	21(12)
pointed and ground	13(04)	8(05)	5(03)
pointed and unground	15(04)	7(04)	8(05)
concave and ground	4(01)	1(01)	3(02)
concave, unground	2(01)		2(01)
square and ground	12(04)	8(05)	4(02)
square and unground	34(10)	21(12)	13(07)
unground side-notch	1(00)	1(01)	
ground tang	2(01)	1(01)	1(01)
unground tang	5(01)	4(02)	1(01)
serrated	7(02)	2(01)	5(03)
fishtailed	1(00)		1(01)
Total	347(101)	171(100)	176(101)

Table 6.51. Early phase knife basal plan.

Type of back	Range total	Forest total	Tundra total
unknown fragment	83(24)	26(15)	57(32)
like opposite edge	264(76)	145(85)	119(68)
Total	347(100)	171(100)	176(100)

Table 6.52. Early phase knife backs.

Platform	Range total	Forest total	Tundra total
unknown fragment	115(33)	45(26)	70(40)
ground and unfacetted	12(04)	2(01)	10(06)
ground and facetted	14(04)	10(06)	4(02)
unground/unfacetted	25(07)	9(05)	16(09)
unground & facetted	19(06)	10(06)	9(05)
retouched away	161(46)	94(55)	67(38)
arcuate facetted	1(00)	1(01)	
Total	347(100)	171(100)	176(100)

Table 6.53. Early phase knive striking platform.

Est.	No.	Min.	Max.	Mean	S.D.	Exclude
L	129	19.00	161.0	79.91	25.25	42 frag.
W	142	16.00	114.0	42.42	16.78	29 frag.
T	156	3.19	45.75	11.99	5.49	15 frag.
Wt	68	1.84	342.4	62.22	65.44	103 frag.

Table 6.54a. Early phase forest knife data (mm and g).

Est.	No.	Min.	Max.	Mean	S.D.	Exclude
L	80	38.00	179.0	81.54	25.20	96 frag.
W	106	21.00	87.00	44.75	14.17	70 frag.
T	148	4.44	28.33	12.61	4.16	28 frag.
Wt	40	7.60	162.1	51.53	35.12	136 frag.

Table 6.54b. Early phase tundra knife data (mm and g).

Material	Range total	Forest total	Tundra total
sandstone	63(88)	51(94)	12(67)
quartzite	9(13)	3(06)	6(33)
Total	72(101)	54(100)	18(100)

Table 6.55a. Early phase chitho material.

Colour	Range total	Forest total	Tundra total
beige	48(67)	42(78)	6(33)
orange	4(06)	1(02)	3(17)
gray	10(14)	6(11)	4(22)
pink	3(04)	3(06)	
black	1(01)		1(06)
brown	3(04)		3(17)
purple	3(04)	2(04)	1(06)
Total	72(100)	54(101)	18(101)

Table 6.55b. Early phase chitho colour.

Faciality	Range total	Forest total	Tundra total
bifacial	64(89)	51(94)	13(72)
unifacial	8(11)	3(06)	5(28)
Total	72(100)	54(100)	18(100)

Table 6.56. Early phase chitho faciality.

Completeness	Range total	Forest total	Tundra total
complete	34(47)	25(46)	9(50)
edge fragment	10(14)	10(19)	
halved	10(14)	7(13)	3(17)
quartered	3(04)	2(04)	1(06)
some spalling	15(21)	10(19)	5(28)
Total	72(100)	54(101)	18(101)

Table 6.57. Early phase chitho completeness.

Plan	Range total	Forest total	Tundra total
unknown/fragment	9(13)	9(17)	
ovoid	31(43)	19(35)	12(67)
round	14(19)	11(20)	3(17)
rectangular/square	8(11)	6(11)	2(11)
triangular	1(01)	1(02)	
tearshaped	5(07)	5(09)	
lanceolate	1(01)		1(01)
bell-shaped	1(01)	1(02)	
pentagonal	2(03)	2(04)	
Total	72(99)	54(100)	18(101)

Table 6.58. Early phase chitho plan.

Section	Range total	Forest total	Tundra total
flat/parallel	50(69)	36(67)	14(78)
uneven/wavy	22(31)	18(33)	4(22)
Total	72(100)	54(100)	18(100)

Table 6.59. Early phase chithos section.

Edge wear	Range total	Forest total	Tundra total
worn	52(72)	43(80)	9(50)
unworn	20(28)	11(20)	9(50)
Total	72(100)	54(100)	18(100)

Table 6.60. Early phase chitho wear

Cortex	Range total	Forest total	Tundra total
present	51(71)	41(76)	10(56)
none	21(29)	13(24)	8(44)
Total	72(100)	54(100)	18(100)

Table 6.61. Early phase chitho cortex.

Est.	No.	Min.	Max.	Mean	S.D.	Exclude
L	33	59.98	124.9	88.19	15.02	21 frag.
W	35	46.97	103.3	62.93	11.99	19 frag.
T	54	4.59	31.99	10.88	5.07	none
Wt	25	28.60	445.1	92.40	91.34	29 frag.

Table 6.62a. Early phase forest chitho data (mm and g).

Est.	No.	Min.	Max.	Mean	S.D.	Exclude
L	11	74.17	152.0	105.3	25.34	7 frag.
W	15	44.12	102.7	71.69	14.31	3 frag.
T	18	4.99	21.64	11.61	4.60	none
Wt	9	35.20	262.9	140.6	78.50	9 frag.

Table 6.62b. Early phase tundra chitho data (mm and g).

Material	Range total	Forest total	Tundra total
quartzite	42(76)	36(75)	6(86)
quartz	9(16)	9(19)	
chert	3(05)	2(04)	1(14)
taconite	1(02)	1(02)	
Total	55(99)	48(100)	7(100)

Table 6.63a. Early phase wedge material.

Colour	Range total	Forest total	Tundra total
beige	12(22)	12(24)	
white	15(27)	12(24)	3(43)
orange	10(18)	10(21)	
gray	8(15)	6(13)	2(29)
pink	6(11)	5(10)	1(14)
red	1(02)	1(02)	
purple	1(02)	1(02)	
green	1(02)		1(14)
clear	1(02)	1(02)	
Total	55(101)	48(98)	7(100)

Table 6.63b. Early phase wedge colour.

Plan	Range total	Forest total	Tundra total
rectangular	17(31)	14(29)	3(43)
square	16(29)	14(29)	2(29)
rhomboid	13(24)	12(25)	1(14)
parallelogram	3(05)	3(06)	
tearshape/triangular	3(05)	3(06)	
biconvex/ovoid	2(04)	1(02)	1(14)
round	1(02)	1(02)	
Total	55(100)	48(99)	7(100)

Table 6.64. Early phase wedge plan.

Section	Range total	Forest total	Tundra total
biplanar	3(05)	3(06)	
biconvex	28(51)	24(50)	4(57)
planoconvex	8(15)	7(15)	1(14)
triangular	7(13)	6(13)	1(14)
concavoconvex	1(02)	1(02)	
rhomboidal	5(09)	4(08)	1(14)
parallelogram	1(02)	1(02)	
biconcave	2(04)	2(04)	
Total	55(101)	48(100)	7(99)

Table 6.65. Early phase wedge section.

Flakescar type	Range total	Forest total	Tundra total
amorphous	20(36)	18(38)	2(29)
flat columnar	11(20)	8(17)	3(43)
channelled	6(11)	6(13)	
" columnar	18(33)	16(33)	2(29)
Total	55(100)	48(101)	7(101)

Table 6.66. Early phase wedge flake scars.

Percussion	Range total	Forest total	Tundra total
bipolar	37(67)	30(63)	7(100)
double bipolar	6(11)	6(13)	
unipolar	10(18)	10(21)	
discoidal	2(04)	2(04)	
Total	55(100)	48(101)	7(100)

Table 6.67. Early phase wedge percussion.

Est.	No.	Min.	Max.	Mean	S.D.	Exclude
L	45	16.85	62.08	31.09	9.65	3 frag.
W	47	12.59	42.33	26.26	7.50	1 frag.
T	47	5.01	17.77	9.87	3.47	1 frag.
Wt	45	1.41	40.47	10.38	9.61	3 frag.

Table 6.68a. Early phase forest wedge data (mm and g).

Est.	No.	Min.	Max.	Mean	S.D.	Exclude
L	7	25.30	58.23	37.06	12.22	none
W	7	17.56	32.60	26.83	5.39	"
T	7	6.73	14.70	9.99	2.85	"
Wt	7	3.50	26.10	12.10	7.99	"

Table 6.68b. Early phase tundra wedge data (mm and g).

Type of tool	Range total	Forest total	Tundra total
adze	7(11)	2(18)	5(10)
adze flakes	51(81)	4(36)	47(90)
chisel	3(05)	3(27)	
gouge	1(02)	1(09)	
pick	1(02)	1(09)	
Total	63(101)	11(99)	52(100)

Table 6.69. Early phase adzelike artifacts.

Material	Range total	Forest total	Tundra total
basalt	50(79)	6(55)	44(85)
chert	1(02)	1(09)	
quartzite	4(06)	3(27)	1(02)
silicious shale	8(13)	1(09)	7(13)
Total	63(100)	11(100)	52(100)

Table 6.70a. Early phase adzelike material.

Colour	Range total	Forest total	Tundra total
beige	1(02)	1(09)	
white	1(02)	1(09)	
orange	1(02)		1(02)
gray	16(25)	6(55)	10(19)
brown	2(03)		2(04)
black	42(67)	3(27)	39(75)
Total	63(101)	11(100)	52(100)

Table 6.70b. Early phase adzelike colour.

Type of striae	Range total	Forest total	Tundra total
none	35(56)	6(55)	29(56)
transverse	13(21)	2(18)	11(21)
diagonal	3(05)		3(06)
longitudinal	4(06)	1(09)	3(06)
transverse and diagonal	2(03)	2(18)	
transverse/diag./longitudinal	2(03)		2(04)
diagonal and longitudinal	1(02)		1(02)
unalligned. No platform	2(03)		2(02)
transverse & longitudinal	1(02)		1(02)
Total	63(101)	11(100)	52(99)

Table 6.71. Early phase adzelike striae.

Flake type	Range total	Forest total	Tundra total
lateral	34(59)	3(50)	31(60)
bit	13(22)	1(17)	12(23)
haft	2(03)		2(04)
ridge	3(05)	1(17)	2(04)
complete tool	6(10)	1(17)	5(10)
Total	58(99)	6(101)	52(101)

Table 6.72. Early phase adze flake type.

Area	Range total	Forest total	Tundra total
none	17(27)	2(18)	15(29)
restricted	13(21)	5(45)	8(15)
widespread	33(52)	4(36)	29(56)
Total	63(100)	11(99)	52(100)

Table 6.73a. Early phase adzelike grinding.

Polish type	Range total	Forest total	Tundra total
none	38(60)	6(55)	32(62)
light	3(05)	1(09)	2(04)
heavy	22(35)	4(36)	18(35)
Total	63(100)	11(100)	52(101)

Table 6.74. Early phase adzelike polish.

Grooved platf.	Range total	Forest total	Tundra total
unknown/fragment	9(14)		9(17)
present	3(05)		3(06)
none	51(81)	11(100)	40(77)
Total	63(100)	11(100)	52(100)

Table 6.75. Early phase adzelike grooved platforms.

Hinge fracture	Range total	Forest total	Tundra total
unknown fragment	61(97)	10(91)	51(98)
present	2(03)	1(09)	1(02)
Total	63(100)	11(100)	52(100)

Table 6.76. Hinge fractures in Early adzelike artifacts.

Est.	No.	Min.	Max.	Mean	S.D.	Exclude
L	4	18.28	39.82	29.31	9.23	none
W	4	18.26	49.83	31.22	13.35	"
T	4	3.57	9.64	6.05	2.58	"
Wt	4	1.56	20.60	8.41	8.36	"

Table 6.77a. Early phase forest adze flake data (mm and g).

Est.	No.	Min.	Max.	Mean	S.D.	Exclude
L	47	5.85	74.64	26.78	16.25	none
W	47	9.45	59.07	22.72	10.04	"
T	47	1.21	9.90	3.86	2.09	"
Wt	47	0.19	19.56	2.84	3.63	"

Table 6.77b. Early phase tundra adze flake data (mm and g).

Material	Range total	Forest total	Tundra total
quartzite	19(86)	8(73)	11(100)
chert	1(05)	1(09)	
quartz	1(05)	1(09)	
basalt	1(05)	1(09)	
Total	22(101)	11(100)	11(100)

Table 6.78a. Early phase core material.

Colour	Range total	Forest total	Tundra total
beige	6(27)	3(27)	3(27)
white	5(23)	4(36)	1(01)
orange	2(09)		2(18)
gray	1(05)		1(09)
pink	3(14)	1(09)	2(18)
black	1(05)	1(09)	
brown	1(05)		1(09)
green	1(05)	1(09)	
purple	2(09)	1(09)	1(09)
Total	22(102)	11(99)	11(101)

Table 6.78b. Early phase core colour.

Texture	Range total	Forest total	Tundra total
normal	17(77)	9(82)	8(73)
banded	5(23)	2(18)	3(27)
Total	22(100)	11(100)	11(100)

Table 6.78c. Early phase core texture.

Plan	Range total	Forest total	Tundra total
unknown fragment	3(14)		3(27)
round cobble	7(32)	6(55)	1(09)
rectangular/square	5(23)	1(09)	4(36)
ovoid	5(23)	3(27)	2(18)
triangular	2(09)	1(09)	1(09)
Total	22(101)	11(100)	11(99)

Table 6.79. Early phase core plan.

Section	Range total	Forest total	Tundra total
unknown	2(09)		2(18)
round	6(27)	5(45)	1(09)
rect./rhomb./square	8(36)	4(36)	4(36)
triangular	2(09)		2(18)
planoconvex	2(09)	2(18)	
biconvex	2(09)		2(18)
Total	22(99)	11(99)	11(99)

Table 6.80. Early phase core section.

Profile	Range total	Forest total	Tundra total
blocky	13(59)	7(64)	6(55)
conical	8(36)	3(27)	5(45)
boat-shaped	1(05)	1(09)	
Total	22(100)	11(100)	11(100)

Table 6.81. Early phase core profile.

Flake removal	Range total	Forest total	Tundra total
blade/bladelike	4(18)	3(27)	1(09)
flakelike	18(82)	8(73)	10(91)
Total	22(100)	11(100)	11(100)

Table 6.83. Early phase core flake removal.

Platform	Range total	Forest total	Tundra total
single	7(32)	4(36)	3(27)
crescentic	14(64)	6(55)	8(73)
bipolar	1(05)	1(09)	
Total	22(101)	11(100)	11(100)

Table 6.84. Early phase core striking platform.

Cortex	Range total	Forest total	Tundra total
present	18(82)	9(82)	9(82)
none/unknown	4(18)	2(18)	2(18)
Total	22(100)	11(100)	11(100)

Table 6.85. Early phase core cortex.

Battering	Range total	Forest total	Tundra total
none/unknown	1(05)		1(09)
unipolar	16(73)	8(73)	8(73)
bipolar	5(23)	3(27)	2(18)
Total	22(101)	11(100)	11(100)

Table 6.86. Early phase core battering.

Edgewear	Range total	Forest total	Tundra total
unknown	7(32)	7(64)	
none	15(68)	4(36)	11(100)
Total	22(100)	11(100)	11(100)

Table 6.87. Early phase core edge wear.

Depleted	Range total	Forest total	Tundra total
no	12(55)	4(36)	8(73)
yes	10(45)	7(64)	3(27)
Total	22(100)	11(100)	11(100)

Table 6.88. Early phase core depletion.

Multi-use	Range total	Forest total	Tundra total
none/unknown	18(86)	10(91)	9(82)
pushplane	2(09)		2(18)
knife	1(05)	1(09)	
Total	22(100)	11(100)	11(100)

Table 6.89. Early phase cores as other tools.

Serration	Range total	Forest total	Tundra total
no	18(82)	7(64)	11(100)
yes	4(18)	4(36)	
Total	22(100)	11(100)	11(100)

Table 6.90. Early phase core serration.

Hinging	Range total	Forest total	Tundra total
no	21(95)	10(91)	11(100)
yes	1(05)	1(09)	
Total	22(100)	11(100)	11(100)

Table 6.91. Early phase core hinge fracturing.

Est.	No.	Min.	Max.	Mean	S.D.	Exclude
L	11	31.80	111.7	59.05	24.49	none
W	11	13.30	82.06	51.92	20.92	"
T	11	8.98	57.28	35.70	13.48	"
Wt	11	4.14	471.4	174.0	172.8	"

Table 6.92a. Early phase forest core (mm and g).

Est.	No.	Min.	Max.	Mean	S.D.	Exclude
L	11	34.20	120.6	79.19	27.52	none
W	11	34.97	81.55	60.12	13.22	" "
T	11	20.50	63.96	42.85	11.82	" "
Wt	11	27.45	632.2	234.4	158.0	" "

Table 6.92b. Early phase tundra core data (mm and g).

Material	Range total	Forest total	Tundra total
quartzite	73(74)	32(62)	41(87)
chert	9(09)	6(12)	3(06)
quartz	6(06)	6(12)	
taconite	6(06)	6(12)	
sandstone	1(01)	1(02)	
silicious shale	4(04)	1(02)	3(06)
Total	99(100)	52(102)	47(99)

Table 6.93a. Early phase regular flake material.

Colour	Range total	Forest total	Tundra total
beige	17(17)	6(12)	11(23)
white	18(18)	13(25)	5(11)
orange	15(15)	5(10)	10(21)
gray	23(23)	14(27)	9(19)
pink	6(06)	4(08)	2(04)
red	7(07)	6(12)	1(02)
brown	6(06)	1(02)	5(11)
purple	3(03)	2(04)	1(02)
black	3(03)		3(06)
clear	1(01)	1(02)	
Total	99(99)	52(102)	47(99)

Table 6.93b. Early phase regular flake colour.

Material	Range total	Forest total	Tundra total
quartzite	92(81)	37(71)	55(89)
chert	15(13)	10(19)	5(08)
quartz	2(02)	2(04)	
taconite	3(03)	3(06)	
silicious shale	2(02)		2(03)
Total	114(101)	52(100)	62(100)

Table 6.93c. Early phase retouched flake material.

Colour	Range total	Forest total	Tundra total
beige	25(22)	9(17)	16(26)
white	16(14)	3(06)	13(21)
orange	23(20)	8(15)	15(24)
gray	17(15)	8(15)	9(15)
pink	13(11)	10(19)	3(05)
red	7(06)	6(12)	1(02)
brown	5(04)		5(08)
purple	6(05)	6(12)	
black	2(02)	2(04)	
Total	114(99)	52(100)	62(101)

Table 6.93d. Early phase retouched flake colour.

Est.	No.	Min.	Max.	Mean	S.D.	Exclude
L	52	11.50	70.96	31.58	15.74	none
W	52	4.01	67.27	22.06	12.89	"
T	52	1.80	22.89	6.75	4.57	"
Wt	52	0.21	64.00	7.79	13.87	"

Table 6.94a. Early phase regular forest flake data (mm and g).

Est.	No.	Min.	Max.	Mean	S.D.	Exclude
L	47	17.81	115.7	37.00	15.99	none
W	47	8.47	55.66	27.82	11.61	"
T	47	2.64	17.68	6.98	3.20	"
Wt	47	0.51	53.26	8.17	9.80	"

Table 6.94b. Early phase regular tundra flake data (mm and g).

Est.	No.	Min.	Max.	Mean	S.D.	Exclude
L	52	13.23	91.99	33.66	14.82	none
W	52	10.51	51.64	26.71	10.43	"
T	52	1.66	18.96	6.77	3.02	"
Wt	52	0.42	43.04	7.19	7.68	"

Table 6.95a. Early phase forest worked flake data (mm and g).

Est.	No.	Min.	Max.	Mean	S.D.	Exclude
L	61	12.10	87.79	44.74	19.41	1 frag.
W	61	9.36	97.13	31.70	16.19	"
T	61	2.61	20.19	8.36	3.93	"
Wt	61	0.30	75.61	14.73	16.79	"

Table 6.95b. Early phase tundra worked flake data (mm and g).

Material	Range total	Forest total	Tundra total
quartzite	5(56)	4(67)	1(33)
granite	3(33)	1(17)	2(67)
sandstone	1(11)	1(17)	
Total	9(100)	6(101)	3(100)

Table 6.96. Early phase hammerstone material.

Plan	Range total	Forest total	Tundra total
unknown/fragment	1(11)		1(33)
square/rectangle	3(33)	2(33)	1(33)
tearshaped	3(33)	2(33)	1(33)
triangular	1(11)	1(17)	
almost ovoid	1(11)	1(17)	
Total	9(99)	6(100)	3(99)

Table 6.97. Early phase hammerstone plan.

Section	Range total	Forest total	Tundra total
round	2(22)	1(17)	1(33)
square/rectangle	2(22)	1(17)	1(33)
biconvex	1(11)	1(17)	
triangular	2(22)	1(17)	1(33)
planoconvex	2(22)	2(33)	
Total	9(99)	6(101)	3(99)

Table 6.98. Early phase hammerstone section.

Pocking	Range total	Forest total	Tundra total
unipolar	7(78)	4(67)	3(100)
bipolar	1(11)	1(17)	
bipolar & equatorial	1(11)	1(17)	
Total	9(100)	6(100)	3(100)

Table 6.99. Early phase hammerstone pocking.

Est.	No.	Min.	Max.	Mean	S.D.	Exclude
L	6	62.92	113.2	87.22	27.93	none
W	6	38.70	97.13	64.24	20.29	"
T	6	35.03	63.74	50.08	9.83	"
Wt	6	113.6	114.4	433.6	361.8	"

Table 6.100a. Early phase forest hammerstone data (mm and g).

Est.	No.	Min.	Max.	Mean	S.D.	Exclude
L	2	95.50	101.5	98.51	4.25	1 frag.
W	2	48.00	68.32	58.61	13.73	"
T	2	43.00	67.06	55.03	17.01	"
Wt	2	279.4	519.4	399.4	16.97	"

Table 6.100b. Early phase tundra hammerstone data (mm and g).

Material	Forest total	Colour	Forest total
sandstone	2(18)	beige	1(09)
schist	1(09)	gray	4(36)
quartzite	1(09)	purple	1(09)
slate	7(64)	red	1(09)
		black	4(36)
Total	11(100)	Total	11(100)

Fig.6.101. Early phase forest whetstone material and colour

Plan	Forest total	Section	Forest total
rectangular bar	9(82)	triangular	1(09)
round/ovoid	1(09)	biplanar	10(91)
triangular	1(09)		
Total	11(100)	Total	11(100)

Table 6.102. Early phase forest whetstone plan and section.

Suspension	Forest total	Edgewear	Forest total
unknown fragment	4(36)		
asymmetric notch	4(36)	none	1(09)
none	3(27)	worn/ground	10(91)
Total	11(99)	Total	11(100)

Table 6.103. Early forest whetstone suspension/edgewear

Facewear	Forest total	Striae	Forest total
unknown/none	2(18)	unknown/none	3(27)
present	9(82)	longitudinal	6(55)
		longitudinal/transverse	2(18)
Total	11(100)		11(100)

Table 6.104. Early phase forest whetstone face wear and striae.

Polish	Forest total	Odd traits	Forest total
unknown/none	1(09)	unknown/none	5(45)
present	10(91)	striated groove	1(09)
Total	11(100)	edge grinder	4(36)
		worn tip	1(09)
		Total	11(99)

Table 6.105a. Early forest whetstone polish/odd traits

Est.	No.	Min.	Max.	Mean	S.D.	Exclude
L	5	54.70	101.5	71.35	20.06	6 frag.
W	10	12.02	54.68	27.81	13.78	1 frag.
T	10	4.13	26.50	9.01	6.39	1 frag.
Wt	5	6.92	144.1	46.16	58.43	6 frag.

Table 6.105b. Early phase forest whetstone data (mm and g).

Colour	Range total	Forest total	Tundra total
beige	2(14)	1(25)	1(10)
orange	2(14)		2(20)
gray	5(36)	2(50)	3(30)
pink	1(07)		1(10)
red	3(21)		3(30)
purple	1(07)	1(25)	
Total	14(99)	4(100)	10(100)

Table 6.106a. Early phase pushplane colour.

Plan	Range total	Forest total	Tundra total
ovoid	9(64)	3(75)	6(60)
rectangular	2(14)	1(25)	1(10)
tearshape/triangular	3(21)		3(30)
Total	14(99)	4(100)	10(100)

Table 6.106b. Early phase pushplane plan.

Section	Range total	Forest total	Tundra total
keeled	5(36)	1(25)	4(40)
tortoise	8(57)	3(75)	5(50)
rectangular	1(07)		1(10)
Total	14(100)	4(100)	10(100)

Table 6.106c. Early phase pushplane section.

Hafting	Range total	Forest total	Tundra total
unknown fragment	2(14)	1(25)	1(10)
thinned	9(64)	3(75)	6(60)
unstemmed	3(21)		3(30)
Total	14(99)	4(100)	10(100)

Table 6.106d. Early phase pushplane hafting.

Edgewear	Range total	Forest total	Tundra total
sharp/serrated	11(79)	2(50)	9(90)
worn/ground	3(21)	2(50)	1(10)
Total	14(100)	4(100)	10(100)

Table 6.107. Early phase pushplane edgetype.

End retouch	Range total	Forest total	Tundra total
abrupt	12(86)	3(75)	9(90)
gradual	2(14)	1(25)	1(10)
Total	14(100)	4(100)	10(100)

Table 6.108. Early phase pushplane end retouch.

Side retouch	Range total	Forest total	Tundra total
abrupt	12(86)	3(75)	9(90)
gradual	2(14)	1(25)	1(10)
Total	14(100)	4(100)	10(100)

Table 6.109. Early phase pushplane side retouch.

Ventral retouch	Range total	Forest total	Tundra total
normal face	11(79)	3(75)	8(80)
haft	1(07)	1(25)	
midsection	2(14)		2(20)
Total	14(100)	4(100)	10(100)

Tables 6.110. Early pushplane ventral retouch

Cortex	Range total	Forest total	Tundra total
none	7(50)	1(25)	6(60)
present	7(50)	3(75)	4(40)
Total	14(100)	4(100)	10(100)

Tables 6.111. Early pushplane cortex

Platform	Range total	Forest total	Tundra total
normal/unidentified	7(50)	1(25)	6(60)
bashed or thin	5(36)	3(75)	2(20)
unusually big	2(14)		2(20)
Total	14(100)	4(100)	10(100)

Table 6.112. Early phase pushplane platform.

Thinning	Range total	Forest total	Tundra total
unknown/none	8(57)	2(50)	6(60)
dorsal haft	4(29)	1(25)	3(30)
both haft faces or edges	2(14)	1(25)	1(10)
Total	14(100)	4(100)	10(100)

Table 6.113. Early phase pushplane thinning.

Est.	No.	Min.	Max.	Mean	S.D.	Exclude
L	3	71.55	81.49	78.09	5.67	1 frag.
W	3	50.56	71.18	62.63	10.75	none
T	4	21.79	36.21	28.58	5.92	"
Wt	3	112.9	240.0	165.0	66.56	1 frag.

Table 6.114a. Early phase forest pushplane data (mm and g).

Est.	No.	Min.	Max.	Mean	S.D.	Exclude
L	9	60.60	84.22	71.40	9.47	1 frag.
W	9	35.55	61.88	49.53	9.60	1 frag.
T	10	14.84	37.92	23.99	7.56	none
Wt	9	10.52	226.0	88.85	73.69	1 frag.

Table 6.114b. Early phase tundra pushplane data (mm and g).

Est.	No.	Min.	Max.	Mean	S.D.	Exclude
L	4	62.08	96.91	81.61	17.74	none
W	4	38.40	67.09	46.59	13.71	"
T	4	11.00	16.52	13.78	2.38	"
Wt	4	40.47	111.1	63.98	32.23	"

Table 6.115a. Early Taltheilei forest skin flexer data (mm and g).

Est.	No.	Min.	Max.	Mean	S.D.	Exclude
L	3	50.71	57.71	54.25	3.50	none
W	3	31.20	34.22	33.07	1.64	"
T	3	11.01	13.48	11.97	1.32	"
Wt	3	22.40	31.90	27.22	4.75	"

Table 6.115b. Early Taltheilei tundra skin flexer data (mm and g).

Type of tool	Range total	Forest total	Tundra total
axe	26(63)	21(72)	5(42)
adze flakes	3(07)	3(10)	
chisel	4(10)	3(10)	1(08)
pick	5(12)	2(07)	3(25)
pick flakes	3(07)		3(25)
Total	41(99)	29(99)	12(100)

Table 7.1a. General phase adzelike tools.

Material	Range total	Forest total	Tundra total
basalt	37(90)	26(90)	11(92)
quartzite	2(05)	2(07)	
silicious shale	2(05)	1(03)	1(08)
Total	41(100)	29(100)	12(100)

Table 7.1b. General phase adzelike artifact material.

Colour	Range total	Forest total	Tundra total
beige	1(02)	1(03)	
red	1(02)		1(08)
green	4(10)	2(07)	2(17)
gray	15(37)	12(41)	3(25)
brown	3(07)	3(10)	
black	17(41)	11(38)	6(50)
Total	41(99)	29(99)	12(100)

Table 7.1c. General phase adzelike artifact colour.

Type of striae	Range total	Forest total	Tundra total
none	35(85)	25(86)	
transverse	3(07)	2(07)	1(08)
diagonal	1(02)	1(03)	
tran./diag./longitudinal	1(02)		1(08)
diagonal & longitudinal	1(02)	1(03)	
Total	41(98)	29(99)	12(99)

Table 7.2. General phase adzelike artifact striae.

Flake type	Range total	Forest total	Tundra total
unknown fragment	5(12)	4(14)	1(08)
lateral	7(17)	4(14)	3(25)
bit	3(07)	3(10)	3(25)
haft	4(10)	4(14)	
ridge	1(02)	1(03)	
complete tool	18(44)	13(45)	5(42)
Total	41(102)	29(100)	12(100)

Table 7.3. General phase adze and pick flake type.

Area	Range total	Forest total	Tundra total
none	21(51)	15(52)	6(50)
restricted	2(05)	1(03)	1(08)
widespread	18(44)	13(45)	5(42)
Total	41(100)	29(100)	12(100)

Table 7.4. General phase adzelike artifact grinding.

Type of polish	Range total	Forest total	Tundra total
none	23(56)	17(59)	6(50)
light	3(07)	1(03)	2(17)
heavy	15(37)	11(38)	4(33)
Total	41(100)	29(100)	12(100)

Table 7.5a. General phase adzelike artifact polish.

Grooved platf.	Range total	Forest total	Tundra total
unknown/fragment	7(17)	7(24)	
none	34(83)	22(76)	12(100)
Total	41(100)	29(100)	12(100)

Table 7.5b. General phase adzelike artifact grooved platforms

Hinge fracture	Range total	Forest total	Tundra total
unknown fragment	36(88)	27(93)	9(75)
present	5(12)	2(07)	3(25)
Total	41(100)	29(100)	12(100)

Table 7.6. General phase adzelike artifact hinge fracturing.

Est.	No.	Min.	Max.	Mean	S.D.	Exclude
L	3	35.61	38.00	37.15	1.34	none
W	3	15.33	18.09	16.41	1.48	"
T	3	3.64	5.34	4.29	0.92	"
Wt	3	2.50	2.98	2.73	0.24	"

Table 7.7a. General phase forest adze flake data (mm and g).

Est.	No.	Min.	Max.	Mean	S.D.	Exclude
L	3	44.84	59.54	50.43	7.96	none
W	3	30.69	67.29	45.32	19.37	"
T	3	10.01	13.69	11.67	1.87	"
Wt	3	17.50	43.70	26.30	15.07	"

Table 7.7b. General phase tundra pick flake data (mm and g).

Est.	No.	Min.	Max.	Mean	S.D.	Exclude
L	12	60.96	156.5	114.6	34.44	9 frag.
W	21	42.18	71.83	58.13	8.11	none
T	21	14.43	36.04	22.16	5.74	"
Wt	12	65.22	368.8	199.9	100.8	9 frag.

Table 7.8a. General phase forest axe data (mm and g).

Est.	No.	Min.	Max.	Mean	S.D.	Exclude
L	3	107.1	131.8	117.8	12.63	3 frag.
W	4	53.17	68.89	59.36	7.61	1 frag.
T	5	12.17	30.30	22.29	7.47	none
Wt	3	165.9	279.3	207.7	62.27	2 frag.

Table 7.8b. General phase tundra axe data (mm and g).

Est.	No.	Min.	Max.	Mean	S.D.	Exclude
L	1	only	one	52.88		2 frag.
W	2	40.93	60.20	50.57	13.63	1 frag.
T	3	10.78	21.24	15.28	5.38	none
Wt	1	only	one	25.40		2 frag.

Table 7.8c. General phase forest chisel data (mm and g).

Est.	No.	Min.	Max.	Mean	S.D.	Exclude
L	2	110	155	132.5		estimated
W	2	33.31	47.02		19.38	none
T	2	20.09	37.91	29.00	12.60	"
Wt	0	both broken. No estimate possible				2 frag.

Table 7.9a. General phase forest pick data (mm and g).

Est.	No.	Min.	Max.	Mean	S.D.	Exclude
L	1	only	one	56.24		2 frag.
W	3	28.64	53.90	39.72	12.91	none
T	3	15.68	39.99	25.81	12.65	"
Wt	1	only one		31.39		2 frag.

Table 7.9b. General phase tundra pick data (mm and g).

Est.	No.	Min.	Max.	Mean	S.D.	Exclude
L	2	36.45	56.59	46.52	14.24	none
W	2	32.71	39.93	36.32	5.11	"
T	2	11.74	24.83	18.29	9.26	"
Wt	2	18.20	72.30	45.25	38.25	"

Table 7.10a. General phase forest shaft polisher data (mm and g).

Est.	No.	Min.	Max.	Mean	S.D.	Exclude
L	2	31.37	48.84	40.11	12.35	none
W	2	21.06	37.33	29.20	11.50	"
T	2	11.37	17.32	14.35	4.21	"
Wt	2	7.62	40.64	24.13	23.35	"

Table 7.10b. General phase tundra shaft polisher data (mm and g).

Material	Range total	Forest total	Tundra total
quartzite	29(20)	4(57)	25(18)
chert	108(76)	2(29)	106(78)
quartz	3(02)		3(02)
silicious shale	3(02)	1(14)	2(01)
Total	143(100)	7(100)	136(99)

Table 8.2. Pre-Dorset point material.

Colour	Range total	Forest total	Tundra total
beige	17(12)	3(43)	14(10)
white	37(26)		37(27)
orange	5(03)	1(14)	4(03)
gray	52(36)	2(29)	50(37)
pink	20(14)	1(14)	19(14)
red	4(03)		4(03)
brown	2(01)		2(01)
green	1(01)		1(01)
purple	1(01)		1(01)
clear	1(01)		1(01)
black	3(02)		3(02)
Total	143(100)	7(100)	136(100)

Table 8.3. Pre-Dorset point colour.

Plan	Range total	Forest total	Tundra total
lanceolate	133(93)	6(86)	127(93)
triangular	8(06)		8(06)
spadelike	2(01)	1(14)	1(01)
Total	143(100)	7(100)	136(100)

Table 8.4. Pre-Dorset point plan.

Type of tip	Range total	Forest total	Tundra total
none/unknown	61(43)	2(29)	59(43)
pointed tip	74(52)	5(71)	69(51)
round	4(03)		4(03)
serrated	3(02)		3(02)
accidental burination	1(01)		1(01)
Total	143(101)	7(100)	136(100)

Table 8.6. Pre-Dorset point tip.

Cross-section	Range total	Forest total	Tundra total
biconvex	133(93)	6(86)	127(93)
planoconvex	9(06)	1(14)	8(06)
biplanar	1(01)		1(01)
Total	143(100)	7(100)	136(100)

Table 8.5. Pre-Dorset point section.

Type of taper	Range total	Forest total	Tundra total
unknown	22(15)		22(16)
tapered to tip	33(23)	2(29)	31(23)
tapered to base	8(06)		8(06)
parallel sided	80(56)	5(71)	75(55)
Total	143(100)	7(100)	136(100)

Table 8.7. Pre-Dorset point taper

Type of base	Range total	Forest total	Tundra total
unknown	33(23)	1(14)	32(24)
unground square	48(34)	3(43)	45(33)
ground square	9(06)		9(07)
unground stem	36(25)	2(29)	34(25)
ground stem	9(06)		9(07)
unground flare	1(01)		1(01)
parallel tang	1(01)		1(01)
unground side-notch	4(03)	1(14)	3(02)
bipointed	1(01)		1(01)
fishtailed	1(01)		1(01)
Total	143(101)	7(100)	136(102)

Table 8.8. Pre-Dorset point base.

Basal edge	Range total	Forest total	Tundra total
unknown	39(27)	1(14)	38(28)
unground flat	43(30)	3(43)	40(29)
ground flat	10(07)		10(07)
unground round	2(01)		2(01)
ungroundconcave	47(33)	3(43)	44(32)
ground concave	1(01)		1(01)
unground & pointed	1(01)		1(01)
Total	143(100)	7(100)	136(99)

Table 8.9. Pre-Dorset point basal edge.

Shoulder type	Range total	Forest total	Tundra total
none/unknown	141(99)	7(100)	134(99)
ground double	2(01)		2(01)
Total	143(100)	7(100)	136(100)

Table 8.10. Pre-Dorset point shoulder.

Breakage type	Range total	Forest total	Tundra total
none	45(31)	4(57)	41(30)
transverse	57(40)	2(29)	55(40)
diagonal	17(12)	1(14)	16(12)
semi-diagonal	10(07)		10(07)
transverse-diagonal	4(03)		4(03)
double transverse	6(04)		6(04)
longitudinal & transverse	4(03)		4(03)
Total	143(100)	7(100)	136(99)

Table 8.11. Pre-Dorset point breakage.

Burination	Range total	Forest total	Tundra total
none/unknown	139(97)	7(100)	132(97)
1 side or face	4(03)		4(03)
Total	143(100)	7(100)	136(100)

Table 8.12. Pre-Dorset point burination.

Special traits	Range total	Forest total	Tundra total
none/unknown	110(77)	6(86)	104(76)
eared	22(15)		22(16)
almost notched	1(01)		1(14)
patinated	3(02)		3(02)
end-thinned	4(03)	1(14)	3(02)
almost tanged	3(02)		3(02)
Total	143(100)	7(100)	136(102)

Table 8.13. Pre-Dorset point special traits.

Other usage	Range total	Forest total	Tundra total
none/unknown	139(97)	7(100)	132(97)
spokeshave	1(01)		1(01)
knife	3(02)		3(02)
Total	143(100)	7(100)	136(100)

Table 8.14. Pre-Dorset points with other functions.

Est.	No.	Min.	Max.	Mean	S.D.	Exclude
L	6	26.00	57.00	39.92	12.33	1 .
W	7	10.30	21.78	15.43	3.83	none
T	6	3.78	5.45	4.64	0.74	1 .
Wt	3	2.30	4.80	3.60	1.25	4

Table 8.15a. Pre-Dorset forest point data (mm and g).

Est.	No.	Min.	Max.	Mean	S.D.	Exclude
L	98	19.98	90.00	35.10	11.73	38
W	112	1.80	33.00	14.12	4.56	24
T	126	2.00	11.67	4.01	1.61	10
Wt	39	0.48	21.07	2.68	3.50	97

Table 8.15b. Pre-Dorset tundra point data (mm and g).

Colour (main)	Range total	Forest total	Tundra total
beige	10(05)	1(17)	9(05)
white	38(20)	4(67)	34(18)
orange	16(08)		16(09)
gray	94(48)	1(17)	93(49)
pink	20(10)		20(11)
red	2(01)		2(01)
green	6(03)		6(03)
brown	3(02)		3(02)
purple	1(01)		1(01)
clear	1(01)		1(01)
black	3(02)		3(02)
Total	194(101)	6(101)	188(102)

Table 8.16b. Pre-Dorset sideblade colour.

Texture	Range total	Forest total	Tundra total
banded	63(93)	1(33)	62(95)
mottled	5(07)	2(67)	3(05)
Total	68(100)	3(100)	65(100)

Table 8.16c. Pre-Dorset sideblade texture.

Faciality	Range total	Forest total	Tundra total
unifacial	13(07)	1(17)	12(06)
bifacial	181(93)	5(83)	176(94)
Total	194(100)	6(100)	188(100)

Table 8.17. Pre-Dorset sideblade faciality.

Completeness	Range total	Forest total	Tundra total
base only	1(01)		1(01)
midsection	12(06)	2(33)	10(05)
tip only	3(02)		3(02)
base and midsection	62(32)	3(50)	59(31)
tip and midsection	33(17)		33(18)
edge fragment	1(01)		1(01)
complete	67(35)	1(17)	66(35)
longitudinally split	3(02)		3(02)
light chipping	12(06)		12(06)
Total	194(102)	6(100)	188(101)

Table 8.18. Pre-Dorset sideblade completeness.

Plan	Range total	Forest total	Tundra total
left-leaning	1(01)		1(01)
lanceolate	1(01)		1(01)
ovoid	13(07)	3(50)	10(05)
triangular	6(03)		6(03)
asymmetric ovoid	162(84)	3(50)	159(85)
notched	11(06)		11(06)
Total	194(102)	6(100)	188(101)

Table 8.19. Pre-Dorset sideblade plan.

Section	Range total	Forest total	Tundra total
biconvex	174(90)	6(100)	168(89)
planoconvex	16(08)		16(09)
tabular	4(02)		4(02)
Total	194(100)	6(100)	188(100)

Table 8.20. Pre-Dorset sideblade section.

Type of edge	Range total	Forest total	Tundra total
serrated preform	37(19)	2(33)	35(19)
unworn bifacial retouch	100(52)	3(50)	97(52)
unworn unifacial retouch	5(03)		5(03)
worn bifacial retouch	45(23)	1(17)	44(23)
worn unifacial retouch	2(01)		2(01)
serrated and worn	5(03)		5(03)
Total	194(101)	6(100)	188(101)

Table 8.21. Pre-Dorset sideblade edge.

Base	Range total	Forest total	Tundra total
unknown	44(23)	1(17)	43(23)
unground dorsal retouch	6(03)		6(03)
unground bifacial retouch	110(57)	3(50)	107(57)
ground dorsal retouch	1(01)		1(01)
ground bifacial retouch	33(17)	2(33)	31(16)
Total	194(101)	6(100)	188(100)

Table 8.22. Pre-Dorset sideblade base.

Midsection	Range total	Forest total	Tundra total
unknown	5(03)		5(03)
unifacial retouch	5(03)		5(03)
bifacial retouch	61(31)	3(50)	58(31)
serrated	123(63)	3(50)	120(64)
Total	194(100)	6(100)	188(101)

Table 8.23. Pre-Dorset sideblade midsection.

Type of tip	Range total	Forest total	Tundra total
unknown	75(39)	5(83)	70(37)
unworn pointed	70(36)		70(37)
worn and round	10(05)		10(05)
worn and pointed	17(09)		17(09)
unworn and round	19(10)	1(17)	18(10)
serrated	2(01)		2(01)
square	1(01)		1(01)
Total	194(101)	6(100)	188(100)

Table 8.24. Pre-Dorset sideblade tip.

Type of break	Range total	Forest total	Tundra total
unknown	67(35)	1(17)	66(35)
transverse	20(10)	1(17)	19(10)
diagonal	16(08)		16(09)
longitudinal	4(02)		4(02)
semi-transverse	8(04)		8(04)
multi-transverse	8(04)	2(33)	6(03)
transverse & longitud.	3(02)		3(02)
multi-diagonal	2(01)		2(01)
light chipping	1(01)		1(01)
split section	1(01)		1(01)
transversely halved	52(27)	2(33)	50(27)
diagonally halved	4(02)		4(02)
longitudinally halved	8(04)		8(04)
Total	194(101)	6(100)	188(99)

Table 8.25. Pre-Dorset sideblade breakage.

Striae to edge	Range total	Forest total	Tundra total
none	191(98)	6(100)	185(98)
perpendicular	2(01)		2(01)
bifacial perpendicular	1(01)		1(01)
Total	194(100)	6(100)	188(100)

Table 8.26. Pre-Dorset sideblade striae.

Cortex	Range total	Forest total	Tundra total
unknown/none	192(99)	6(100)	186(99)
midsection face	2(01)		2(01)
Total	194(100)	6(100)	188(100)

Table 8.27. Pre-Dorset sideblade cortex.

Basal plan	Range total	Forest total	Tundra total
unknown	55(28)	2(33)	53(28)
tapered, flat and ground	4(02)		4(02)
tapered, round, unground	1(01)		1(01)
tapered, flat & unground	7(04)		7(04)
round and ground	7(04)		7(04)
round and unground	28(14)	2(33)	26(14)
pointed and ground	17(09)	1(17)	16(09)
pointed and unground	60(31)	1(17)	59(31)
square and ground	1(01)		1(01)
square and unground	5(03)		5(03)
ground side-notched	3(02)		3(02)
unground side-notched	6(03)		6(03)
Total	194(102)	6(101)	188(102)

Table 8.28. Pre-Dorset sideblade base.

Type of back	Range total	Forest total	Tundra total
unknown	27(14)		27(14)
like opposite edge	167(86)	6(100)	161(86)
Total	194(100)	6(100)	188(100)

Table 8.29. Pre-Dorset sideblade back.

Platform	Range total	Forest total	Tundra total
unknown fragment	46(24)	2(33)	44(23)
ground/unfacetted	1(01)		1(01)
ground and facetted	5(03)		5(03)
unground & facetted	3(02)		3(02)
retouched away	138(71)	4(67)	134(71)
arcuate and facetted	1(01)		1(01)
Total	194(102)	6(100)	188(101)

Table 8.30. Pre-Dorset sideblade platform.

Est.	No.	Min.	Max.	Mean	S.D.	Exclude
L	6	22.00	42.00	34.83	7.65	none
W	6	16.00	18.00	16.67	0.82	"
T	5	3.88	6.26	4.44	1.03	1 .
Wt	1	only	one	1.60		5

Table 8.31a. Pre-Dorset forest sideblade data (mm and g).

Est.	No	Min.	Max.	Mean	S.D.	Exclude
L	166	14.00	60.00	28.60	8.77	22
W	174	6.00	30.00	13.42	4.46	14
T	183	1.78	9.73	3.68	1.51	5
Wt	69	0.20	15.53	1.81	2.68	119 s

Table 8.31b. Pre-Dorset tundra sideblade data (mm and g).

Substance	Range total	Forest total	Tundra total
quartzite	239(42)	18(53)	221(41)
chert	270(47)	13(38)	257(44)
quartz	56(10)	3(09)	53(10)
silicious shale	9(02)		9(02)
copper	1(00)		1(00)
Total	575(101)	34(100)	541(97)

Table 8.33a. Pre-Dorset scraper material.

Colour	Range total	Forest total	Tundra total
clear	21(04)		21(04)
beige	92(16)	5(15)	87(16)
white	119(21)	6(18)	113(21)
orange	31(05)	1(03)	30(06)
gray	213(37)	17(50)	196(33)
pink	41(07)	2(06)	39(07)
red	6(01)		6(01)
brown	6(01)		6(01)
green	27(05)		27(05)
purple	10(02)	2(06)	8(01)
unknown	1(00)	1(03)	
black	8(01)		8(01)
Total	575(100)	34(98)	541(99)

Tables 8.33b. Pre-Dorset scraper colour.

Texture	Range total	Forest total	Tundra total
banded	141(94)	10(91)	131(94)
mottled	8(05)	1(09)	7(05)
speckled	1(01)		2(01)
Total	150(100)	11(100)	139(100)

Table 8.33c. Pre-Dorset scraper texture.

Plan	Range total	Forest total	Tundra total
unknown	9(02)		9(02)
rhomboid	125(22)	5(15)	120(22)
tearshape	98(17)	12(35)	86(16)
triangular	71(12)	3(09)	68(13)
ovoid	62(11)	3(09)	59(11)
rectangle/bladelike	73(13)	2(06)	71(13)
square	9(02)	1(03)	8(01)
ululike	88(15)	2(06)	86(16)
discoid	40(07)	6(18)	34(06)
Total	575(101)	34(101)	541(100)

Table 8.34. Pre-Dorset scraper plan.

Cross-section	Range total	Forest total	Tundra total
tabular	208(36)	7(21)	201(37)
keeled	81(14)	7(21)	74(14)
tortoise	190(33)	17(50)	173(32)
biconvex	81(14)	3(09)	78(14)
planoconvex	14(02)		14(03)
concavoconvex	1(00)		1(00)
Total	575(99)	34(101)	541(100)

Table 8.35. Pre-Dorset scraper section.

Serration	Range total	Forest total	Tundra total
unknown	5(01)		5(01)
serrated	126(22)	4(12)	122(23)
unserrated	424(74)	30(88)	394(73)
Total	575(97)	34(100)	541(97)

Table 8.36. Pre-Dorset scraper serration.

Base	Range total	Forest total	Tundra total
unknown	16(03)		16(03)
unretouched/unground	118(21)	2(06)	116(21)
unretouched/ground	68(12)	1(03)	67(12)
dorsal retouch	243(42)	24(71)	219(40)
discoidal	5(01)		5(01)
alternate retouch	1(00)		1(00)
bifacial retouch	14(02)	6(18)	8(01)
ventrally retouch	110(19)	1(03)	109(20)
Total	575(100)	34(101)	541(98)

Table 8.37. Pre-Dorset scraper base.

Basal grinding	Range total	Forest total	Tundra total
none/unknown	19(03)	1(03)	18(03)
ground	317(55)	18(53)	299(55)
very ground	51(09)	4(12)	47(09)
unground	188(33)	11(32)	177(33)
Total	575(100)	34(100)	541(100)

Table 8.38. Pre-Dorset scraper basal grinding.

Cortex	Range total	Forest total	Tundra total
none	518(90)	28(82)	490(91)
present	57(10)	6(18)	51(09)
Total	575(100)	34(100)	541(100)

Table 8.39. Pre-Dorset scraper cortex.

Bit wear	Range total	Forest total	Tundra total
unknown	18(03)		18(03)
worn	318(55)	23(68)	295(55)
very worn	90(16)	3(09)	87(16)
unworn	149(26)	8(24)	141(26)
Total	575(100)	34(101)	541(100)

Table 8.40. Pre-Dorset scraper bit wear.

Striae	Range total	Forest total	Tundra total
none-unknown	505(88)	32(94)	473(87)
over the edge	70(12)	2(06)	68(13)
Total	575(100)	34(100)	541(100)

Table 8.41. Pre-Dorset scraper striae.

Bifacial platform	Range total	Forest total	Tundra total
unknown	443(77)	30(88)	413(76)
present	132(23)	4(12)	128(24)
Total	575(100)	34(100)	541(100)

Tble 8.42 Pre-Dorset scrapers made from thinning flakes

Spurring	Range total	Forest total	Tundra total
unspurred	377(66)	29(85)	348(64)
single spur	115(20)	5(15)	110(20)
double spur	83(14)		83(15)
Total	575(100)	34(100)	541(99)

Table 8.43. Pre-Dorset scraper spurring.

Est.	No.	Min.	Max.	Mean	S.D.	Exclude
L	33	14.00	52.00	29.72	9.97	4
W	34	12.12	35.26	22.77	6.21	all
T	33	4.92	12.20	7.34	2.08	1
Wt	30	1.80	13.19	5.85	4.08	4

Table 8.44a. Pre-Dorset forest scraper data (mm and g).

Est.	No.	Min.	Max.	Mean	S.D.	Excl
L	488	12.00	104.0	30.75	13.28	53
W	499	2.00	66.19	26.11	8.94	42
T	531	1.49	17.46	6.83	2.48	10
Wt	380	0.10	172.6	6.95	11.54	161

Table 8.44b. Pre-Dorset tundra scraper data (mm and g).

Material	Range total	Forest total	Tundra total
quartzite	345(65)	20(71)	325(64)
chert	159(30)	6(21)	153(30)
quartz	17(03)	2(07)	15(03)
slate	1(00)		1(00)
silicious shale	10(02)		10(02)
Total	532(100)	28(99)	504(99)

Table 8.45a. Pre-Dorset knife material.

Colour (main)	Range total	Forest total	Tundra total
beige	113(21)	3(11)	110(22)
white	122(23)	7(25)	115(23)
orange	51(10)	3(11)	48(10)
gray	139(26)	11(39)	128(25)
pink	54(10)	1(04)	53(11)
red	8(02)	1(04)	7(01)
green	9(02)		9(02)
brown	11(02)		11(02)
purple	10(02)	2(07)	8(02)
clear	10(02)		10(02)
black	5(01)		5(01)
Total	532(101)	28(101)	504(101)

Table 8.45b. Pre-Dorset knife colour.

Texture	Range total	Forest total	Tundra total
solid colour	413(78)	21(75)	392(78)
veined	1(00)		1(00)
banded	98(18)	7(25)	91(18)
mottled	9(02)		9(02)
speckled	1(00)		1(00)
Total	532(98)	28(100)	504(98)

Table 8.45c. Pre-Dorset knife texture.

Faciality	Range total	Forest total	Tundra total
unifacial	100(19)	7(25)	93(18)
bifacial	432(81)	21(75)	411(82)
Total	532(100)	28(100)	504(100)

Table 8.46. Pre-Dorset knife faciality.

Completeness	Range total	Forest total	Tundra total
base only	27(05)		27(05)
midsection	27(05)	3(11)	24(05)
tip only	27(05)	1(04)	26(05)
base and midsection	81(15)		81(16)
tip and midsection	93(18)	1(04)	92(18)
edge fragment	20(05)		20(04)
complete	217(41)	22(79)	195(39)
longitudinally split	4(01)		4(01)
light chipping	36(07)	1(04)	35(07)
Total	532(101)	28(102)	504(100)

Table 8.47. Pre-Dorset knife completeness.

Plan	Range total	Forest total	Tundra total
unknown	36(07)	1(04)	35(07)
lanceolate	94(18)	1(04)	93(18)
ovoid	150(28)	10(36)	140(28)
semilunar	52(10)	5(18)	47(09)
rectangle or square	47(09)	4(14)	43(09)
triangular/tearshaped	37(07)	5(18)	32(06)
pentagonal	3(01)		3(01)
left-leaning	32(06)	2(07)	30(06)
asymmetric ovoid	32(06)		32(06)
discoidal	21(04)		21(04)
uni-shouldered	7(01)		7(01)
bi-shouldered	2(00)		2(00)
notched	4(01)		4(01)
spadelike	1(00)		1(00)
bladelike	13(02)		13(03)
rhomboid	1(00)		1(00)
Total	532(100)	28(101)	504(98)

Table 8.48. Pre-Dorset knife plan.

Section	Range total	Forest total	Tundra total
unknown	1(00)		1(00)
biconvex	375(70)	20(71)	355(70)
planoconvex	114(21)	5(18)	109(22)
tabular	11(02)	1(04)	10(02)
concavoconvex	1(00)		1(00)
keeled	16(03)		16(03)
tortoise	10(02)	2(07)	8(02)
sinuous	1(00)		1(00)
biconvex C-F*	1(00)		1(00)
planoconvex C-F	1(00)		1(00)
tabular C-F	1(00)		1(00)
Total	532(98)	28(100)	504(100)

8.49. Pre-Dorset knife section (*C-F=channel-flaked).

Type of edge	Range total	Forest total	Tundra total
unknown fragment	3(01)		3(01)
serrated preform	107(20)	7(25)	100(20)
unworn bifacial retouch	164(31)	11(39)	153(30)
unworn unifacial retouch	25(05)	1(04)	24(05)
worn bifacial retouch	178(33)	7(25)	171(34)
worn unifacial retouch	46(09)	2(08)	44(09)
alternate retouch/unworn	1(00)		1(00)
serrated and worn	7(01)		7(01)
alternate retouch & worn	1(00)		1(00)
Total	532(100)	28(101)	504(100)

Table 8.50. Pre-Dorset knife edge.

Base	Range total	Forest total	Tundra total
unknown	149(28)	5(18)	144(29)
unground unretouched	11(02)	1(04)	10(02)
unground dorsal retouch	49(09)	3(11)	46(09)
unground ventral retouch	2(00)		2(00)
unground bifacial retouch	178(33)	12(43)	166(33)
unground alternate retouch	1(00)	1(04)	
ground dorsal retouch	18(03)		18(04)
ground ventral retouch	2(00)		2(00)
ground bifacial retouch	120(23)	6(21)	114(23)
ground alternate retouch	1(00)		1(00)
bifacial thinning	1(00)		1(00)
Total	532(98)	28(101)	504(100)

Table 8.51. Pre-Dorset knife basal retouch.

Midsection	Range total	Forest total	Tundra total
unknown/none	57(11)	1(04)	56(11)
unifacial retouch	54(10)	4(14)	50(10)
bifacial retouch	267(50)	14(50)	253(50)
alternate retouch	11(02)	9(32)	2(00)
serrated	143(27)		143(28)
Total	532(100)	28(100)	504(99)

Table 8.52. Pre-Dorset knife midsection.

Type of tip	Range total	Forest total	Tundra total
unknown	152(29)	3(11)	149(30)
unworn pointed	99(19)	8(29)	91(18)
worn and round	71(13)	6(21)	65(13)
worn and pointed	77(14)	1(04)	76(15)
unworn and round	76(14)	5(18)	71(14)
serrated	24(05)	2(08)	22(04)
square	33(06)	3(11)	30(06)
Total	532(100)	28(102)	504(100)

Table 8.53. Pre-Dorset knife tip.

Type of break	Range total	Forest total	Tundra total
unknown	213(40)	22(79)	191(38)
transverse	131(25)	1(04)	130(26)
diagonal	47(09)		47(09)
transverse-diagonal	18(03)	1(04)	17(03)
longitudinal	15(03)		15(03)
semi-transverse	42(08)	1(04)	41(08)
multi-transverse	18(03)	1(04)	17(03)
transverse & longitudinal	14(03)		14(03)
multi-diagonal	12(02)	1(04)	11(02)
diagonal and longitudinal	8(02)		8(02)
light chipping	5(01)	1(04)	4(01)
transversely halved	4(01)		4(01)
diagonally halved	1(00)		1(00)
longitudinally halved	4(01)		4(01)
Total	532(101)	28(103)	504(100)

Table 8.54. Pre-Dorset knife breakage.

Striae	Range total	Forest total	Tundra total
none	531(100)	28(100)	503(100)
over the edge	1(00)		1(00)
Total	532(100)	28(100)	504(100)

Table 8.55. Pre-Dorset knife striae.

Cortex	Range total	Forest total	Tundra total
unknown/none	486(91)	25(89)	461(91)
most of dorsal face	4(01)		4(01)
most of edge	4(01)		4(01)
tip face	2(00)		2(00)
basal face	4(01)	1(04)	3(01)
midsection edge	1(00)	1(04)	
basal edge	2(00)		2(00)
striking platform	29(05)	1(04)	28(06)
Total	532(99)	28(101)	504(100)

Tables 8.56. Pre-Dorset knife cortex.

Basal plan	Range total	Forest total	Tundra total
unknown	176(33)	5(18)	171(34)
tapered, round & ground	24(05)	3(11)	21(04)
tapered, flat and ground	30(06)		30(06)
tapered, round, unground	17(03)	3(11)	14(03)
tapered, flat & unground	55(10)	3(11)	52(10)
tapered. No basal edge	2(00)		2(00)
round and ground	30(06)		30(06)
round and unground	51(10)	2(08)	49(10)
pointed and ground	28(05)	3(11)	25(05)
pointed and unground	21(04)	2(08)	19(04)
concave and ground	1(00)		1(00)
concave and unground	3(01)		3(01)
square and ground	23(04)	1(04)	22(04)
square and unground	44(08)	5(18)	39(08)
ground side-notched	2(00)		2(00)
unground side-notched	2(00)		2(00)
ground tang	6(01)		6(01)
unground tang	9(02)		9(02)
serrated	7(01)	1(04)	6(01)
unground corner-notch	1(00)		1(00)
Total	532(99)	28(104)	504(99)

Table 8.57. Pre-Dorset knife base.

Platform	Range total	Forest total	Tundra total
unknown fragment	177(33)	4(14)	173(34)
ground unfacetted	8(02)		8(02)
ground and facetted	29(05)	1(04)	28(06)
unground unfacetted	32(06)	2(08)	30(06)
unground & facetted	35(07)	1(04)	34(07)
on raised side	1(00)		1(00)
on unraised side	1(00)		1(00)
retouched away	247(46)	20(71)	227(45)
arcuate unground facets	2(00)		2(00)
Total	532(99)	28(101)	504(100)

Tables 8.58. Pre-Dorset knife platform.

Type of back	Range total	Forest total	Tundra total
unknown	86(16)	1(04)	85(17)
like opposite edge	442(83)	27(96)	415(82)
blunted cortex	3(01)		3(01)
blunted retouch	1(00)		1(00)
Total	532(100)	28(100)	504(100)

Tables 8.59. Pre-Dorset knife back.

Est.	No.	Min.	Max.	Mean	S.D.	Excl
L	26	23.0	98.00	57.04	18.04	2
W	"	15.0	54.00	30.96	10.26	2
T	"	3.22	14.33	9.32	2.92	2
Wt	"	2.8	71.70	24.18	18.23	6

Table 8.60a. Pre-Dorset forest knife data (mm and g).

Est.	No	Min.	Max.	Mean	S.D.	Excl
L	385	20.00	160.0	65.28	24.89	118
W	441	10.00	92.00	32.94	15.03	63
T	485	2.00	23.65	8.50	3.30	19
Wt	195	0.75	155.5	29.41	30.28	309

Table 8.60b. Pre-Dorset tundra knife data (mm and g).

Material	Tundra total	Colour	Tundra total
sandstone	7(64)	beige	5(45)
quartzite	3(27)	white	1(09)
silicious shale	1(09)	gray	1(09)
		pink	1(09)
		brown	3(27)
Total	11(100)	Total	11(100)

Table 8.61. Pre-Dorset chitho material and colour.

Faciality	Tundra total	Completeness	Tundra total
bifacial	4(36)	complete	6(55)
unifacial	7(64)	edge fragment	2(18)
		quartered	1(09)
		some spalling	2(18)
Total	11(100)	Total	11(100)

Table 8.62. Pre-Dorset chitho faciality and completeness.

Plan	Tundra total	Section	Tundra total
unknown/fragment	2(18)	flat/parallel	7(64)
ovoid	2(18)	uneven/wavy	4(36)
round	5(45)		
rectangular/square	2(18)		
Total	11(99)	Total	11(100)

Table 8.63. Pre-Dorset chitho plan and section.

Edge wear	Tundra total	Cortex	Tundra total
worn	7(64)	present	8(73)
unworn	4(36)	none	3(27)
Total	11(100)	Total	11(100)

Table 8.64. Pre-Dorset chitho wear and cortex.

Est.	No.	Min.	Max.	Mean	S.D.	Exclude
L	8	49.59	175.5	85.39	41.14	3
W	6	48.01	87.20	63.73	14.63	5
T	11	5.39	31.92	12.98	7.17	none
Wt	6	44.90	115.2	76.91	29.31	5

Table 8.65. Pre-Dorset tundra chitho data (mm and g).

Material	Range total	Forest total	Tundra total
quartzite	18(56)	2(67)	16(55)
quartz	10(31)	1(33)	9(31)
chert	4(13)		4(14)
Total	32(100)	3(100)	29(100)

Table 8.66a. Pre-Dorset wedge material.

Colour	Range total	Forest total	Tundra total
beige	6(19)		6(21)
white	9(28)	1(33)	8(28)
orange	3(09)		3(10)
gray	3(09)	1(33)	2(07)
pink	1(03)	1(33)	
red	2(06)		2(07)
purple	1(03)		1(03)
green	2(06)		2(07)
clear	5(16)		5(17)
Total	32(99)	3(99)	29(100)

Table 8.66b. Pre-Dorset wedge colour.

Plan	Range total	Forest total	Tundra total
rectangular	9(28)		9(31)
square	5(16)		5(17)
rhomboid	3(09)	1(33)	2(07)
parallelogram	3(09)	1(33)	2(07)
tearshaped triangular	2(06)	1(33)	1(03)
biconvex/ovoid	6(19)		6(21)
round	4(13)		4(14)
Total	32(100)	3(99)	29(100)

Table 8.67. Pre-Dorset wedge plan.

Section	Range total	Forest total	Tundra total
biplanar	3(09)		3(10)
biconvex	13(41)	1(33)	12(41)
planoconvex	12(38)	1(33)	11(38)
concavoconvex	1(03)		1(03)
rhomboidal	2(06)	1(33)	1(03)
parallelogram	1(03)		1(03)
Total	32(100)	3(99)	29(98)

Table 8.68. Pre-Dorset wedge section.

Flakescar type	Range total	Forest total	Tundra total
amorphous	9(28)		9(31)
flat columnar	10(31)	2(67)	8(28)
channelled	2(06)		2(07)
" columnar	11(34)	1(33)	10(34)
Total	32(99)	3(100)	29(100)

Table 8.69. Pre-Dorset wedge flake scars.

Percussion	Range total	Forest total	Tundra total
bipolar	22(69)	2(67)	20(69)
double bipolar	1(03)		1(03)
unipolar	6(19)	1(33)	5(17)
discoidal	3(09)		3(10)
Total	32(100)	3(100)	29(99)

Table 8.70. Pre-Dorset wedge percussion.

Est.	No.	Min.	Max.	Mean	S.D.	Exclude
L	3	27.03	49.65	36.66	11.68	none
W	3	15.48	52.05	31.57	18.67	"
T	3	9.78	13.86	11.81	2.04	"
Wt	3	5.23	43.12	19.86	20.37	"

Table 8.71a. Pre-Dorset forest wedge data (mm and g).

Est.	No.	Min.	Max.	Mean	S.D.	Exclude
L	28	14.34	59.66	29.69	10.26	1
W	"	13.75	43.33	23.61	6.94	"
T	"	5.48	20.49	9.21	3.15	"
Wt	27	1.29	63.80	9.40	12.04	2

Table 8.71b. Pre-Dorset tundra wedge data (mm and g).

Type-tool	Tundra total	Material	Tundra
adze	9	basalt	17(55)
adze flakes	11	chert	10(32)
chisel	10	quartzite	1(03)
gouge	1	silicious shale	3(10)
Total	31	Total	31(100)

Table 8.72a. Pre-Dorset adzelike artifacts and material.

Colour	Tundra	Type-striae	Tundra total
beige	3(10)	none	14(45)
white	1(03)	transverse	2(06)
orange	1(03)	diagonal	4(13)
gray	13(42)	longitudinal	3(10)
pink	1(03)	double diagonal	2(06)
black	12(39)	transverse/diag./longitudinal	2(06)
		diagonal and longitudinal	1(03)
		transverse/longitudinal	3(10)
Total	31(100)	Total	31(99)

Table 8.72b. Pre-dorset adzelike artifact colour and striae.

Flake type	Tundra total	Ground areas	Tundra total
unknown	2(06)	none	6(19)
lateral	9(29)	restricted	12(39)
bit	5(16)	widespread	13(42)
haft	1(03)		
complete tool	14(45)		
Total	31(99)	Total	31(100)

Table 8.73. Pre-Dorset adze flakes and grinding.

Polish	Tundra total	Hinged fractured	Tundra total
none	7(23)	unknown/none	29(94)
light	3(10)	present	2(06)
heavy	21(68)		
Total	31(101)	Total	31(100)

8.74. Pre-Dorset adzelike artifact polish and hinging

Est.	No.	Min.	Max.	Mean	S.D	Exclude
L	11	15.80	56.20	39.97	11.81	none
W	11	6.08	39.37	23.85	10.48	"
T	11	3.05	12.45	7.13	3.78	"
Wt	10	0.40	24.50	9.17	8.75	1

Table 8.75. Pre-Dorset tundra adze flake data (mm and g).

Material	Range total	Forest total	Tundra total
quartzite		4(50)	18(20)
chert	65(66)	1(13)	64(70)
quartz	12(12)	3(38)	9(10)
Total	99(100)	8(101)	91(100)

Table 8.78a. Pre-Dorset core and microcore material.

Colour	Range total	Forest total	Tundra total
beige	20(20)	2(25)	18(20)
white	25(25)	4(50)	21(23)
orange	3(03)		3(03)
gray	30(30)	2(25)	28(31)
pink	7(07)		7(08)
red	1(01)		1(01)
brown	1(01)		1(01)
green	8(08)		8(09)
blue	1(01)		1(01)
clear	2(02)		2(02)
black	1(01)		1(01)
Total	99(99)	8(100)	91(100)

Table 8.78b. Pre-Dorset core and microcore colour.

Texture	Range total	Forest total	Tundra total
normal	69(69)	8(100)	61(67)
mottled	1(01)		1(01)
banded	29(29)		29(32)
Total	99(99)	8(100)	91(100)

Table 8.78c. Pre-Dorset core and microcore texture.

Plan	Range total	Forest total	Tundra total
unknown	11(11)		11(12)
round cobble	15(15)	1(13)	14(15)
rectangular/square	43(43)	3(38)	40(44)
ovoid	12(12)	2(25)	10(11)
triangular	18(18)	2(25)	16(18)
Total	99(99)	8(101)	91(100)

Table 8.79. Pre-Dorset core and microcore plan.

Section	Range total	Forest total	Tundra total
unknown	6(06)		6(07)
round	6(06)		6(07)
rectang./rhomb./square	45(45)	5(63)	40(44)
triangular	16(16)	1(13)	15(16)
planoconvex	11(11)	2(25)	9(10)
biconvex	15(16)		15(16)
Total	99(99)	8(101)	91(100)

Table 8.80. Pre-Dorset core and microcore section.

Profile	Range total	Forest total	Tundra total
unknown	5(05)		5(05)
blocky	31(31)	1(13)	30(33)
conical	24(24)	4(50)	20(22)
spherical	2(02)		2(02)
boatshaped	32(32)	2(25)	30(33)
lenticular	5(05)	1(13)	4(04)
Total	99(99)	8(101)	91(99)

Table 8.81. Pre-Dorset core and microcore profile.

Flake removal	Range total	Forest total	Tundra total
blade/bladelike	54(54)	6(75)	48(53)
flakelike	45(45)	2(25)	43(47)
Total	99(99)	8(100)	91(100)

8.82. Pre-Dorset core and microcore flake/blade removal.

Striking platform	Range total	Forest total	Tundra total
unknown	3(03)		3(03)
single	28(28)	1(13)	27(30)
crescentic	58(58)	6(75)	52(57)
bipolar	10(10)	1(13)	9(10)
Total	99(99)	8(101)	91(100)

Table 8.83. Pre-Dorset core and microcore platform.

Cortex	Range total	Forest total	Tundra total
present	41(41)	3(38)	38(42)
none/unknown	58(58)	5(63)	53(58)
Total	99(99)	8(101)	91(100)

Table 8.84. Pre-Dorset core cortex.

Battering	Range total	Forest total	Tundra total
none/unknown	26(26)	1(13)	25(27)
unipolar	57(57)	6(75)	51(56)
bipolar	16(16)	1(13)	15(16)
Total	99(99)	8(100)	91(99)

Table 8.85. Pre-Dorset core and microcore battering

Edgewear	Range total	Forest total	Tundra total
unknown	13(13)		13(14)
present	13(13)	2(25)	11(12)
none	73(73)	6(75)	67(74)
Total	99(99)	8(100)	91(100)

Table 8.86. Pre-Dorset core and microcore edgewear.

Depleted	Range total	Forest total	Tundra total
no	23(23)	1(13)	22(24)
yes	76(76)	7(88)	69(76)
Total	99(99)	8(100)	91(100)

Table 8.87. Pre-Dorset core and microcore depletion

Multiple use	Range total	Forest total	Tundra total
none/unknown	91(91)	7(88)	84(92)
wedge	5(05)		5(05)
pushplane	2(02)	1(13)	1(01)
knife	1(01)		1(01)
Total	99(99)	8(101)	91(99)

Table 8.88. Pre-Dorset core and microcore multi-use.

Serration	Range total	Forest total	Tundra total
no	83(83)	7(88)	76(84)
yes	16(16)	1(13)	15(16)
Total	99(99)	8(101)	91(100)

Table 8.89. Pre-Dorset core and microcore serration.

Hinging	Range total	Forest total	Tundra total
no	70(70)	7(88)	63(69)
yes	29(29)	1(13)	28(31)
Total	99(99)	8(101)	91(100)

Table 8.90. Pre-Dorset core and microcore hinging

Est.	No.	Min.	Max.	Mean	S.D.	Exclude
L	40	19.22	120.5	55.15	23.94	none
W	40	17.10	129.0	44.60	22.18	"
T	40	9.44	86.47	26.33	16.00	"
Wt	40	3.25	1404	131.4	280.1	"

Table 8.91. Pre-Dorset tundra core data (mm and g).

Est.	No.	Min.	Max.	Mean	S.D.	Exclude
L	8	21.14	53.67	32.47	10.03	non
W	8	12.49	37.08	26.05	10.14	"
T	8	7.83	22.59	14.88	5.27	"
Wt	8	4.10	53.70	17.60	16.22	"

Table 8.92a. Pre-Dorset forest microcore data (mm and g).

Est.	No.	Min.	Max.	Mean	S.D.	Exclude
L	41	12.99	47.98	27.23	7.37	none
W	41	6.65	39.22	22.59	7.38	"
T	38	4.56	28.00	11.83	6.00	"
Wt	39*	1.05	33.24	9.02	7.99	1

Table 8.92b. Pre-Dorset tundra microcore data (mm and g).
* includes weighed unassembled fragments of one core.

Material	Range total	Forest total	Tundra total
quartzite	149(24)		149(24)
chert	442(71)	9(100)	433(71)
quartz	12(02)		12(02)
basalt	2(00)		2(00)
sandstone	2(00)		2(00)
silicious shale	14(02)		14(02)
Total	621(99)	9(100)	612(99)

Table 8.94a. Pre-Dorset regular, worked & sharpening flake material

Colour	Range total	Forest total	Tundra total
beige	76(12)		76(12)
white	80(13)	2(22)	78(13)
orange	21(03)		21(03)
gray	342(55)	7(78)	335(55)
pink	59(10)		59(10)
red	4(01)		4(01)
brown	10(02)		10(02)
purple	3(00)		3(00)
blue	1(00)		1(00)
green	14(02)		14(02)
black	4(01)		4(01)
clear	7(01)		7(01)
Total	621(100)	9(100)	612(100)

Table 8.94b. PreDorset regular, worked and sharpening flake colour.

Texture	Range total	Forest total	Tundra total
solid colour	408(66)	1(11)	407(67)
banded	208(33)	8(89)	200(33)
mottled	4(01)		4(01)
speckled	1(00)		1(00)
Total	621(100)	9(100)	612(101)

Table 8.94c. Pre-Dorset flake texture.

Est.	No.	Min.	Max.	Mean	S.D.	Exclude
L	9	18.52	49.63	29.56	11.96	none
W	9	13.92	37.02	23.26	8.14	"
T	9	3.36	12.29	7.92	3.20	"
Wt	9	0.80	14.78	5.65	4.56	"

Table 8.94d. Pre-Dorset regular forest flake data (mm and g).

Est.	No.	Min.	Max.	Mean	S.D.	Exclude
L	603	5.84	125.3	25.66	13.65	9
W	608	3.03	66.45	18.80	10.50	4
T	608	0.64	21.18	5.11	3.19	4
Wt	604	0.05	155.5	4.09	9.54	8

Table 8.94e. Pre-Dorset regular tundra flake data (mm and g).

Material	Range total	Forest total	Tundra total
quartzite	42(47)		42(47)
chert	48(53)	1(100)	47(53)
Total	90(100)	1(100)	89(100)

Table 8.95a. Pre-Dorset blade material.

Colour	Range total	Forest total	Tundra total
beige	25(28)		25(28)
white	13(15)		13(15)
orange	12(13)		12(13)
gray	29(33)		29(33)
pink	6(07)		6(07)
blue	3(02)	1(100)	2(02)
green	1(01)		1(01)
purple	1(01)		1(01)
Total	90(100)	1(100)	89(100)

Table 8.95b. Pre-Dorset blade colour.

Texture	Range total	Forest total	Tundra total
solid colour	62(69)	1(100)	61(69)
banded	25(28)		25(28)
mottled	2(02)		2(02)
speckled	1(01)		1(01)
Total	90(100)	1(100)	89(100)

Table 8.95c. Pre-Dorset blade texture.

Est.	No.	Min.	Max.	Mean	S.D.	Exclude
L	49	21.10	74.20	45.77	16.25	41 s
W	90	8.79	37.41	18.20	6.32	none
T	90	1.46	14.97	5.22	2.67	none
Wt	49	0.41	25.67	7.00	7.34	41 s

Table 8.95d. Pre-Dorset forest and tundra blade data (mm and g).

Material	Range total	Forest total	Tundra total
quartzite	12(05)	3(30)	9(04)
chert	236(89)	3(30)	233(91)
silicious shale	2(01)	2(20)	
quartz	16(06)	2(20)	14(05)
Total	266(101)	10(100)	256(100)

8.96a. Pre-Dorset forest and tundra microblade material.

Colour	Range total	Forest total	Tundra total
beige	15(06)	1(10)	14(05)
white	35(13)	3(30)	32(13)
orange	6(02)	1(10)	5(02)
gray	155(58)	1(10)	154(60)
pink	28(11)		28(11)
red	1(00)		1(00)
green	1(00)		1(00)
black	9(03)	2(20)	7(03)
clear	16(06)	2(20)	14(05)
Total	266(99)	10(100)	256(99)

8.96b. Pre-Dorset forest and tundra microblade colour

Texture	Range total	Forest total	Tundra total
solid colour	170(64)	9(10)	161(63)
banded	92(35)	1(10)	91(36)
mottled	4(02)		4(02)
Total	266(101)	10(100)	256(101)

Table 8.96c. Pre-Dorset forest and tundra microblade texture.

Est.	No.	Min.	Max.	Mean	S.D.	Exclude
L	4	25.50	46.00	32.06	9.40	6
W	10	7.07	17.00	11.16	2.97	none
T	9	1.82	4.80	3.37	1.13	1
Wt	3	0.40	1.20	0.83	0.40	7

Table 8.96d. Pre-Dorset forest microblade data (mm and g).

Est.	No.	Min.	Max.	Mean	S.D.	Exclude
L	139	8.93	44.88	22.85	7.00	117
W	253	2.00	13.07	5.95	2.00	3
T	253	0.54	5.32	1.99	0.82	3
Wt	147	0.01	1.94	0.31	0.32	109

Table 8.96e. Pre-Dorset tundra microblade data (mm and g).

Material	Range total	Forest total	Tundra total
quartzite	6(86)	2(67)	4(100)
granite	1(14)	1(33)	
Total	7(100)	3(100)	4(100)

Table 8.98a. Pre-Dorset hammerstone material.

Colour	Range total	Forest total	Tundra total
beige	1(14)		1(25)
white	3(43)	1(33)	2(50)
gray	2(29)	1(33)	1(25)
black	1(14)	1(33)	
Total	7(100)	3(99)	4(100)

Table 8.98b. Pre-Dorset hammerstone colour

Plan	Range total	Forest total	Tundra total
round	2(29)		2(50)
tearshaped	1(14)	1(33)	1(25)
triangular	1(14)		1(25)
almost ovoid	3(43)	2(67)	1(25)
Total	7(100)	3(100)	4(100)

Table 8.99. Pre-Dorset hammerstone plan.

Section	Range total	Forest total	Tundra total
round	2(29)	1(33)	1(25)
ovoid	3(43)	1(33)	2(50)
square/rectangle	1(14)		1(25)
triangular	1(14)	1(33)	
Total	7(100)	3(99)	4(100)

8.100. Pre-Dorset hammerstone section.

Pocking	Range total	Forest total	Tundra total
unipolar	1(14)		1(25)
bipolar	4(57)	3(100)	1(25)
bipolar & equatorial	2(29)		2(50)
Total	7(100)	3(100)	4(100)

Table 8.101. Pre-Dorset hammerstone pocking.

Est.	No.	Min.	Max.	Mean	S.D.	Exclude
L	3	49.51	64.65	54.57	8.73	none
W	3	32.46	45.01	37.87	6.45	"
T	3	25.65	34.29	29.12	4.56	"
Wt	3	58.39	103.7	81.37	22.64	"

Table 8.102a. Pre-Dorset forest hammerstone (mm and g).

Est.	No.	Min.	Max.	Mean	S.D.	Exclude
L	4	39.90	79.50	63.74	17.34	none
W	4	34.74	54.80	45.43	9.96	"
T	4	21.50	41.10	31.79	8.22	"
Wt	4	46.60	260.0	148.9	87.34	"

Table 8.102b. Pre-Dorset tundra hammerstone (mm and g).

Material	Range total	Forest total	Tundra total
chert	14(93)		14(100)
silicious shale	1(07)	1(100)	
Total	15(100)	1(100)	14(100)

8.103a. Pre-Dorset forest and tundra graver material.

Colour	Range total	Forest total	Tundra total
beige	1(07)		1(07)
white	3(20)		3(21)
gray	11(73)	1(100)	10(71)
Total	15(100)	1(100)	14(99)

Table 8.103b. Pre-Dorset forest and tundra graver colour.

Est.	No.	Min.	Max.	Mean	S.D.	Exclude
L	14	18.14	59.53	28.64	10.15	1 .
W	15	3.61	27.83	14.70	8.77	none
T	15	2.33	9.95	4.70	2.14	"
Wt	14	0.16	10.62	2.37	2.74	1 .

Table 8.103c. Pre-Dorset forest and tundra graver data (mm and g).

Material	Range total	Forest total	Tundra total
quartzite	3(01)		3(01)
chert	563(99)	4(100)	559(99)
silicious shale	2(00)		2(00)
Total	569(100)	4(100)	565(100)

8.105a. Pre-Dorset rangewide burin-related artifact mat.

Colour	Range total	Forest total	Tundra total
beige	25(04)	1(25)	24(04)
white	119(21)	2(50)	117(21)
orange	4(01)		4(01)
gray	393(69)	1(25)	392(69)
pink	16(03)		16(03)
green	3(01)		3(01)
brown	3(01)		3(01)
black	6(01)		6(01)
Total	569(101)	4(100)	565(101)

8.105b Pre-Dorset rangewide burin-related art. colour

Texture	Range total	Forest total	Tundra total
solid colour	355(62)	3(75)	352(62)
banded	209(37)	1(25)	208(37)
mottled	1(00)		1(00)
veined	1(00)		1(00)
patinated	3(01)		3(01)
Total	569(100)	4(100)	565(100)

8.105c. Pre-Dorset rangewide burin-related texture.

Est.	No.	Min.	Max.	Mean	S.D.	Exc
L	83	13.5	52.29	30.62	7.42	26
W	92	8.99	24.36	17.05	3.33	17
T	102	2.98	9.80	6.06	1.38	7
W	72	0.47	9.35	3.40	1.86	37

Table 8.106. Pre-Dorset rangewide burin plane data (mm and g).

Est.	No.	Min.	Max	Mean	S.D	Exclude
edge 1 scars	85	1	12	3.45	2.4	23 without spallscars
edge 2 scars	10	1	4	2.00	1.05	10 dihedral burins
scar group	89	1	3	1.13	0.36	19 scar groups
tip angle	24	30	135	64.2	28.0	84 without pointed tips

Table 8.108. Pre-Dorset tundra burin plane scars and tip angles.

Attribute	Yes	Absent	Unkn'n	Implication
carinated	42(37)	68(60)	4(04)	many beaked burins
spallface	102(89)	11(10)	1(01)	1/10 burins destroyed
retouch	13(11)	82(72)	19(17)	" " =ret. tools
ground haft	86(75)	37(32)	11(10)	3/4 are socket worn
backed	88(77)	19(17)	7(06)	3/4 high pressure use
back wear	88(77)	19(17)	7(06)	" " " "
back retouch	100(88)	10(09)	4(04)	9/10 " " " "
multiple use	7(06)	107(94)		knife, graver, 4 side-blades and skin flexer

Table 8.110. Pre-Dorset tundra burin slotter attributes.

Estimate	No.	Min.	Max	Mean	S.D	Exclude
edge 1 scars	85	1	12	2.55	2.08	29 without spallscars
edge 2 scars	6	1	7	2.38	2.34	6 dihedral burins
scar groups	87	1	2	1.09	0.29	27 with scar groups
tip angle	31	30	110	76.4	20.5	83 without pointed tips

Table 8.111. Pre-Dorset tundra burin slotter attributes.

Est.	No.	Min.	Max.	Mean	S.D.	Exclude
L	87	15.77	60.49	29.40	8.38	27
W	96	9.18	24.21	16.15	2.87	18
T	109	2.46	10.80	4.73	1.43	5
Wt	80	0.43	15.30	2.50	2.19	34

Table 8.112. Pre-Dorset tundra burin slotter data (mm and g).

Est.	No.	Min.	Max.	Mean	S.D.	Exclude
L	3	25.84	38.38	31.24	6.45	none
W	3	9.64	17.64	13.37	4.03	"
T	3	4.85	7.35	5.92	1.29	"
Wt	3	1.57	4.50	2.58	1.67	"

Table 8.113a. Pre-Dorset forest unburinated plane data(mm/g

Est.	No.	Min.	Max.	Mean	S.D.	Exclude
L	52	20.41	76.45	33.22	10.37	48
W	73	9.75	38.11	17.52	4.52	27
T	52	3.33	9.73	5.90	1.18	48
Wt	47	0.77	25.03	4.02	4.34	53

Table 8.113b. Pre-Dorset tundra unburinated plane data (mm and g).

Est.	No.	Min.	Max.	Mean	S.D.	Exclude
L	5	22.62	60.49	32.75	15.82	none
W	5	13.06	24.21	17.25	4.43	"
T	5	2.61	9.75	5.04	2.74	"
Wt	5	1.00	15.30	4.11	6.27	"

Table 8.114a. Pre-Dorset tundra slotter blank data (mm and g).

Est.	No.	Min.	Max.	Mean	S.D.	Exclude
L	22	12.00	29.63	19.43	5.51	16
W	38	2.00	5.65	3.85	0.89	none
T	38	1.59	4.53	2.70	0.69	"
Wt	22	0.09	0.36	0.18	0.08	16

Table 8.114c. Pre-Dorset tundra plane blank primary spall data.

Est.	No.	Min.	Max.	Mean	S.D.	Excl
L	6	15.30	32.48	20.68	6.47	none
W	6	3.03	5.92	4.02	1.04	"
T	6	2.05	3.20	2.68	0.41	"
Wt	6	0.09	0.33	0.20	0.08	"

Table 8.114d. Pre-Dorset tundra slotter blank primary spall data.

Est.	No.	Min.	Max.	Mean	S.D.	Exclude
L	183	8.98	38.47	18.91	5.07	none
W	183	2.00	8.84	4.75	1.16	"
T	183	1.14	6.27	2.12	0.71	"
Wt	183	0.03	1.37	0.21	0.71	"

Table 8.115a. Pre-Dorset tundra plane spall data (mm and g).

Est.	No.	Min.	Max.	Mean	S.D.	Exclude
L	27	7.58	31.10	18.52	5.55	25
W	52	1.62	7.64	4.79	1.34	none
T	52	0.98	4.83	2.00	0.65	"
Wt	27	0.03	0.41	0.20	0.11	25

Table 8.115b. Pre-Dorset tundra slotter spall data (mm and g).

Material	Range total	Forest total	Tundra total
quartzite	112(96)	50(94)	62(97)
chert	3(03)	1(02)	2(03)
Total	117(101)	53(100)	64(100)

Table 9.2a. Shield Archaic point material.

Colour	Range total	Forest total	Tundra total
beige	30(26)	15(28)	15(23)
white	44(38)	15(28)	29(45)
orange	4(03)	3(06)	1(02)
gray	18(15)	11(21)	7(11)
pink	8(07)	6(11)	2(03)
red	6(05)		6(09)
brown	6(05)	2(04)	4(06)
purple	1(01)	1(02)	
Total	117(100)	53(100)	64(99)

Table 9.2b. Shield Archaic point colour.

Texture	Range total	Forest total	Tundra total
solid colour	110(94)	52(98)	58(91)
banded	7(06)	1(02)	6(09)
Total	117(100)	53(100)	64(100)

Table 9.2c. Shield Archaic point texture.

Plan	Range total	Forest total	Tundra total
lanceolate	26(22)	11(21)	15(23)
spadelike	91(78)	42(79)	49(77)
Total	117(100)	53(100)	64(100)

Table 9.3. Shield Archaic point plan.

Cross-section	Range total	Forest total	Tundra total
biconvex	111(95)	52(98)	59(92)
planoconvex	6(05)	1(02)	5(08)
Total	117(100)	53(100)	64(100)

Table 9.4. Shield Archaic point section.

Type of tip	Range total	Forest total	Tundra total
none/unknown	52(44)	18(34)	34(53)
pointed tip	44(38)	23(43)	21(33)
round	7(06)	5(09)	2(03)
flat	2(02)	1(02)	1(02)
intentionally burinated	1(01)	1(02)	
accidentally burinated	11(09)	5(09)	6(09)
Total	117(100)	53(99)	64(100)

Table 9.5. Shield Archaic point tip.

Type of taper	Range total	Forest total	Tundra total
unknown fragment	14(12)	5(10)	9(14)
tapered to tip	46(39)	23(43)	23(36)
tapered to base	3(03)	2(04)	1(02)
parallel sided	54(46)	23(43)	31(48)
Total	117(100)	53(100)	64(100)

Table 9.6. Shield Archaic point taper.

Type of base	Range total	Forest total	Tundra total
unknown fragment	11(09)	4(08)	7(11)
ground stem	3(03)		3(05)
unground side-notch	3(03)	1(02)	2(03)
ground side-notch	100(85)	48(91)	52(81)
Total	117(100)	53(101)	64(100)

Table 9.7. Shield Archaic point base.

Basal edge	Range total	Forest total	Tundra total
unknown fragment	27(23)	15(28)	12(19)
unground flat	1(01)	1(02)	
ground flat	16(14)	6(11)	10(16)
unground round	2(02)	1(02)	1(02)
ground round	71(61)	30(57)	41(64)
Total	117(101)	53(100)	64(101)

Table 9.8. Shield Archaic point basal edge.

Shoulder type	Range total	Forest total	Tundra total
none/unknown	116(99)	53(100)	63(98)
ground double	1(01)		1(02)
Total	117(100)	53(100)	64(100)

Table 9.9. Shield Archaic point shoulder.

Breakage type	Range total	Forest total	Tundra total
none	36(31)	21(40)	15(23)
transverse	45(38)	20(38)	25(39)
diagonal	5(04)		5(08)
semi-diagonal	11(09)	3(06)	8(13)
double diagonal	1(01)	1(02)	
transverse-diagonal	5(04)	1(02)	4(06)
double transverse	11(09)	6(11)	5(08)
longitudinal & transverse	2(02)	1(02)	1(02)
intentionally burinated	1(01)		1(01)
Total	117(99)	53(101)	64(100)

Table 9.10. Shield Archaic point breakage.

Burination	Range total	Forest total	Tundra total
none/unknown	96(82)	45(85)	51(80)
1 side or face	18(15)	7(13)	11(17)
2 sides or faces	3(03)	1(02)	2(03)
Total	117(100)	53(100)	64(100)

Table 9.11. Shield Archaic point burination.

Special traits	Range total	Forest total	Tundra total
none/unknown	39(33)	20(38)	19(30)
eared	76(65)	32(60)	44(69)
almost notched	1(01)		1(02)
end-thinned	1(01)	1(02)	
Total	117(100)	53(100)	64(101)

Table 9.12. Shield Archaic point special traits.

Other usage	Range total	Forest total	Tundra total
none/unknown	98(84)	46(87)	52(81)
burin	16(14)	5(09)	11(17)
bifacial scraper	1(01)	1(02)	
chisel	2(02)	1(02)	1(02)
Total	117(101)	53(100)	64(100)

Table 9.13. Shield Archaic points having other functions.

Est.	No.	Min.	Max.	Mean	S.D.	Exclude
L	47	27.58	115.0	54.51	17.24	6 frag.
W	50	17.35	36.06	22.95	3.64	3 frag.
T	53	5.78	11.20	7.96	1.26	none
Wt	21	1.90	17.68	8.52	4.29	32 frag.

Table 9.14a. Shield Archaic forest point data (mm and g).

Est.	No.	Min.	Max.	Mean	S.D.	Exclude
L	53	23.71	134.0	56.65	21.39	11 frag.
W	57	16.38	35.00	22.13	3.57	7 frag.
T	62	4.45	10.70	7.65	1.46	2 frag.
Wt	12	2.82	10.49	6.26	2.77	52 frag.

Table 9.14c. Shield Archaic tundra point data (mm and g).

Substance	Range total	Forest total	Tundra total
quartzite	92(89)	54(86)	38(95)
chert	5(05)	4(06)	1(03)
quartz	5(05)	5(08)	
sandstone	1(01)		1(01)
Total	103(100)	63(100)	40(101)

Table 9.15a. Shield Archaic scraper material.

Colour	Range total	Forest total	Tundra total
beige	30(29)	16(25)	14(35)
white	24(23)	15(24)	9(23)
orange	9(09)	6(10)	3(08)
gray	14(14)	11(17)	3(08)
pink	10(10)	7(11)	3(08)
red	7(07)	1(02)	6(15)
brown	3(03)	1(02)	6(15)
green	3(03)	3(05)	
purple	3(03)	3(05)	
Total	103(101)	63(101)	40(100)

Table 9.15b. Shield Archaic scraper colour.

Texture	Range total	Forest total	Tundra total
banded	16(16)	15(24)	1(03)
mottled	1(01)		1(03)
speckled	1(01)	1(02)	
solid colour	85(83)	47(75)	38(95)
Total	103(101)	63(101)	40(101)

Table 9.15c. Shield Archaic scraper texture.

Plan	Range total	Forest total	Tundra total
unknown fragment	1(01)		1(03)
rhomboid	11(11)	5(08)	6(15)
tearshape	34(33)	16(25)	18(45)
triangular	4(04)	3(05)	1(03)
ovoid	27(26)	17(27)	10(25)
rectangular/bladelike	8(08)	6(10)	2(05)
square	12(12)	11(17)	1(03)
ululike	3(03)	3(05)	
discoid	3(03)	3(05)	
Total	103(101)	63(100)	40(102)

Table 9.16. Shield Archaic scraper plan.

Cross-section	Range total	Forest total	Tundra total
tabular	53(51)	29(46)	24(60)
keeled	13(13)	9(14)	4(10)
tortoise	27(26)	15(24)	12(30)
biconvex	2(02)	2(03)	
planoconvex	8(08)	8(13)	
Total	103(100)	63(100)	40(100)

Table 9.17. Shield Archaic scraper section.

Edge type	Range total	Forest total	Tundra total
serrated	18(17)	13(21)	5(13)
unserrated	85(83)	50(79)	35(88)
Total	103(100)	63(100)	40(101)

Table 9.18. Shield Archaic scraper edge type.

Base	Range total	Forest total	Tundra total
unknown fragment	2(02)	1(02)	1(03)
unretouched/unground	12(12)	10(16)	2(05)
unretouched/ground	14(14)	8(13)	6(15)
dorsal retouch	58(56)	33(52)	25(63)
ventral retouch	4(04)	3(05)	1(03)
bifacial retouch	12(12)	8(13)	4(10)
discoidal	1(01)		1(03)
Total	103(101)	63(100)	40(102)

Table 9.19. Shield Archaic scraper base edge.

Cortex	Range total	Forest total	Tundra total
none	78(76)	43(68)	35(88)
present	25(24)	20(32)	5(13)
Total	103(100)	63(100)	40(101)

Table 9.20. Shield Archaic scraper cortex.

Bit wear	Range total	Forest total	Tundra total
worn	65(63)	36(57)	29(73)
very worn	21(20)	15(24)	6(15)
unworn	17(17)	12(19)	5(13)
Total	103(100)	63(100)	40(101)

Table 9.21. Shield Archaic scraper bit wear.

Basal grinding	Range total	Forest total	Tundra total
none/unknown	2(02)	1(02)	1(03)
ground	70(68)	40(63)	30(75)
very ground	10(10)	5(08)	5(13)
unground	21(20)	17(27)	4(10)
Total	103(100)	63(100)	40(101)

Table 9.22. Shield Archaic scraper basal grinding.

Striae	Range total	Forest total	Tundra total
none-unknown	90(87)	55(87)	35(88)
over the edge	13(13)	8(13)	5(13)
Total	103(100)	63(100)	40(101)

Table 9.23. Shield Archaic scraper striae.

Bifac. platform	Range total	Forest total	Tundra total
unknown	88(85)	54(86)	34(85)
present	15(15)	9(14)	6(15)
Total	103(100)	63(100)	40(100)

Table 9.24. Shield Archaic scrapers made from thinning flakes

Spurring	Range total	Forest total	Tundra total
unspurred	90(87)	53(84)	37(93)
single spur	11(11)	9(14)	2(05)
double spur	2(02)	1(02)	1(03)
Total	103(100)	63(100)	40(101)

Table 9.25. Shield Archaic scraper spurring.

Est.	No.	Min.	Max.	Mean	S.D	Exclude
L	62	16.83	90.20	45.47	18.99	1 fragment
W	62	15.00	56.22	32.13	8.51	1 fragment
T	63	4.39	21.61	10.15	3.46	none
Wt	50	2.00	128/6	21.06	21.16	12 frag.

Table 9.26a. Shield Archaic forest scraper data (mm and g).

Est.	No.	Min.	Max.	Mean	S.D	Exclude
L	38	24.62	75.42	41.89	12.54	2 frag.
W	38	13.42	52.96	30.84	7.24	2 frag.
T	40	4.58	16.62	7.82	2.55	none
Wt	32	3.47	66.27	13.19	13.80	8 frag.

Table 9.26b. Shield Archaic tundra scraper data (mm and g).

Material	Range total	Forest total	Tundra total
quartzite	351(96)	223(95)	128(98)
chert	9(02)	7(03)	2(02)
quartz	2(01)	2(01)	
silicious shale	2(01)	2(01)	
Total	364(100)	234(100)	130(100)

Table 9.27a. Shield Archaic knife material.

Colour	Range total	Forest total	Tundra total
beige	89(24)	64(27)	25(19)
white	68(19)	43(18)	25(19)
orange	29(08)	19(08)	10(08)
gray	78(21)	57(24)	21(16)
pink	25(07)	19(08)	6(05)
red	34(09)	5(02)	29(22)
green	4(01)	4(02)	
brown	18(05)	9(04)	9(07)
purple	19(05)	14(06)	5(04)
Total	364(99)	234(99)	130(100)

Table 9.27b. Shield Archaic knife colour.

Texture	Range total	Forest total	Tundra total
solid colour	327(90)	203(87)	124(95)
banded	33(09)	27(12)	6(05)
mottled	3(01)	3(01)	
speckled	1(00)	1(00)	
Total	364(100)	234(100)	130(100)

Table 9.27c. Shield Archaic knife texture.

Faciality	Range total	Forest total	Tundra total
unifacial	30(08)	15(06)	15(12)
bifacial	334(92)	219(94)	115(88)
Total	364(100)	234(100)	130(100)

Table 9.28. Shield Archaic knife faciality.

Completeness	Range total	Forest total	Tundra total
base only	23(06)	11(05)	12(09)
midsection	27(07)	17(07)	10(08)
tip only	23(06)	8(03)	15(12)
base-midsection	81(22)	56(24)	25(19)
tip-midsection	89(24)	51(22)	38(29)
edge fragment	6(02)	4(02)	2(02)
complete	98(27)	75(32)	23(18)
longitudinally split	1(00)	1(00)	
light chipping	16(04)	11(05)	5(04)
Total	364(98)	234(100)	130(101)

Table 9.29. Shield Archaic knife completeness.

Plan	Range total	Forest total	Tundra total
unknown fragment	28(08)	17(07)	11(08)
lanceolate	231(63)	142(61)	89(68)
ovoid	43(12)	28(12)	15(12)
semilunar	2(01)	1(00)	1(01)
rectangular or square	12(03)	9(04)	3(02)
triangular	8(02)	8(03)	
asymmetrical ovoid	5(01)	4(02)	1(01)
discoidal	9(02)	7(03)	2(02)
uni-shouldered	2(01)	2(01)	
bi-shouldered	1(00)		1(01)
notched	4(01)	2(01)	2(02)
sinuous	19(05)	14(06)	5(04)
Total	364(99)	234(100)	130(101)

Table 9.30. Shield Archaic knife plan.

Section	Range total	Forest total	Tundra total
biconvex	301(83)	189(81)	112(86)
planoconvex	46(13)	34(15)	12(09)
concavoconvex	2(01)	1(00)	1(01)
keeled	9(02)	4(02)	5(04)
tortoise	4(01)	4(02)	
sinuous	1(00)	1(00)	
planoconvex C-F	1(00)	1(00)	
Total	364(100)	234(100)	130(100)

9.31. Shield Archaic knife section. *=channel-flaked

Type of edge	Range total	Forest total	Tundra total
unknown fragment	9(02)	5(02)	4(03)
serrated preform	111(30)	60(26)	51(39)
unworn bifacial retouch	108(30)	80(34)	28(22)
unworn unifacial retouch	14(04)	8(03)	6(05)
worn bifacial retouch	112(31)	75(32)	37(28)
worn unifacial retouch	7(02)	3(01)	4(03)
serrated and worn	2(01)	2(01)	
alternate retouch & worn	1(00)	1(00)	
Total	364(100)	234(99)	130(100)

Table 9.32. Shield Archaic knife edge.

Base	Range total	Forest total	Tundra total
unknown fragment	135(37)	74(32)	61(47)
unground-unretouched	6(02)	4(02)	2(02)
ground and unretouch	1(00)	1(00)	
unground dorsal ret.	15(04)	10(04)	5(04)
unground ventral ret.	3(01)	1(01)	2(02)
unground bifacial ret.	133(37)	94(40)	39(30)
ground dorsal retouch	3(01)	2(01)	1(01)
ground bifacial retouch	68(19)	48(21)	20(15)
Total	364(100)	234(101)	130(101)

Table 9.33. Shield Archaic knife basal edge

Midsection	Range total	Forest total	Tundra total
unknown fragment	45(12)	19(08)	26(20)
unifacial retouch	17(05)	11(05)	6(05)
bifacial retouch	168(46)	125(53)	43(33)
alternate retouch	1(00)	1(00)	
serrated	133(37)	78(33)	55(42)
Total	364(100)	234(99)	130(100)

Table 9.34. Shield Archaic knife midsection.

Type of tip	Range total	Forest total	Tundra total
unknown fragment	131(36)	84(36)	47(36)
unworn pointed	84(23)	54(23)	30(23)
worn and round	38(10)	26(11)	12(09)
worn and pointed	57(16)	35(15)	22(17)
unworn and round	38(10)	28(12)	10(08)
serrated	9(02)	6(03)	3(02)
square	7(02)	1(00)	6(05)
Total	364(99)	234(100)	130(100)

Table 9.35. Shield Archaic knife tip.

Type of break	Range total	Forest total	Tundra total
unknown/fragment	74(20)	59(25)	15(12)
transverse	139(38)	81(35)	58(45)
diagonal	40(11)	31(13)	9(07)
transverse-diagonal	18(05)	10(04)	8(06)
longitudinal	11(03)	8(03)	3(02)
semi-transverse	51(14)	25(11)	26(20)
multi-transverse	20(05)	13(06)	7(05)
transverse & longitudinal	5(01)	2(01)	3(02)
multi-diagonal	2(01)	2(01)	
diagonal and longitudinal	2(01)	2(01)	
light chipping	1(00)	1(00)	
longitudinally halved	1(00)	1(00)	
Total	364(99)	234(99)	130(100)

Table 9.36. Shield Archaic knife breakage.

Striae	Range total	Forest total	Tundra total
none	363(100)	233(100)	130(100)
bifacial scraper	1(00)	1(00)	
Total	364(100)	234(100)	130(100)

Table 9.37. Shield Archaic knife striae.

Cortex	Range total	Forest total	Tundra total
unknown/none	335(92)	211(90)	124(95)
most of dorsal face	5(01)	4(02)	1(01)
most of edge	1(00)	1(00)	
tip face	2(01)	1(00)	1(01)
midsection face	1(00)	1(00)	
basal face	1(00)	1(00)	
midsection edge	1(00)	1(00)	
basal edge	2(01)		2(02)
striking platform	16(04)	14(06)	2(02)
Total	364(99)	234(98)	130(101)

Table 9.38. Shield Archaic knife cortex.

Basal plan	Range	Forest	Tundra
unknown fragment	145(40)	86(37)	59(45)
tapered, round & ground	13(04)	9(04)	4(03)
tapered, flat and ground	19(05)	10(04)	9(07)
taper, round & unground	16(04)	8(03)	8(06)
taper, flat and unground	30(08)	18(08)	12(09)
tapered. No basal edge	1(00)	1(01)	
round and ground	23(06)	18(08)	5(04)
round and unground	54(15)	35(15)	19(15)
pointed and ground	3(01)	3(01)	
pointed and unground	12(03)	10(04)	2(02)
concave and unground	1(00)		1(01)
square and ground	8(02)	6(03)	2(02)
square and unground	30(08)	25(11)	5(04)
unground corner-notch	1(00)	1(00)	
ground side-notch	1(00)	1(00)	
unground side-notch	1(00)	1(00)	
unground tang	3(01)	1(00)	2(02)
serrated	3(01)	2(01)	1(01)
Total	364(98)	234(100)	130(102)

Table 9.39. Shield Archaic knife base.

Type of back	Range total	Forest total	Tundra total
unknown fragment	44(12)	24(10)	20(15)
like opposite edge	320(88)	210(90)	110(85)
Total	364(100)	234(100)	130(100)

Table 9.40. Shield Archaic knife back.

Striking platform	Range	Forest	Tundra
unknown fragment	144(40)	84(36)	60(46)
ground & unfacetted	7(02)	3(01)	4(03)
ground and facetted	9(02)	5(02)	4(03)
unground & unfacetted	20(05)	12(05)	8(06)
unground & facetted	22(06)	16(07)	6(05)
retouched away	159(44)	111(47)	48(37)
unraised lateral	3(01)	3(01)	
Total	364(100)	234(99)	130(100)

Table 9.41. Shield Archaic knife platform.

Est.	No.	Min.	Max.	Mean	S.D.	exe
L	172	18.00	146.0	83.54	22.34	22 frag.
W	207	17.00	85.00	33.64	10.83	27 frag.
T	231	5.31	33.51	12.14	4.01	3 frag.
Wt	74	2.83	291.2	47.74	48.77	160 frag.

Table 9.41a. Shield Archaic forest knife data (mm and g).

Est.	No.	Min.	Max.	Mean	S.D.	exe
L	64	28.00	125.0	75.31	20.23	66 frag.
W	109	19.00	68.00	30.23	6.64	21 frag.
T	126	3.76	16.66	10.70	2.42	4 frag.
Wt	25	6.39	70.40	24.66	15.24	105 frag.

Table 9.41b. Shield Archaic tundra knife data (mm and g).

Material	Warden' Grove	Whitefish-Lynx	Remarks
sandstone	2(67)	5(100)	Lynx-Whitefish, Warden's Grove have quartzite river cobbles
quartzite	1(33)		
Total	3(100)	5(100)	

Table 9.42a. Shield Archaic chitho material.

Colour	Warden's Grove	Whitefish-Lynx	Remarks
beige	2(67)	4(80)	very similar in both areas
purple	1(33)	1(20)	
Total	3(100)	5(100)	

Table 9.42b. Shield Archaic chitho colour.

Faciality	Warden's Grove	Whitefish-Lynx	Remarks
bifacial	3(100)	3(60)	emphasis on unifaces to south
unifacial		2(40)	
Total	3(100)	5(100)	

Table 9.43. Shield Archaic chitho faciality.

Plan	Warden's Grove	Whitefish-Lynx	Remarks
ovoid	2(67)	5(100)	all Whitefish-Lynx chithos are ovoid
round	1(33)		
Total	3(100)	5(100)	

Table 9.44. Shield Archaic chitho plan.

Edge wear	Warden's Grove	Whitefish-Lynx	Remarks
worn	2(67)	5(100)	all Whitefish-Lynx chithos are worn
unworn	1(33)		
Total	3(100)	5(100)	

Table 9.45. Shield Archaic chitho wear.

Est.	No.	Min.	Max.	Mean	S.D.	Exclude
L	3	110.2	163.9	131.5	28.48	none
W	3	73.84	135.5	95.16	34.92	"
T	3	27.18	34.73	30.76	3.79	"
Wt	3	222.1	669.8	404.5	235.1	"

Table 9.46a. Shield Archaic Warden's Grove chitho data (mm and g).

Est.	No.	Min.	Max.	Mean	S.D.	Exclude
L	5	78.87	120.1	100.2	17.09	none
W	5	64.44	81.32	71.84	5.40	"
T	5	11.57	16.89	14.59	2.32	"
Wt	5	71.00	173.2	119.6	40.36	"

Table 9.46b. Shield Archaic Whitefish-Lynx chitho data (mm and g).

Material	Range total	Forest total	Tundra total
quartzite	19(90)	17(94)	2(100)
quartz	1(10)	1(10)	
Total	20(100)	18(100)	2(100)

Table 9.47a. Shield Archaic wedge material.

Colour	Range total	Forest total	Tundra total
beige	2(10)	2(11)	
white	9(45)	7(39)	2(100)
orange	3(15)	3(17)	
gray	6(30)	6(33)	
Total	20(100)	18(100)	2(100)

Table 9.47b. Shield Archaic wedge colour.

Plan	Range total	Forest total	Tundra total
rectangular	3(15)	3(17)	
square	12(60)	11(61)	1(50)
rhomboid	1(05)	1(06)	
parallelogram	1(05)	1(06)	
tearshaped/triangular	2(10)	1(06)	1(50)
round	1(05)	1(06)	
Total	20(100)	18(102)	2(100)

Table 9.48a. Shield Archaic wedge plan.

Section	Range total	Forest total	Tundra total
biplanar	1(05)	1(06)	
biconvex	12(60)	10(56)	2(100)
planoconvex	4(20)	4(22)	
triangular	1(05)	1(06)	
square	1(05)	1(06)	
rhomboidal	1(05)	1(06)	
Total	20(100)	18(102)	2(100)

Table 9.48b. Shield Archaic wedge section.

Flakescar type	Range total	Forest total	Tundra total
amorphous	5(25)	4(22)	1(50)
flat columnar	7(35)	6(33)	1(50)
channelled	2(10)	2(11)	
" columnar	6(30)	6(33)	
Total	20(100)	18(99)	2(100)

Table 9.49. Shield Archaic wedge flake scars.

Percussion	Range total	Forest total	Tundra total
bipolar	8(40)	6(33)	2(100)
double bipolar	2(10)	2(11)	
unipolar	10(50)	10(56)	
Total	20(100)	18(100)	2(100)

Table 9.50. Shield Archaic wedge percussion.

Est.	No.	Min.	Max.	Mean	S.D.	Exclude
L	18	20.18	41.86	29.87	6.59	none
W	18	14.80	36.68	23.82	5.91	"
T	18	6.06	20.84	11.20	4.60	"
Wt	18	2.68	21.40	10.19	5.53	"

Table 9.51a. Shield Archaic forest wedge data (mm and g).

Est.	No.	Min.	Max.	Mean	S.D.	Exclude
L	2	25.36	34.02	29.69	6.12	none
W	2	20.75	24.22	22.49	2.45	"
T	2	7.22	9.34	8.28	1.50	"
Wt	2	5.28	5.55	5.42	0.19	"

Table 9.51c. Shield Archaic tundra wedge data (mm and g).

Material	Range total	Forest total	Tundra total
quartzite	28(97)	20(95)	8(100)
granite	1(03)	1(05)	
Total	29(100)	21(100)	8(100)

Table 9.52a. Shield Archaic core material.

Colour	Range total	Forest total	Tundra total
beige	3(10)	2(10)	1(13)
white	9(31)	7(33)	2(25)
orange	4(14)	2(10)	2(25)
gray	10(34)	9(43)	1(13)
pink	2(07)	1(05)	1(13)
purple	1(03)		1(13)
Total	29(99)	21(101)	8(102)

Table 9.52b. Shield Archaic core colour.

Plan	Range total	Forest total	Tundra total
unknown fragment	4(14)	1(05)	3(38)
round cobble	11(38)	9(43)	2(25)
rectangular/square	8(28)	5(24)	3(38)
ovoid	5(17)	5(24)	
triangular	1(03)	1(05)	
Total	29(100)	21(101)	8(101)

Table 9.53. Shield Archaic core plan.

Section	Range total	Forest total	Tundra total
unknown	3(10)		3(38)
round	5(17)	3(14)	2(25)
rect./rhomb./square	15(52)	12(57)	3(38)
triangular	1(03)	1(05)	
planoconvex	4(14)	4(19)	
biconvex	1(03)	1(05)	
Total	29(99)	21(100)	8(101)

Table 9.54. Shield Archaic core section.

Profile	Range total	Forest total	Tundra total
blocky	15(52)	14(67)	1(13)
conical	8(28)	3(14)	5(63)
spherical	2(07)	2(10)	
boatshaped	2(07)	1(05)	1(13)
lenticular	2(07)	1(05)	1(13)
Total	29(101)	21(101)	8(102)

Table 9.55. Shield Archaic core profile.

Flake removal	Range total	Forest total	Tundra total
blade/bladelike	4(14)	3(14)	1(13)
flakelike	25(86)	18(86)	7(88)
Total	29(100)	21(100)	8(101)

Table 9.56. Shield Archaic core flake removal.

Platform	Range total	Forest total	Tundra total
single	6(21)	6(29)	
crescentic	17(59)	11(52)	6(75)
bipolar	6(21)	4(19)	2(25)
Total	29(101)	21(100)	8(100)

Table 9.57. Shield Archaic core platform.

Cortex	Range total	Forest total	Tundra total
present	23(79)	20(95)	3(38)
none/unknown	6(21)	1(05)	5(63)
Total	29(100)	21(100)	8(101)

Table 9.58. Shield Archaic core cortex.

Battering	Range total	Forest total	Tundra total
unipolar	19(66)	15(71)	4(50)
bipolar	10(34)	6(29)	4(50)
Total	29(100)	21(100)	8(100)

Table 9.59. Shield Archaic core battering.

Edgewear	Range total	Forest total	Tundra total
unknown	6(21)	6(29)	
present	10(34)	10(48)	
none	13(45)	5(24)	8(100)
Total	29(100)	21(101)	8(100)

Table 9.60. Shield Archaic core edge wear.

Depleted	Range total	Forest total	Tundra total
no	9(31)	7(33)	2(25)
yes	20(69)	14(67)	6(75)
Total	29(100)	21(100)	8(100)

Table 9.61. Shield Archaic core depletion.

Hinging	Range total	Forest total	Tundra total
no	25(86)	18(86)	7(88)
yes	4(14)	3(14)	1(13)
Total	29(100)	21(100)	8(100)

Table 9.62. Shield Archaic core tools.

Serration	Range total	Forest total	Tundra total
no	18(62)	12(57)	6(75)
yes	11(38)	9(43)	2(25)
Total	29(100)	21(100)	8(100)

Table 9.63. Shield Archaic core serration.

Multiple use	Range total	Forest total	Tundra total
none or unknown	20(69)	13(62)	7(88)
wedge	5(17)	4(19)	1(13)
chopper	4(14)	4(19)	
Total	29(100)	21(100)	8(101)

Table 9.64. Shield Archaic core multiple use

Est.	No.	Min.	Max.	Mean	S.D	Exclude
L	20	28.01	96.55	59.44	19.87	1 frag.
W	21	29.10	81.40	50.81	15.48	none
T	21	17.73	68.07	33.56	12.29	"
Wt	20	15.90	352.7	125.4	94.70	1 frag.

Table 9.65a. Shield Archaic forest core data (mm and g).

Est.	No.	Min.	Max.	Mean	S.D	Exclude
L	8	32.12	107.7	56.13	29.70	none
W	8	20.75	90.13	46.13	25.55	"
T	8	9.34	64.56	34.78	19.20	"
Wt	8	5.55	619.8	176.8	260.6	"

Table 9.65b. Shield Archaic tundra core data (mm and g).

Colour	Range total	Forest total	Tundra total
beige	18(25)	11(28)	7(21)
white	26(36)	10(26)	16(47)
orange	11(15)	8(21)	3(09)
gray	11(15)	7(18)	4(12)
pink	3(04)	2(05)	1(03)
red	1(01)		1(03)
brown	2(02)		2(06)
purple	1(01)	1(03)	
Total	73(99)	39(101)	34(101)

Table 9.66c. Shield Archaic regular flake colour.

Colour	Range total	Forest total	Tundra total
beige	11(30)	9(45)	2(12)
white	9(24)	3(15)	6(35)
orange	3(08)	2(10)	1(06)
gray	4(11)	2(10)	2(12)
pink	6(16)	3(15)	3(18)
red	1(03)	1(05)	
green	1(03)		1(06)
brown	1(03)		1(06)
purple	1(03)		1(06)
Total	37(101)	20(100)	17(101)

Table 9.66d. Shield Archaic retouched flake colour.

Est.	No.	Min.	Max.	Mean	S.D	Exclude
L	39	12.31	79.25	45.81	18.97	none
W	39	10.05	60.87	35.42	16.06	"
T	39	1.64	30.48	11.17	5.82	"
Wt	39	0.26	122.5	22.88	26.51	"

Table 9.67a. Shield Archaic regular forest flake data (mm and g).

Est.	No.	Min.	Max.	Mean	S.D	Exclude
L	34	11.50	74.23	36.68	12.65	none
W	34	14.66	72.38	31.42	14.09	"
T	34	2.67	15.32	7.17	3.44	"
Wt	34	0.87	45.67	8.64	10.01	"

Table 9.67b. Shield Archaic regular tundra flake data (mm and g).

Est.	No.	Min.	Max.	Mean	S.D	Exclude
L	20	26.04	137.9	53.02	24.67	none
W	20	18.04	94.84	39.13	17.98	"
T	20	5.68	24.41	12.71	5.44	"
Wt	20	4.83	241.0	32.63	52.43	"

Table 9.68a. Shield Archaic forest worked flake data (mm and g).

Est.	No.	Min.	Max.	Mean	S.D	Exclude
L	17	23.15	70.82	38.60	11.70	none
W	17	19.21	79.19	35.63	13.76	"
T	17	4.03	22.64	8.99	5.30	"
Wt	17	2.13	108.5	15.76	25.43	"

Table 9.69. Shield Archaic forest pebble data (mm and g).

Est.	No.	Min.	Max.	Mean	S.D	Exclude
L	11	21.63	41.63	32.79	6.98	none
W	11	19.40	30.95	23.31	4.29	none
T	11	9.00	23.33	15.61	4.99	none
Wt	10	5.80	26.40	13.31	8.27	1 frag.

Table 9.68b. Shield Archaic tundra worked flake data (mm and g).

Colour	Range total	Forest total	Tundra total
beige	1(20)	1(25)	
white	3(60)	3(75)	
brown	1(20)		1(100)
Total	5(100)	4(100)	1(100)

Table 9.71. Shield Archaic hammerstone colour.

Plan	Range total	Forest total	Tundra total
square/rectangular	1(20)	1(25)	
tearshaped	1(20)		1(100)
triangular	1(20)	1(25)	
almost ovoid	2(40)	2(50)	
Total	5(100)	4(100)	1(100)

Table 9.72. Shield Archaic hammerstone plan.

Section	Range total	Forest total	Tundra total
square/rectangular	3(60)	3(75)	
triangular	1(20)		1(100)
planoconvex	1(20)	1(25)	
Total	5(100)	4(100)	1(100)

Table 9.73. Shield Archaic hammerstone section.

Pocking	Range total	Forest total	Tundra total
unipolar	3(60)	2(50)	1(100)
bipolar	1(20)	1(25)	
unipolar & equatorial	1(20)	1(25)	
Total	5(100)	4(100)	1(100)

Table 9.74. Shield Archaic hammerstone pocking.

Est.	No.	Min.	Max.	Mean	S.D	Exclude
L	4	44.10	103.2	60.85	28.36	none
W	4	36.88	68.38	45.58	15.24	none
T	4	29.62	56.03	39.06	11.64	none
Wt	4	71.96	463.3	178.1	190.3	none

Table 9.75a. Shield Archaic forest hammerstone data (mm and g).`

Est.	No.	Min.	Max.	Mean	S.D	Exclude
L	1			62.75		only one
W	1			52.60		" "
T	1			43.75		" "
Wt	1			185.0		" "

Table 9.75b. Shield Archaic tundra hammerstone data (mm and g).

Material	Range total	Forest total	Tundra total
schist	1(17)		1(100)
silicious shale	1(17)	1(20)	
slate	3(50)	3(60)	
basalt	1(17)	1(20)	
Total	6(101)	5(100)	1(100)

Fig. 9.76a. Shield Archaic whetstone material.

Colour	Range total	Forest total	Tundra total
gray	5(83)	4(80)	1(100)
purple	1(17)	1(20)	
Total	6(100)	5(100)	1(100)

Table 9.76b. Shield Archaic whetstone colour.

Suspension	Range total	Forest total	Tundra total
unknown fragment	2(33)	2(40)	
notch inferred	2(33)	1(20)	1(100)
none	2(33)	2(40)	
Total	6(99)	5(100)	

Table 9.76c. Shield Archaic whetstone suspension.

Striae	Range total	Forest total	Tundra total
unknown/none	2(33)	2(40)	
longitudinal	4(67)	3(60)	1(100)
Total	6(100)	5(100)	1(100)

Table 9.77. Shield Archaic whetstone striae.

Added traits	Range total	Forest total	Tundra total
unknown/none	1(17)	1(20)	
wide striated groove (1)	1(17)	1(20)	
edge abrader (2)	2(33)	1(20)	1(100)
both 1 and 2	2(33)	2(20)	
Total	6(100)	5(100)	1(100)

Table 9.78. Shield Archaic whetstone multi-use.

Est.	No.	Min.	Max.	Mean	S.D	Exclude
L	4	21.76	91.10	65.03	31.59	1 frag.
W	5	13.33	32.35	20.45	7.67	none
T	5	5.04	12.84	8.84	3.15	"
Wt	4	3.38	37.86	16.44	15.47	1 frag.

Table 9.79a. Shield Archaic forest whetstone data (mm and g).

Est.	No.	Min.	Max.	Mean	S.D	Exclude
L	1			121.4		only one
W	1			27.50		" "
T	1			12.00		" "
Wt	1			60.10		" "

Table 9.79b. Shield Archaic tundra whetstone data (mm and g).

Est.	No.	Min.	Max.	Mean	S.D	Exclude
L	4	33.21	87.08	54.47	22.99	2 frag.
W	6	21.12	43.74	28.18	8.20	none
T	6	7.88	15.72	12.18	2.63	none
Wt	4	6.30	41.20	23.15	15.71	2 frag.

Table 9.80. Shield Archaic forest skin flexc.r data (mm and g).

Material	Range total	Forest total	Tundra total
quartzite	152(96)	17(89)	135(97)
chert	5(03)	2(11)	3(02)
basalt	1(01)		1(01)
Total	158(100)	19(100)	139(100)

Table 10.2a. Northern Plano point material.

Colour	Range total	Forest total	Tundra total
beige	69(44)	5(26)	64(46)
white	48(30)	3(16)	45(32)
orange	3(02)	3(16)	
gray	20(13)	6(32)	14(10)
pink	9(06)		9(06)
red	4(03)	2(11)	2(02)
brown	3(02)		3(02)
black	2(01)		2(02)
Total	158(101)	19(101)	139(100)

Table 10.2b. Northern Plano point colour.

Cross-section	Range total	Forest total	Tundra total
biconvex	147(93)	19(100)	128(92)
planoconvex	9(06)		9(06)
concavoconvex	1(01)		1(01)
keeled	1(01)		1(01)
Total	158(101)	19(100)	139(100)

Table 10.3. Northern Plano point section.

Type of tip	Range total	Forest total	Tundra total
none/unknown	118(75)	12(63)	106(76)
pointed tip	19(12)	1(05)	18(13)
round	1(01)		1(01)
burinated	19(12)	5(26)	14(10)
retouched tip tool	1(01)	1(05)	
Total	158(101)	19(99)	139(100)

Table 10.4. Northern Plano point tip

Type of taper	Range total	Forest total	Tundra total
unknown fragment	14(09)	2(11)	12(09)
tapered to tip	9(06)	1(05)	8(06)
tapered to base	86(54)	7(37)	79(57)
parallel sided	49(31)	9(47)	40(29)
Total	158(100)	19(100)	139(101)

Table 10.5. Northern Plano point taper.

Type of base	Range total	Forest total	Tundra total
unknown fragment	10(06)	4(21)	6(04)
ground stem	142(90)	14(74)	128(92)
ground square	2(01)		2(01)
unground stem	4(03)	1(05)	3(02)
Total	158(100)	19(100)	139(99)

Table 10.6. Northern Plano point base.

Basal edge	Range total	Forest total	Tundra total
unknown fragment	25(16)	8(42)	17(12)
unground flat	1(01)		1(01)
ground flat	105(66)	10(53)	95(68)
unground round	4(03)	1(05)	3(02)
ground round	23(15)		23(17)
Total	158(101)	19(100)	139(100)

Table 10.7. Northern Plano point basal edge.

Shoulder type	Range total	Forest total	Tundra total
none or unknown	157(99)	19(100)	138(99)
ground double	1(01)		1(01)
Total	158(100)	19(100)	139(100)

Table 10.8. Northern Plano point shoulder.

Breakage type	Range total	Forest total	Tundra total
none	14(09)	1(05)	13(09)
transverse	100(63)	7(37)	93(67)
diagonal	15(09)		15(11)
semi-diagonal	10(06)		10(07)
double diagonal	3(02)	1(05)	2(01)
transverse-diagonal	3(02)	3(16)	
double transverse	4(03)	3(16)	1(01)
longitudinal & transverse	7(04)	4(21)	3(02)
accidentally burinated	2(01)		2(01)
Total	158(99)	19(100)	139(99)

Table 10.9. Northern Plano point breakage.

Burination	Range total	Forest total	Tundra total
none/unknown	113(72)	9(47)	104(75)
1 side or face	20(13)	6(32)	14(10)
2 sides or faces	25(16)	4(21)	21(15)
Total	158(101)	19(100)	139(100)

Table 10.10. Northern Plano point burination.

Special traits	Range total	Forest total	Tundra total
none/unknown	140(89)	11(58)	129(93)
eared	2(01)		2(01)
burnt	1(01)		1(01)
channel-flaked	5(03)	3(16)	2(01)
thinned	10(06)	5(26)	5(04)
Total	158(100)	19(100)	139(101)

Table 10.11. Northern Plano point special traits.

Other usage	Range total	Forest total	Tundra total
none/unknown	115(73)	9(47)	106(76)
wedge	4(03)	1(05)	3(02)
knife	1(01)		1(01)
burin	31(20)	3(16)	3(03)
graver	6(04)	3(16)	3(02)
endscraper	1(01)		1(01)
Total	158(102)	19(100)	139(100)

Table 10.12. Northern Plano point multi-tools

Est.	N	Min.	Max.	Mean	S.D	Exclude
L	14	54.16	100	73.35	11.93	5 frag.
W	19	20.38	27.0	23.99	1.97	none
T	18	6.00	12.55	8.45	1.39	1 frag.
Wt	2	4.10	10.64	7.37	4.62	17 frag.

Table 10.13a. Northern Plano forest point data (mm and g).

Est.	N	Min.	Max.	Mean	S.D	Exclude
L	38	40.00	95.61	61.72	13.44	101 frag.
W	86	17.40	46.78	23.64	3.52	53 frag.
T	126	5.31	11.72	8.05	1.23	13 frag.
Wt	11	7.73	19.24	12.58	3.82	13 frag.

Table 10.13b. Northern Plano tundra point data (mm and g).

Substance	Range total	Forest total	Tundra total
quartzite	36(84)	3(75)	33(85)
chert	7(16)	1(25)	6(15)
Total	43(100)	4(100)	39(100)

Table 10.14a. Northern Plano scraper material.

Colour	Range total	Forest total	Tundra total
beige	24(56)	2(50)	22(56)
white	6(14)	1(25)	5(13)
orange	2(05)		2(05)
gray	3(07)	1(25)	2(05)
pink	1(02)		1(03)
red	2(05)		2(05)
brown	3(07)		3(08)
black	2(05)		2(05)
Total	43(101)	4(100)	39(100)

Table 10.14b. Northern Plano scraper colour.

Texture	Range total	Forest total	Tundra total
banded	8(19)	1(25)	7(18)
solid colour	35(81)	3(75)	32(82)
Total	43(100)	4(100)	39(100)

Table 10.14c. Northern Plano scraper texture.

Plan	Range total	Forest total	Tundra total
unknown fragment	1(02)		1(03)
rhomboid	14(33)	4(100)	10(26)
tearshape	1(02)		1(03)
triangular	16(37)		16(41)
ovoid	4(10)		4(10)
rectangular/bladelike	6(14)		6(15)
parallelogram	1(02)		1(02)
Total	43(100)	4(100)	39(101)

Table 10.15. Northern Plano scraper plan.

Cross-section	Range total	Forest total	Tundra total
tabular	29(67)	2(50)	27(69)
keeled	7(16)	1(25)	6(15)
tortoise	5(12)		5(13)
biconvex	1(02)		1(03)
planoconvex	1(02)	1(25)	
Total	43(99)	4(100)	39(100)

Table 10.16. Northern Plano scraper section.

Edge type	Range total	Forest total	Tundra total
serrated	5(12)	1(25)	4(10)
unserrated	38(88)	3(75)	35(90)
Total	43(100)	4(100)	39(100)

Table 10.17. Northern Plano scraper edge.

Base	Range total	Forest total	Tundra total
unretouched/unground	11(26)	1(25)	10(26)
unretouched/ground	6(14)	1(25)	5(13)
dorsal retouch	19(44)	2(50)	17(44)
bifacial retouch	7(16)		7(18)
Total	43(100)	4(100)	39(101)

Table 10.18. Northern Plano scraper basal retouch.

Cortex	Range total	Forest total	Tundra total
none	38(88)	3(75)	35(90)
present	5(12)	1(25)	4(10)
Total	43(100)	4(100)	39(100)

Table 10.19. Northern Plano scraper cortex.

Bit wear	Range total	Forest total	Tundra total
worn	27(63)	2(50)	25(64)
very worn	9(21)	1(25)	8(21)
unworn	7(16)	1(25)	6(15)
Total	43(100)	4(100)	39(100)

Table 10.20. Northern Plano scraper bit.

Basal grinding	Range total	Forest total	Tundra total
ground	33(77)	4(100)	29(74)
very ground	1(02)		1(03)
unground	9(21)		9(23)
Total	43(100)	4(100)	39(100)

Table 10.21. Northern Plano scraper basal grinding.

Striae	Range total	Forest total	Tundra total
none/unknown	41(95)	4(100)	37(95)
over the edge	2(05)		2(05)
Total	43(100)	4(100)	39(100)

Table 10.22. Northern Plano scraper striae.

Bifacial platform	Range total	Forest total	Tundra total
unknown	36(84)	4(100)	32(82)
present	7(16)		7(18)
Total	43(100)	4(100)	39(100)

Table 10.23. North Plano scrapers made from thinning flakes

Spurring	Range total	Forest total	Tundra total
unspurred	40(93)	4(100)	36(92)
single spur	2(05)		2(05)
double spur	1(02)		1(03)
Total	43(100)	4(100)	39(100)

Table 10.24. Northern Plano scraper spurring

Est.	No.	Min.	Max.	Mean	S.D	Exclude
L	4	32.87	44.69	38.45	5.04	none
W	4	19.54	36.99	31.71	8.29	"
T	4	6.34	9.72	8.06	1.38	"
Wt	4	4.19	13.20	10.07	4.08	"

Table 10.25a. Northern Plano forest scraper data (mm and g).

Est.	No.	Min.	Max.	Mean	S.D	Exclude
L	35	24.17	76.07	43.07	11.55	4 frag.
W	38	13.81	58.25	32.24	8.89	1 frag.
T	39	3.95	12.15	7.29	1.57	none
Wt	31	1.93	68.81	13.02	11.60	8 frag.

Table 10.25b. Northern Plano tundra scraper data (mm and g).

Material	Tundra total	Colour	Tundra total
quartzite	38(95)	beige	19(48)
chert	2(05)	white	9(23)
Total	40(100)	orange	1(02)

Table 10.26a. Northern Plano knife material.

Texture	Tundra total	gray	4(10)
solid colour	38(95)	pink	2(05)
banded	2(05)	red	3(08)
Total	40(100)	Total	40(102)

Table 10.26b. Northern Plano knife texture.

Completeness	Tundra total	Plan	Tundra total
base only	2(05)	unknown frag.	15(38)
midsection	8(20)	lanceolate	6(15)
tip only	4(10)	ovoid	9(23)
base and midsection	4(10)	pentagonal	2(05)
tip and midsection	8(20)	rect.or square	1(03)
edge fragment	6(15)	triangular	1(03)
complete	6(15)	asymmet. ovoid	1(03)
longitudinally split	1(03)	discoidal	4(10)
light chipping	1(03)	rhomboid	1(03)
Total	40(100)	Total	40(103)

Table 10.27. Northern Plano knife completeness

Section	Tundra	Type of edge	Tundra
biconvex	28(70)	unknown fragment	1(03)
planoconvex	8(20)	serrated preform	5(13)
concavoconvex	2(05)	unworn bifacial retouch	7(18)
keeled	1(03)	unworn unifacial retouch	3(08)
sinuous	1(03)	worn bifacial retouch	21(53)
Total	40(101)	worn unifacial retouch	3(08)

Table 10.28a-b. Northern Plano knife section and edge type.

Faciality	Tundra
unifacial	7(18)
bifacial	33(83)
Total	40(101)

Table 10.28c. Northern Plano knife faciality

Base	Tundra	Midsection	Tundra
unknown fragment	24(60)	unknown fragmen	11(28)
unground and unretouched	1(03)	unifacial retouch	5(13)
bladelike retouch	1(03)	bifacial retouch	21(53)
unground dorsal retouch	1(03)	serrated	3(08)
unground bifacial retouch	8(20)	Total	40(102)
ground bifacial retouch	5(13)		
Total	40(102)		

Table 10.29a-b. Northern Plano knife base and midsection.

Type of tip	Tundra	Break	Tundra
unknown fragment	19(48)	unknown/fragment	5(13)
unworn and pointed	4(10)	transverse	7(18)
worn and round	6(15)	diagonal	6(15)
worn and pointed	6(15)	transverse-diagonal	5(13)
unworn and round	3(08)	longitudinal	3(08)
serrated	1(03)	semi-transverse	4(10)
square	1(03)	multi-transverse	1(03)
Total	40(101)	transversely halved	2(05)
		longitudinally halved	2(05)
		Total	40(103)

Table 10.30a-b. Northern Plano knife tip and break.

Cortex	Tundra	Basal plan	Tundra
none/unknown	37(93)	unknown fragment	26(65)
dorsal face	2(05)	tapered, round & ground	1(03)
platform	1(03)	tapered, flat and ground	2(05)
Total	40(102)	tapered, flat and unground	1(03)
Type of back	Tundra	round and ground	2(05)
unknown frag.	6(40)	round and unground	2(05)
like oppos. edge	4(60)	unground pointed	1(03)
Total	40(100)	square and ground	1(03)
		square and unground	4(10)
		Total	40(102)

10.31a-c. Northern Plano knife cortex, base plan and back

Platform	Tundra
unknown fragment	26(65)
ground and unfacetted	1(03)
unground and unfacetted	1(03)
unground and facetted	2(05)
retouched away	10(25)
Total	40(101)

Table 10.32. Northern Plano knife platform.

Est.	No.	Min.	Max.	Mean	S.D	Exclude
L	17	36.00	110.0	66.76	19.17	23 frag.
W	17	22.00	65.00	40.41	13.45	23 frag.
T	35	4.39	15.39	9.26	2.53	5 frag.
Wt	6	6.45	41.72	25.09	12.47	34 frag.

Table 10.33. Northern Plano tundra knife data (mm and g).

Material	Range total	Forest total	Tundra total
sandstone	28(97)	10(91)	18(100)
quartzite	1(03)	1(09)	
Total	29(100)	11(100)	18(100)

Table 10.34a. Northern Plano chitho material.

Colour	Range total	Forest total	Tundra total
beige	7(24)	6(55)	1(06)
pink	2(07)	2(18)	
red	14(48)	2(18)	12(67)
brown	5(17)		5(28)
green	1(03)	1(09)	
Total	29(99)	11(100)	18(101)

Table 10.34b. Northern Plano chitho colour.

Faciality	Range total	Forest total	Tundra total
bifacial	20(69)	10(91)	10(56)
unifacial	9(31)	1(09)	8(44)
Total	29(100)	11(100)	18(100)

Table 10.35. Northern Plano chitho faciality.

Completeness	Range total	Forest total	Tundra total
complete	14(48)	8(73)	6(33)
edge fragment	2(07)		2(11)
central fragment	2(07)		2(11)
halved	1(03)		1(06)
quartered	4(14)	1(09)	3(17)
some spalling	6(21)	2(18)	4(22)
Total	29(100)	11(100)	18(100)

Table 10.36. Northern Plano chitho completeness.

Plan	Range total	Forest total	Tundra total
unknown/fragment	4(14)		4(22)
ovoid	5(17)	1(09)	4(22)
round	20(69)	10(91)	10(56)
Total	29(100)	11(100)	18(100)

Table 10.37. Northern Plano chitho plan.

Section	Range total	Forest total	Tundra total
unknown fragment	1(03)		1(06)
flat or parallel	22(76)	11(100)	11(61)
uneven or wavy	6(21)		6(33)
Total	29(100)	11(100)	18(100)

Table 10.38. Northern Plano chitho section.

Edge wear	Range total	Forest total	Tundra total
unknown fragment	1(03)		1(06)
worn	16(55)	8(73)	8(44)
unworn	12(41)	3(27)	9(50)
Total	29(99)	11(100)	18(100)

Table 10.39. Northern Plano chitho wear.

Cortex	Range total	Forest total	Tundra total
present	20(69)	9(82)	11(61)
none	9(31)	2(18)	7(39)
Total	29(100)	11(100)	18(100)

Table 10.40. Northern Plano chitho cortex.

Est.	N	Min.	Max.	Mean	S.D	Exclude
L	9	45.28	78.78	60.56	12.61	2
W	8	40.34	66.69	55.12	9.07	3
T	11	4.90	11.26	7.95	2.22	none
Wt	8	15.01	68.90	39.07	19.39	3

Table 10.41a. Northern Plano forest chitho data (mm and g).

Est.	N	Min.	Max.	Mean	S.D	Exclude
L	8	69.01	86.93	79.73	5.66	10
W	8	60.03	79.03	66.74	7.24	10
T	17	3.98	7.69	6.16	1.11	1
Wt	6	41.41	61.51	51.72	8.93	12

Table 10.41b. Northern Plano tundra chitho data (mm and g).

Material	Range total	Forest total	Tundra total
quartzite	29(88)	5(71)	24(92)
quartz	4(12)	2(29)	2(08)
Total	33(100)	7(100)	26(100)

Table 10.42a. Northern Plano wedge material.

Colour	Range total	Forest total	Tundra total
beige	15(45)	2(29)	13(50)
white	8(24)	3(43)	5(19)
orange	1(03)		1(04)
gray	4(12)	1(14)	3(12)
pink	2(06)		2(08)
red	1(03)		1(04)
green	2(06)	1(14)	1(04)
Total	33(99)	7(100)	26(101)

Table 10.42b. Northern Plano wedge colour.

Plan	Range total	Forest total	Tundra total
unknown plan	1(03)		1(04)
rectangular	8(24)	3(43)	5(19)
square	6(18)	3(43)	3(12)
rhomboid	9(27)	1(14)	8(31)
parallelogram	2(06)		2(08)
tearshaped/triangular	5(15)		5(19)
biconvex or ovoid	2(06)		2(08)
Total	33(99)	7(100)	26(101)

Table 10.43. Northern Plano wedge plan.

Section	Range total	Forest total	Tundra total
biplanar	7(21)	3(43)	4(15)
biconvex	15(45)	3(43)	12(46)
planoconvex	5(15)	1(14)	4(15)
triangular	2(06)		2(08)
rhomboidal	3(09)		3(12)
parallelogram	1(03)		1(04)
Total	33(99)	7(100)	26(100)

Table 10.44. Northern Plano wedge section.

Flakescar type	Range total	Forest total	Tundra total
unknown fragment	1(03)		1(04)
amorphous	18(54)	4(57)	14(54)
flat columnar	5(15)		5(19)
channelled	3(09)	1(14)	2(08)
" columnar	6(18)	2(29)	4(15)
Total	33(99)	7(100)	26(100)

Table 10.45. Northern Plano wedge flake scars.

Percussion	Range total	Forest total	Tundra total
bipolar	22(67)	4(57)	18(69)
double bipolar	3(09)		3(12)
unipolar	6(18)	3(43)	3(12)
discoidal	2(06)		2(08)
Total	33(100)	7(100)	26(101)

Table 10.46. Northern Plano wedge percussion.

Est.	No.	Min.	Max.	Mean	S.D	Exclude
L	7	26.51	67.70	39.86	15.11	none
W	7	26.91	43.61	33.17	5.56	"
T	7	6.05	15.01	9.83	3.00	"
Wt	7	6.50	81.10	21.66	26.77	"

Table 10.47a. Northern Plano forest wedge data (mm and g).

Est.	No.	Min.	Max.	Mean	S.D	Exclude
L	26	17.88	65.31	32.13	10.47	none
W	26	9.14	38.22	25.38	6.82	"
T	26	5.70	14.73	7.90	1.84	"
Wt	26	0.98	19.53	7.60	4.40	"

Table 10.47b. Northern Plano tundra wedge data (mm and g).

Type of tool	Tundra	Ground areas	Tundra
adze	1(03)	none	2(07)
adze flakes	27(93)	restricted	7(24)
chisel	1(03)	widespread	20(69)
Total	29(99)	Total	29(100)

Table 10.48. Northern Plano adzelike tools and grinding.

Flake type	Tundra	Type of striae	Tundra
unknown fragment	1(03)	none	14(48)
lateral (side)	13(45)	transverse	3(10)
bit	13(45)	diagonal	2(07)
complete tool	2(07)	longitudinal	4(14)
Total	29(100)	double diagonal	1(03)
Type-polish	Tundra	diagonal and longitudinal	1(03)
none	2(07)	transverse & longitudinal	4(14)
light	3(10)	Total	29(99)
heavy	23(79)	Hinged fractures	Tundra
facial ridges	1(03)	unknown/fragment	29(100)
Total	29(99)	Total	29(100)

Table 10.49. Northern Plano adze flake type, polish, striae, hinging

Est.	No.	Min.	Max.	Mean	S.D	Exclude
L	27	13.67	62.43	27.03	12.86	none
W	27	9.84	36.25	20.94	6.60	"
T	27	0.17	9.88	4.10	2.18	"
Wt	27	0.45	12.60	3.19	3.76	"

Table 10.50a. Northern Plano tundra adze flake data (mm and g).

Est.	No.	Min.	Max.	Mean	S.D.	Exclude
L	10	5.86	63.33	31.07	17.43	none
W	10	8.55	43.19	25.48	10.75	"
T	10	1.93	13.40	7.69	3.46	"
Wt	10	0.16	17.52	7.32	6.04	"

Table 10.52a. Northern Plano tundra regular flake data (mm and g).

Est.	No.	Min.	Max.	Mean	S.D	Exclude
L	4	21.13	63.61	45.01	19.29	none
W	4	18.73	56.72	29.38	18.35	"
T	4	6.27	13.60	8.62	3.36	"
Wt	4	3.11	47.89	16.44	21.18	"

Table 10.52b. Northern Plano tundra worked flake data (mm and g).

Material	Range total	Forest total	Tundra total
quartzite	3(18)	2(67)	1(07)
granite	14(82)	1(33)	13(93)
Total	17(100)	3(100)	14(100)

Table 10.53. Northern Plano hammerstone material.

Colour	Range total	Forest total	Tundra total
beige	10(59)	1(33)	9(64)
white	1(06)	1(33)	1(07)
gray	2(12)	1(33)	1(07)
red	1(06)		1(07)
brown	2(12)		2(14)
purple	1(06)		1(07)
Total	17(101)	3(99)	14(99)

Table 10.54. Northern Plano hammerstone colour.

Plan	Range total	Forest total	Tundra total
round	5(29)	1(33)	4(29)
triangular	2(12)		2(14)
almost ovoid	10(59)	2(67)	8(57)
Total	17(100)	3(100)	14(100)

Table 10.55. Northern Plano hammerstone plan.

Section	Range total	Forest total	Tundra total
square/rectangle	3(18)		3(21)
triangular	1(06)		1(07)
ovoid	10(59)	3(100)	7(50)
round	3(18)		3(21)
Total	17(101)	3(100)	14(99)

Table 10.56. Northern Plano hammerstone section.

Pocking	Range total	Forest total	Tundra total
unipolar	1(06)		1(07)
bipolar	10(59)	2(67)	8(57)
bipolar and equatorial	6(35)	1(33)	5(36)
Total	17(100)	3(100)	14(100)

Table 10.57. Northern Plano hammerstone pocking.

Est.	No.	Min.	Max.	Mean	S.D	Exclude
L	3	82.88	90.09	87.28	3.86	none
W	3	54.33	80.54	67.69	13.11	"
T	3	44.29	53.41	49.86	4.88	"
Wt	3	262.3	462.2	380.0	104.5	"

Table 10.58a. Northern Plano forest hammerstone data (mm and g).

Est.	No.	Min.	Max.	Mean	S.D	Exclude
L	14	82.08	126.7	106.7	14.97	none
W	14	51.52	99.80	85.26	15.24	"
T	14	34.02	96.21	72.09	18.17	"
Wt	14	232.1	1625	984.1	430.5	"

Table 10.58b. Northern Plano tundra hammerstone data (mm and g).

Material	Range total	Forest total	Tundra total
sandstone	2(50)		2(67)
silicious shale	1(25)	1(100)	
slate	1(25)		1(33)
Total	5(100)	1(100)	3(99)

Table 10.59a. Northern Plano whetstone material.

Colour	Range total	Forest total	Tundra total
beige	1(25)		1(33)
gray	1(25)	1(100)	
brown	1(25)		1(33)
red	1(25)		1(33)
Total	4(100)	1(100)	3(99)

Table 10.59b. Northern Plano whetstone colour.

Edge wear	Range total	Forest total	Tundra total
none	1(25)		1(33)
worn/ground	3(75)	1(100)	2(67)
Total	4(100)	1(100)	3(100)

Table 10.60a. Northern Plano whetstone edge.

Facial wear	Range total	Forest total	Tundra total
none	1(25)		1(33)
worn/ground	3(75)	1(100)	2(67)
Total	4(100)	1(100)	3(100)

Table 10.60b. Northern Plano whetstone face.

Striae	Range total	Forest total	Tundra total
unknown/none	2(50)		2(67)
longitudinal	1(25)		1(33)
longitudinal/transverse	1(25)	1(100)	
Total	4(100)	1(100)	3(100)

Table 10.61. Northern Plano whetstone striae.

Estimated	No.	Measures 89.2x22.3x14.5 mm/43.6g	Exclude
length	1		one
width	1		"
thickness	1		"
weight	1		"

Table 10.62a. Northern Plano forest whetstone data (mm and g).

Est.	No.	Min.	Max.	Mean	S.D	Exclude
L	3	70.83	106.4	83.78	19.64	1
W	3	26.12	68.97	48.47	21.50	"
T	3	8.85	20.45	13.14	6.36	"
Wt	3	34.38	132.3	70.23	53.93	"

Table 10.62b. Northern Plano tundra whetstone data (mm and g).

Material	Range total	Forest total	Tundra total
quartzite	29(94)	6(86)	23(96)
chert	2(06)	1(14)	1(04)
Total	31(100)	7(100)	24(100)

Table 10.64a. Northern Plano burin material.

Colour	Range total	Forest total	Tundra total
beige	16(52)	3(43)	13(54)
white	8(26)	1(14)	7(29)
orange	1(03)	1(14)	
gray	3(10)	1(14)	2(08)
brown	1(03)		1(04)
red	2(06)	1(14)	1(04)
Total	31(100)	7(99)	24(100)

Table 10.64b. Northern Plano burin colour.

Texture	Range total	Forest total	Tundra total
solid colour	29(94)	6(86)	23(96)
banded	1(03)	1(14)	
speckled	1(03)		1(04)
Total	31(100)	7(100)	24(100)

Table 10.64c. Northern Plano burin-related artifact texture.

Est.	No.	Min.	Max.	Mean	S.D	Exclude
L	29	14.94	94.72	42.16	17.44	2 frag.
W	31	16.54	30.74	22.59	3.07	none
T	31	5.92	11.55	8.58	1.17	"
Wt	28	1.61	24.50	9.61	5.48	3 frag.

Table 10.65a. Northern Plano forest burin data (mm and g).

Est.	No.	Min.	Max.	Mean	S.D	Exclude
L	23	14.94	94.72	39.83	17.96	1 frag.
W	24	16.60	30.74	22.63	3.11	none
T	24	5.92	11.55	8.56	1.29	"
Wt	23	1.61	24.50	9.43	5.91	1 frag.

Table 10.65b. Northern Plano tundra burin data (mm and g).